RESERVATION OF TITLE

AUSTRALIA
The Law Book Company Ltd.
Sydney : Melbourne : Brisbane : Perth

CANADA
The Carswell Company Ltd.
Toronto : Calgary : Vancouver : Ottawa

INDIA
N. M. Tripathi Private Ltd.
Bombay
and
Eastern Law House Private Ltd.
Calcutta *and* Delhi

M.P.P. House
Bangalore

Universal Book Traders
Delhi

ISRAEL
Steimatzky's Agency Ltd.
Jerusalem : Tel Aviv : Haifa

PAKISTAN
Pakistan Law House
Karachi

RESERVATION OF TITLE

BY

GERARD McCORMACK
B.C.L., LL.M.,
of the King's Inn, Dublin, Barrister-at-Law,
Lecturer in Law, University of Southampton

WITH CHAPTER 12 BY

BRICE DICKSON
B.A., B.C.L.,
Barrister-at-Law,
Senior Lecturer in Law at Queens University, Belfast

LONDON
SWEET & MAXWELL
1990

Published in 1990 by
Sweet & Maxwell Limited of
South Quay Plaza, 183 Marsh Wall,
London E14 9FT
Phototypeset by
MFK Typesetting of
Hitchin, Herts.
Printed in England by
Clays Ltd., St. Ives plc

British Library Cataloguing in Publication Data
McCormack, Gerard
  Reservation of title
  1. Great Britain. Goods. Title. Retention. Law.
  I. Title
  344.10672

ISBN 0–421–42140–1

PREFACE

The law relating to reservation of title clauses in sale of goods contracts has been described judicially "as a maze if not a minefield." Moreover, the committee under the chairmanship of Sir Kenneth Cork, which reviewed the state of Insolvency Law and Practice in 1982 came to a similar conclusion. The committee viewed this area of the law as highly technical, encompassing as it did the law relating to sale of goods, bailment, agency, trusts, mortgages and charges and the principles of tracing. To this might be added the law of property, both real and personal.

This book attempts to thread a path through the minefield. The practice of reserving title in the seller even though the goods have been delivered to the buyer is even older than the codification of sale of goods law in 1893. Such reservation of title clauses are also frequently referred to as "retention of title clauses" or "*Romalpa* clauses" after the seminal *Romalpa* decision in 1976. It was also after the Romalpa litigation that the full potentialities of the practice were realised in English law. Since then the fortunes of the draft-persons of reservation of title clauses have waxed and waned as successive decisions have been handed down by the courts. Chapter 5 of this book looks in detail at the influential *Romalpa* decision and its progeny as well as analysing the various types of reservation of title clause individually. Earlier chapters set the matter in context by looking, *inter alia*, at the general principles that govern the passing of property as well as situations analogous to reservation of title. Tracing and admixture of goods are also discussed together with the important issue of incorporation of a reservation of title clause into a sale of goods contract. Later chapters detail particular aspects of the reservation of title phenomenon such as company charge registration, the effect of restrictions imposed by the Insolvency Act 1986 and the question of resale.

Finally the various strands are brought together in the concluding chapter. This chapter aims to provide pointers towards the drafting of more effective reservation of title clauses having regard to the principles discussed in the work as a whole.

In writing this book I must acknowledge a heavy indebtedness to the published writings of others, particularly those of Professor R.M. Goode. Thanks are especially due to Brice Dickson of Queen's University Belfast for contributing Chapter 12, as well as providing a first draft of Chapter 13 together with more general advice in relation to the entirety of the work. The advice, assistance and encouragement offered in various ways by Peter Birks, Norman Palmer and William Swadling is gratefully acknowledged.

Preface

The editorial staff at Sweet & Maxwell, both past and present, have been extremely helpful. Especial thanks are also due to Miss Alison Lampard for typing the manuscript.

I have endeavoured to state the law on the basis of the materials available to me on June 1, 1990. It should be noted however that the House of Lords heard the appeal in *Armour* v. *Thyssen Edelstahlwerke A.G.* during the last week of June. At the time of writing the detailed reasons for the decision are not available but the House of Lords upheld the claim of the German supplier and overturned the ruling of the Scottish Court of Session 1989 S.L.T. 182. The decision confirms the effectiveness of "all-liabilities" reservation of title clauses and supports the burden of the argument advanced in Chapter 6 at pages 104–109.

This book is dedicated to my mother and to the memory of my father.

Gerard McCormack
Southampton
July 1990

CONTENTS

Contents

Contents

Contents

Contents

TABLE OF CASES

Table of Cases

Table of Cases

Table of Cases

Table of Cases

Table of Cases

TABLE OF STATUTES

Table of Statutes

Chapter 1

INTRODUCTION

A reservation of title clause, sometimes called a retention of title clause, is a clause in an agreement whereby the party who is transferring property under that agreement seeks to reserve to itself the ownership of that property until certain specified conditions have been met. In recent years the clause has become a common feature both of standard form contracts and of contracts freely negotiated, though it has certainly been employed in the past as well. Continental systems of law have had a long experience of regulating such clauses,[1] but in the United Kingdom there is still a great deal of uncertainty as to when they are legally valid and effective.

The focus of this book is on contracts for the sale of goods. The law relating to the sale of goods was codified in 1893 with the passing of the Sale of Goods Act of that year. The relevant provisions are now contained in the Sale of Goods Act 1979.[2]

Section 19 of the same Act provides the legislative basis for reservation of title clauses. The section provides that where there is a contract for the sale of specific goods or where goods are subsequently appropriated to the contract, the seller may, by the terms of the contract or appropriation, reserve the right of disposal of the goods until certain conditions are fulfilled. In such a case, notwithstanding the delivery of the goods to the buyer, the property in the goods does not pass to the buyer until the conditions imposed by the seller are fulfilled.

"Reserving a right of disposal of goods" may be an inapt way of describing the operation under discussion but the intention behind this provision is relatively clear—a seller may reserve title in certain goods until certain conditions are met despite the fact that physical possession of the goods has passed to the buyer. Some preliminary considerations have to be dealt with before one considers the purpose behind the use of reservation of title clauses.

Types of Reservation of Title Clause

Basically, there are five different types of reservation of title clause, four

---

[1] See generally, Pennington, "Retention of Title to the Sale of Goods under European Law" (1978) 27 I.C.L.Q. 277.
[2] There is a definition of goods in s. 41 of the Act. The expression is defined to include all personal chattels other than things in action and money, and in Scotland all corporeal movables except money, and in particular "goods" includes emblements, industrial growing crops and things attached to or forming part of the land which are agreed to be severed before sale or under the contract of sale.

of them purporting to go one step further than the original "simple" clause. The objectives of each of these clauses may be summarised thus:

1. *Simple clause*: the seller retains ownership in the goods delivered as against the buyer until the full purchase price for goods has been paid.

2. *Current account clause*: the seller retains ownership in the goods delivered as against the buyer until all debts or other obligations owed by the buyer to the seller have been paid.

3. *Extended (or "continuing") clause*: the seller retains ownership in the goods delivered as against the buyer and any sub-buyer either until the full purchase price for goods has been paid or until all debts owed by the buyer to the seller have been paid.

4. *Tracing (or "prolonged") clause*: the seller retains ownership in the goods delivered as against the buyer either until the full purchase price for those goods has been paid or until all debts owed by the buyer to the seller have been paid, but, *if the goods are resold to a sub-buyer*, then the seller acquires ownership either of the proceeds of sale or of the right to sue the sub-buyer for the proceeds of sale.

5. *Aggregation (or "enlarged") clause*: the seller retains ownership in the goods delivered as against the buyer either until the full purchase price for those goods has been paid, but, if the goods are manufactured into some other property, with or without the addition of other goods, then the seller acquires ownership of the resulting property or of a proportionate part of it equal to the contribution made to the manufacturing process by the original goods.

As the wording of the summaries indicates, a current account clause (No. 2) may be combined with an extended clause (No. 3), a tracing clause (No. 4) or an aggregation clause (No. 5). In addition, an extended clause (No. 3) or a tracing clause (No. 4) may be added to an aggregation clause (No. 5). However, No. 3 and No. 4 cannot be combined in the same clause. In the end, therefore, one might have a clause that represents No. 2 and (No. 3 or No. 4) and No. 5.

Reasons for the Use of Reservation of Title Clauses

Why, one may ask, has "reservation of a right of disposal" become a matter of great moment to business people and their advisors. Undoubtedly the principal reason underlying the insertion in a contract for the sale of goods of a term retaining title until certain requirements have been met is to provide security for payment of the purchase price. However, in *Clough Mill Ltd.* v. *Martin*[3] Oliver L.J. questioned the correctness of the assumption that

[3] [1985] 1 W.L.R. 111, 122.

2

the whole purpose of a reservation of title condition is to give the seller security for the payment of the purchase price. Indeed, he suggested that the purpose of the clause goes well beyond a mere security for payment of the price. In more general terms its purpose was to protect the seller from the insolvency of the buyer in circumstances where the price remains unpaid.

The remedy of repossession is available against the goods, the subject-matter of the contract of sale. Alternatively, if the goods have been sold, the original seller's claim lies against the proceeds of sale. Where the goods have been incorporated into other products, or formed part of the raw material for a process of manufacture, the seller may have an entitlement to the finished product, either alone or in common with others.

The important point to note is that the seller is not left with an unsecured claim in respect of the purchase price in the event of the buyer's insolvency. There is often a jungle of competing claims in an insolvency and any device which puts a supplier of goods ahead of the queue is very much welcomed from the supplier's point of view.

The point becomes more apparent if one looks more closely at the large variety of secured and preferential debts which are a normal concomitant of corporate insolvency. When a company is wound up the assets of the company are distributed in the following order:

(1) expenses of winding up;
(2) fixed charge holders;
(3) preferential debts;
(4) floating charges; and
(5) unsecured debts.

Persons with unsecured claims against the assets of the company come at the end of the posse. There will be little, if anything, left for them in the corporate carcass.

In the retention of title scenario, most buyers of goods will be corporate enterprises and the above-mentioned state of affairs is the order of the day. Even if the buyer is an individual or a partnership, the general picture holds good. The main difference lies in the fact that it is not possible for individuals or partnerships to create floating charges over their assets.[4]

The unsecured supplier of goods to a company is also vulnerable to an operation known as "hiving down." The principal remedy of the floating charge holder lies in the appointment of a receiver whose task it is to realise the assets of the company subject to the floating charge.

[4] A floating charge enables a company to dispose of assets within the category covered by the charge in the ordinary course of its business without reference to, or the consent of the person entitled to the benefit of the charge. The person who acquires the assets in such an eventuality gets a good title unimpaired by the charge. This state of affairs continues until the charge is said to crystallise, *i.e.* becomes converted into a fixed charge on the assets then in the possession of the company and within the scope of the charge. See generally, *Re Yorkshire Woolcombers Association Ltd.* [1903] 2 Ch. 284; *Illingsworth* v. *Houldsworth* [1904] A.C. 355; *Re Brightlife Ltd.* [1987] Ch. 200; Eilis Ferran, "Floating charges—the nature of the security" [1988] C.L.J. 213.

It has become the practice of a receiver on his appointment to "hive down" the assets of the company which fall within the reach of a floating charge to a new and independent company. The first part in the process is for the receiver to acquire an "off-the-peg" £100 nominal shareholding limited liability company which adopts a trading name similar to that possessed to the original company. The next stage is for the receiver to assign or otherwise to transfer to this new company, all the assets including goodwill possessed by the original insolvent company. Such assets would include goods in the physical possession of the insolvent company but not yet paid for. As Parris suggests in his work on *Effective Retention of Title Clauses*,[5] the new company is thus enabled to carry on the business without the inconvenience of meeting the debts of its predecessor. The unsecured creditor's only claim is against the company with which he contracted. In metaphorical terms, he is left with a claim against an empty shell from which all the crabmeat has been skilfully extracted. The observations of Templeman L.J. in *Re Southard and Co. Ltd.*,[6] though specifically addresssed to the issue of the parent/subsidiary company relationship, may be thought to apply with some suitable modification in this context. He said[7]:

> "English company law possesses some curious features which may generate curious results. A parent company may spawn a number of subsidiary companies, all controlled directly or indirectly by the shareholders of the parent company. If one of the subsidiary companies, to change the metaphor, turns out to be the runt of the litter and declines into insolvency to the dismay of its creditors, the parent company and the other subsidiary companies may prosper to the joy of the shareholders without any liability for the debts of the insolvent subsidiary."

The state of affairs which gave rise to the litigation in *Re Bond Worth Ltd.*[8] bears all the hallmarks of a "hiving-down" operation. Over £500,000 was owed to a supplier of goods in respect of deliveries of acrilan fibre for use in the manufacture of carpets. A receiver went into possession of the assets of the company after having been appointed by the National Westminster Bank. The business of Bond Worth was hived down to a £100 nominal shareholding company with no assets, Glixcroft Ltd. An agreement was made whereby Bond Worth agreed to sell, and Glixcroft agreed to purchase free from all liens, charges and incumbrances, the goodwill, undertaking and all other property and assets of Bond Worth.

Criticisms of the Reservation of Title Phenomenon

Retention of title clauses represent a weapon in the hands of a supplier of

[5] *Op. cit.* p. 4.
[6] [1979] 1 W.L.R. 1198.
[7] *Ibid.* 1208.
[8] [1980] Ch. 228.

goods to stave off the claims of secured creditors. Indeed, much of the criticism levelled at the retention of title clauses has come from those not over-anxious about the possible abuses associated with the use of floating charges. Robert Goff L.J. put the point well in *Clough Mill Ltd.* v. *Martin*[9] when he said that the mechanism of the floating charge, on which secured creditors are content to rely, is perhaps as much open to criticism as the mechanism of the retention of title clause, at which they now express their dismay.

The concern is not confined to charge holders, however. It was shared by the Department of Trade Review Committee on Insolvency Law and Practice which reported in June 1982.[10] This committee is commonly called the Cork Committee after the Chairman, Sir Kenneth Cork. It pointed out that while the supplier of goods is able to protect himself by adopting reservation of title clauses, no similar protection is available to the supplier of consumables or of services. The report went on[11]:

> "Fuel supplied to heat furnaces, or fodder supplied for livestock, disappears on consumption and paint supplied to the fabric of a factory becomes attached to the reality; the supplier on credit is necessarily left with an unsecured claim in the insolvency of the customer. The canteen operator, the contractor who cleans the factory, the pensions consultant all extend credit with no means of protection similar to that of the supplier of goods."

Lack of Registration Requirement

One of the principal grievances against reservation of title clauses lies in the fact that there is no need to register such clauses in a central register open to inspection by anybody who might be contemplating the supply of services to a company. Thus a potential supplier of services to a company may be misled as to its creditworthiness by the number of goods in the physical possession of the company.

In the case of certain charges created by a company there is an obligation to file details of the instrument by which the charge was created with the registrar of companies. This registration requirement is embodied in section 395 of the Companies Act 1985.[12] If registration is not effected the charge becomes void against an administrator or liquidator of the company, and any person who for value acquires an interest in or right over property subject to the charge.[13] In other words, the charge holder loses his priority.

If a reservation of title clause were to be regarded as constituting a registrable charge then it would be difficult if not impossible to conform with

[9] [1985] 1 W.L.R. 111, 121.
[10] Cmnd. 8558.
[11] *Op. cit.* para. 1619.
[12] Pt. XII of the Companies Act 1985 which takes in s. 395 has been redrawn by Pt. IV of the Companies Act 1989.
[13] s. 399(1)—inserted into the Companies Act 1985 by s. 91 of the Companies Act 1989.

the registration specifications in the Companies legislation. The difficulty flows from the fact that there may be a large number of contracts between seller and buyer. It has been argued that it is absurd to expect a seller to register each contract separately instead of filing a single notice at the outset that he will be financing that buyer's periodic purchases of specified types of materials or goods and will have a security interest in them and their proceeds for whatever amount is currently owed to him.[14]

Reform of the Law Relating to Reservation of Title Clauses

The Crowther Report which looked at this area in 1971 recommended reform along the lines of Article 9 of the American Uniform Commercial Code. The Code was first promulgated in 1951 by two sponsoring organisations, the National Conference of Commissioners on Uniform State Laws and the American Law Institute. It has since been adopted by every State in the Union except Louisiana, with its civil law system. Article 9 adopts the generic concept of a security interest. The test under the Article is the substantive purpose and effect of the agreement and not the nomenclature applied to it. If the essence of the agreement is to secure payment or performance of an obligation, then it is characterised as a security interest and will be governed by Article 9. Sellers who have included a reservation of title clause in their conditions can safeguard their rights, not only in goods sold but also in products and proceeds of sale by registering a "financing statement" which details the type of property over which they are to be regarded as having a security interest.[15]

The latest government-inspired review of security interests in property is that undertaken by Professor Aubrey Diamond for the Department of Trade and Industry.[16] Diamond took the view that the present law relating to security interests should be replaced by new legislation containing a simpler and unified system.[17] Similar rules should apply to all types of security interest except where the security interest otherwise provides or where there were good policy reasons for the differences.

Under the new régime priorities would depend on a system of notice filing.[18] The proposal is for a register of security interests with the register

[14] Thornely, "Reservation of Title and Tracing—Romalpa Clauses" [1980] C.L.J. 48.
[15] For a discussion of Art. 9 of the Uniform Commercial Code as a possible model for reform of personal property security law, see Davies, "The Reform of Personal Property Security Law: Can Article 9 of the U.S. Uniform Commercial Code be a precedent" (1988) 37 I.C.L.Q. See also, Goode, "The Modernisation of Personal Property Security Law" (1984) 100 L.Q.R. 324.
[16] *A Review of Security Interests in Property* (1989); on which see Lawson, "The Reform of the Law Relating to Security Interests in Property" [1989] J.B.L. 287. See also Diamond, "The Reform of the Law of Security Interests" (1989) 42 C.L.P. 231.
[17] Para. 9.2.1. He suggested that the legislation should be based closely on Art. 9 of the American Uniform Commercial Code and the Personal Property Security Acts introduced into several Canadian provinces, though it need not slavishly follow any of the precedents, since the needs in the U.K. were not necessarily the same as those in North America.
[18] Chap. 11.

consisting of a collection of forms submitted by applicants. The form submitted is not to be a security agreement but rather a "financing statement," the function of which is to put on record that a named debtor may have created a security interest in favour of a named creditor. It is sufficient if the types of property affected are described in the document. The financing statement need not be tied to any specific timespan, unlike the American position. In general, priority in the queue of creditors is dependent upon the date of registration of the financing statement. No mandatory requirement to file a financing statement is proposed. A financing statement should not operate, however, to protect a security interest created more than 21 days before the filing if insolvency occurs within 12 months of the date of filing.[19]

The recommendations are that reservation of title by the seller under a contract of sale of goods should be treated as a security interest taken by the seller.[20] The legislation should spell this out. A reservation of title clause should be regarded as an effective security interest without the need for further documentation. If the seller resold the goods on the buyer's failure to pay, mortgage principles would apply and any surplus would be payable to the buyer.[21] It is intended to subject clauses reserving title to the obligation to file a financing statement but "simple" clauses in the first category, as outlined earlier in this chapter, would receiver favourable treatment.[22]

Such clauses are to be afforded a priority over pre-existing security interests which include after-acquired property. The justification for this favouritism is that whereas a security interest granted over property already owned may remove that property from the debtor's estate, a security interest over newly-acquired property to secure the price paid for that property is neutral in its effect. The debt in respect of the price is offset by the addition of the property. Moreover, if the new property helped the debtor's business to earn extra profits it would strengthen the position of existing creditors by swelling their security interest.[23] Diamond also suggested that the special treatment should extend to a claim in respect of the proceeds generated by an on-sale of the goods in their unprocessed state.

Implementation of the package of reforms proposed by Diamond is likely to be some years hence, if at all. The provisions relating to the registration of company charges have recently been overhauled by the Companies Act 1989 and it is difficult to imagine any legislative action on the reservation of title front, at least in the short-term. Originally the Government suggested the inclusion in the company charge provisions of a provision stating that a clause purporting to retain title should be deemed to create a charge unless it

---

[19] Para. 11.3.9.
[20] Chap. 17 of the Report.
[21] Enforcement of security is discussed in Chap. 14.
[22] Para. 17.7.
[23] It was also argued that if an earlier creditor could rely on an after-acquired property clause to the prejudice of a "simple" reservation of title creditor, he would obtain a wholly unjustified windfall at the expense of the later creditor whose money enabled the additional property to be acquired.

did no more than retain title to the goods sold under the contract, while they remained in their original state in the buyer's possession, with or without a claim to be entitled to the proceeds of sale of such goods, for the purpose of obtaining the price of those goods.[24] The idea was later dropped however.[25] The justification advanced for this change of heart was that the Act did not single out other examples of security which constituted a charge, but did not do so expressly and which were not in fact registrable.

Title and Property

So far we have used the terms "title" and "property" interchangeably. However, Part III of the 1979 Act which is set out in the appendix is divided into two groups of sections. Sections 16 to 20 are grouped together under the heading "Transfer of Property as between Seller and Buyer" and sections 21 to 26 appear under the heading "Transfer of Title." The term "property" is defined by section 61 as "the general property in goods." There is no definition of title anywhere in the Act. The language adopted in these sections is somewhat at variance with common terminology. The expression "the property in the goods" is generally used to denote the rights of ownership which can be asserted against the world at large. The term "title to the goods," on the other hand, is generally taken as referring to the rights that pass between seller and buyer.

Atiyah in his treatise *The Sale of Goods* points out that the distinguishing feature of property rights is that they bind not merely the immediate parties to the transaction but also all third parties.[26] He asks how then can there be such a legal phenomenon as a transfer of property as between seller and buyer? Either there is a mere transfer of rights and duties from seller to buyer, or there is a transfer of property which affects the whole world.[27]

The Sale of Goods Act, however, is not so respectful of linguistic niceties. For present purposes the expressions "title" or "property" can be used as alternatives. A further synonym is the phrase "ownership." The latter is a lay person's term and there is not much in the way of satisfactory definition. In the *Oxford English Dictionary* it is defined simply as "the fact or state of being an owner." An owner is defined as "one who owns or holds something as his own"; a proprietor "one who has the rightful claim or title to a thing."

A. M. Honoré in his essay on "Ownership" in the *Oxford Essays on Jurisprudence*[28] defines ownership as the residue of legal rights in an asset

---

[24] Release from the DTI dated September 2, 1987. See also, the Diamond Report, para. 23.6.10.

[25] DTI statement dated July 7, 1988.

[26] (7th ed., 1985), p. 217.

[27] See also, Lawson, "The Passing of Property and Risk in Sale of Goods—A Comparative Study" (1949) 65 L.Q.R. 362; Battersby & Preston, "The Concepts of 'Property,' 'Title,' and 'Owner' used in the Sale of Goods Act 1893" (1972) 35 M.L.R. 268.

[28] First series (1961), p. 108. The essay is reprinted in Honoré, *Making Law Bind* (1987), p. 161. See also, Waldron, "What is Private Property" (1985) 5 O.J.L.S. 313; J. W. Harris, "Ownership of Land in English Law" in McCormick and Birks, *The Legal Mind* (1986), p. 143.

remaining in a person (or persons) after specific rights over the assets have been granted to others. Any person with specific rights in property is said to have an interest in the goods but not ownership. After this look at a dictionary definition and also the views of an academic commentator there remains to be considered the views of the judiciary. In *Clough Mill Ltd.* v. *Martin*[29] Robert Goff L.J. was faced with a reservation of title clause which stipulated that:

> "the ownership of the material shall remain with the seller, which reserves the right to dispose of the material until payment in full for all the material has been received by it in accordance with the terms of this contract or until such time as the buyer sells the material to its customers by way of *bona fide* sale at full market value."

He said that prima facie, in a commercial document, "ownership" means quite simply, the property in the goods.[30]

However, a slightly different view was taken by Slade J. in *Re Bond Worth Ltd.*[31] of a different set of contractual terms. In this case the words used in the contract were that "equitable and beneficial ownership" was to remain with the sellers until payment. The judge viewed this clause as meaning that legal title would pass to the buyers and that the sellers would retain only an equitable one.

A gloss was put on this judgment by Staughton J. in *Hendy Lennox (Industrial Engines) Ltd.* v. *Grahame Puttick Ltd.*[32] He said[33]:

> "If these words had occurred in a document prepared by commercial men, one might perhaps have concluded that they simply meant ownership. But this occurred in a document which evidently had a legal provenance and Slade J. accordingly held that the legal property in the fibre passed to the buyers on delivery."

Slade J.'s judgment in *Bond Worth* has come under attack from many quarters. One of the most vehement and outspoken critics is John Parris in his book *Effective Retention of Title Clauses*.[34] He suggests that it contains more errors in law than any other judgment before or since. One of many was that there is such a thing as an equitable title in goods as distinct from legal ownership of them, consisting of "property" or "title" in the goods. This somewhat extravagant criticism should be tempered by reference to *Chase Manhattan Bank N.A.* v. *Israel-British Bank (London) Ltd.*[35] There,

---

[29] [1985] 1 W.L.R. 111.
[30] *Ibid.* 115.
[31] [1980] Ch. 228.
[32] [1984] 1 W.L.R. 485.
[33] *Ibid.* 493.
[34] (1986), p. 11. See also, *Re Wait* [1927] 1 Ch. 606.
[35] [1981] Ch. 105.

9

Introduction

Goulding J. was clearly of the opinion that where property, including presumably goods, is transferred under a mistake of fact, the transferor retains an equitable proprietary interest in the property. In other words, equitable property is retained.

CHAPTER 2

PASSING OF PROPERTY AND SITUATIONS
ANALOGOUS TO RESERVATION OF TITLE

Passing of Property

The main object of a contract of sale is the passing of property from buyer
to seller. One writer has, however, described the results which flow from the
mere passing of property as "for the most part, if not essentially, illusory."[1]
This is something of an exaggeration. Indeed, there would be little reason
for the employment of reservation of title clauses that postpone the passing
of property for as long as possible if the consequences were almost entirely
illusory. The following are important practical consequences that result
from the mere passing of property:

(1) As we have stated earlier, a person who has sold goods subject to a
    reservation of title clause should be able to recover them in the event
    of the buyer's insolvency.
(2) Where the seller is a company, the buyer will generally have a good
    title in the goods against the liquidator of the seller if the seller is in
    liquidation and the goods are still in its possession.
(3) The right to sue a third party for damage to or loss of the goods may
    turn on who has the property.
(4) Prima facie, the risk passes with the property.
(5) In general terms, a seller can only sue for the price if the property has
    passed.[2]

Specific Goods

In looking at the rules relating to the passing of property a distinction has
to be drawn between specific goods and unascertained goods.[3] Section 61(1)
of the Sale of Goods Act 1979 defines the latter as meaning goods which are
identified and agreed upon at the time a contract of sale is made. If,
therefore, the parties have agreed that a precise individual item should form
the subject matter of a contract of sale, then there is a contract for the sale of
specific goods.[4] There is no definition in the act of "unascertained goods"
but it would appear that three categories are included within the term. The

[1] See Lawson (1949) 65 L.Q.R. 352, 359.
[2] s. 49 of the Sale of Goods Act 1979.
[3] See generally, on the passing of property, *Benjamin's Sale of Goods* (3rd ed., 1987), Chap. 5;
Atiyah's Sale of Goods (7th ed., 1985), Chap. 17.
[4] See *Kursell* v. *Timber Operators & Contractors Ltd.* [1927] 1 K.B. 298; *Lord Eldon* v. *Hedley
Bros.* [1935] 2 K.B. 1; *Joseph Reid Pty. Ltd.* v. *Schultz* (1949) S.R. (N.S.W.) 231.

first category is purely generic goods. Here the buyer is not concerned with which items he gets so long as it tailors with the description he applies. An example would be a contract for the sale of "200 boxes of canned fruit."

The second situation is where the goods to be supplied are an unidentified part of a larger quantity. An example often proffered relates to a contract for the sale of "50 tonnes of wheat out of the consignment of 200 tonnes now on board a certain ship."[5]

The third category is that of particular kinds of future goods. Section 5(1) defines future goods as goods to be manufactured or acquired by the seller after the making of the contract of sale. Future goods may either be specific or unascertained. If the goods do not yet exist, as in the case of a crop to be grown, they will clearly be unascertained. If they are in existence, they may be specific or unascertained. An example of a specific future good would arise in a sale of an individualised item where the parties know that it belongs to a third party at the time of sale. An example of the latter would be the sale of a Triumph 20 bicycle where the parties know that the seller will have to acquire one from the manufacturer.

Section 17 provides that where there is a contract for the sale of specific or ascertained goods the property in them is transferred to the buyer at such time as the parties to the contract intend it to be transferred. The section goes on to provide that for the purpose of ascertaining the intention of the parties, regard shall be had to the terms of the contract, the conduct of the parties and the circumstances of the case. Channell J. commented in *Varley* v. *Whipp*[6] that it is impossible to imagine a clause more vague than this. The clause does however stress the primacy of the terms of the contract. If the contract contains an express provision on the matter then this concludes the issue.

Often the parties have made no express statement on the matter in which case the rules stated in section 18 will come into play. These so-called rules are best described as presumptions since the law permits the parties to settle the point for themselves by any intelligible expression of their intention.

Rule 1 states that where there is an unconditional contract for the sale of specific goods in a deliverable state, the property in the goods passes to the buyer when the contract is made and it is immaterial whether the time of payment or the time of delivery, or both, is postponed. However, in *R.V. Ward Ltd.* v. *Bignall*[7] Diplock L.J. observed that in modern times very little is needed to give rise to the inference that the property in specific goods is to pass only on delivery or payment. To be effective, nonetheless, an expression of contrary intention must be made manifest at or before the time of the contract. In *Dennant* v. *Skinner and Collom*[8] a car was knocked down to a

---

[5] See *Re Wait* [1927] 1 Ch. 606.
[6] [1900] 1 Q.B. 513, 517 but he added that it correctly represents the state of the authorities when the Act was passed.
[7] [1967] 1 Q.B. 534, 545. See also, *Ingram* v. *Little* [1961] 1 Q.B. 31; *Lacis* v. *Cashmarts* [1969] 2 Q.B. 400; *Davis* v. *Leighton* [1978] Crim.L.R. 575; *Re Anchor Line Ltd.* [1937] Ch. 1.
[8] [1948] 2 K.B. 164.

swindler at an auction. He gave a false name and address and was allowed to take the car away in return for a cheque, after he had signed a form that no property in the car would pass until the cheque was met. It was held that when the swindler signed the form the property had already passed to him under section 18, rule 1. Therefore, the form which he signed had no legal effect.

In the context of rule 1 there remain questions as to the meaning of "unconditional" and "deliverable state." The phrase "unconditional contract" may mean either (a) a contract not containing any condition suspensive of the passing of property or (b) a contract containing no conditions in the sense of key provisions the breach of which may generate a right of repudiation on the part of the buyer. It seems clear that the former interpretation is the correct one despite some uncertainty in the authorities.[9] This view is held partly because few, if any, contracts do not contain conditions in the second sense.[10]

In relation to "deliverable state" section 62(5) stipulates that goods are in a "deliverable state" within the meaning of the 1979 Act when they are in such a state that the buyer would under the contract be bound to take delivery of them. As Atiyah points out this sub-section does not purport to give a comprehensive definition of deliverable state.[11] In particular, there is no statement that if the buyer would not be bound to take delivery of the goods, the goods are not in a deliverable state.

Again the authorities are not of great assistance. The leading case is *Underwood Ltd.* v. *Burgh Castle Brick and Cement Syndicate.*[12] Here, a contract was made for the sale of a condensing engine to be delivered free on rail in London. At the time of the contract the engine was affixed to the seller's trade premises. It had to be separated from its concrete bed and dismantled before it could be delivered on rail. The holding was that the engine was not in a deliverable state and that the property had not passed when the contract was made. Bankes L.J. said[13]:

> "A 'deliverable state' does not depend upon the mere completeness of the subject matter in all its parts. It depends on the actual state of the goods at the date of the contract and the state in which they are to be delivered by the terms of the contract."

Rule 2 refers to the situation where there is a contract for the sale of

[9] See *Varley* v. *Whipp* [1900] 1 Q.B. 513; *Ollet* v. *Jordan* [1918] 2 K.B. 41; *Leaf* v. *International Galleries* [1950] 2 K.B. 86; *Long* v. *Lloyd* [1958] 1 W.L.R. 753.
[10] See Atiyah, *op. cit.* pp. 224–225; *Benjamin's Sale of Goods*, paras. 282–283. It appears that the difficulty in the authorities arose because s. 11(1)(c) of the Sale of Goods Act 1893 took away from the buyer the right to reject goods for breach of condition "where the contract is for specific goods, the property in which has passed to the buyer." The crucial limitation on the right to reject was removed by s. 4 of the Misrepresentation Act 1967.
[11] *Op. cit.* p. 226.
[12] [1912] 1 K.B. 343; see also, *Phillip Head & Sons Ltd.* v. *Showfronts Ltd.* [1970] 1 Lloyd's Rep. 140.
[13] *Ibid.* 345.

specific goods and something needs to be done to put the goods into a deliverable state. Property does not pass until whatever needs to be done has been done, and the buyer has been advised that it has been done. The rule is negative in form. It does not for instance say that property automatically passes when the goods have been put in a deliverable state. The rule was applied by the Court of Appeal in the case referred to above—*Underwood Ltd.* v. *Burgh Castle Brick and Cement Syndicate.*

Rule 3 states that there is a contract for the sale of specific goods in a deliverable state, but the seller is bound to weigh, measure, test or do some other act or thing with reference to the goods for the purpose of ascertaining the price, the property does not pass until such act or thing be done and the buyer has notice thereof. The rule only caters for acts to be done by the seller.[14] Apart from that, Rule 3 is pretty self-explanatory.

Rule 4 talks about a situation where goods have been delivered to the buyer "on approval or on sale or return." The rule specifies that property passes to the buyer in two instances. The first instance is where he does any act which signifies his approval or acceptance of the goods. In the *locus classicus Kirkham* v. *Attenborough*[15] it was held that the act of pledging the goods was an act adopting the transaction because it was inconsistent with the buyer's power to return the goods. Lopes L.J. made the following comment[16]:

> "The position of a person who has received goods on sale or return is that he has the option of becoming the purchaser of them, and may become so in three different ways. He may pay the price, or he may retain the goods beyond a reasonable time for their return, or he may do an act inconsistent with his being other than a purchaser."

It must be remembered, however, that this rule, like the other rules in section 18, yields to the expression of a contrary intention. If it is laid down in the contract that property is not to pass until the goods are paid for, the pledging of the goods by the buyer will not transfer the property. This is the effect of *Weiner* v. *Gill.*[17]

The alternative hypothesis, mentioned in Rule 4, provides for property to pass if the buyer retains the goods without giving notice of rejection and retains the goods after the date given for their return, or where no such date is given, retains them for more than a reasonable time. A reasonable time is a question of fact to be determined in the light of all the circumstances of the case.[18] For this alternative to operate, the goods have to be "retained" by the

---

[14] [1926] A.C. 77.

[15] [1877] 1 Q.B. 201. See also, *London Jewellers Ltd.* v. *Attenborough* [1934] 2 K.B. 206; *Genn* v. *Winkel* (1912) 28 T.L.R. 483; *Weiner* v. *Harris* [1910] 1 K.B. 285.

[16] *Ibid.* 204. The judge added that the words of the Act are difficult to construe but if the recipient of the goods retains them for an unreasonable time he does something inconsistent with the exercise of his option to return them, and thereby adopts the transaction.

[17] [1906] 2 K.B. 574.

[18] *Heilbutt* v. *Hickson* (1872) L.R. 7 C.P. 438; *Poole* v. *Smith's Car Sales (Balham) Ltd.* [1962] 1 W.L.R. 744.

buyer. A clue as to the meaning of "retain" is provided by *Re Ferrier*.[19] Here goods delivered on sale or return were seized by the sheriff in an execution against the buyer's property. This meant that they could not be returned within the time fixed by the contract. It was held that the goods had not been "retained" by the buyer. Therefore property had not passed to him.

Unascertained Goods

When considering the passing of property in unascertained goods the starting point is section 16.[19a] The section provides that property cannot pass until the goods are ascertained. Property does not necessarily pass when this eventuality occurs. All depends on the intention of the parties. Rule 5 of section 18 says that whereas a contract for the sale of unascertained or future goods by description, property passes when goods of that description and in a deliverable state are "unconditionally appropriated" to the contract, by either party with the assent of the other. Such assent may be express or implied and may be given before or after appropriation.

There is a large question as to the meaning of "unconditionally appropriated." The rule supplies one illustration of unconditional appropriation. That is where the seller delivers the goods to the buyer or to a carrier for transmission to the buyer and does not reserve the right of disposal. Leaving aside this one bit of statutory guidance we have to fall back on a wealth of case law. The clearest path through the thicket of precedent seems to be that mapped out by Pearson J. in *Carlos Federspiel & Co. S.A.* v. *Charles Twigg & Co. Ltd.*[20] This was a case where sellers agreed to sell to overseas buyers a quantity of bicycles. The bicycles were packed at the sellers' premises and marked with the name of the buyers. The buyers were also informed by the sellers of the shipping marks of the consignment and that the goods had been registered for shipment. Before shipment took place, the sellers became insolvent. It was held that property in the bicycles had not passed to the buyers. Pearson J. spoke thus[21]:

> "A mere setting apart or selection by the seller of the goods which he expects to use in performance of the contract is not enough. If that is all, he can change his mind and use those goods in performance of such other contract and use some other goods in performance of this contract. To constitute an appropriation of the goods to the contract the parties must have had, or be reasonably supposed to have had, an intention to attach the contract irrevocably to those goods, so that those

[19] [1944] Ch. 295. See also, *Ray* v. *Barker* (1879) 4 Ex.D. 279; *Genn* v. *Winkel* (1912) 28 T.L.R. 483.
[19a] The relevant Sale of Goods Act provisions on passing of property are contained in the appendix.
[20] [1957] 1 Lloyd's Rep. 240.
[21] *Ibid.* 255. See also, *Healey* v. *Howlett & Sons* [1917] 1 K.B. 337; *National Coal Board* v. *Gamble* [1959] 1 Q.B. 11; *Edwards* v. *Ddin* [1976] 1 W.L.R. 942.

goods and not others are the subject of the sale and become the property of the buyer."

However, it was made clear recently in *Karlshamns Oliefabriker* v. *Eastport Navigation Corp.*[22] that the only essential requirements are that the goods are ascertained, and that the parties should intend that property is to be transferred. There is, Mustill J. said, no independent third requirement of unconditional appropriation of the goods to the contract.[23] Property may pass even though goods are not appropriated under rule 5. Rule 5 did not make appropriation a pre-condition of the passing of property.

Reservation of a Right of Disposal

Section 19 of the Sale of Goods Act permits a seller under a contract for the sale of specific goods, or under a contract for the sale of unascertained goods where goods are subsequently appropriated to the contract, to reserve a right of disposal of the goods until certain conditions are fulfilled. This reservation may be done by the terms of the contract or appropriation.

"Right of disposal" is nowhere defined in the 1979 Act. However, it clearly encompasses a situation where ownership is retained as well as the reservation of a power to resell the goods. This section provides one of the legislative foundations for reservation of title at least insofar as the simple reservation of title clause is concerned. There are other statutory pillars which support the institution of simple reservation of title clauses.

First, in the case of specific or ascertained goods, the parties may agree when ownership shall pass by virtue of section 17 of the Sale of Goods Act 1979. Secondly, in the case of unascertained goods ownership cannot pass to the purchaser until the goods are ascertained—a consequence of section 18. Thirdly, the implied terms as to the passing of property stated in section 18 only apply where a different intention has not been made manifest.

Analogous Concepts—The Purchase-Money Security Interest

Reservation of title clauses may be used in a situation where bank loans for buyers are not readily available. In Germany during the nineteenth century it appears that reservation of title clauses were common because buyers were not able to borrow money very easily from lending institutions.[24] Clauses in contracts came to be worded so as to provide for the retention of ownership, rather than just allowing ownership to be reclaimed if a condition was not fulfilled. This was partly because the first codification of Prussian law in 1794 had laid down the requirement that the latter type of clause could be operative only when the seller had first of all re-obtained

---

[22] [1982] 1 All E.R. 208, *following Wait & James* v. *Midland Bank* (1926) 31 Com.Cas. 172.
[23] *Ibid.* 215. For commentary on the case see Adams (1982) 45 M.L.R. 690; Thornely [1982] C.L.J. 239.
[24] See generally, Pennington, "Retention of Title to the Sale of Goods under European Law" (1978) 27 I.C.L.Q. 277.

possession of the goods.[25] Such a restrictive condition made the reservation of title clause a more attractive proposition.

Used in the fashion that we have described, the reservation of title clause bears very definite similarities to what Professor Roy Goode has characterised as the purchase money security interest.[26] In both cases one might say loosely that money has been advanced to facilitate the purchase of property in return for the lender having an interest in the property. The purchase money security interest has come before the courts in a situation where A makes an advance to the debtor on the security of its future property and the debtor subsequently acquires an asset with funds provided by B on the security of that asset. A priority dispute arises between the interests of A and B. A case often cited in this connection is that of *Re Connolly Bros. Ltd. (No. 2)*.[27]

Here a company issued debentures subject to a condition that it would not create any other charge in priority to those debentures. A couple of years later when the company wished to purchase some premises but did not have enough money for that purpose, it "borrowed" £1,000 from a Mrs. O'Reilly upon terms that she should have a charge upon the premises when purchased, a memorandum of this equitable charge being duly executed. A contest arose as to whether the debenture holders had priority over Mrs. O'Reilly's claim. It was held by the Court of Appeal that they did not. When the company purported to purchase the premises it in fact acquired only an equity of redemption in the property subject to the equitable charge of Mrs. O'Reilly. The full ownership of the premises never formed part of the company's assets for the purpose of the floating charge in favour of the debenture holders. The money contributed by Mrs. O'Reilly was therefore not so much a loan like the money lent by debenture holders but rather a part payment for the premises. She acquired an interest in the premises at the very moment when the company purported to purchase them.

Another case to the same effect is *Wilson* v. *Kelland*.[28] In this instance a vendor gave up his lien as unpaid seller over property he had agreed to sell for £5,350, in return for £2,350 and a contractual promise that he would be granted an equitable charge over the property of £3,000. The subsequently-created charge was unregistered. However, it was held to prevail over a floating charge over all the assets, present or future of the company, which was duly registered and prior in point of time. The *raison d'etre* of the decision was that the company had only acquired an equity of redemption in the property.

The same principle was applied by the Judicial Committee of the Privy Council in *Security Trust Co.* v. *Royal Bank of Canada*.[29] The difficulty with

[25] Prussian *Allgemeines Landrecht*, First Part, Title 7, s. 58 and Title 10, s. 1.
[26] See generally, Goode, *Legal Problems of Credit and Security* (2nd ed., 1988), pp. 98–101.
[27] [1912] 2 Ch. 25.
[28] [1910] 2 Ch. 306.
[29] [1976] A.C. 503.

these decisions was that priority was determined by a matter largely divorced from the merits of the situation; namely the order in which the transactions took place. A person was relegated, priority-wise, if he did not bargain for his purchase-money security in advance but rather, without any prior binding agreement, took it on completion of the purchase. A case in point was *Church of England Building Society* v. *Piskor*.[30]

Piskor has recently been overruled by the House of Lords in *Abbey National Building Society* v. *Cann*.[31] Lord Oliver recognised that as a matter of legal theory, a person could not charge a legal estate that he did not have, so that there was an attractive legal logic in the *ratio* of *Piskor*. Nevertheless, his Lordship felt that it flew in the face of reality. The reality was that, in the huge majority of cases, acquisition of the legal estate and the charge were not only precisely simultaneous, but indissolubly bound up together. The purchaser who relied on a loan for the completion of his purchase never in fact acquired anything but an equity of redemption, for the property was, from the very inception, charged with the amount of the loan without which it could never have been transferred at all and it had never been intended that it should be otherwise. *Piskor* was held to have been wrongly decided and the reasoning of the Court of Appeal in *Connolly* was adopted.

Hire-purchase

The hire-purchase agreement bears strong similarities to a sale subject to a reservation of title clause.[32] In *Lee* v. *Butler*[33] it was held that a person who is in possession of goods under a conditional sale agreement has "agreed to buy" within the meaning of section 9 of the Factors Act 1989 and section 25(1) of the Sale of Goods Act 1979. The consequence was that he could pass a good title to third parties under those sections.[34] This holding revealed deficiencies in the conditional sale agreement as a security to the seller for the unpaid purchase price. The result was more ingenuity on the part of commercial practitioners and the devising of the hire-purchase agreement.

---

[30] [1954] 1 Ch. 533.
[31] *The Times*, March 30, 1990. See also, Goode, *op. cit.* pp. 98–99 and *Coventry Permanent Economic Building Soceity* v. *Jones* [1951] 1 All E.R. 901. Professor Diamond in paras. 11.7.5–11.7.7 of his DTI commissioned "A Review of Security Interests in Property" recommended that "purchase money security interests" should be afforded a priority over pre-existing security interests which include after-acquired property. The justification for this recommendation was that while a security interest granted over property already owned could effectively remove the property from the debtor's estate, a security interest over newly-acquired property to secure the price paid for that property was neutral in its effect.
[32] On hire-purchase see generally, Bennion, *Consumer Credit Control*; Goode, *Consumer Credit Legislation*; Goode, *Consumer Credit Law* (1989); Guest, *The Law of Hire-Purchase* (1966); Goode, *Hire-Purchase Law and Practice* (2nd ed., 1970); Guest and Lloyd, *Encyclopedia of Consumer Credit Law*.
[33] [1893] 2 Q.B. 318.
[34] See *infra*, Chap. 10.

The Crowther Committee on Consumer Credit pointed out[35] that if the Court of Appeal in *Lee* v. *Butler* had interpreted section 9 of the Factories Act 1889 in the restrictive manner subsequently adopted in *Newtons of Wembley Ltd.* v. *Williams*[36] it is highly probable that hire-purchase as distinct legal form would not have been invented, since there would have been no need for it. However, the outcome of *Lee* v. *Butler* dictated the present form of hire-purchase agreement in which the hirer is given the option to purchase without being under any obligation to do so.

A hire-purchase agreement has been defined at common law as a contract for the hiring of goods under which there is conferred on the hirer an option to buy the goods.[37] During the subsistence of the agreement the property in the goods remains in the owner while the hirer has no power to dispose of them. Secondly, the hirer has an option to purchase the goods but is not subject to a binding obligation to do so. The practice differs somewhat from the legal form. The notion that a hire purchase agreement is a hiring with an option to purchase has been authoritatively described as a legal fiction bearing no relation to reality.[38] Often the option to purchase is for a trifling sum.

Two House of Lords cases decided in 1895 cemented the foundations of the modern form of hire-purchase agreement. In *Helby* v. *Matthews*[39] it was held that where the hirer of goods had no obligation but rather an option to buy the goods, he had not "agreed to buy" them even conditionally. This meant that he had no power to confer good title to the goods on a third party and so the *Lee* v. *Butler* point was met.

In order to provide protection against loss in value through depreciation of goods repossessed or returned to them it is normal practice for finance companies to insert clauses in their hire-purchase agreements that impose a liability upon the hirer to make payment over and above the arrears of hire-rent if the agreement or hiring has been brought to an end before the property in the goods has passed to the hirer. If depreciation is mentioned as the *raison d'etre* of the payment then it is referred to as a depreciation clause. In other cases it is called simply a minimum payment clause.

In the agreement which came before the court in *Helby* v. *Matthews* there was no minimum payment clause. In the Crowther Report it is argued that if the agreement had contained such a clause this fact might have led the court to treat the agreement as in reality a conditional sale agreement, again making unnecessary the development of hire-purchase as a separate instrument.[40] However, once the accolade had been bestowed, hire-purchase was destined for a lasting presence. When minimum payment clauses came into

[35] Cmnd. 4569, p. 182.
[36] [1965] 1 Q.B. 560. The Court of Appeal held that a seller, to pass a good title under s. 9 of the Factors Act 1889 must act in the way that a mercantile agent would act in the ordinary course of business even if, in fact, he is not a mercantile agent.
[37] *Benjamin's Sale of Goods* (3rd ed., 1987), p. 45, para. 53.
[38] See generally, Crowther Committee Report, pp. 175–176.
[39] [1895] A.C. 471.
[40] *Ibid.* 182.

vogue, the courts countered merely by devising ways of offsetting the worst excesses of such clauses by the development of a rule against penalties.[41]

The second case which forms the basis of the modern hire-purchase agreement and the first in point of time is *McEntire* v. *Crossley Bros. Ltd.*[42] The agreement considered in this case was in reality a conditional sale agreement rather than a hire-purchase agreement. It provided that the "hirer" acquired ownership automatically when his rental payments reached a stated amount. However, he had no right to terminate the agreement before the property in the goods became vested in him. The importance of the case is that it makes it clear that the Bills of Sale Acts 1878 and 1882 have no application in a hire-purchase or conditional sale situation. The rationale of these statutory dispensations was to protect persons who extended credit on the strength of the debtor's apparent ownership of goods which the debtor had in fact secretly transferred to a third party while himself remaining in possession.[43]

Bills of sale require to be registered within seven days of their execution. If the registration requirements are not complied with, the bills are void against creditors if the grantor is still in possession of the chattels comprised in the bill at the time of bankruptcy.[44] The House of Lords in *McEntire* v. *Crossley Bros. Ltd.* said that a hire-purchase or conditional sale transaction was not caught by the Bills of Sale Act because there was no assignment or right to seize granted to another by the owner of the goods. The Lord Chancellor, Lord Herschell, opined that if the property never passed to the bankrupt he can never have conveyed it or assigned it, or given the right to seize, or have given any rights over it within the meaning of the Bills of Sale Acts.[45]

In this century we have witnessed the development of a corpus of legislation regulating the hire-purchase transaction.[46] Coupled with this development was the assimilation in treatment of hire-purchase and conditional sales to a considerable degree. Scotland led the way in 1932 with the Hire-Purchase and Small Debt (Scotland) Act 1932. This was the first United Kingdom enactment dealing specifically with hire-purchase. England followed suit with the 1938 Hire-Purchase Act. This was followed by the Hire-Purchase Acts of 1954 and 1964. The legislation was consolidated in 1965 with the Hire-Purchase Act 1965 of that year. The 1965 Act was finally repealed on May 19, 1985,[47] though many of its provisions continue to apply to agreements made before that date.

The Hire-Purchase Act 1965 was superseded by the Consumer Credit Act 1974. Basically the Acts embodied a whole host of matters for the protection

[41] See generally, *Bridge* v. *Campbell Discount Co. Ltd.* [1962] A.C. 600; Goode, *Hire-Purchase Law and Practice* (2nd ed., 1970), pp. 383–399.
[42] [1895] A.C. 457.
[43] See generally, *infra*, Chap. 8.
[44] 1878 Act, s. 4.
[45] [1895] A.C. 457, 462.
[46] See generally, the textbooks mentioned in n. 32 for an account of this development.
[47] Consumer Credit Act 1974 (Commencement No. 8) Order 1983 (S.I. 1983 No. 1551).

of the hirer or conditional buyer. The legislation is of some complexity but in essence it regulates all hire-purchase and conditional sale agreements under a certain financial ceiling provided that they are not exempt agreements. There are measures dealing with formalities of contracts and the right of cancellation of a hirer or buying signing the agreement elsewhere than at appropriate trade premises.

Conditional Payments

So far most of the cases we have considered have been concerned with sales of chattels. It is worth remembering, however, that the same kind of problems can easily arise in the context of money-lending or other situations of payment of money. If a lender lends money on condition that it is used for a particular purpose and/or paid back out of a particular fund, or if a purchaser pays in advance on condition that the money is used to provide something he wants, to what extent can the lender or payer enforce the conditional agreement?[48] Conditional loans or payments are usually discussed under the rubric of the *Quistclose* trust and it is perhaps convenient to continue this classification.

The *locus classicus* is *Barclays Bank Ltd.* v. *Quistclose Investments Ltd.*[49] This is a case where Quistclose lent a company, Rolls Razor Ltd., some £210,000 to allow Rolls Razor to pay a dividend it had already declared. Rolls Razor sent the money to its bank, asking it to pay it into a separate dividend account and stating that the money was to be used only to pay the dividend. But before the dividend could be paid Rolls Razor went into voluntary liquidation, leaving Quistclose and the bank to dispute ownership of the £210,000. The company's bank claimed a right to set off the £210,000 credit against a debit balance in another account.

The claim failed. The money was held to be impressed with a trust in favour of Quistclose should the primary purpose of the payment fail. Lord Wilberforce said that the mutual intention of Quistclose and of Rolls Razor Ltd. and the essence of the bargain was that the sum advanced should not become part of the assets of Rolls Razor Ltd. but should be used exclusively for payment of a particular class of its creditors, namely, those entitled to the dividend. This entailed the necessary consequence that if, for any reason, the dividend could not be paid, the money was to be returned to Quistclose. The word "only" was not capable of bearing any other effect.[50]

[48] The link between reservation of title clauses in sales of goods and conditional loans or payments has not always been borne in mind when one or other of the two phenomena have been examined. However, the two are brought together in the excellent article by Goodhart and Jones, "The Infiltration of Equitable Doctrine into English Commercial Law" (1980) 43 M.L.R. 489. See also, Priestley, "The Romalpa Trust and the Quistclose Trust" in P. D. Finn, *Equity in Commercial Relationships* (1987) and Milman and Durrant, *Corporate Insolvency Law and Practice* (1987), Chap. 8. What follows on the subject of conditional payments has appeared substantially in the form of an article by the present author "Conditional Payments and Insolvency" (1990) 134 S.J. 216.
[49] [1970] A.C. 567.
[50] *Ibid.* 580.

His Lordship was emphatic in his disavowal of the idea that a transaction giving rise to a legal action for debt could not also create a trust. He said[51]:

"There is surely no difficulty in recognising the co-existence in one transaction of legal and equitable rights and remedies; when the money is advanced, the lender requires an equitable right to see that it is applied for the primary designated purpose . . . : when the purpose has been carried out (*i.e.* the debt paid) the lender has his remedy against the borrower in debt; if the primary purpose cannot be carried out, the question arises if a secondary purpose (*i.e.* repayment to the lender) had been agreed, expressly or by implication: if it has, the remedies of equity may be invoked to give effect to it, if it has not (and the money) is intended to fall within the general fund of the debtor's assets) then there is the appropriate remedy for recovery of a loan. I can appreciate no reason why the flexible interplay of law and equity cannot let in these practical arrangements, and other variations if desired; it would be to the discredit of both systems if they could not."

In upholding the claim put forward by Quistclose, the House of Lords followed a long line of cases dating back to the beginning of the last century. *Toovey* v. *Milne*[52] marks the *fons et origo* of this stream of authority. Abbott C.J. said[53]:

"I thought at the trial, and still think, that the fair inference from the facts proved was that this money was advanced for a specific purpose, and that being so clothed with a specific trust, no property in it passed to the assignee of the bankrupt. Then the purpose having failed, there is an implied stipulation that the money shall be repaid."

If the primary purpose of the payment had been carried out in *Quistclose* then the result achieved is one of credit substitution.[54] A, the payer, becomes a creditor of B, the person to whom the payment is made, instead of C, the third party creditors who are the ultimate intended recipients of the payment. Before the payment was made, there was no pre-existing relationship of debt between A and B. *Carreras Rothmans Ltd.* v. *Freeman Matthews Treasure Ltd.*[55] involves an extension of the *Quistclose principle* in that A stood in a relationship of debt to B prior to the time of making the payment. The facts of that case are as follows.

---

[51] *Ibid.* 581–582.
[52] (1819) 2 B. & Ald. 683. See also, *Edwards* v. *Glynn* (1859) 2 E. & E. 29; *Giber* v. *Gonard* (1884) 54 L.J. Ch. 439; *Re Rogers* (1891) 8 Morr. 243; *Re Drucker* [1902] 2 K.B. 237; *Re Watson* (1912) 107 L.T. 783 and *Re Hooley* [1915] 84 L.J.K.B. 181. See also *Re Pallitt* [1893] 1 Q.B. 455; *Re Mid-Kent Fruit Factory* [1896] 1 Ch. 567; *Re City Equitable Fire Insurance Co. Ltd. (No. 2)* [1930] Ch. 293.
[53] (1819) 2 B. & Ald. 684.
[54] See Priestley, *op. cit.* 230 who points out that the attitude of other sources of finance might change if the credit substitution were known, but this is unlikely in the case of unsecured credit.
[55] [1985] Ch. 207. See also, *Re E.V.T.R.* [1987] B.C.L.C. 646 and *Re Northern Development Holdings Ltd.* unreported, October 6, 1978, but discussed by Millett, "The Quistclose Trust: Who can Enforce it?" (1985) 101 L.Q.R. 269.

The plaintiff tobacco manufacturer arranged that the defendant advertising agency would place advertisements for it in newspapers, periodicals and by means of posters. The advertising agency thereby incurred debts to various media creditors as principal. These debts it recharged to the plaintiff along with its own fees. The plaintiff became concerned about the solvency of the advertising agency. If the agency went into liquidation leaving media creditors unpaid the plaintiff's reputation would suffer. Alternatively, it would have to pay off the media creditors to avoid disruption of a major advertising campaign that it had launched. Therefore, with the agreement of the defendant the plaintiff paid into a special account a sum equivalent to the money due to the third party creditors. The advertising agency went into insolvent liquidation but before the media creditors could be paid the liquidator froze the special account. The plaintiff, as had been feared was forced to discharge the sums due to the media people so as to maintain its advertising initiative. Thereupon it sought to recoup the moneys in the special account; a claim resisted by the defendant and its liquidator.

Peter Gibson J. acknowledged the factual differences between *Quistclose* and the present case.[56] In *Quistclose* the transaction was one of loan with no contractual obligation on the part of the lender to make payment prior to the agreement for the loan. In the present case there was no loan but there was an antecedent debt owed by the plaintiff. He held however that this factual difference was not legally material. The principal in all these cases is that equity fastens on the conscience of the person who receives from another property transferred for a specific purpose only and not therefore for the recipient's own purposes, so that such person would not be permitted to treat the property as his own or to use it for other than the stated purpose.[57]

Carreras Rothmans has attracted some criticism on the score that it ignores the possible application of the improper preference provisions in the insolvency legislation.[58] Basically the legislation invalidates acts done by a company within six months prior to the commencement of winding up which had the effect of giving a creditor a preference over other creditors and which were influenced by a desire to achieve that result.[59] The argument in the *Carreras Rothmans* context is that the consensual element in the payment transforms it into an act done by the recipient of the payment.[60] This conclusion is by no means inevitable. If the payment is made only on

---

[56] *Ibid.* 222.

[57] *Ibid.*

[58] See Priestley, *op. cit.* 235–236.

[59] ss. 239–241 of the Insolvency Act 1986. The relevant period is two years in the case of payment made in favour of a person connected with the company otherwise than by reason only of being its employee. For the definition of connected person see s. 249 of the Act. Prior to the Insolvency Act reforms, the law concerned itself only with fraudulent preferences as defined in s. 615 of the Companies Act 1985 re-enacting earlier legislation. In *Re M.C. Bacon Ltd. The Times*, December 1, 1989, Jinelott J. denied the relevance of the old cases on fraudulent preferences to the new statutory dispensation.

[60] It should be noted that Priestley's argument is made in the context of s. 122 of the Australian Bankruptcy Act which is worded differently than its U.K. counterpart.

condition that it is applied for a specific purpose the recipient can hardly be said to have bargained away the right to receive the payment without strings attached. Moreover, the "influenced by a desire to" criterion may not be satisfied.[61]

Failure to take account of the invalidating provisions of insolvency legislation is also a criticism levelled at *Re Kayford Ltd.*[62] This case concerned a company which carried on a mail-order business. The company was in financial difficulties and took advice on how best to protect customers. The customers were sending money to the company in anticipation of being supplied with goods. The company was advised by accountants to open a Customers Trust Deposit Account into which all further sums of money sent by customers for goods not yet delivered should be paid, so that should the company be forced into liquidation, these sums could be refunded to the customers who had sent them. The company largely accepted that advice but instead of opening a new account used a dormant deposit account in the company's name.

Megarry J. held that a trust in favour of the customers had been created. The whole object of what was done was to ensure that the monies remained in the beneficial ownership of those who sent them and a trust was the obvious means of achieving this.[63] The sender could create a trust by using appropriate words when he sends the money or the company could do it by taking suitable steps on or before receiving the money. If either was done the obligations in respect of the money were transformed from contract to property, from debt to trust.

Megarry J. said that no question of an improper preference arose. One was concerned here not with the question of preferring creditors but of preventing those who pay money from becoming creditors, by making them beneficiaries under a trust.[64]

This analysis has not been universally accepted. Attention may have been diverted from the question of who owned the monies at the time that the company declared itself trustee of them. If the company owned the monies at that time, then the declaration of trust had the effect of impermissibly altering the statutory order of priorities for payment of creditors.[65]

---

[61] For instance, it has been suggested that payments made in response to pressure escape invalidation as improper preferences in that the element of pressure vitiates any desire to prefer but see Sealy and Milman, *An Annotated Guide to the 1986 Insolvency Legislation*, p. 253.
[62] [1975] 1 W.L.R. 279. See Priestley, *op. cit.* 233; Jones and Goodhart, *op. cit.* 495–497; Waters, "Trusts in the Setting of Business, Commerce and Bankruptcy" (1893) 21 Alberta Law Review 395, 417: Heydon, Gummow and Austin, *Cases and Materials on Equity and Trusts* (2nd ed., 1982), p. 353; *Jacobs' Law of Trusts in Australia* (5th ed., 1986), pp. 17–18.
[63] *Ibid.* 282. He said that payment into a separate bank account was a useful (though by no means conclusive) indication of an intention to create a trust, but there was nothing to prevent the company from binding itself by a trust even if there were no effective banking arrangements.
[64] *Ibid.* 281. See also, Goode, *Payment Obligations in Commercial and Financial Transactions* (1983), p. 18, n. 64.
[65] See Waters, *op. cit.* 417.

Re Kayford Ltd. may be distinguished from *Re Nanwa Gold Mines Ltd.*[66] which is safe from criticism. There money was advanced on the faith of a promise to keep it in a separate account and Harman J. held that a trust had been created. He contrasted *Moseley* v. *Cressey's Co.*[67] where a simple statement that application monies would be refunded was held not to bind monies standing in a bank to the credit of the company, with a trust in favour of the depositors. The intent of the promise to keep in a separate account meant that the monies would not be mixed with the company's monies.[68]

Despite all the criticisms *Re Kayford Ltd.* was followed by the Court of Appeal in *Re Chelsea Cloisters Ltd.*[69] This was a case where the company which was the underlessee of a block of flats granted numerous tenancies. It took a deposit from individual tenants in respect of any sum which might be due from the tenant at the end of the tenancy for damage, breakages and compensation. Initially there were no special arrangements for dealing with deposits of the tenants but when the company got into financial difficulties they were segregated from the company's general assets and paid into a Tenant's Deposit Account. The company went into liquidation and it was held that the deposits were held by the company on trust for the tenants.

Lord Denning said that the deposits were not impressed with a trust from the very beginning.[70] The creation of the special arrangements, however, established a trust.[71] No issue of improper preference was raised.

There remains to be considered the pre-requisites for the creation of a valid express trust, namely the three certainties—certainty of intention, certainty of subject-matter and certainty of objects. Moreover, if the declaration of trust relates to land, signed written evidence must be available before the trust can be enforced.[72]

Certainty of Intention

This issue was discussed in *Re Kayford Ltd.* Megarry J. said that a trust can be created without using the words "trust" or "confidence" or the like. The pertinent question was whether a sufficient intention to create a trust had been manifested.[73] Sufficiency of intention to create a trust was not manifested in *Swiss Bank Corporation* v. *Lloyds Bank Ltd.*[74]

[66] [1955] 3 All E.R. 219. See also, *National Bolivian Navigation Co.* v. *Wilson* [1880] 5 A.C. 176. *Elkins* v. *Capital Guarantee Society* (1900) 16 T.L.R. 423; *Re Independent Air Travel Ltd.* [1961] 1 Lloyd's Rep. 604 and *Smith* v. *Liquidator of James Birrell Ltd.* 1968 S.L.T. 174.
[67] (1865) L.R. 1 Eq. 405.
[68] [1955] 3 All E.R. 219, 223.
[69] (1981) 41 P. & C.R. 98.
[70] *Ibid.* 101. He referred to *Potters* v. *Loppert* [1973] Ch. 399. See also, Bridge L.J. at 102 and Oliver L.J. at 104 who were disinclined to express an opinion on this point.
[71] Referring to *Henry* v. *Hammond* [1913] 2 K.B. 515 and *Hughes* v. *Stubbs* (1842) 1 Hare 478 as well as *Re Kayford Ltd.* [1975] 1 W.L.R. 279.
[72] s. 53(1)(b) of the Law of Property Act 1925.
[73] [1975] 1 W.L.R. 279, 282.
[74] [1982] A.C. 584.

The facts of the case are complicated but the nub of the issue was whether a lender of money, the Swiss Bank Corpn. had obtained any kind of proprietary interest in securities which the borrower, as the lender knew, wished to use the loan to invest in.

The loan agreement did not actually confer such a proprietary interest, but in it the borrower did promise that it would observe all the conditions attached by the Bank of England to its consent for the loan. These conditions included the requirements that the loan was to be used exclusively for the purchase of certain foreign securities (F.I.B.I. securities) and that the interest on and capital of the loan were to be repaid to the Swiss Bank Corpn. out of the F.I.B.I. securities or the proceeds of their sale. The borrower subsequently charged the F.I.B.I. securities to Lloyds Bank as security for a guarantee given in respect of a further loan from that bank. When the Swiss Bank Corpn. sought repayment of the loan, it claimed to have a better interest in the securities than Lloyds Bank. Although the judge at first instance, Browne-Wilkinson J., held in the plaintiffs' favour both the Court of Appeal and the House of Lords held against them.

None of the appellate judges in the *Swiss Bank* case could see anything in the loan which specifically said that the borrowers would repay the loan out of the F.I.B.I. securities, nor would they imply any such promise. Both the Court of Appeal and the House of Lords judges were content to apply the law as stated by Lord Wrenbury in *Palmer* v. *Carey*.[75]

> "An agreement for valuable consideration that a fund shall be applied in a particular way may found an injunction to restrain its application in another way. But if there be nothing more, such a stipulation will not amount to an equitable assignment. It is necessary to find further, that an obligation has been imposed in favour of the creditor to pay the debt out of the fund."

Certainty of Subject-matter

The property which is said to form the subject-matter of the alleged trust must be identifiable. A trust claim failed on this ground in *Re London Wine Shippers Ltd.*[76] This case involved a wine merchant who appropriated part of its general wine stock to a specific customer order only when the customer came in to collect the wine. The wine merchant went into receivership. Oliver J. held that the customers could not claim to be beneficiaries under a trust of the wine as the essential element of certainty of subject-matter was absent.

Certainty of Objects

Although the requirements of certainty of intention and certainty of

[75] [1926] A.C. 703, 706–707.
[76] [1986] P.C.C. 212. The case was decided on November 7, 1975. See also, *Export Credits Guarantee Dept.* v. *Turner* 1981 S.L.T. 286.

subject-matter are satisfied there cannot be a valid trust for beneficiaries or purposes if those beneficiaries or purposes are themselves insufficiently certain.[77] In such a situation of uncertainty the property is held on a resulting trust for the settlor. The word "resulting" is used in the sense of "springing back."[78] The beneficial interest is said to spring back to the grantor but in reality it never left him. In *Quistclose* itself the primary purpose of the payment was held to have failed so that the property was held on a resulting trust for the grantor.[79]

Controversy has dogged the *Quistclose* trust in relation to the right of the settlor, recognised in the *locus classicus* itself, to see that the property is applied for the primary stated purpose.[80] It has been suggested that the right is not the right of a beneficiary under the resulting trust, for if the primary purpose is fulfilled there is no resulting trust and the payer is a mere creditor. It is axiomatic that a grantor or settlor who retains no beneficial interest cannot enforce the trust which he has created but the beneficiaries can.[81]

P. J. Millett, Q.C. has argued persuasively that *Quistclose* does not necessitate the recognition of a new *genus* of enforceable purpose trust which a settlor may enforce.[82] The question of enforceability involves an examination of the payer's intention which is to be gleaned from the conduct of the parties, the language used and the circumstances of the case. The following have been suggested as guidelines by which the payer's intention may be ascertained.[83]

> "1. If [the payer's] intention was to benefit [the third party], or his object would be frustrated if he were to retain a power of revocation, the transaction will create an irrevocable trust in favour of [the third party] enforceable by [the third party], but not by [the payer]. The beneficial interest in the trust property will be in [the third party].
>
> 2. If [the payer's] intention was to benefit [the recipient] (though without vesting a beneficial interest in him), or to benefit himself by furthering some private or commercial interest of his own and not

---

[77] Generally the only type of valid purpose trusts are charitable trusts because of the beneficiary principle, *i.e.* there must be beneficiaries who can apply to the court to enforce their rights. In the case of a charitable trust the Attorney General, as guardian of the public interest, may enforce. However, the courts have recognised a certain anomalous category of non-charitable trusts. See generally, *Re Astor's Settlement Trusts* [1952] Ch. 534; *Leahy v. Attorney General for New South Wales* [1959] A.C. 457; *Re Denley's Trust Deed* [1969] 1 Ch. 373 and *Wicks v. Firth* [1983] A.C. 214.

[78] "Resulting" is derived from the Latin verb *resalire*.

[79] See also, *Re E.V.T.R.* [1987] B.C.L.C. 646.

[80] See Heydon, Gummow and Austin, *op. cit.* 357; Millett, *op. cit.* 287.

[81] This principle forms the basis of the rule against non-charitable purpose trusts and also is at the heart of the doctrine enunciated in *Saunders v. Vautier* (1841) Cr. & Ph. 240. Under this doctrine beneficiaries of full age and consent who are all ascertained and between them entitled to the entire beneficial interest in the trust property, may have the property transferred to themselves absolutely and bring the trust to an end.

[82] *Op. cit.* particularly p. 290. Mr. Millett is now a High Court Judge.

[83] *Ibid.* 290.

(except incidentally) to benefit [the third party], then the transaction will create a trust in favour of [the payer] alone, and [the recipient] will hold the trust property in trust to comply with [the payer's] directions. The trust will be enforceable by [the payer] but not by [the third party]. The beneficial interest will remain in [the payer]."

Constructive Trusts

Constructive trusts arise independently of the intention of the parties. In certain circumstances equity deems the legal owner of property to be constructive trustee for another: the United States judge, Carozo J. put it grandiloquently when he said in *Beatty* v. *Guggenheim Exploration Co.*[84]:

"A constructive trust is the formula through which the conscience of equity finds expression. When property has been acquired in such circumstances that the holder of the legal title may not in good conscience retain the beneficial interest, equity converts him into a trustee."

Constructive trusts or principles analogous thereto have been argued in certain payment of money cases, particularly where money has been paid under a mistake of fact. In *Chase Manhattan Bank N.A.* v. *Israel-British Bank (London) Ltd.*[85] Goulding J. held that a payment actuated by a factual error was recoverable. Such recovery was based on a persistent equitable proprietary interest on the payer. The judge said that a person who paid money to another, under a mistake of fact, retained an equitable proprietary interest in it and the conscience of the payee was subjected to a fiduciary duty to respect that continuing proprietary interest.[86]

The principles governing recovery of payments made under a mistake of fact were summed up by Robert Goff J. in *Barclays Bank Ltd.* v. *W.J. Simms Son & Cooke (Southern) Ltd.*[87] He said[88]:

[84] 225 N.Y. 380, 386 (1919).
[85] [1981] Ch. 105.
[86] *Ibid.* 119.
[87] [1980] 2 W.L.R. 218. See also, *Rover International Ltd.* v. *Cannon Film Sales Ltd.* [1989] 1 W.L.R. 912 and *Australian and New Zealand Banking Group Ltd.* v. *Westpac Banking Corp.* (1988) 78 A.L.R. 577. Here the High Court of Australia reiterated that the mistake need not be shared by the payee or that the mistake be as to a fact which, if it had existed, would have resulted in the payee being under a legal obligation to make the mistake. The Court, however, postponed consideration of the question "whether the requirement that the mistake be fundamental involves any more than that it appears that without the mistake on the part of the payee, the payment would not have been made." In other words, the shift from the notion of "fundamental mistake" to "causative mistake" evidenced in *Barclays Bank* v. *Simms* was left in the air so far as Australia is concerned. See generally, on this whole area, Beatson and Bishop, "Mistaken Payments in the Law of Restitution" (1986) 36 U. of Toronto L.J. 149; Sutton, "Mistaken Payments: An Inner Logic infringed" (1987) 37 U. of Toronto L.J. 389; Birks, *An Introduction to the Law of Restitution* (paperback ed., 1989), pp. 149–159 and 452–454.
[88] *Ibid.* 232. The learned judge deduced these principles from a formidable line of authority. Proposition 1 was founded on three House of Lords cases: *Kleinwort, Sons & Co.* v. *Dunlop Rubber Co.* (1907) 97 L.T. 263; *Kerrison* v. *Glyn, Mills, Currie & Co.* (1911) 81 L.J.K.B. 465; and *Jones (R.E.) Ltd.* v. *Waring & Gillow Ltd.* [1925] 2 K.B. 612. Proposition 2(a) was founded

"(1) If a person pays money to another under a mistake of fact which causes him to make the payment, he is *prima facie* entitled to recover it as money paid under a mistake of fact. (2) His claim may however fail if (a) the payer intends that the payee shall have the money at all events, whether the fact be true or false, or is deemed in law so to intend; or (b) the payment is made for good consideration, in particular if the money is paid to discharge, and does discharge, a debt owed to the payee (or a principal on whose behalf he is authorised to receive the payment) by the payer or by a third party to whom he is authorised to discharge the debt; or (c) the payee has changed his position in good faith, or is deemed in law to have done so."

The recognition of equitable proprietary claims leads in consequence to a diminution of a debtor's estate available for distribution to general creditors. When one considers the question whether a payment should be impressed with a trust, it must be remembered that the real contest is not between payer and recipient but between the payer and the recipient's creditors.[89] A constructive trust claim was upheld however in *Neste Oy* v. *Lloyds Bank plc*.[90] This was a case where a principal made various payments to its agent, a company called P.S.L. At the time that the last payment was made, the directors of P.S.L. had resolved to discontinue trading and to seek the appointment of a receiver.

Bingham J. decided that this last payment was subject to a constructive trust. P.S.L. could not in good conscience, at the time of receipt of the payment, retain it. It would have seemed little short of sharp practice for them to take any advantage from the payment. Moreover, it would be contrary to any ordinary notion of fairness, according to the learned judge, that the general body of creditors should profit from the accident of a payment at a time when there was bound to be a total failure of consideration.[91]

It has been suggested that the position of a payer in a *Quistclose* situation is to be equated with that of a person who pays for property in advance of transfer and, without acquiring ownership, invests in the seller indefeasible title to the money.[92] The courts, however, have recoiled from the analogy, taking the view that there is no good reason to accord the buyer real rights

---

on *Kelly* v. *Solari* (1841) 9 M. & W. 54 and *Morgan* v. *Ashcroft* [1938] 1 K.B. 49. Proposition 2(b) was based upon the decision in *Aiken* v. *Short* and upon dicta in *Kerrison* v. *Glyn, Mills, Currie & Co.* (1911) 81 L.J.K.B. 465. Proposition 2(c) has as its foundation the statement of principle by Lord Loreburn L.C. in *Kleinwort Sons & Co.* v. *Dunlop Rubber Co.* (1907) 97 L.T. 263.

[89] See generally, Goode, "Ownership and Obligation in Commercial Transactions" (1987) 103 L.Q.R. 433.

[90] [1983] 2 Lloyd's Rep. 658. See also, *Re Irish Shipping Ltd.* [1986] I.L.R.M. 518.

[91] *Ibid.* 666.

[92] See Birks, *An Introduction to the Law of Restitution* (1985), p. 387; Goode (1987) 103 L.Q.R. 433, 440.

over the seller's assets merely because insolvency supervenes.[93] A leading case is the Irish Supreme Court decision in *Re Barrett Apartments Ltd.*[94]

Barrett Apartments Ltd. owned a site on which it proposed to build a block of flats. "Booking deposits" were paid by prospective purchasers of the flats and a further sum was to be paid on the execution of a building agreement. Building agreements were signed in only a couple of cases. A receiver was appointed to the company and the question arose whether the depositors had secured claims against the company. A distinction was drawn between depositors who had, and those who had not, signed a legally enforceable contract for the purchase of premises.[95]

Henchy J. said that the rationale behind allowing a purchaser a lien on the purchased property in respect of a deposit paid to the vendor was that by paying the deposit in pursuance of the contract, the purchaser acquired an equitable estate or interest in the property.[96] Therefore he should be allowed to follow that estate or interest by being accorded a lien on it.[97] Where no contract of purchase was entered into by the depositor, the payment of the booking deposit did not give the payer any estate or interest, legal or equitable, in the property—as would have been the case if a written contract had been entered into and the booking deposit had been converted into a deposit paid on foot of the contract.

The depositors relied heavily on the words of Vaughan Williams L.J. in *Whitbread and Co. Ltd.* v. *Watt*[98] that the lien was a right invented for the purpose of doing justice. The Supreme Court, however, were unmoved by this argument. Henchy J. stated that depositors as a class did not have an equity to be treated as secured creditors, while other creditors, whose debts could be more deserving of payment and no less closely connected with the

---

[93] *Cf.* however, Lord Templeman in *Space Investments Ltd.* v. *Canadian Imperial Bank of Commerce Trust Co. (Bahamas) Ltd.* [1986] 3 All E.R. 75, 76–77.

[94] [1985] I.R. 350; on which see McCormack (1986) 7 Co. Law 113; Coughlan (1988) 10 D.U.L.J. 90.

[95] The Supreme Court appears to have decided that an equitable lien was claimable only by persons with a continuing right to specific performance. This view is at variance with the opinion of the High Court of Australia in *Hewett* v. *Court* (1983) 57 A.L.J.R. 211 who decided by a majority that the availability of specific performance to a purchaser was not essential in deciding upon an equitable lien. Specific performance results in fulfilment of the contract whereas an equitable lien came about in the event of the contract not being performed. Logically the two were quite distinct. A decree of specific performance may be withheld from an innocent purchaser on grounds which had nothing to do with the question whether he should be accorded security for the return of the purchase money. See generally, Hardingham, "Equitable Liens for the Recovery of Purchase Money" (1985) 15 M.U.L.R. 65.

[96] *Ibid.* 357–358. Reference was made to *Rose* v. *Watson* (1864) 10 H.L.C. 672 and *Tempany* v. *Hynes* [1976] I.R. 101.

[97] It has been argued that this view is at odds with the accepted learning that equitable charges are not dependent on possession or ownership, either at law or in equity. See Coughlan, *op. cit.* 96.

[98] [1902] 1 Ch. 835, 838. See also, *Combe* v. *Lord Swaythling* [1947] 1 Ch. 625. McCarthy J. pointed out at 360 that the learned Lord Justice merely meant to say that an express agreement for the grant of a lien was not necessary. He did not purport to remove the necessity of a contractual setting.

property, were left to languish as unsecured creditors without hope of payment at the tail-end of the queue of creditors.[99]

McCarthy J. subscribed to the same idea. Those who paid advances in respect of an anticipated contract should not be placed in a more advantageous position than that of trading creditors or professional creditors who put their goods or their services at the disposal of the self-same debtor without payment and whose claims could only rank as those of unsecured creditors.[1]

Conditional Payments—A Summing Up

It is certainly possible for a person who has paid money to a company under particular conditions to secure the return of that money if the stated conditions are not fulfilled. This right of return takes precedence over company creditors if the payments have been clothed with a trust—the so-called *Quistclose* trust. An express trust in the *Quistclose* mould arises only if the necessary intention to create a trust has been manifested with sufficient certainty. Moreover, the money forming the subject-matter of the trust must be identified with certainty. The payment should be clothed with a trust at the outset—otherwise the improper preference provisions in the Insolvency Act may apply.

A conditional might also be able to argue that his payments have been impressed with a constructive trust. The courts, however, in deciding whether or not to impose a constructive trust are likely to take account of the fact that the real contest is not between payer and payee but between the payer and the payee's general creditors.

---

[99] [1985] I.R. 350, 358–359. For an argument supporting a more individuated claim to a lien, see Couglan, *op. cit.* 104–106.
[1] *Ibid.* 361.

CHAPTER 3

TRACING AND ADMIXTURE OF GOODS

It may be that a person to whom goods have been supplied subject to a reservation of title clause has passed those goods on to somebody else receiving other goods or a monetary sum in exchange. This matter is usually discussed under the rubric of tracing.[1] In many sale of goods cases there will be an express "tracing clause" which talks about rights in relation to proceeds. Even apart from the existence of such a clause the matter of tracing falls to be considered. A "tracing clause," though, is realistic in recognising that a buyer of goods must usually be accorded, if not expressly, then by necessary implication of law, the right to resell those goods. It may also be the case that the goods supplied have been incorporated into other goods or form all or part of the raw material of a process of manufacture. In this chapter both tracing and admixture of goods will be addressed in fairly general terms. The discussion will be applied more specifically to particular problems arising in the reservation of title context in Chapters 5 and 6.

Tracing Rights

The right to trace arises both at common law and in equity. The common law right to trace is largely undeveloped. In recent times, far greater attention has been directed at its equitable equivalent. Nevertheless, the common law remedy may yield a positive result from the point of view of a claimant where equity holds no such hope. Therefore, the position at common law merits some discussion.

Common Law Right to Trace

The *locus classicus* of the common law right to trace is *Taylor* v. *Plumer*.[2] In this case, one Walsh was entrusted by Sir Thomas Plumer with money for investment in exchequer bills. Walsh instead purchased bullion and American stock with which he attempted to abscond. In this attempt he was unsuccessful and was forced to surrender the property to Plumer. An action

---

[1] For periodical literature on tracing see, *inter alia*, R. H. Maudsley, "Proprietary Remedies for the Recovery of Money" (1959) 75 L.Q.R. 234; M. Scott, "The Right to 'Trace' at Common Law" (1966) 7 Univ. of W.A.L.R. 63; F. O. B. Babafemi, "Tracing Assets: A Case for the Fusion of Common Law and Equity in English Law" (1971) 34 M.L.R. 12; R. Pearce, "A Tracing Paper" [1976] *Conveyancer* 277; R. M. Goode, "The Right to Trace and its Impact on Commercial Transactions" (1976) 92 L.Q.R. 360, 528; S. Khurshid and P. Matthews, "Tracing Confusion" (1979) 95 L.Q.R. 98.
[2] (1815) 3 M. & S. 562.

in trover was brought by Walsh's assignees in bankruptcy to recapture the property from Plumer but the action failed. According to Lord Ellenborough C.J.[3]:

> "He has repossessed himself of that, of which, according to the principles established in the cases I have cited, he never ceased to be the lawful proprietor; and having so done we are of opinion, that the assignees cannot in this action recover that which, if an action were brought against them, the assignees, by the defendant, they could not have effectually retained against him, inasmuch as it was trust property of the defendant, which, as such, did not pass to them under the commission."

Taylor v. *Plumer* has given rise to the "exchange-product" theory of common law tracing. Under this theory legal title to the exchange product vests in the owner of the original goods.[4] The difficulty with this analysis is that property passes to the person to whom the transferor intended it to pass, even if the person with whom he deals has falsely assumed the identity of another.[5] Therefore, a right to trace based on legal ownership of the product exchanged for the original goods would have little scope for application.

Professor Goode has argued eloquently, however, that the right to follow an asset at common law is not a proprietary right but rather a right to assert against another a personal right of some kind (whether possessory or purely personal) by reason of his receipt and retention or disposal of the asset.[6] In Goode's view each movement of the asset from one recipient to another brings into existence a distinct personal right of the original owner against that recipient and a separate new duty of account by the recipient to the owner. The right to follow an asset at common law may be lost though. One such situation is where a subsequent transferee has given value at a time that he is unaware that the transmission is in breach of the transferor's duty of account to the original owner.

The original asset may have altered in form or become unidentifiable thereby making necessary a claim to the proceeds of the assets instead. A big question is when the "means of ascertainment" of proceeds fails. This is the major difficulty associated with the common law right to trace.

Commentators have talked about the materialism of the common law. The common lawyer has been depicted as the "poor mutt . . . able to grasp the identity of specific coins but retiring mouth agape in baffled amazement once they are mixed with other coins."[7]

The judgment of Lord Ellenborough in *Taylor* v. *Plumer* contributes to this characterisation. He suggests that the means of ascertainment fail and

---

[3] *Ibid.* 579. Lord Ellenborough referred to a case including *L'Apostre* v. *Le Plaistrier* (1708) 1 P. Wms. 318 and *Scott* v. *Surman* (1743) Willes 400.
[4] See generally, Kurshid and Matthews, *op. cit.*; Goode (1976) 92 L.Q.R. 360, 365–68.
[5] See *Lewis* v. *Averay* [1972] 1 Q.B. 198.
[6] See Goode, *op. cit.* 369–370.
[7] See *Scott, op. cit.* 470; see also, Lord Greene M.R. in *Re Diplock* [1948] Ch. 465, 520.

with that the right to trace is lost when the subject is turned into money and mixed and confounded in a general mass of the same description.[8] He explained the earlier case of *Scott* v. *Surman*[9] by pointing out that the difficulty was one of fact and not of law. The dictum that money was no earmark must be understood as predicated on the existence only of an undivided and undistinguishable mass of current money. He went on to say that money, marked or kept apart from other money, could be followed. Money which remained as a debt and so was identifiable could also be traced and so was money laid out in the purchase of specific goods.[10]

The matter of identifiability becomes acute when the proceeds of the original goods are mixed in a bank account with other monies. The traditional view is that the common law is helpless in this respect.[11] Professor Goode takes a different view, however.[12] He has contended forcefully that the inability of the common law to allow money to be followed into a mixed fund is a myth and that in the common case of mixing in a bank or other account the rule in *Clayton's* case,[13] which will be discussed later, should apply.

Others have argued for application of the principles operative in the case of admixture of goods.[14] According to *Spence* v. *Union Marine Insurance Co. Ltd.*,[15] where it is impossible to identify or separate the goods the original owners are treated as tenants in common of the mixed whole in proportion to the value of their contributions to it.

The point is, nonetheless, that the common law right to trace has not been relied upon in recent times. Equitable intervention is the order of the day. Consequently, in the words of Goff and Jones,[16] the courts have not had the opportunity to develop "mature and consistent" common law rules for tracing money into a mixed fund in a bank account.

It is possible to envisage cases where this state of affairs might change. The common law right to trace has advantages not associated with its equitable equivalent. One drawback, however, is that the common law does not take cognisance of equitable interests in property. Hence a beneficiary under a trust could not at common law follow the property in the hands of the trustee. The big plus is the absence of any requirement of a fiduciary relationship as a foundation of the right to trace which equity, unlike the common law, requires.

In the academic literature there is mention of two situations where a common law duty to account may be of avail to a "*Romalpa*-type" supplier.

---

[8] (1815) 3 M. & S. 562, 575.
[9] (1743) Willes 400. See in particular the statement of Lord Willes at 404.
[10] See *Ryall* v. *Rolle* (1749) 1 Atk. 165.
[11] The *locus classicus* is *Banque Belge pour L'Etranger* v. *Hambrouck* [1921] 1 K.B. 321.
[12] Goode, *op. cit.* 378 *et seq.*
[13] (1816) 1 Mer. 572.
[14] See Pearce, *op. cit.* 282–283.
[15] (1868) L.R. 3 C.P. 427.
[16] See Goff and Jones, *Law of Restitution* (3rd ed., 1986), p. 67.

The first is where a purchaser of goods subject to a reservation of title clause sub-sells payment for the goods being set off against a previous debt owed by the purchaser to the sub-purchaser.[17] It is difficult to conceive of the availability of an equitable proprietary remedy in this situation for such a remedy assumes the existence of assets in the hands of the defendant and a set-off can hardly constitute this.

The second instance is in relation to *Romalpa* itself. The question of the common law right to follow proceeds was not raised. It has been suggested, though, that would equally have been available to the plaintiffs. It is argued that had the receiver applied the money he collected in meeting the running expenses of the business the right to trace in equity would have been lost. In this event the plaintiffs would have had to fall back on the personal common law remedy against the receiver in an action for money had and received.[18]

Equitable Tracing

Equitable tracing has formed the subject-matter of extensive discussion in reservation of title cases. Much of the heat and controversy has turned on the question of a fiduciary relationship. It is a strongly entrenched proposition that the equitable right to trace is not available to every owner. The remedy obtains only where the owner can show that a fiduciary duty is owed to him by the person to whom he has entrusted his property. Some have argued to the contrary[19] and suggested that it is possible to interpret the leading case, *Re Diplock*,[20] in a way which does not require, as a general rule, the finding that there is a fiduciary relationship. However, this view has been dismissed as an ingenious rationalisation not present in the mind of the Court of Appeal.[21] Furthermore, the proponent of this idea has mended the error of his ways.[22]

The fiduciary relationship requirement was accepted as inviolable by Goulding J. in *Chase Manhattan Bank N.A.* v. *Israel-British Bank (London) Ltd.*[23] The judge, however, gave a generous interpretation to the phrase. In this case the plaintiff bank paid some two million dollars by mistake to the defendant bank, which later was the subject of a winding-up order. The plaintiffs discovered their mistake and sought to trace the sum paid. They also claimed for it in the winding-up proceedings on the basis of an action for money had and received. As the defendant bank was insolvent, the latter claim, being a purely personal one, was insufficient to compensate

---

[17] See I. R. Davies "Reservation of Title Clauses: A Legal Quagmire" [1985] L.M.C.L.Q. 49, 70.

[18] Goode (1976) 92 L.Q.R. 528, 551.

[19] See Pearce [1976] Conv. 277, 287 *et seq*. See also, Oakley, "The Prerequisites of an Equitable Tracing Claim" (1975) 28 C.L.P. 64.

[20] [1948] Ch. 465.

[21] See Goff and Jones, *The Law of Restitution* (3rd ed., 1986), p. 71, n. 66.

[22] See Pearce, "Reservation of Title on the Sale of Goods in Ireland" (1985) 20 Ir.Jur. (n.s.) 264, 288.

[23] [1981] Ch. 105.

the plaintiffs, so they pressed ahead with their tracing action. The action proved successful.

Goulding J. observed that there was no judicial decision in England on the question of whether a person who mistakenly paid money could be granted the restitutionary proprietary remedy of tracing.[24] He then proceeded to examine *Re Diplock*[25] to see if it supported the argument of counsel for the defendants that there was no equitable right to trace property unless some initial fiduciary relationship existed. The judge's conclusion was that, in order to be traced, a fund need not have been the subject of fiduciary obligations before falling into the wrong hands: it was enough that the payment into the wrong hands itself gave rise to a fiduciary relationship.[26] *Sinclair* v. *Brougham*[27] was mentioned in support of this proposition. There did not have to be any consensual arrangement involved. Applied to the facts of the *Chase Manhattan* case this principle meant that "a person who pays money to another under a factual mistake retains an equitable property in it and the conscience of that other is subjected to a fiduciary duty to respect his proprietary right."

At the moment, sellers of goods have fitted themselves into the category of a bailee or agent to satisfy the fiduciary relationship requirement. The finding of a fiduciary relationship does not follow automatically from the fact of an agency of bailment, however, as we shall discover later.[28] In this context too, one should bear in mind the words of Robert Goff L.J. in *Clough Mill Ltd.* v. *Martin*[29] that concepts like bailment and fiduciary duty are our tools, not our masters.

Identifying the "Trust" Property

Equity's greatest contribution has been to clear up matters on the identi-fiability agenda or in identifying the surviving enrichment as has been stated elsewhere.[30] Whereas the common law may have stopped at the banker's door, equity was able to open the latch, walk in and inspect the books.[31] Equity, so to speak, is able to draw up a balance sheet, on the right hand side of which appears the composite fund and on its left hand side the two or

[24] *Ibid.* 116. But see *Barclays Bank Ltd.* v. *W.J. Simms Son & Cooke (Southern) Ltd.* [1980] 2 W.L.R. 218.
[25] [1948] Ch. 465.
[26] [1981] Ch. 105, 119.
[27] [1914] A.C. 398. This well-known case involved a situation where a building society carried on an *ultra vires* banking business. It was held that depositors retained an equitable property in funds they parted with, and fiduciary relationships arose between them and the directors. A sufficient fiduciary relationship to support a tracing right was found to exist between the depositors and the directors by reason of the fact that the purposes for which the depositors had handed their money to the directors were by law incapable of fulfilment.
[28] *Supra.*
[29] [1985] 1 W.L.R. 111, 116.
[30] See Birks, *Introduction to the Law of Restitution* (1985), p. 358.
[31] See *Banque Belge Pour l'Etranger* v. *Hambrouck* [1921] 1 K.B. 321, 335 *per* Atkins L.J.

more funds of which it is deemed to be made up.[32] Equity may order the restoration of an unmixed sum of money (or property acquired by means of such a sum). Alternatively, it may declare a charge on a mixed fund (or property acquired by means of such a fund).

If the fiduciary uses the proceeds of the goods to purchase another asset, the original owner may adopt the purchase and claim the purchase property entirely as his own.[33] Alternatively, he may claim a lien on the property to secure recoupment of the value of his original asset. Normally, what the fiduciary receives in return for the goods is money and he may mix this money with his own money in a bank or other running account. The original owner, O, is entitled to a charge on the account to secure recoupment of the proceeds of his asset.[34]

Usually withdrawals from a bank account are taken as representing the earliest credit item. This is the rule in *Clayton's* case.[35] However, the principle is not applied in the tracing situation that we have outlined. The presumption is that the fiduciary did not intend to commit a breach of trust. Consequently, in working out which funds have been expended *Clayton's* case is inapplicable and the monies remaining in the account will be taken to be the monies belonging to O. This is known as the rule in *Re Hallett's Estate*.[36]

The presumption against a breach of trust is not carried very far. If subsequently, the trustee were to replenish the fund there is no assumption that in doing so he intended to replace the monies withdrawn in breach of trust. O is entitled to a charge on the bank account only to the extent of the lowest intermediate balance. This principle was formulated in *James Roscoe (Bolton) Ltd.* v. *Winder*.[37] Sargant J. held that payments into a general account cannot, without proof of express intention, be appropriated to the replacement of trust money which has been improperly mixed with that account and drawn out. In the words of the American Professor Scott, "there is no reason for subjecting other property of the wrongdoer to the claimant's claim any more than to the claims of other creditors merely because the money happens to be put in the same place where the claimant's money formerly was unless the wrongdoer actually intended to make restitution to the claimant."[38]

Re Hallett's Estate does not take away from the fundamental principle that O has an entitlement to a charge on the mixed fund or any property which is

[32] *Re Diplock* [1948] Ch. 465, 520 *per* Lord Greene M.R. The Master of the Rolls stated that it was the metaphysical approach of equity coupled with and encouraged by the far-reaching remedy of a declaration of charge that enabled equity to identify money in a mixed fund.

[33] *Re Hallett's Estate* (1880) 13 Ch.D. 696, 709 *per* Sir George Jessel M.R.

[34] *Ibid.* It was explained that the charge was quite independent of the fact of the amount laid out by the fiduciary. The moment you got a substantial portion of it furnished by the fiduciary, the right to a charge followed.

[35] (1817) 1 Mer. 572.

[36] (1880) 13 Ch.D. 696. The Court of Appeal (Thesiger L.J. dissenting) on this point refused to follow the earlier decision in *Pennell* v. *Deffell* (1853) 4 De G.M. & G. 372.

[37] [1915] 1 Ch. 62.

[38] A. W. Scott, *The Law of Trusts* (3rd ed., 1967), Vol. 5, p. 3638.

purchased thereout. A case in point is *Re Oatway*[39] where the trustee had mixed his own and trust monies in a banking account. The account was drawn upon to further the purchase of shares but a balance was left that exceeded the amount of trust monies paid in. Further drawings were made which exhausted the account. Therefore, it was useless to proceed against the account. These later drawings were dissipated and did not result in any assets which could be traced. The court took the view that the *cestuis que trust* had a charge on the shares from the trust money paid into the account. It was held that the original charge on the mixed fund continued on each and every part thereof, despite changes of form, unless and until the restoration of the trust money paid into the mixed account and reinstatement of the trust fund by the proper investment of the money in the joint names of the appropriate trustees. Joyce J. put the matter bluntly. He said[40]:

> "It is, in my opinion, . . . clear that when any of the money drawn out has been invested, and the investment remains in the name or under the control of the trustee, the rest of the balance having been afterwards dissipated by him, he cannot maintain that the investment which remains represents his own money alone, and that what has been spent and can no longer be traced and recovered was the money belonging to the trust."

If the entirety of a mixed fund is used in the acquisition of property which increases in value, then according to the opinion expressed by Ungoed Thomas J. in *Re Tilley's Will Trusts*[41] the claim will be for a proportionate part of the enhanced value and not just for the amount of the trust money expended in the purchase. So, in general, O may claim a proportionate share of a new asset purchased out of the trust money. The judge held that this right of election by a beneficiary also applied where an asset was purchased by a trustee in part out of his own money and in part out of the trust money. The beneficiary could, if he wished, require the asset to be treated as trust property with regard to that proportion of it which the trust monies contributed to its purchase.[42]

If a dispute arises between two claimants to a mixed fund consisting of monies held on behalf of the two of them and mingled together by the trustee, they share *pari passu*. Moreover, if property is acquired by means of the mixed fund, each is entitled to a charge rateably. Neither gains over the other. The same principle holds if the property of O and an innocent volunteer are mixed. In *Re Diplock* it was said[43]:

> "It would be inequitable for the volunteer to claim priority for the reason that he is a volunteer: it would be equally inequitable for the true

[39] [1903] 2 Ch. 356.
[40] *Ibid.* 360.
[41] [1967] 1 Ch. 1179.
[42] *Ibid.* 1189.
[43] [1948] Ch. 465, 539.

owner of the money to claim priority over the volunteer for the reason that the volunteer is innocent and cannot be said to act unconscionably if he claims equal treatment for himself. The mutual recognition of one another's rights is what equity insists upon as a condition of giving relief."

Where the funds of two separate trusts or the funds of one trust and those of an innocent volunteer are mixed in the context of an active banking account then the rule in *Clayton's* case, namely, first in, first out, will apply.[44] This application tends to produce unjust results causing loss to fall on the shoulders of one or other innocent party.[45]

Tracing rights subsist only so long as the fund can be followed, in the legally understood sense of that term. Dissipation may occur leaving no traceable assets. In *Re Diplock* itself the court spoke thus[46]:

"The equitable remedies presuppose the continued existence of the money either as a separate fund or as part of a mixed fund or as latent in property acquired by means of such a fund. If ... such continued existence is not established, equity is as helpless as the common law itself. If the fund, mixed or unmixed, is spent upon a dinner, equity, which dealt only in specific relief and not in damages, can do nothing."

Re Diplock is also important in highlighting equitable bars to a tracing claim. The remedy awarded by equity is a declaration of charge enforceable by sale. If an innocent volunteer has spent the trust money on altering or improving his own land or buildings, it would not be equitable to allow O to trace the monies. A charge on the land or buildings is backed up by a power to compel a sale. This would mean the volunteer being forced to exchange his land or buildings for money and often their market value will not have increased in line with the monetary amount of the alterations.[47]

Relevance of Traditional Tracing Rules in the Modern World

The relevance of the rules for ascertaining the surviving enrichment in this modern world of mass communications and instantaneous transfer of funds has been questioned by Professor Jones.[48] He suggests that it may no longer

---

[44] See *Re Diplock* [1948] Ch. 465, 554. See also, Fry J. in *Hallett's Case* (1880) 13 Ch.D. 696, 699 and North J. in *Re Stenning* [1895] 2 Ch. 433. The justification advanced for not treating two claimants rateably was that this would lead to the greatest difficulty and complication in practice.
[45] For a critical view see Goff and Jones (3rd ed., 1986), p. 75 who quote the words of Judge Learned Hand in *Re Walter J. Schmidt & Co.* 298 F. 314, 316 (1923) that to adopt the fiction of first in, first out, is "to apportion a common misfortune through a test which has no relation whatever to the justice of the case." See also, Birks, *op. cit.* p. 364 who alludes to the "undemonstrated strength of the reasons of convenience and so-called presumed intention."
[46] [1948] Ch. 465, 521.
[47] See generally, *op. cit.* 546–550.
[48] "Tracing Claims in the Modern World" [1988] King's Counsel 15. See also, Goff and Jones, *op. cit.* 79 and 116.

be necessary, to "identify" in accordance with equity's traditional rules and presumptions, assets in the hands of the defendant. The rules may be found wanting in the context of a volatile and active banking.

For illustration one might refer to the *Chase Manhattan* case.[49] Here the defendant had traded for over a month after it had received the mistaken payment with daily inflows and outflows surely in excess of millions of pounds. Goulding J. left aside for another day the question of whether any part of the *corpus* of the mistaken payment remained to form the subject-matter of a tracing order.[50] Jones reasons that the other day never dawned in the Chancery Division for the very probable reason that there were no unsecured assets over which a lien could be imposed in favour of the plaintiff.[51]

Professor Jones' arguments are very much in line with the prescription of Jessel M.R. in *Re Hallett's Estate*.[52] He pointed out that the rules of Court of Equity were not established from time immemorial. On the contrary they had been established from time to time as well as altered, improved and refined from time to time. Moreover, to discover the principles of equity one had to refer to the more modern rather than the more ancient cases.

On the other hand the rules have been firmly established over the past 100 years; it would require an extremely daring judge to cast these principles aside and to go back to the drawing board. Moreover, the traditional approach has been vigorously defended by distinguished academic as well as judicial theorists. The influential American Professor A. W. Scott, has contended there is no good reason to prefer a tracing claimant to an insolvent's general creditors where it could not be proved at the time of the action that the insolvent's assets consisted wholly or in part, of funds originally provided by the plaintiff.[53]

Bailment

Bailment is important in the reservation of title context because it may provide a foundation for a claim against the proceeds of sale of the original goods supplied or the products thereof. However, it has been pointed out that more recent cases mark a shift in emphasis in the direction of enquiry

[49] [1981] Ch. 105.
[50] *Ibid.* 128.
[51] Jones, *op. cit.* 16.
[52] (1880) 13 Ch.D. 696, 710.
[53] *Law of Trusts* (3rd ed., 1967), Vol. 5, s. 521 quoted by Jones, *op. cit.* 16. There are faint indications however, in the Privy Council case of *Space Investments Ltd.* v. *Canadian Imperial Bank of Commerce Trust Co. (Bahamas) Ltd.* [1987] 1 W.L.R. 1072 that the courts may redesign equity's traditional tracing rules. Professor Goode points out: "The implication in Lord Templeman's speech seems to be that all the assets of the bank constitute one enormous fund so that the infusion of any part of the trust property into those assets impresses the totality of the assets with a charge in favour of the beneficiaries," "Ownership and Obligation in Commercial Transactions" (1987) 103 L.Q.R. 433, 447. See also Birks, *An Introduction to the Law of Restitution* (paperback ed., 1989), pp. 472–473.

from whether there was a bailment to the more relevant examination of the relationship between the parties to see if it was fiduciary in character.[54]

The starting point for our discussion must be a brief examination of the nature of bailment. It has been said that, in many respects, bailment is at the intersection point of contract, property and tort.[55] In the classical situation of bailment, we have a conveyance of personal property, created by contract and enforceable in tort. The doctrine is confined to personal property. Bailment connotes a divergence between the actual physical possession of goods and some ultimate or reversionary possessory right. A number of obligations are imposed by law upon a person in possession of goods as a bailee.

In the landmark case of *Aluminium Industrie Vaassen B.V.* v. *Romalpa Aluminium Ltd.*[56] the concession was made by counsel for the receiver that the intending purchaser of goods, subject to a clause reserving title in the seller until payment, was the bailee of the goods for the owner. This concession was accepted as well founded by the Court of Appeal and is supported by authority from other common law jurisdictions.

In the New Zealand case of *Motor Mart Ltd.* v. *Webb*[57] it was held that a person who had agreed to purchase goods subject to a retention of title clause was a bailee of the goods for the owner. Turner J. made some pertinent observations on the nature and development of the bailment relationship. He said[58]:

> "There are few transactions in the terminology of the law whose defini-
> tion proves so difficult as that of bailment, and few to which so little
> careful attention has been given in recent years . . . I think . . . it would
> be a mistake to conclude that the transaction of bailment is one which
> has refused, and can still refuse, to undergo the evolution and adapta-
> tion which the Common Law imposes upon every legal institution . . . I
> think . . . development in our day of the commercial process of the
> instalment-purchase of goods, with concurrent evolution of the legal
> concepts of hire-purchase and . . . the wider use of the (conditional
> sale), may all combine to compel the evolution in the law of bailment of
> a new type of bailment different in some respects from other types
> hereto existing."

The basic nature of a bailment is that the property bailed should be returned to the bailor or applied in accordance with his instructions when the bailment comes to an end. It is not necessary that the goods be returnable in their precise original form. It *is* essential, however, that the bailor is subject to a duty to return the goods themselves, be it in original or altered form, and not merely a monetary sum or goods of equivalent characteristics. The

[54] See J. H. Farrar and Chiah Kim Chai [1985] J.B.L. 160.
[55] Palmer, *Bailment*, p. 1. This is a lengthy and detailed treatise on the modern law of bailment.
[56] [1976] 1 W.L.R. 676.
[57] [1958] N.Z.L.R. 772.
[58] *Ibid.* 780, 784–785.

leading case is the Privy Council decision *South Australian Insurance Co. Ltd.* v. *Randell*.[59] There the view was taken that, where there was a delivery of property on a contract in exchange for an equivalent in money, or some valuable commodity, and not for the return of the identical subject-matter in its original form or an altered form, then this was a sale and not a bailment.

Much criticism has been directed at the judgment of Slade J. in *Re Bond Worth Ltd.*[60] for alleging advancing the proposition that there can only be a bailment when the very goods themselves have to be returned to the bailor. However, it is submitted that this perception of the judgment rests upon a misconception. Granted Slade J. cited certain cases where a bailment was held not to exist and regarded them as providing assistance for the resolution of the issues before him.[61] The cases, though, were adduced in support of the statement that where an alleged trustee has the right to mix tangible assets or monies with his own assets or monies, and to deal with them as he pleases, this is incompatible with the existence of a presently subsisting fiduciary relationship in regard to such particular assets or moneys. In other words the cases were relevant to the issue of fiduciary relationship and not just to bailment *per se*.

In more recent cases the debate has moved on explicitly to the fiduciary relationship plane. Both Staughton J. in *Hendy Lennox (Industrial Engines) Ltd.* v. *Grahame Puttick Ltd.*[62] and Peter Gibson J. in *Re Andrabell Ltd.*[63] refuted the idea that the bailor/bailee relationship was necessarily a fiduciary one. In doing so, they rejected the submission that the judgments of the Court of Appeal in *Romalpa* supported a contrary proposition.

Staughton J. believed that it was implicit in the reasoning of the Court of Appeal in *Romalpa* that some bailees and some agents do not occupy a fiduciary position. He referred in some detail to the reasoning of Jessel M.R. in *Re Hallett's Estate*.[64] In that case the Master of the Rolls expressed himself in the following terms[65]:

> "Has it ever been suggested, until very recently, that there is any distinction between an express trustee, or an agent, or a bailee, or a collector of rents, or anybody else in a fiduciary position? I have never heard, until quite recently, such a distinction suggested. . . . It can have no foundation in principle. . . ."

Staughton J. understood these remarks as not referring to every agent or every bailee. The reference rather was to persons in a fiduciary position who receive money not for their own account but for another's account. In

[59] (1869) L.R. 3 P.C. 101.
[60] [1980] Ch. 228.
[61] The cases he mentions are *Foley* v. *Hill* (1848) 2 H.L. Cas. 28; *Re Nevill, ex parte White* (1871) 6 Ch.App. 397; *South Australian Insurance Co. Ltd.* v. *Randell* (1869) L.R. 3 P.C. 101 and *Henry* v. *Hammond* [1913] 2 K.B. 515.
[62] [1984] 1 W.L.R. 485.
[63] [1984] 3 All E.R. 407.
[64] (1880) 13 Ch.D. 676.
[65] *Ibid.* 708.

support of this analysis he referred to the speech of Lord Upjohn in *Board-man* v. *Phipps*[66] where the latter said[67]:

> "The facts and circumstances must be carefully examined to see whether in fact a purported agent and even a confidential agent is in a fiduciary relationship to his principal. It does not necessarily follow that he is in such a position. ...."

There was some disagreement between Staughton J. and Peter Gibson J. about the probability or otherwise that bailees occupy a fiduciary position. Staughton J. opined, at one point in his judgment, that there is a presumption that bailees are fiduciary.[68] But at a later stage he said that one had to examine the relationship in each individual case to see whether it is of a fiduciary nature.[69] Peter Gibson J. in *Re Andrabell Ltd.* preferred the latter view. He said one should deal with each case on its merits unencumbered by any kind of presumption.[70]

Agency

Agency is again important in the reservation of title context because it may provide a basis for the claim to proceeds. In many reservation of title clauses the buyer in effecting sub-sales is referred to as the seller's "fiduciary agent." But as we have seen, the courts are not so much concerned with labelling as with the true nature of the relationship between the parties. That relationship must be examined to see whether it is fiduciary in character. Not all fiduciaries are agents and not all agents are fiduciaries. The two terms are not synonymous but neither are the terms mutually exclusive. Perhaps the best course of action is to indicate factors that provide pointers for and against the existence of a fiduciary relationship in the agency context.[71]

First, there is authority for the view that it is not necessarily inconsistent with an agency or with a fiduciary relationship that the alleged agent is entitled to set resale prices or to pocket profits on resales. In this respect there is a divergence between *Re Nevill, ex parte White*[72] and *Re Smith, ex parte Bright*,[73] or at least a conflict between dicta in the two cases.

Take *Re Nevill* initially. For instance Sir George Mellish L.J. said that if a consignee was at liberty, according to the contract between him and his consignor to sell at any price he likes and receive payment at any time he

---

[66] [1967] 2 A.C. 46.
[67] *Ibid.* 127.
[68] At 498.
[69] *Ibid.*
[70] [1984] 3 All E.R. 407, 415.
[71] For an extremely useful discussion see Watts, "Reservation of Title Clauses in England and New Zealand" (1985) 5 O.J.L.S. 456, who refers in detail to a New Zealand case *Len Vidgen Ski & Leisure Ltd.* v. *Timaru Marine Supplies (1982) Ltd.* (1985) 2 N.Z.C.L.C. 99, 438.
[72] (1871) L.R. 6 Ch.App. 397. The decision in this case was confirmed by the House of Lords where it is reported *sub nom. Towle & Co.* v. *White* (1873) 29 L.T. 78.
[73] (1879) 10 Ch.D. 566.

likes, but was bound, if he sold the goods, to pay the consignor for them at a fixed price and a fixed time, the relationship between the parties was not that of principal and agent.[74] The contract of sale which the alleged agent makes with his purchasers was not a contract made on account of his principal. The learned Lord Justice went so far as to say that, in such a case, the alleged agent was making, on his own account, a contract of purchase with his alleged principal and again reselling.[75]

James L.J. was a party to the decision in *Re Nevill*. He was also party to the decision in *Re Smith* where he was at pains to relegate the earlier case to the realm of cases decided on their special facts. James L.J. voiced the view that such cases when quoted and argued only tend to waste the time of the court and divert its attention from the principle upon which the case should be decided.[76]

Jessel M.R. did not refer directly to *Re Nevill*. However, he enunciated the following principle[77]:

> "There is nothing to prevent the principal from remunerating the agent by a commission varying according to the amount of the profit obtained by the sale. *A fortiori* there is nothing to prevent his paying a commission depending upon the surplus which the agent can obtain over and above the price which will satisfy the principal. The amount of commission does not, turn the agent into a purchaser."

A *del credere* agency was found to exist in *Re Smith*. The characteristics of a *del credere* agency is that the agent guarantees the performance of obligations by the third parties with whom he contracts on behalf of the principal.[78]

Re Smith enjoys some support from the decision of the New Zealand Court of Appeal in *Westpac Banking* v. *Savin*.[79] In this case two boat owners authorised Aqua Marine to sell their boats. Aqua Marine's commission was to be whatever price the company achieved above a certain stated sum. The court held that the company was a fiduciary in respect of the proceeds of sale and was not entitled to pay them into its overdrawn trading account.

The *Westpac* case also supports the proposition that if a particular relationship is deemed fiduciary, then the fiduciary comes under an obligation to segregate his assets from the principal's. It is a counsel of prudence, however, to spell this separation obligation out clearly. Such a statement will stiffen the resolve of the court in coming to a fiduciary relationship conclu-

[74] (1871) L.R. 6 Ch.App. 397, 403.
[75] *Ibid.* 404.
[76] (1879) 10 Ch.D. 566, 572.
[77] *Ibid.* 570.
[78] *Morris* v. *Cleasby* (1816) 4 M. & S. 566; *Hornby* v. *Lacy* (1817) 6 M. & S. 166. See generally the section on Agency and Undisclosed Principals in F. Reynolds, *Bowstead on Agency* (15th ed.).
[79] [1985] 2 N.Z.L.R. 41. See also, *Fraser-Ramsay (N.Z.) Ltd.* v. *De Renzy* (1912) N.Z.L.R. 553; *Re Conway (a bankrupt)* [1936] N.Z.L.R. 334 and *Ticki Paaka* v. *MacLarn* [1937] N.Z.L.R. 369.

sion. *Henry* v. *Hammond*[80] attests to this state of affairs. There Channell J. expressed himself thus[81]:

> "It is clear that if the terms upon which the person receives the money are that he is bound to keep it separate, either in a bank or elsewhere, and to hand that money so kept as a separate fund to the person entitled to it, then he is a trustee of the money and must hand it over to the person who is his *cestui que trust*. If, on the other hand, he is not bound to keep the money separate, but is entitled to mix it with his own money and deal with it as he pleases, and when called upon to hand over an equivalent sum of money, then, in my opinion, he is not a trustee of the money, but merely a debtor."

The same principle was applied more recently in *Neste Oy* v. *Lloyd's Bank PLC*.[82] Bingham J. accepted that where money was, with the consent of the principal paid by agents into a general account containing their own funds the proper inference was that the relationship was one of debtor and creditor, not trustee and beneficiary.[83]

A right in an agent to alter the nature of the goods was treated as a pointer against a fiduciary relationship in *Re Nevill*. Mellish L.J. said that if an agent is allowed to change the character of the goods—if he may turn wheat into flour, or grey goods into dyed or bleached goods, and sell those changed goods on any terms and at any price he pleases—that makes it still clearer that he was not selling on account of a principal.[84] Instead, he was selling on his own account. As reinforcement for this view, the Lord Justice argued that if the agent was selling on account of his principal, then the principal must be liable to be sued. That was regarded as an absurd proposition.

Two points may be made. First, in *Romalpa*[85] the court saw nothing strange in a situation where a person who agreed to buy goods conditionally was the buyer's fiduciary agent but, in making sales to third parties, acted as an independent principal. Secondly, as we have seen, *Re Nevill* was almost stigmatised subsequently by the Court of Appeal in *Re Smith*.[86]

Many of the discussions on the reservation of title assume the absence of a House of Lords decision directly in point. In fact, this is not so. There is a Scottish case which went to the House of Lords in 1917 that deals with reservation of title issues: *Michelin Tyre Co. Ltd.* v. *Macfarlane (Glasgow) Ltd.*[87] The case however, deals with quite a narrow point. Basically we had the supply of tyres subject to a reservation of title agreement but no express duty to account for the proceeds of sub-sales of the tyres. The buyer

---

[80] [1913] 2 K.B. 515.
[81] *Ibid.* 521.
[82] [1983] 2 Lloyd's Rep. 658.
[83] See also, *The Wilsons and Furness-Leyland Line Ltd.* v. *The British and Continental Shipping Co. Ltd.* (1907) 23 T.L.R. 397.
[84] (1871) L.R. 6 Ch.App. 397, 404.
[85] [1976] 1 W.L.R. 676. See also, *infra*, Chap. 10.
[86] (1879) 10 Ch.D. 566, 572.
[87] 1917 2 S.L.T. 205.

(defender) became insolvent. The supplier (pursuer) contended that the buyer was merely its agent and thus obliged to account for the proceeds of resales.

The submission did not pass muster with a majority of the House of Lords though their Lordships were split 3–2. The majority placed reliance upon the fact that the particular agreement required that the stockist or agent should pay for the goods sold either immediately upon sale or when Michelin requested him to do so, irrespective of whether the stockist or agent had been paid or not. For example, Lord Dunedin said[88]:

> "The fact that the moment that the stockist sells to a retail purchaser, which he may do either for cash or on credit, as he pleases, he at once becomes debtor to the manufacturer for the wholesale price, seems to me quite inconsistent with *del credere* agency, and only consistent with sale and return. A *del credere* agent, who has sold to a third party does not become debtor to the principal; he only guarantees that the debtor will meet his engagement."

The hurdle presented by the *Michelin* decision is one that may be surmounted with ease however. One way of overcoming the barrier is expressly to constitute the buyer a *del credere* agent. This designation should be followed up by an obligation to pay the supplier the price of the goods at the end of the credit period irrespective of whether the goods have been resold or whether the *del credere* agent has received payment from sub-buyers.[89]

Admixture of Goods

In discussing admixture of goods the first thing to note is confused and varying terminology. Latin tags are employed to differentiate between various situations. However, there is no unanimity as to the terms to be employed or whether particular examples come under one head or another. Parris in his treatise on *Effective Retention of Title Clauses* distinguishes between three separate situations.[90] In his analysis, *accessio* involves the addition of something trifling in value to a more substantial article: for example, the addition of writing ink to a parchment. Parris continues[91]:

> "*Confusio* dealt with the position where goods were so combined as to be inseparable: the admixture of two liquids, or where A's purple was used for dyeing B's garment. The third situation, *commixtio*, was where there was the admixture of the chattels of two owners in such a way that they could readily be separated.

---

[88] *Ibid.* 212.
[89] See generally, Watts, *op. cit.* 462; *Churchill & Sim* v. *Goddard* [1937] K.B. 92 and *Kelly* v. *Enderton* [1913] A.C. 191.
[90] (1986), p. 89. An earlier version of this section on mixture of goods appears in the form of an article by the author in [1990] *Legal Studies*.
[91] *Ibid.*

In modern times, where A's paint is used to paint B's motor car we have *accessio*. A's resin is mixed with B's dessicated wood: *confusio*. An engine and new tyres are put by B on A's motor car: *commixtio*."

Others theorise rather differently. For instance, in one article the author talks about the mixing of materials belonging to different owners (*confusio* or *commixtio*); secondly, attachment of one thing belonging to one owner on to another's (*accessio* or *adjunctio*) and lastly the creation of a *nova species* or *specificatio*.[92]

A. G. Guest draws a distinction between accession and confusion (the doctrine thereof). In his view, accession arises when one chattel is annexed to another. Confusion of goods, on the other hand, occurs where the goods of two or more persons are so intermingled that the several parts or portions can no longer be distinguished.[93]

The Romans distinguished between *confusio* (wet mixtures) and *commixtio* (dry mixtures). An example of *confusio* would be the mixing of A's wine and B's wine whereas *commixtio* would arise where A's sheep were mixed with B's sheep.[94]

In this chapter a distinction is made between the following:

(1) Accession—the addition of one chattel to a dominant chattel.
(2) Confusion or commingling without a loss of physical identity subdivided into fluid mixtures and dry mixtures.
(3) Processing involving a loss of physical identity.

There is a certain degree of arbitrariness about any scheme of classification adopted in this area. For instance, in relation to accession how does one distinguish between the dominant and inferior chattel. The test cannot simply depend on the relative value of the two items. Take the situation where gold plating is added to a motor vehicle.[95] The vehicle must remain the dominant object for the purpose of the law of accession, notwithstanding the fact that the gold plating may be infinitely greater in value. Another element of arbitrariness arises with respect to the distinction between (2) and (3) above. By what test does one determine that a loss of physical integrity has occurred?

Accession—The Addition of an Item of Personalty to a More Substantial Chattel

Accession gives rise to the least difficulties partly on account of the fact that there is some common ground as to what the term entails. Even here, though, it is not all plain sailing. Cases of accession are rarely encountered in

---

[92] See I. R. Davies, "Reservation of title clauses: a legal quagmire?" [1985] L.M.C.L.Q. 49, 64.
[93] See generally, "Accession and Confusion in the Law of Hire Purchase" (1964) 27 M.L.R. 505.
[94] See Whittaker, "Retention of Title and Specificatio" (1984) 100 L.Q.R. 35.
[95] See generally, R.M. Goode, *Hire Purchase Law and Practice* (2nd ed., 1970), p. 751.

practice. This is largely because it is standard practice to include in a hire-purchase agreement to the effect that any accessories or goods supplied with, or for, or attached to, or repairs executed to the hired goods shall become part of the hired goods. There is no reason why such a clause should not be included in the case of a sale of goods subject to a reservation of title clause.

An agreement of this nature was held effective in *Akron Tyre Co. Pty. Ltd.* v. *Kittson.*[96] In this case the hirer fitted some tyres to the vehicle. Subsequently he removed the tyres and sold them to the defendant who refused to hand them over to the plaintiffs. A successful conversion action was brought. The High Court of Australia took the view that by virtue of the express provision in the hire-purchase agreement the legal title in the new tyres passed to the owner of the truck to which they were fitted.

Often, of course, the parties have stayed silent on the matter and in such circumstances we must fall back on the accession doctrine. Basically, accessions become the property of the owner of the principal goods.[97] The question remains what degree of annexation is necessary to cause an accession. The test may vary depending on whether the goods attached were the property of the hirer or conditional buyer or else the property of some third party.

First of all, in the hirer/conditional buyer situation, A. G. Guest in his influential article on "Accession and Confusion in the Law of Hire Purchase" suggests a number of possible tests.[98] The first test is one of injurious removal, which holds that accession applies where one chattel is added to another chattel so that it cannot be separated without serious injury to or destruction of the whole so formed. A second test is one of separate existence which asks whether the chattel which has been incorporated in another chattel ceased to exist as a separate chattel. A third test, wider than that of injurious removal, is one of destruction of utility. It asks whether the removal of the article annexed would destroy the practical usability of the principal chattel. A fourth and final test analogises with fixtures to land and looks at the degree and purpose of annexation.

The preponderance of judicial support in the common law world is for what might be described as the "injurious removal" test. A case often cited in this connection is the Australian case *Rendell* v. *Associated Finance Pty. Ltd.*[99] This is a case where C acquired both an engine and a truck on hire-purchase. He affixed the engine to the truck. The engine was acquired from A and the truck from B. C never exercised his option to purchase the

---

[96] (1951) 82 C.L.R. 477.
[97] Reference might be made to accessions by natural increase. In *Tucker* v. *Farm and General Investment Trust Ltd.* [1966] 2 Q.B. 421—that lambs bred to ewes during the currency of a hire agreement belonged to the hirer of the ewes. Diplock L.J. said at 431 that where there is a lease of livestock and where, accordingly, property and possession are divided, the English rule and the rule in the civil law is that the progeny and the produce of the livestock belong to the person entitled to the possession: that is to say the lessee in English law, the usufructuary in civil law.
[98] (1964) 27 M.L.R. 505, 507–509.
[99] [1957] V.R. 604.

engine. Also he failed to pay the hire-purchase instalments in relation to the truck which led to its repossession by B. A brought an action in conversion against B. The defence to the action was that the engine, in consequence of having been installed in the truck, ceased to be the property of A. The Supreme Court of Victoria held that the defence failed. The judgment contains a fairly full discussion and repays careful study.

First, O'Bryan J. pointed out that the views of the Roman jurists were not necessarily helpful in the present case.[1] The common law looked at matters from the point of view of the law of property whereas Roman law perceived matters from a property perspective. Roman commentators addressed not so much the question of a remedy against a wrongdoer who had taken another's property and added it to or mixed it with his own, but rather the question of who was entitled to the product thus increased in value.

In determining whether accession had occurred the judge referred to two New South Wales decisions. In *Bergougnan* v. *British Motors Ltd.*[2] it was held that tyres did not merge in a motor vehicle so that the ownership in them passed to the owner of the lorry. The decision was based on the fact that there was no change in ownership because they were readily identifiable and could be detached without damage to the lorry.

The same principle was applied in *Lewis* v. *Andrews and Rowley Pty. Ltd.*[3] with respect to tyres and other accessories which had been attached to a motor-trailer. The majority of the court rejected the submission that if the attached articles are essential to the operation of the vehicle, they became, when affixed, incorporated with it so that the property in them thereby passed to the owner of the vehicle.

Manning J. dissented. He preferred the test of whether the chattel which had been added to or incorporated in another chattel ceased to exist as a separate chattel. But as O'Bryan J. pointed out in *Rendell* this test is very difficult to apply. Did a battery or fan belt put in a car cease to have a separate existence?[4] Likewise, he rejected as inappropriate the test propounded by the Court of Appeal of Saskatchewan in *Regina Chevrolet Sales Ltd.* v. *Riddell.*[5]

That court held that tyres fitted to a truck became the property of the truckowner because they were an integral part of the truck and necessary for its proper working.

Incidentally, the *Riddell* test of accession has been disapproved of by the Supreme Court of Canada in *Firestone Tyre and Rubber Co.* v. *Industrial Acceptance Corporation.*[6] Again this was a case of tyres and motor vehicles but this time, the dispute was between two security holders. Laskin J. expressed himself thus[7]:

[1] *Ibid.* 606.
[2] (1929) 30 S.R. (N.S.W.) 61.
[3] (1956) 56 S.R. (N.S.W.) 439.
[4] [1957] V.R. 604, 609.
[5] [1942] 3 D.L.R. 159.
[6] (1971) 17 D.L.R. (3d) 229.
[7] *Ibid.* 1.

"The present case is unembarrassed by any suggestion that the accessory chattels have lost their identity. Nor are we concerned with an accession to the title of the purchaser of a fabricated product, be it a ship or other chattel, by the maker thereof. Again, we are not concerned with the enhancement of a security holder's position against a conditional buyer or chattel mortgagor who improves the burdened chattel in some way. In my opinion, whatever be the rationale of the doctrine of accession in taking effect in the foregoing situations, it ought not to be applied to the present case where removable and identifiable accessory chattels are claimed by the holder of an original title thereto, retained as security for their value, against the prior security title holder of the principal chattel."

The Supreme Court of New Zealand had occasion to consider the issue of accession in *Thomas* v. *Robinson*.[8] The case concerned the attachment of replacements for essential working components of a motor vehicle. Speight J. held that the accessories had not become part of the motor vehicle. After reviewing the authorities, the judge appears to have plumped for an "injurious removal" test. He cited a dictum in *Rendell* v. *Associated Finance Pty. Ltd.* to the effect that[9]:

"The accessories continue to belong to their original owner unless it is shown that as a matter of practicability they cannot be identified, or, if identified, they have been incorporated to such an extent that they cannot be detached from the vehicle."

Thomas v. *Robinson* goes some way towards recognising a *via media*. Speight J. opined that a consideration of the remedies available to the court showed that a practical and just solution could be had of conflicting rights.[10] He pointed to *Munro* v. *Willmott*[11] where in an action for detinue and conversion of a motor car, damages for improper sale were offset by credit for amounts spent by the defendant for work done and material supplied. The same result was obtained in *Greenwood* v. *Bennett*[12] where an allowance for compensation was made to the mistaken improver of a motor vehicle.

The Torts (Interference With Goods) Act 1977 has something to say about the matter. Section 3(6) stipulates that an order for delivery of goods may contain such conditions as may be determined by the court. Moreover, relief may be afforded by way of giving the defendant the alternative of paying damages calculated with the reference to the value of the goods. In addition section 6(1) provides that if in proceedings for wrongful interference against a person who has improved the goods, it is shown that the

[8] [1977] 1 N.Z.L.R. 385. See also, *McKeown* v. *Cavalier Yachts Pty. Ltd.* (1988) 13 N.S.W.L.R. 303.
[9] *Ibid.* 391. The quotation is at [1975] V.R. 604, 610.
[10] [1977] 1 N.Z.L.R. 392.
[11] [1949] 1 K.B. 295.
[12] [1973] 1 Q.B. 195. See also, *Rendell* v. *Associated Finance Pty. Ltd.* [1957] V.R. 604, 607 and *Whiteley Ltd.* v. *Hilt* [1918] 2 K.B. 808, 818 and 824.

improver acted in the mistaken but honest belief that he had a good title to them, an allowance for his work shall be made. The amount of the allowance is determined by the extent to which the value of the goods is attributable to the improvement, at the time at which the goods fall to be valued in assessing damages.

All this is very well when the *Romalpa* supplier is seeking the return of goods which have been improved or to which accessories have been attached. But what if the goods supplied have been incorporated in a dominant chattel. Title thereto would appear to be lost by virtue of the doctrine of accession. Sections 3(6) and 6(1) of the Act of 1977 seem to be of no avail. To protect his position, a *Romalpa* supplier should consider inserting in the conditions of sale a clause precluding the incorporation of his goods in a major chattel.[13]

Confusion or Commingling Without Loss of Physical Identity

Where a supplier's goods and those of a conditional buyer are mixed up, but not so as to affect the physical characteristics of the commingled goods, the position differs depending on whether the buyer acted wrongfully in bringing about the commingling. The old rule was taken to be that where the conditional buyer was guilty of intentional wrongdoing the supplier could claim the entirety.

A case in point is *Lupton* v. *White*.[14] There the view was expressed that if a person, having undertaken to keep the property of another distinct, mixes it with his own, the whole must, both at law and in equity, be taken to be the property of the other, until the former puts the subject under such circumstances, that it may be distinguished as satisfactorily as it might have been before that unauthorised mixture upon this part.

However, under section 3(6) of the Torts (Interference with Goods) Act 1977, which has already been mentioned above, the court has an extensive discretion to impose conditions on making a specific delivery order. It may bear in mind the value added by the conditional buyer in calculating damages for conversion. These discretionary powers reflect the common law position. Thus the forfeiture rule, as it might be termed, is not as absolute as it appears at first. A recent case in point is *Indian Oil Corporation* v. *Greenstone Shipping S.A. (Panama)*[15] where there is a very full discussion of

---

[13] If the buyer goes ahead and incorporates the goods disregarding the clause then the supplier might lay claim to the dominant chattel under the doctrine of *Lupton* v. *White* (1808) 15 Ves. 432 discussed shortly. If the dominant chattel belongs to a third party then the courts might adopt a tenancy in common in proportionate shares solution. See generally, Matthews, "Proprietary Claims at Common Law for Mixed and Improved Goods" [1981] C.L.P. 159 who sounds a dissentient note in the area of accession. He rejects the view that the owner of the dominant chattel becomes the owner of the whole to the entire exclusion of the other party. His suggestion is that, on principle, those who have contributed to mixed property should become owners in common of the whole in accordance with their respective contributions.
[14] (1808) 15 Ves. 432.
[15] [1988] 1 Q.B. 345. On this case see Stein (1987) 46 C.L.J. 369; Brown [1988] L.M.C.L.Q. 286.

the authorities although no reference was made to the Torts (Interference with Goods) Act 1977.

This was a case where the owners of a vessel which was chartered to transport a quantity of Russian crude oil from a Russian port to India, mixed the Russian oil with crude oil, which was their own property, already on board the vessel. Staughton J. held that where a party wrongfully mixed the goods of another with his own goods which were substantially of the same nature and quality, and they could not be separated for practical purposes, the mixture was held in common. The innocent party was entitled to receive from it a quantity equal to that of his goods which had gone into the mixture. If doubt remained as to either quantity or quality, the matter should be resolved in the innocent party's favour. Moreover, he was entitled to claim damages from the wrongdoer for losses suffered, in respect of quality of otherwise, as a result of the admixture.

The judge observed that in the days when corn and hay were to be found in heaps which could not be measured accurately and when such disputes were tried to jury and witnesses might be illiterate or ignorant, a rough and ready punitive rule may have been the best that the law could find.[16] A primitive rule however, was no longer appropriate in an age when modern and sophisticated methods of measurement were available. It was not the function of civil justice to punish or discourage crime by awarding a victim more than he had lost, unless it be a special case which fell within the ambit of an award of exemplary damages.[17]

In circumstances where commingling has been effected in good faith or with the consent of the supplier then there is a strong current of authority supporting the view that the two parties become tenants in common of the mass in proportion to their respective contributions. Cases usually cited in this connection are *Buckley* v. *Gross*[18] and *Spence* v. *Union Marine Insurance Co.*[19] In *Buckley* v. *Gross*, tallow in a warehouse belonging to a number of persons flowed out as a result of a fire into a common sewer. Blackburn J. said[20]:

> "The tallow of the different owners was indeed mixed up into a molten mass, so that it might be difficult to apportion it among them. ... Probably the legal effect of such a mixture would be to make the owners tenants in common in equal portions of the mass, but at all events they do not lose their property in it."

In this case there was no proof of the respective contributions of the

---

[16] *Ibid.* 370. It should be noted that the punitive rule was extant in this century. For example, in *Sandeman & Sons* v. *Tyzack and Branfoot S.S. Co. Ltd.*, Lord Moulton insisted that if the mixing was the fault of one party, then the other could claim the entirety of the goods.
[17] *Ibid.* 369.
[18] (1863) 3 B. & S. 566; 122 E.R. 213.
[19] (1868) L.R. 3 C.P. 427.
[20] (1863) 3 B. & S. 566, 574–575; 122 E.R. 213, 216.

owners of the separate goods. Therefore, a tenancy in common in equal shares solution was adopted.

In *Spence* v. *Union Marine Insurance Co.* such proof was forthcoming and a tenancy in common was declared in line with the contribution of each party to the whole.

This was a case where a ship carrying a cargo of cotton from the American South to Liverpool became shipwrecked. Consequently, distinguishing marks on the bales of cotton were obliterated. The court took the view that[21]:

> ". . . by the mixture of the bales, and their becoming undistinguishable by reason of the action of the sea, and without the fault of the respective owners, these parties became tenants in common of the cotton, in proportion to their respective interests."

More generally, the court enunciated the proposition that[22]:

> "(I)f . . . separation is not practicable, then the former proprietors of the things now connected will be joint owners of the whole, whenever the mixture has been made with the consent of both parties, or by accident."

This tenancy in common in proportionate shares solution should obtain irrespective of whether the supplier's goods and those of a conditional buyer have been mixed, or whether mixing has occurred between the goods of a supplier and those of a third party.

In this connection however, it is as well to bear in mind the cautionary comment of Lord Moulton in *Sandeman & Sons* v. *Tyzack and Branfoot Steamship Co. Ltd.*[23] that the whole matter is far from being within the domain of settled law. He suggested that the conclusions of the courts in such cases were little more than instances of cutting the Gordian knot— reasonable adjustments of the rights of the parties in cases where complete justice was impracticable of attainment.

Fluid Mixtures and Dry Mixtures

There has been a suggestion that the courts should reinstate the Roman distinction between *confusio* (wet mixtures) and *commixtio* (dry mixtures).[24] Professor P. B. H. Birks has argued for acceptance of a rule to the effect that, if the constituent units lose their integrity in the mixture as happens in fluid mixtures, common ownership supervenes while, if the units retain their integrity as in granular mixtures, ownership of the units remains

---

[21] (1868) L.R. 3 C.P. 427, 438–439.
[22] *Ibid.* 438.
[23] [1913] A.C. 680, 695. See also, *Jones* v. *Moore* (1841) 4 Y. & C. Ex. 351; *Gill & Duffus (Liverpool) Ltd.* v. *Scruttons Ltd.* [1953] 1 W.L.R. 1407.
[24] See Birks, "Admixture of Goods in English Law" in *Proceedings of the Anglo–Polish Legal Symposium 1989.*

unchanged although in practice difficult to demand for want of identifiability. He sees no place for common ownership in the latter situation.[25]

What are the merits of restoring the Roman position apart of course from symmetry with Roman law, whatever might be the attractions of that course of action. The principle reason advanced for making the distinction is consistency with certain judicial decisions, in particular *Wiles* v. *Woodward*.[26] This was a case where a partnership was dissolved and a dispute arose over paper belonging to the former partnership. Dissolution was effected by deed which deed recited that a physical act of partition had taken place. It was held that the parties were estopped by the deed from saying that no partition had occurred. Secondly, as the defendant had converted the whole, the plaintiff might maintain an action in conversion, although no specific proportion had been set apart for him. As a general rule one co-owner cannot maintain an action in conversion against the other,[27] so Birks argues that the relationship of the parties in the mixture were those of owners of separate entities, which separate entities happened to be intermingled.

On the other hand *Wiles* v. *Woodward* may not be a case of consensual or good faith mixing. The jute and cotton bales cases *Sandeman & Sons* v. *Tyzack and Branfoot Steamship Co. Ltd.*[28] and *Spence* v. *Union Marine Insurance Co. Ltd.*[29] are pretty adamant that in instances of consensual or good faith mixing, co-ownership arises.

Birks also points to *Taylor* v. *Plumer*[30] on common law tracing which suggests that where one's money is mixed and confounded in a general mass of the same description, one does not become an owner of the whole so formed. Rather one's right to trace is lost. *Per contra*, it might be argued that the courts never had the opportunity to develop comprehensive rules for common law tracing and that, in any event, money behaves differently. It is submitted that to draw a distinction between fluid and granular intermixtures in terms of legal results is to complicate the law unnecessarily.

Remedies of Co-owners

Undoubtedly, there are difficulties with co-ownership in relation to remedies. One co-owner excluded from possession has the right to a "rent" from the other.[31] What about sale and division of the proceeds? Section 188 of the Law of Property Act 1925 empowers the court to order a division of chattels according to a valuation or otherwise but only on the application of a person or persons interested in a moiety or upwards.

[25] *Op. cit.*
[26] (1850) 5 Exch. 557.
[27] See pp. 55–56, *infra*.
[28] [1913] A.C. 680.
[29] (1868) L.R. 3 C.P. 427.
[30] (1815) 3 M. & S. 562.
[31] See generally, *Jones (A.E.)* v. *Jones (F.W.)* [1977] 1 W.L.R. 438; *Dennis* v. *McDonald* [1982] Fam. 63; *Chhokar* v. *Chhokar* [1984] F.L.R. 313.

McLelland J. in *Ferrari* v. *Beccaris*[32] had cause to interpret similar New South Wales legislation. He said that the section was open to two interpretations. The first was that it did not apply to a case where the chattel or chattels are not susceptible to physical division. The second view, and the view he adopted, was that the expression "division" embraces, where appropriate, a division by conversion into money and distribution of that money, being in many cases the only method of carrying out a division. It is likely that an English court would afford the Law of Property Act a similar purposive construction.

Section 188 is limited however, to cases where a party is interested in a half or upwards. It is unclear whether or not the courts have power to order a sale on the application of a person with less than a 50 per cent. stake in the chattel.[33]

Can one co-owner maintain an action in conversion against another? The general rule is not, but this principle has been so eaten away by exceptions that one may ask which is the general rule and which the exception. Section 10 of the Torts (Interference with Goods) Act 1977 provides as follows:

(1) Co-ownership is no defence to an action founded on conversion or trespass where the defendant without the authority of the other co-owner—
(a) destroys the goods, or disposes of the goods in a way giving a goods title to the entire property in the goods, or otherwise does anything equivalent to the destruction of the other's interest in the goods; or
(b) purports to dispose of the goods in a way which would give a good title to the entire property in the goods if he was acting with the authority of all co-owners of the goods.

Subsection (1)(a) purports to be a restatement of existing law whereas subsection (1)(b) seems to signify a change from the pre-existing position. To put the change in context, it is appropriate to state the régime applicable to co-owners which was replaced by the new statutory dispensation. The pre-1977 law was set out by Parke B. in *Morgan* v. *Marquis*.[34] He said[35]:

"It is well established that one tenant in common cannot maintain an action against his companion unless there has been a destruction of the particular chattel or something equivalent to it."

A reason for the rule was adduced in *Frazer* v. *Kershaw*[36]—namely that a sale by one co-owner cannot convey the other co-owner's interest; the buyer can only acquire the seller's interest and become a co-owner with the

---

[32] [1979] 2 N.S.W.L.R. 181.
[33] See generally, *Ryan* v. *King* [1932] Q.W.N. 1 and Sackville and Neave, *Property Law: Cases and Materials* (4th ed., 1988), pp. 670–671.
[34] (1854) 9 Ex. 145.
[35] *Ibid.* 148. See generally, Derham, "Conversion by Wrongful Disposal as Between Co-owners" (1952) 68 L.Q.R. 507.
[36] (1856) 2 K. & J. 49. See also, *Heath* v. *Hubbard* (1803) 4 East 110 and *Farrar* v. *Beswick* (1836) 1 M. & W. 682 and the other cases referred to by Derham, *op. cit.*

plaintiff. As pointed out by Somers J. in the recent New Zealand case *Coleman* v. *Harvey*[37] this justification is not entirely convincing. The same could be said of a case where the defendant sells property belonging entirely to the plaintiff but that fact affords no defence to an action. Moreover, there were authorities in which the supposed rule against an action in conversion was not so unequivocally stated.[38]

The old idea against an action in conversion by one co-owner against another came to be considered by the New Zealand Court of Appeal in *Coleman* v. *Harvey*.[39] The rule was reviewed in the light of contemporary conditions and it was found wanting. The Court developed the common law to the stage where it corresponded with the rule laid down by statute in this jurisdiction in the shape of section 10 of the Torts (Interference with Goods) Act 1977.

Processing Involving Loss of Physical Identity

Where goods have been mixed so as to result in a loss of physical identity opinions differ about the principles to be applied. Professor Goode has contended that subject to possible forfeiture of the buyer's interest where he has been guilty of intentional wrongdoing in processing the supplier's goods, the parties become tenants in common of the new product in the proportions of their respective contributions.[40] In other words, the rules applicable in the context of commingling obtain equally here. In support he can refer to a dictum of Latham C.J. in the Australian case of *Farnsworth* v. *Federal Commissioner of Taxation*[41] but arguably that passage is directed to a situation of commingling of goods without loss of physical identity. The Australian Chief Justice simply referred to a statement in *Halsbury's Laws of England*[42] to the effect that:

> "[W]here the chattels of two persons are intermixed by consent or agreement, so that the several portions can be no longer distinguished, the proprietors have an interest in common in proportion to their respective shares."

The co-ownership conclusion is also supported by the decision of the New Zealand Court of Appeal in *Coleman* v. *Harvey*.[43] This is a case of consensual mixing where silver coins belonging to one Harvey were mixed with silver belonging to a company for whom Coleman acted as agent. The mass

[37] [1989] 1 N.Z.L.R. 723.
[38] See, *e.g. Mayhew* v. *Herrick* (1849) 7 C.B. 229, 247–248 *per* Maule J.
[39] [1989] 1 N.Z.L.R. 723. Somers J. as instances of changing conditions pointed to population growth, increased industrialisation, the ease of transport and the increase in the variety of tangible goods.
[40] Goode, *Proprietary Rights and Insolvency in Sale Transactions* (2nd ed., 1989), p. 92.
[41] (1949) 78 C.L.R. 504, 510.
[42] (2nd ed.), Vol. 1, p. 746.
[43] [1989] 1 N.Z.L.R. 723.

was mixed so as to produce ingots and the question arose whether Harvey could sustain an action in conversion against Coleman. The court held that the parties became tenants in common of the ingots and that a conversion action was maintainable. There is not a great deal of discussion though on the co-ownership point.

Cooke P. referred to the passage from *Halsbury's Laws Of England* cited earlier. He accepted that in this particular case there were complications such as the intended destruction of the identity of the coins by chemical means. In the judge's opinion, however, this should not be treated as changing the essence of the transaction.

The other substantive judgment was delivered by Somers J. He noted that the refined product contained silver supplied by Harvey and silver which was the property of the company represented by Coleman. Moreover, the constituent parts were not capable of segregation or identification after refinement. Nevertheless, the judge concluded that the parties were co-owners of the products of the refining process; *i.e.* the ingots.

Another view holds that where a loss of physical identity has been perpetrated with no reduction possible, the maker of the new product becomes its owner regardless of whether any of the materials used were his. The Scottish case of *International Banking Corp.* v. *Ferguson Shaw and Sons*[44] may be taken as offering some support to this idea. This is a case where A purchased bona fide from B oil which in fact belonged to C. With the oil and other materials, A manufactured lard. An action was brought by C against A for delivery of the oil. The Court of Session held that the defender, by creating in the process of manufacture a new species which could not be resolved into its original elements, had become proprietor of the substance manufactured under the doctrine of *specificatio*.[45]

The Court was unanimous in this conclusion though Lord Low conceded that there was singularly little judicial authority on the question. Lord Dundas opined that the case was a pure type for the application of the Roman doctrine of *specificatio*.[46] The oil no longer existed in its original and proper form. A new species had been created, of which the oil was only an ingredient. After the creation the new product could not be restored to its original elements.

A major difficulty arises in relation to the test to be applied in determining whether a new product has been created.[47] The Scottish court in the *International Banking Corp.* cases appears to have applied a test of reversibility.

[44] 1910 S.C. 182.
[45] *Ibid.* 192. Lord Law quoted the Scottish institutional writer Erskine to the effect that when by the mixing together of two or more substances of different kinds, belonging to different proprietors, a new species is formed, which cannot be brought back again to the first condition of these substances, the mixer, whether he be one of the proprietors or a third party, must, as the maker of the new species, become the sole proprietor of the subjects mixed.
[46] *Ibid.* 194.
[47] See Matthews (1981) 10 *Anglo-American Law Review* 121: see generally, also, Wylie [1978] Conv. 37.

This is in line with the Justinian school of Roman jurisprudence. Justinian propounded the view that if the new product was reducible to its constituent elements, ownership vested in the supplier of the materials, whereas if reduction was not possible, then ownership vested in the maker.[48] Other tests have been suggested such as whether the substance is chemically different from the previous one, whatever the form. Another test asks whether the new product can be identified in substance as being the supplier's goods.[49] Ultimately, the issue is one of policy. Should a supplier who has inserted a reservation of title clause into a contract for the sale of goods be protected over and above other creditors?

One scenario where the commentators seem at one is where a buyer simply applies his labour to convert the supplier's materials into a different product. In this situation, even Goode accepts that the buyer, if acting innocently becomes the owner of the product, albeit with a duty to compensate the supplier for the value of the materials.[50]

A case in point is *Thorogood* v. *Robinson*[51] where chalk was turned into lime. A dug chalk from B's land and burnt it, thereby leaving lime. The Court of Queen's Bench held that the limeburner rather than the landowner had a right to the goods.

Summary—Mixture of Goods

Before leaving the subject of mixtures of goods, it may be useful to summarise the principles which apply in this area. It is suggested that these principles may be stated as follows:

1. Where a chattel is attached to a more substantial chattel, it becomes the property of the owner of the dominant chattel, unless it can be removed without serious damage to the dominant chattel.

2. The court, however, may impose conditions on a specific delivery order under the Torts (Interference with Goods) Act 1977. In addition, the owner of the inferior chattel may have a restitutionary claim against the owner of the dominant chattel according to the principle in *Greenwood* v. *Bennett*.[52]

3. The parties, moreover, may stipulate as to where ownership of the whole consisting of the dominant and inferior chattel shall lie.

4. Where goods are mixed together without producing a loss of physical identity the owners of the goods so mixed become tenants in common of the resultant mass in accordance with the value of their contributions to the same.

[48] See generally, Whittaker (1984) 100 L.Q.R. 35, 40.
[49] Matthews (1981) 10 *Anglo-American Law Review* 121, 123.
[50] Goode, *Proprietary Rights and Insolvency in Sale Transactions* (2nd ed., 1989), p. 92.
[51] [1845] 6 Q.B. 769.
[52] [1973] 1 Q.B. 195.

5. Where a party is guilty of intentional wrongdoing in bringing about the mixing, the old rule was that the other party could then claim the entirety of the goods. Now, however, the mixture is held in common according to the parties' respective contributions. Where there are uncertainties about either the quantity or quality of the goods which have gone into the mixture, the matter should be resolved in the innocent party's favour. In addition, an innocent party is entitled to claim from the wrongdoer for losses suffered as a result of the admixture.

6. Where commingling results in a loss of physical identity and the formation of a new product, the better view appears to be that the maker of the new product becomes its owner, regardless of whether any of the materials used were his. But there is no consensus as to the test to be applied in determining whether a new product has been created.

7. Where a party simply applies his labour in the conversion of another party's raw materials into a different product the worker, as it were, becomes the owner of the new product if acting innocently in bringing about the formation of the new product.

CHAPTER 4

INCORPORATION OF A RESERVATION OF TITLE CLAUSE INTO A SALE OF GOODS CONTRACT

Having purported to reserve title until certain conditions are fulfilled, it is necessary to ensure, however, that this provision forms part of the contract of sale. Well-drafted clauses are hardly worth the paper they are written on if they have not been properly incorporated into the contract between the parties.[1] The incorporation issue will be discussed in this chapter.

Reasonable Notice of the Clause

In accordance with standard principle, reasonably sufficient notice of the clause must be given to the other party before, or at the time when, the contract is made. If the document in which the clause is contained has been signed, and if it is indeed a contractual document rather than say just a publicity leaflet or a receipt, then the law presumes that the party who has signed has read and understood the clause. This is the effect of the decision in *L'Estrange* v. *Graucob*.[2] The principle holds good even if the clause is in very small print and couched in legal jargon.

It is clear from *Curtis* v. *Chemical Cleaning and Dyeing Co.*[3] that the presumption can be rebutted if there has been a misrepresentation as to the effect of the clause. Furthermore, if there has been an oral statement purporting to override the clause then, according to *Couchman* v. *Hill*,[4] this can be given precedence. These last two cases involved exemption clauses, *i.e.* clauses purporting to negative or limit the liability of one of the contracting parties. Nonetheless, the same principles should apply to all types of clauses. The same cannot be said of Schedule 2 to the Unfair Contract Terms Act 1977, paragraph (c) of which says that, when deciding whether it is fair and reasonable to allow one party to rely on an exemption clause, the court can bear in mind whether the other party knew or ought reasonably to have known of the existence and extent of the clause in question.

---

[1] But see J. R. Bradgate [1988] J.B.L. 477 who argues that post-contractual reservation of title may be effective in certain circumstances. His argument is based on s. 19 of the Sale of Goods Act 1979 which appears to permit a seller in a contract for the sale of non-specific goods to reserve a "right of disposal" when goods are subsequently appropriated to the contract. Bradgate admits that a reservation of title at this stage may be in breach of contract but he suggests that the right will be valuable where other sums are due to the seller from an insolvent buyer. An instance of this would be where there has been a continuous trading relationship between the parties. Even Bradgate concedes though that sellers should still be advised to endeavour to incorporate their terms of business into sale contracts.

[2] [1934] 2 K.B. 394.

[3] [1951] 1 K.B. 805.

[4] [1947] K.B. 554.

If the relevant contractual document has not been signed then the party wishing to rely upon the reservation of title clause will have to show that the other party was supplied with reasonably sufficient notice of the clause's existence. The leading case is *John Snow and Co. Ltd.* v. *DBG Woodcroft and Co. Ltd.*[5] where the material principles are helpfully summarised by Boreham J. He said that to entitle a party to rely upon a particular term, he must prove that the term was brought to the notice of the party sought to be bound, before or at the time that the contract was made. Where the term was contained in a standard form document the following general propositions operated with respect to notice[6]:

(1) If the party sought to be bound was, at the material time, unaware of any writing or printing on the document relied upon, he is not regarded as having notice of the term in question and thus is not bound by it.

(2) If the party sought to be bound was aware, at the material time, that the document relied upon contained or referred to terms and conditions (albeit that he was unaware of their purport) he is taken to have notice of the term in question and is bound by it.

(3) If the party sought to be bound knew that the document relied upon contained writing or printing, but was unaware that it contained terms or conditions, he will be taken to have notice of and thus be bound by the term in question, only if the party seeking to bind him had done all that was reasonably sufficient to bring the terms and conditions to his notice. Whether what was done was reasonably sufficient for that purpose is to be judged by all the circumstances of the case, including the situation of the parties, the layout and contents of the documents relied upon and whether or not the term in question is unusually wide or unusually stringent.

Boreham J. added that some clauses may be so unusual that they require attention drawn to them in the most explicit manner. He went on to hold that a simple reservation of title clause, which had become quite a common term in commercial transactions, was not to be stigmatised as unusual thereby warranting stringent notice requirements.

A view favourable to the party proferring a reservation of title clause was adopted by Slade J. in *Re Bond Worth Ltd.*[7] at least as regards the incorporation point. In this case, the suppliers, Monsanto, wrote to the buyers Bond Worth, stating that with effect from a certain date they were amending their standard terms of contract insofar as all future business was concerned. Notwithstanding the letter, Monsanto continued to issue, with their confirmation notes, conditions of sale which made no reference to the altered terms. Nevertheless, Slade J. held that the title retention clause contained in

[5] [1985] B.C.L.C. 54.
[6] *Ibid.* 58.
[7] [1980] Ch. 228. See also, *Aluminium Industrie Vaassen B.V.* v. *Romalpa Aluminium Ltd.* [1976] 1 W.L.R. 676.

the letter was a term of the contracts of sale. Parris' comment seems a valid one. He says[8]:

"Another judge might well on those facts have concluded that the retention of title terms formed no part of the contract of sale since the offer was made by the issue of a confirmation note to which was attached the unamended conditions of sale, purporting to be as inviolable as the law of the Medes and Persians and the acceptance was by the act of receiving delivery of goods, and each delivery constituted a separate contract."

More generally, the observations of Megaw L.J. in *Thornton* v. *Shoe Lane Parking Ltd.*[9] should be borne in mind in the context of incorporation. He said that where the particular condition relied on involves a sort of restriction which was usual in that class of contract, a defendant must show that his intention to attach an unusual condition of that particular nature was fairly brought to the notice of the other party. Lord Denning went even further as was his wont. He said that some terms are so wide and so destructive of rights that in order to give sufficient notice they would need to be printed in red ink with a red hand pointing to them, or something equally startling.[10]

Thornton v. *Shoe Lane Parking Ltd.* was applied by the Court of Appeal in *Interfoto Picture Library Ltd.* v. *Stiletto Visual Programmes Ltd.*[11] The court emphasised that issues concerning incorporation revolved around whether reasonably sufficient notice of a clause had been given in the particular circumstances. Where a particular clause was untypically wide or onerous, then it would be only fair and reasonable to draw a parties' attention specifically to that clause.

Bingham L.J. suggested that the well-known cases on sufficiency of notice like *Parker* v. *South Eastern Ry Co.*[12] and *Hood* v. *Anchor Line (Henderson Bros.) Ltd.*[13] could be read in two ways. At one level they were concerned with a question of pure contractual analysis, whether one party has done enough to give the other notice of the incorporation of a term into the contract. At another level they were concerned with a somewhat different question, whether it would in all the circumstances be fair (or reasonable) to hold a party bound by any conditions or by a particular condition of an unusual and stringent nature.

Irish Cases

The incorporation issue has arisen in a number of Irish cases on retention

---

[8] *Effective Retention of Title Clauses* (1986), p. 142.
[9] [1971] 2 Q.B. 163.
[10] *Ibid.* 170.
[11] [1988] 1 All E.R. 348.
[12] (1877) 2 C.P.D. 416.
[13] [1918] A.C. 837.

of title. In *Union Paper Co. Ltd.* v. *Sunday Tribune Ltd.*[14] Barron J. held that, as the defendant company had never been supplied with any document setting out the reservation of title clause, the clause could not be taken to be part of the contract. The case related to supplies of newsprint. Confirmation notes were sent by the paper company's head office to the Irish agent which notes referred to the paper company's general terms including a reservation of title clause. These were not, however, sent forward to the *Sunday Tribune*.

In two other Irish cases a pro-incorporation result has been reached. In the first case *Sugar Distributors Ltd.* v. *Monaghan Cash and Carry Ltd.*,[15] a retention of title clause was added to standard terms after about two years trading, without it being drawn specifically to the defendant's attention. It was argued on behalf of the defendants that reasonable notice of the new term had not been given. This contention was rejected. Carroll J. held that the clause was duly incorporated by inclusion on the face of invoices over 15 months and the defendants ought reasonably to have known the terms on which the goods were supplied. In other words, the reservation of title clause was not treated as an usual term which should have been brought specifically to the attention of the purchaser. The court ruled inapplicable the earlier Irish case of *Western Meats Ltd.* v. *National Ice and Cold Storage Co. Ltd.*[16] There it was held that a businessperson offering a specialist service but accepting no responsibility for it must bring the terms home clearly to the other party. An important point in *Sugar Distributors Ltd.* was that the two firms involved had been dealing with each other over an extended period. The same held true in *Kruppstahl AG* v. *Quitmann Products Ltd.*[17]

In that case the plaintiff's Irish agent sought out an order for steel from the defendants. The order was confirmed in writing from Germany. Before receiving the confirmation note the defendants placed a second order and later placed further orders. The confirmation of order material issued for each order drew attention in red print to conditions on the reverse written in German.

These conditions included provision for retention of title. Gannon J. concluded that the buyer must have been aware of these terms and must have expected to find such-like since this was the normal practice of German firms. The conclusion was aided by the fact that the principals acting on each side of the negotiations were Germans. Both were accustomed to making contracts in this manner.

It was also argued unsuccessfully that the contracts for the supply of steel were made as soon as each order was placed—the corollary being that the confirmation notes arrived too late to be part of the contracts. Gannon J. would have none of this, tartly remarking that the buyers did not object to

---

[14] High Court, April 27, 1983.
[15] [1982] I.L.R.M. 399.
[16] [1982] I.L.R.M. 99.
[17] [1982] I.L.R.M. 551.

the terms but accepted them without demur. The conclusion was that the first and all subsequent contracts incorporated the reservation of title terms.[18]

A couple of points need to be made. It might be argued that the more complicated a reservation of title clause the greater the degree of notice required. For instance, one might distinguish between a simple reservation of title clause like that involved in *John Snow and Co. Ltd.* v. *DBG Woodcroft and Co. Ltd.*[19] and also in *Sugar Distributors Ltd.* v. *Monaghan Cash and Carry Ltd.* and more extensive clauses giving rights in relation to products and proceeds. However, the cases hitherto do not support such a distinction.

The second point is that some of the cases we have been discussing like *Kruppstahl* might be taken as supporting the implication of contractual terms by a consistent course of dealing between the parties. Donaldson J. in *SIAT Di Del Ferro* v. *Tradax Overseas SA*,[20] suggests that the test for incorporation by a "consistent course of dealing" should be "what each party by his words and conduct would have led the other party as a reasonable man to believe he was accepting." This test in turn echoes the words of Lord Reid in *McCutcheon* v. *David MacBrayne Ltd.*[21]

Incorporation by a Course of Dealing

A well-known case of incorporation by a "consistent course of dealing" is the exemption clause case *J. Spurling Ltd.* v. *Bradshaw*.[22] Here the defendant had sent eight casks of orange juice for storage in the plaintiff's warehouse. When the casks were collected it was discovered that the juice was either gone or ruined. After being sued by Spurling for the storage charge Bradshaw counterclaimed for breach of contract by negligent storage. To stave off the counterclaim Spurling produced an exclusion clause which appeared in a document sent to Bradshaw some days after the conclusion of the contract. The court were of the view that the past dealings between the parties had to be taken into account and that the apparent lateness of the clause was not decisive. Shades of *Kruppstahl* one might suggest. Bradshaw admitted to receiving such documents in the past. The clause was part of the contract by the course of business and conduct of the parties.

Another case in point is *British Crane Hire Ltd.* v. *Ipswich Plant Hire Ltd.*[23] Here two previous transactions had taken place between the parties

---

[18] On the Irish cases see Robert Pearce (1985) 20 Ir.Jur. (n.s.) 264, 267–270.
[19] Arguably however, the clause in *Woodcraft* reserved title until all obligations owed by the buyer to the seller had been discharged and not just those flowing from the particular contract of sale.
[20] [1980] 1 Lloyd's Rep. 53.
[21] [1964] 1 W.L.R. 125. See also, *Hardwick Game Farm* v. *Agricultural Poultry Producers Association* [1969] 2 A.C. 31.
[22] [1956] 1 W.L.R. 461.
[23] [1974] 2 W.L.R. 856. The authorities on incorporation by a course of dealing were reviewed by the Court of Appeal in *Circle Freight International Ltd.* v. *Medeast (Gulf Exports) Ltd.*

using British Crane's standard terms. In the instance which gave rise to the litigation the contract was made over the telephone in an emergency with no mention of British Crane's standard terms. Both concerns were in the same trade and of equal bargaining power; each had hired out plant on occasion. Furthermore, British Crane's conditions were similar to those used by Ipswich Plant Hire themselves. Lord Denning suggested that incorporation rested on the common understanding which was derived from the conduct of the parties.

Incorporation by course of dealing was unsuccessfully argued in the reservation of title context in *Wavin Nederland BV* v. *Excomb Ltd.*[24] In this case *W. Ltd.* the manufacturer of certain games, delivered a quantity of them to *E. Ltd.* under a contract of sale. W's general conditions included a term stating: "*Passing of Property*: Until payment in full has been effected, the goods remain our property. If customer fails to fulfil any obligation, we are entitled to recover our goods at all times and wherever they may be, notwithstanding our right to claim damages from Customer." A dispute arose about whether the condition formed part of the contract by reason of the parties' course of dealing with each other. Leggatt J. expressed the view that to discern in the rag-bag of contracts any pattern or course of dealing from which the requisite contractual intention could be inferred was impossible. The salesmen concerned in the contracts were more interested in the goods being sold than in lawyers' provisions designed to guard against a calamity which none of them foresaw.

Apart from what are basically "consistent course of dealing" cases, a reservation of title clause will not be implied into a contract if it is not expressly mentioned. The test for implying terms is whether an implication is necessary for the sake of business efficacy. This should never be the case as regards reservation of title, even where there are other indications in the contract suggesting that the reserving of title has been in the seller's mind. The House of Lords has remained adamant in its opposition to a reasonableness test for the implying of contractual terms—witness *Liverpool City Council* v. *Irwin*.[25] If it were to relent in its opposition, this would still not allow for more frequent implication of reservation of title claims. They are not yet a common enough feature of sales of goods for their omission to be regarded as unreasonable.

Battle of the Forms

One aspect of incorporation that gives rise to particular problems is the

[1988] 2 Lloyd's Rep. 427, 433. Taylor L.J. concluded that "it is not necessary to the incorporation of trading terms into a contract that they should be specifically set out provided that they are conditions in common form or usual terms in the relevant business. It is sufficient if adequate notice is given identifying and relying upon the conditions and they are available on request. Other considerations apply if the conditions or any of them are particularly onerous or unusual."

[24] [1983] New L.J. 937.
[25] [1977] A.C. 239.

so-called "battle of the forms." The following is a typical order of events in this conflict striven situation.

Round One Prospective buyer seeks quotation on his standard form which embodies the terms on which he is prepared to do business.

Round Two Prospective supplier quotes on his own standard form contract which incorporates a reservation of title clause.

Round Three Buyer places an order on his own standard form which usually states that the terms set out in the buyer's order form alone shall govern the contract, thereby excluding any retention of title term.

Round Four Goods are supplied accompanied by a delivery note that reiterates supplier's terms and conditions, including the reservation of title clause. The goods are signed for by the buyer's gateman.

Difficulties arise if the two sets of terms are inconsistent. Is there any contract between the parties and, if so, which set of terms applies? One solution is to say that there is no contract because there is no agreement on terms or *consensus ad idem* to use the expression favoured by contract lawyers. If a no-contract solution is adopted then it appears that the "buyer" would be under a restitutionary obligation to pay for the use of the goods. It does not appear, however, that title passes in this situation. The "mistake in contract" cases like *Cundy* v. *Lindsay*[26] are in point.

Cundy v. *Lindsay* is a case where a rogue called Blenkarn wrote to the plaintiffs and offered to buy certain goods. He masked his signature so as to resemble that of Blenkiron & Co., a substantial undertaking carrying on business in the same street and with whom the plaintiffs had previously dealt. The plaintiffs forwarded the goods under the assumption that they were dealing with Blenkiron & Co. The goods eventually came into the possession of the defendant, an innocent purchaser. The House of Lords held that the contract between the plaintiffs and Blenkiron was void for mistake. No property in the goods passed and the plaintiff was entitled to recover them.

So where a contract is void for mistake, no property passes. The principle is well established but the application of the principle has occasioned difficulties particularly where parties are dealing *inter praesentes*.[27] The reservation of title scenario that is somewhat analogous in that there is a fundamental divergence of view about the nature of the contact which vitiates the contract formation process and so, arguably, prevents property from passing. If the "buyer" becomes insolvent and a liquidator or trustee in bankruptcy, (or indeed a receiver or administrator) purports to withhold the goods from the seller, then he is personally liable under the Torts (Interference with Goods) Act 1977. The goods are not among the property of the "buyer" available for distribution among its creditors. The doctrine of

---

[26] [1878] 3 A.C. 459; *cf. King's Norton Metal Co.* v. *Eldridge Merrett & Co. Ltd.* (1897) 14 T.L.R. 98.
[27] *Lake* v. *Simmons* [1927] A.C. 487 and *Ingram* v. *Little* [1961] 1 Q.B. 31 should be contrasted with *Phillips* v. *Brook* [1919] 2 K.B. 243 and *Lewis* v. *Averay* [1972] 1 Q.B. 198.

reputed ownership never applied in the corporate context (see *Gorringe* v. *Irwell India Rubber Works*)[28] and in the individual insolvency situation was swept away by the Insolvency Act reforms of 1985/1986—see now Insolvency Act 1986, s. 283.

The "no-contract" view has a respectable pedigree in tradition behind it. It is supported by the old cases of *Hyde* v. *Wrench*,[29] and *Neale* v. *Merrett*,[30] though these cases also succumb to an offer-acceptance analysis, which, when applied in the modern "battle of the forms" context, favours he who fires the final salvo. *Hyde* v. *Wrench* is a case where the defendant offered to sell his farm for £1000 but the plaintiff offered £950 which the defendant refused to accept. Later the plaintiff agreed to give £1000 but there appeared to be no assent on the part of the defendant though there had been no withdrawal of the first offer. Lord Langdale M.R. held that there existed no valid binding contract between the parties for the sale of the property.

The preponderance of modern opinion is in support of a contractual rather than a quasi-contractual result being reached. In the "battle of the forms" the courts have tended to award the spoils of victory to the last past the post. Two cases in point may be mentioned.[31]

In *British Road Services Ltd.* v. *Arthur Crutchley & Co. Ltd.*,[32] a load of whiskey was delivered by British Road Services to a warehouse belonging to the defendants. The latter stamped the plaintiff's delivery note "Received on AVC's conditions." The whiskey was stolen while in the possession of the defendants.

The issue of liability turned partly on whether the plaintiff's or defendant's terms and conditions prevailed; the two sets of conditions being entirely incompatible. It was held by the Court of Appeal that the defendants' conditions were incorporated in their contract with the plaintiffs' by reason of the rubber stamp. The decision on this point is complicated by the fact that there was a long-established course of business between the parties. The plaintiffs' driver was their agent to accept the defendants' special contractual terms because of the frequency of deliveries over the years and the mode in which they had been carried out.

In the subsequent case of *Butler Machine Tool Co. Ltd.* v. *Ex-Cell-O Corporation (England) Ltd.*,[33] a last past the post solution was again adopted. Here the sellers of a machine tool quoted a price of £7500. The offer included a price variation clause. The clause provided for an increase in

[28] (1888) 34 Ch.D. 128.
[29] (1840) 49 E.R. 132.
[30] [1930] W.N. 189.
[31] See also, *Kingsley and Keith Ltd.* v. *Glynn Bros. (Chemicals) Ltd.* [1953] 1 Lloyd's Rep. 211; *A. Davies and Co. (Shopfitters) Ltd.* v. *Williams Old Ltd.* (1969) 67 L.G.R. 395; *Transmotors Ltd.* v. *Robertson Buckley & Co.* [1970] 1 Lloyd's Rep. 224; *O.T.M. Ltd.* v. *Hydronautics* [1981] 2 Lloyd's Rep. 211; *Uniroyal Ltd.* v. *Miller and Co. Ltd.* 1985 S.L.T. 101 and *Sauter Automation Ltd.* v. *H. C. Goodman (Mechanical Services) Ltd., Financial Times*, May 10, 1986; noted by Bragg (1986) 7 Co. Law 209.
[32] [1968] 1 All E.R. 811.
[33] [1979] 1 W.L.R. 401.

price if costs rose for the sellers before delivery, which was to take place 10 months later. The buyers struck back by accepting the offer on their own standard order form which had no price fluctuation clause. The sellers returned a portion of the buyers' printed form acknowledging that the contract was made on the basis of the buyers' conditions. The decision was in favour of the buyers. In the classic language of offer, counter-offer and acceptance the sellers' quotation was held to be an offer. The buyers' response was adjudged a counter-offer which was accepted by returning the slip. The fact that the sellers included a covering note which reasserted that their own terms of contract applied was held not to affect the position.

The above analysis commended itself to Lord Justices Lawton and Bridge. Lord Denning, while not dissenting from this approach, put forward an alternative view. He said that the documents comprised in a "battle of forms" were to be considered as a whole to discover the consensus of the parties by reasonable implication if the conflicting terms and conditions of both parties were irreconcilable. On that basis the acknowledgment of the order was the decisive document since it made it clear that the contract was to be on the buyers' and not the sellers' terms.

Lord Denning also believed that in some cases the battle ought to be won by the man who gets the blow in first. If he offers to sell at a named price on the terms and conditions stated on the back and the buyer orders the goods purporting to accept the offer on an order form with his own different terms and conditions on the back, then if the difference is so material that it would affect the price, the buyer ought not to be allowed to take advantage of the difference unless he draws it specifically to the attention of the seller.

A variety of criticisms have been levelled at the Denning approach and it is submitted that these criticisms are in the main well founded.[34] It is said to occasion uncertainty and to be of insufficient assistance to the court in determining whether or not an agreement has been reached. Moreover, it does not discourage the firing of salvos, and almost any term can affect the price. The "last past the post" formula, for all its mechanical rigour, has much to commend it.

Conclusion

What is the moral of the story for those attempting to insert reservation of title clauses? If an offer to supply goods is made on the sellers' standard form which includes a reservation of title clause, and an acceptance is received on the buyers' standard terms which exclude a reservation of title clause, then this is deemed not an acceptance of the offer but rather a counter-offer. If the goods are then supplied without any further interchange between the parties, the contract is regarded as having been made on the buyers' conditions. The supply is taken as an acceptance by conduct of the counter-offer.

[34] See generally, Rawlings (1979) 42 M.L.R. 715; Adams (1979) 95 L.Q.R. 481; [1983] J.B.L. 297 and McKendrick (1988) 8 O.J.L.S. 197, 198.

Conclusion

In a situation where orders are placed on the buyers' terms, the supplier is faced with two possibilities. He may refuse the offer and, in doing so, overcome considerable reluctance at having to turn down business. Alternatively, he may send a written "confirmation of order" note which makes it clear that the goods are supplied on the sellers' terms as previously made known to the buyers.[35]

---

[35] An earlier version of this chapter appeared in the form of an article at (1989) 133 S.J. 1052.

Chapter 5

ROMALPA AND ITS PROGENY

As we have seen in Chapter 1, while the concept of reservation of title is older than the Sale of Goods Act 1893[1] it was not until the mid 1970s that the legal consequences of the concept began to be explored fully by the courts.[2] The seminal case is *Aluminium Industrie Vaassen BV* v. *Romalpa Aluminium Ltd.*[3] The case is generally referred to as *Romalpa* and has given rise to a popular shorthand expression for reservation of title clauses—"Romalpa" clauses. While the potentialities of this decision were appreciated immediately by a number of commentators, the insight offered passed unnoticed insofar as the compilers of the Official Law Reports were concerned. Remarkably, *Romalpa* was not reported in the official series of Law Reports. In this chapter *Romalpa* and the mainstream reservation of title cases that followed it will be examined. More detailed points will be picked up in succeeding chapters.

Romalpa

Basically the facts are that the plaintiffs, a Dutch company, supplied aluminium foil to the defendants, an English company. Some of this aluminium foil was resold to third parties. A receiver was appointed to the defendant company. The plaintiffs were owed over £122,000 by the defendants. The receiver certified that approximately £35,000 was held in an account in his name as receiver-manager of the defendants, representing the proceeds of sub-sales of aluminium foil supplied by the plaintiffs. Moreover, unused foil to the value of £50,000 was held by him. The plaintiffs sought the return of the unused foil and a declaration that they were entitled to a charge on the sum of £35,000. The latter claim was based on a right to trace on the principle established in *Re Hallett's Estate.*[4]

The plaintiffs' submissions were grounded on clause 13 of their general selling terms and conditions. Because of the significance of this clause to the decision in the case and the results reached in other cases, it is useful to set out the clause in full. It provided as follows:

"The ownership of the material to be delivered by A.I.V. will only be

---

[1] See for instance the case of *Bateman* v. *Green and King* (1868) I.R. 2 Ch. 607. The case is discussed by Phillips and Schuster, "Reservation of Title in the Commercial Laws of England and Ireland" (1979–1980) D.U.L.J. 1.
[2] A short account of reservation of title pre-*Romalpa* is provided by Diamond in *Security Over Corporeal Movables* (ed. Sauveplanne, 1974), Sijthoff, Chap. 2.
[3] [1976] 1 W.L.R. 676.
[4] (1880) 13 Ch.D. 696.

transferred to purchaser when he has met all that is owing to A.I.V., no matter on what grounds. Until the date of payment, purchaser, if A.I.V. so desires, is required to store this material in such a way that it is clearly the property of A.I.V. A.I.V. and the purchaser agree that, if purchaser should make (a) new object(s) from the material, mix this material with (an)other object(s) or if this material in any way whatsoever becomes a constituent of (an)other object(s) A.I.V. will be given the ownership of this (these) new object(s) as surety of the full payment of what purchaser owes A.I.V. To this end A.I.V. and purchaser now agree that the ownership of the article(s) in question, whether finished or not, are to be transferred to A.I.V. and that this transfer of ownership will be considered to have taken place through and at the moment of the single operation or event by which the material is converted into (a) new object(s), or is mixed with or becomes a constituent of (an)other object(s). Until the moment of full payment of what purchaser owes A.I.V. purchaser shall keep the object(s) in question for A.I.V. in his capacity of fiduciary owner and, if required, shall store this (these) object(s) in such a way that it (they) can be recognised as such. Nevertheless, purchaser will be entitled to sell these objects to a third party within the framework of the normal carrying on of his business and to deliver them on condition that—if A.I.V. so requires—purchaser, as long as he has not fully discharged his debt to A.I.V. shall hand over to A.I.V. the claims he has against his buyer emanating from this transaction."

Mocatta J. decided that the clause applied to the transactions between the parties. This being so, it was admitted that the plaintiffs were the owners of the remaining unsold aluminium foil held by the receiver and they were entitled to an order for its delivery up to them.[5] More heat was engendered by the tracing claim. Two concessions by the defendants proved crucial to the disposal of this claim. First, it was accepted that clause 13 rendered the defendants' bailees of any foil in their possession while money was still owing to the plaintiffs. Secondly, the defendants were accepted as having authority to resell the foil to sub-purchasers. Clause 13 catered for the situation where foil was mixed with other materials and then resold, but there was no express provision dealing with the position where foil had been resold in its original condition.

The judge held that the tracing claim succeeded. While accepting the necessity for a fiduciary relationship, he said that the reservation of ownership clause demonstrated an intention to create such a relationship, thereby bringing into play the principle stated in *Re Hallett's Estate*.[6] In his view the clause contained unusual and fairly elaborate provisions departing substantially from the debtor/creditor relationship.

[5] [1976] 1 W.L.R. 676, 680.
[6] Mocatta J. recognised that he found himself in a "most unfamiliar field"—*ibid.* 682.

The Court of Appeal confirmed the first instance decision. The principal area of controversy revolved around the terms on which a power of resale of the aluminium foil supplied was to be implied. Were the defendants obliged to account to the plaintiffs for the resale proceeds? The defendants submitted that no accounting obligation could be inferred. This submission placed reliance on a 75-day credit period afforded in the conditions of sale.

The Court of Appeal was attracted by, but did not succumb to this contention. According to Roskill L.J. it was a formidable argument if one looked at the matter solely from the point of view of the defendants. The matter had to be regarded in the light of the contractual provisions agreed upon by both parties. The whole purpose of clause 13 would be undermined if no accounting obligation was inferred. Roskill L.J. expressed himself thus[7]:

> "I see no difficulty in the contractual concept that as between the defendants and their sub-purchasers, the defendants sold as principals, but that, as between themselves and the plaintiffs, those goods which they were selling as principals within their implied authority from the plantiffs were the plaintiffs' goods which they were selling as agents for the plaintiffs to whom they remained fully accountable. If an agent lawfully sells his principal's goods, he stands in a fiduciary relationship to his principal and remains accountable to his principal for those goods and their proceeds."

Goff and Megaw L.JJ. agreed with the conclusion that the defendants were accountable for the proceeds of subsales.

A number of matters in relation to the Court of Appeal decision merit attention. First, the Court seemed unperturbed by the consideration that as a matter of business the plaintiffs would not have required the defendants to account immediately. Roskill L.J. said that it was only upon insolvency that the question of what the powers are under clause 13 comes into play. The clause was not directed as to the halcyon days of solvency.[8] Goff L.J. accepted that in practice, so long as all went well, the plaintiffs would allow the defendants to use proceeds of sale in their business as they did. He seemed to think, however, that this matter of practice had no bearing on the strict rights of the parties.

Secondly, the details of the tracing remedy were not addressed by the Court of Appeal. Roskill L.J. referred simply to *Re Hallett's Estate*[9] and said that it was not necessary to quote the Master of the Roll's famous judgment or from the various restatements of principle in the many textbooks.[10] No reference was made to tracing at common law where a fiduciary relationship is not necessary.

[7] *Ibid.* 690.
[8] *Ibid.*
[9] *Ibid.* 692.
[10] *Ibid.* 687.

Thirdly, not a lot of energy was expended in expounding the capacity in which the defendants "handled" the plaintiffs' goods. The defendants accepted that they were bailees. Clause 13, however, referred to them as "fiduciary owner" while Roskill L.J. said that they resold as agents albeit still as fiduciaries. Perhaps, it is to the good that the Court of Appeal was not obsessed by considerations of terminological consistency.[11]

Fourthly, the private international law aspect was ignored.[12] The conditions of sale were expressed to be governed by Dutch law. No evidence though was adduced as to Dutch law and the case was decided in the light of English law.

Fifthly, the decision of the Court of Appeal leads to the conclusion that even profits made by the defendants on resales were to be held for the account of the plaintiffs.[13] The issue was not expressly adverted to however.

Sixthly, relevant provisions of company law were not weighed in the balance by the Court of Appeal. The argument that the reservation of title clause constituted a charge which was invalid for want of registration was made at first instance before Mocatta J. He rejected it on the ground that the ownership of the foil never left the plaintiffs so that the proceeds of subsales belonged in equity to them.[14]

Re Bond Worth Ltd.

Slade J. proved more sympathetic to company law contentions in *Re Bond Worth Ltd.*[15] The case concerned acrilan fibre which was manufactured into carpets. In a blockbuster judgment he held that a reservation of title clause imposed by the sellers constituted an unregistered charge on four categories of assets in the hands of the defendants, namely raw fibre, the proceeds of sale of such fibre, carpets into which the fibre was manufactured, and the proceeds of sale of the carpets. Detailed matters of company charge registration will be left to the next chapter but *Bond Worth* provides a suitable focus for discussing the impact of *Romalpa* on subsequent case law. A thematic

---

[11] Note in this context the observations of Robert Goff L.J. in *Clough Mill Ltd.* v. *Martin* [1985] 1 W.L.R. 111, 116 who says that concepts like bailment and fiduciary duty are our tools not our masters. See also the judgment of Goulding J. in *Chase Manhattan Bank N.A.* v. *Israel-British Bank (London) Ltd.* who holds that an initial fiduciary obligation is not necessary in relation to the right to trace. It suffices if say, for instance, payment into the wrong hands gives rise to a fiduciary obligation. There is an extensive discussion of the prerequisites of a valid equitable tracing claim in Chap. 3.

[12] The private international law angle is discussed *infra*, Chap. 13.

[13] For criticism on this score see Atiyah, *The Sale of Goods* (7th ed., 1985), pp. 361–362.

[14] [1976] 1 W.L.R. 676, 682–683. Many important issues in relation to reservation of title are touched upon in the Irish case *Re Interview Ltd.* [1975] I.R. 382. This case was decided by the Irish High Court in March 1975—after Mocatta J's decision in the *Romalpa* case but before the Court of Appeal's pronouncement. The *Interview* case is discussed by Dickson, *Reservation of Title Clauses* (1987), pp. 12–15. The later Irish cases are discussed by Dickson, *op. cit.* pp. 29–35 and also by Pearce, "Reservation of Title on the Sale of Goods in Ireland" (1985) 20 Ir.Jur. (n.s.) 264.

[15] [1980] Ch. 228.

approach will be discussed in relation to the treatment of the different types of reservation of title clause.

"Simple" Clauses

As we have seen above it was conceded in *Romalpa* that if the reservation of title clause formed part of the conditions of sale, the aluminium foil which had not been resold belonged to the plaintiff sellers. The reservation of ownership point is not really discussed in the judgments. The relevant portion of the clause read: "The ownership of the material . . . will only be transferred to purchaser when he has met all that is owing to A.I.V. no matter on what grounds."

Subsequent cases have affirmed the effectiveness of "simple" reservation of title clauses with one major hiccup. The hiccup occurred in *Re Bond Worth Ltd.* where a clause purported to reserve "equitable and beneficial ownership." It was held that legal and equitable title to the goods passed to the buyers and a equitable interest was granted back to the sellers by way of security.[16] The judgment is discussed in more detail in the next chapter as are the other cases on "simple" reservation of title. The *locus classicus* is now the decision of the Court of Appeal in *Clough Mill Ltd.* v. *Martin.*[17] There the Court rejected the notion, propounded by Judge O'Donoghue at first instance, that if the purpose of a reservation of title clause is to provide security for the payment of the purchase price, then the clause should be construed as creating a charge.[18]

In *Romalpa* ownership was retained by the seller until the buyer met "all that is owing . . . no matter on what grounds." Although there is no discussion on this point in the judgment, the clause is clearly what is known as an extended reservation of title clause. Such a clause reserves ownership even beyond the time when all obligations under the particular contract of sale have been met. The precise status of such clauses remains unclear. Again the issue is more fully discussed in the succeeding chapter.

Clauses Conferring an Entitlement to Proceeds of Resales of the Original Goods Supplied

The main area of dispute in *Romalpa* centred around the accounting obligation with respect to resale proceeds. The controversy on the issue has continued since *Romalpa*. It is important to distinguish between two types of "proceeds of resale" clauses. First, there is a clause affording a right to proceeds of resale of the original goods supplied. Secondly, we have a clause

[16] [1980] Ch. 228, 252–256. In this connection Slade J. cites *Re Connolly Bros. Ltd. (No. 2)* [1912] 2 Ch. 25; *Capital Finance Co. Ltd.* v. *Stokes* [1969] 1 Ch. 261; *Coborn* v. *Collins* (1887) 35 Ch.D. 373 and *McEntire* v. *Crossley Bros. Ltd.* [1895] A.C. 457.
[17] [1985] 1 W.L.R. 111.
[18] The first instance decision is reported at [1984] 1 W.L.R. 1967.

relating to proceeds of sale of manufactured goods. Clearly, if the original supplier has no title to manufactured goods, then he will not be able to establish a claim to the proceeds of sale of such goods.

Romalpa was a case where the goods supplied had not been processed in any form.

In *Re Bond Worth Ltd.*, on the other hand, acrilan fibre supplied had formed part of the process of manufacture of carpets. Nonetheless, much of what Slade J. had to say is of general application in relation to the essentials of a valid tracing claim, more particularly a claim to the proceeds of sale of unprocessed goods. The fibre was sold subject, *inter alia*, to the following condition.

> "(a) The risk in the goods passes to the buyer upon delivery, but equitable and beneficial ownership shall remain with us until full payment has been received (each order being considered as a whole), or until prior resale, in which case our beneficial entitlement shall attach to the proceeds of resale or to the claim for such proceeds. (b) Should the goods become constituents of or be converted into other products while subject to our equitable and beneficial ownership we shall have the equitable and beneficial ownership in such other products as if they were solely and simply the goods and accordingly subclause (a) shall as appropriate apply to such other products."

A fiduciary relationship appears to have been accepted as a foundation of the right to trace. The judge went on to hold that where an alleged fiduciary had the right to mix assets or money with his own assets or money this was incompatible with the existence of a fiduciary relationship with respect to such assets or money.[19] Four cases were cited in support of this proposition. The first is *Re Nevill*[20] where James L.J. said *a propos* an alleged fiduciary[21]:

> "It does not appear that he ever was expected to return any particular contract, or the names of the persons with whom he had dealt. He pursued his own course in dealing with the goods, and frequently before sale he manipulated them to a very considerable extent by pressing, dyeing and otherwise altering their character, changing them as much as wheat would be changed by being turned into flour, and he sold them on what terms he pleased as to price and length of credit. ... This is quite inconsistent with the notion that he was acting in a fiduciary character in respect of those goods."

Foley v. *Hill*,[22] *South Australia Insurance Co.* v. *Randell*[23] and *Henry* v. *Hammond*[24] were also cited in this connection. In *Foley* v. *Hill* the House of

[19] [1980] Ch. 228, 261.
[20] (1871) L.R. 6 Ch. App. 397.
[21] *Ibid.* 400.
[22] (1848) 2 H.L. Cas. 28.
[23] (1869) L.R. 3 P.C. 101.
[24] [1913] 2 K.B. 515.

Lords held that the banker-customer relationship was that of debtor and creditor. Lord Cottenham L.C. said money paid to a banker becomes the banker's money. He makes what profit of it he can, which profit he retains to himself, paying back only the principal, or the principal and a small rate of interest as may be.[25]

In *South Australian Insurance Co.* v. *Randell* the Privy Council opined that an indelible incident of trust property is that a trustee can never make use of it for his own benefit.[26] The crescendo of concurring voices was added to by Channell J. in *Henry* v. *Hammond*. He said that if a person is not bound to keep money separate, but is entitled to mix it with his own money and deal with it as he pleases, and when called upon, to hand over an equivalent sum of money, then he is not a trustee of the money, but merely a debtor.[27]

The sellers tried to counter this line of authority by reference to *Romalpa*. Slade J. accepted that the facts in *Romalpa* had much in common with the facts in the present case. In each instance the purchaser was left at liberty both to sell the relevant goods and to use them unrestrictedly for the purposes of manufacture, at least in the ordinary course of business. The quartet of cases mentioned above were not cited in *Romalpa*. If they had been, then as Slade J. suggestively remarked, the Court of Appeal would have had the opportunity of explaining specifically why the principles exemplified in these earlier decisions did not bar the crucial conclusion that at all material times, up to and including sale, a presently subsisting fiduciary relationship existed between vendor and purchaser in regard to the goods or their proceeds.[28]

This comes pretty close to saying that *Romalpa* was wrongly decided but the judge steered clear of that statement. First, a bailment relationship had been conceded in *Romalpa* whereas there was no such concession in *Bond Worth*. The buyers were referred to as "fiduciary owner." If the goods supplied became a constituent part of new objects the purchaser was required to store them in such a way that they could be recognised as such. Furthermore, the monies which formed the subject-matter of the action in *Romalpa* had been kept separate by the receiver from other monies in his hands.[29] Some of these supposed distinctions do not carry a great deal of conviction. This is especially true of the last one in that in *Romalpa* the buyers were left free to use resale proceeds in the course of their business without being obliged to account during the golden days of solvency.[30]

---

[25] (1848) 2 H.L. Cas. 28, 36–37.

[26] (1869) L.R. 3 P.C. 101.

[27] [1913] 2 K.B. 515, 521. See also, *supra*, Chap. 3, pp. 43–46.

[28] [1980] Ch. 228, 263.

[29] Slade J. also relied on the fact that in *Romalpa* full legal ownership was reserved whereas in *Bond Worth* the sellers purported to retain only "equitable and beneficial" ownership. The draftsperson of the clause in *Bond Worth* may have felt that reservation of equitable and beneficial ownership made it easier to establish a fiduciary relationship between buyer and seller.

[30] See [1976] 1 W.L.R. 676, 690 *per* Roskill L.J. and 692 *per* Goff L.J.

Also Slade L.J. was somewhat selective in his reference to earlier authority. While he cites approvingly *Re Nevill*, no mention is made of *Re Smith*.[31] To some extent, forgiveness is possible on this score in that *Re Smith* does not appear to have been referred to in argument in *Bond Worth*. In any event, as explained in the previous chapter, *Re Nevill*[32] came in for some criticism in *Re Smith*. James L.J. was a party to both decisions. He suggested that *Re Nevill* was a "special facts" decision and that citation of such cases engages the attention of the court unnecessarily while deflecting concern away from the true underlying principles.[33]

Re Bond Worth Ltd. was not fated to be the last word on fiduciary relationships and the right to trace. The next instalment of the saga came with the decision of Staughton J. in *Hendy Lennox (Industrial Engines) Ltd. v. Grahame Puttick Ltd.*[34] The case related to the sale of diesel engines. These were then fitted into generating sets and resold. The defendant buyers went into receivership owing some £46,000 to the plaintiff suppliers in respect of diesel engines. Only three of the engines were on the defendants' premises at the time the receiver was appointed and of these two had been incorporated into generating sets. The diesel engines had been supplied subject, *inter alia*, to the following conditions of sale:

> "10. Payment. . . . Unless the company shall otherwise specify in writing all goods sold by the company to the purchaser shall be and remain the property of the company until the purchase price thereof shall be paid to the company. In the case of default in payment by the purchaser, the company shall have the right to take possession of and permanently retain any unpaid for goods and to revoke all liability of the company to the purchaser on the contract of sale and delivery of such goods."

Staughton J. held that as between the plaintiffs and defendants, the plaintiffs' proprietary rights were not lost by incorporation of the diesel engines in the generating sets—on which more anon. Title however, had passed to the defendants' customers with respect to two of the diesel engines on the defendants' premises at the time of the appointment of the receiver. The plaintiffs were therefore entitled only to delivery of one diesel engine; more correctly, to its resale value as it had been sold off by the receiver as part of a generating set.

The big debate in the case turned on the wider issue of entitlement to resale proceeds of the generating sets. The key question could be phrased better as revolving around that portion of the price fetched for generating sets which represented the diesel engines incorporated therein. The judge ruled that the claim failed. Some of Staughton J.'s reasoning has been

---

[31] (1879) 10 Ch.D. 566. There is an invaluable treatment by Watts, "Reservation of Title Clauses in England and New Zealand" (1985) 5 O.J.L.S. 456. See also, *supra*, Chap. 3, pp. 43–44.
[32] (1871) L.R. 6 Ch. App. 397.
[33] (1879) 10 Ch.D. 566, 572. See also, Sir George Jessel M.R. at 570.
[34] [1984] 1 W.L.R. 485.

adumbrated in the preceding chapter.[35] First, he said that one had to examine the relationship in each individual case to see whether it was of a fiduciary nature. *Romalpa* was distinguished on a number of grounds which are not altogether convincing.[36] One point was that the clauses in this case, unlike those in *Romalpa*, did not purport to deal with mixed or manufactured goods. It is difficult to see how this is a relevant consideration or why the sellers in *Hendy Lennox* should be penalised for limited ambition.

Other factors relied upon by Staughton J. in *Hendy Lennox* was the absence of an express obligation on the buyers to store the goods in such a way that they were clearly the property of the sellers. Moreover, there was no mention of the buyers as "fiduciary owner." Furthermore, the conferral in the conditions of sale of an express right to repossess the diesel engines, was taken as excluding any implied right to the proceeds of resales. The agreement between the parties that the buyers should have at least a one-month credit period was taken as ruling out any implied obligation to keep resale proceeds separate.[37]

In the previous chapter, the argument has been made that if a fiduciary label is ascribed to a particular relationship then the fiduciary comes under a duty to segregate the principal's assets from his own.[38] So an express statement stating this separation obligation is not necessary to the establishment of a right to trace proceeds—indeed in *Romalpa* there was no such express obligation. Given, however, the subsequent course of judicial decisions, clearly it is a counsel of prudence to spell out the duty to separate.

This counsel of prudence becomes even clearer in the light of *Re Andrabell Ltd.*[39] Here the plaintiff sold travel bags on credit terms to a company Andrabell Ltd. The bags were then resold by the company in the ordinary course of its business as a retailer and exporter of travel bags. The resale proceeds were paid into the company's general bank account where they were mixed with its other monies. The company later went into liquidation leaving the plaintiffs unpaid. The plaintiffs sought to establish a claim to the resale proceeds but the claim proved unsuccessful before Peter Gibson J. The supply contract stipulated, *inter alia*, that "sales terms will be 45 days

---

[35] See *supra*, Chap. 3, pp. 42–43.
[36] [1984] 1 W.L.R. 485, 498–499.
[37] *Ibid.* 499. Staughton J. referred to the observations of Buckley L.J. in *Borden (U.K.) Ltd.* v. *Scottish Timber Products Ltd.* [1981] Ch. 25, 46:

> "If any term is to be implied, that must be a term which is necessary to give the contract business efficacy, but it must also be a term which the court can see unambiguously to be a term which the parties would have inserted into their contract had they thought it appropriate to express it."

[38] See *supra*, Chap. 3, pp. 44–45. Reference is made to the New Zealand cases *Westpac Banking* v. *Savin* [1985] 2 N.Z.L.R. 41 and *Len Vidgen Ski & Leisure Ltd.* v. *Timarn Marine Supplies (1982) Ltd.* (1985) 2 N.Z. Co. Law Cases 99, 438 as well as to *Neste Oy* v. *Lloyd's Bank plc* [1983] 2 Lloyd's Rep. 658 and *Henry* v. *Hammond* [1913] 2 K.B. 515.
[39] [1984] 3 All E.R. 407.

net" and ". . . ownership of the goods covered shall not pass to the Company until the Company has paid . . . the total purchase price including VAT."

The judge accepted that there were a number of similarities between the present case and *Romalpa*. These similarities were listed as follows[40]:

> "(1) In each case there was an ordinary commercial contract for the sale of goods, subject only to a retention of title clause; (2) in each case the obvious purpose of the clause was to give protection to the seller in the case of insolvency of the purchaser before the seller had been paid; (3) in each case the contracts provided for a credit period; (4) in each case there was no express provision allowing sale by the purchaser of the goods supplied; yet such a provision had to be implied; (5) in each case the goods were simply sold on without mixing with or incorporation into other goods."

Nevertheless, Peter Gibson J. decided that the right to trace proceeds recognised in *Romalpa* should not be afforded recognition in the present case. With the greatest of respect the suggested grounds of distinction do not carry much weight.[41] First, he noted that the reservation of title clause upheld in *Romalpa* was an all-liabilities clause whereas here, property passed when the particular consignment of goods to which the contract related had been paid for. If anything, this should have strengthened the fiduciary relationship argument in *Andrabell*. Secondly, he harped back to the fact that the buyers were not bound to store the goods in such a way as to manifest the continued ownership of the sellers. Also there was no express acknowledgment of a fiduciary relationship nor the assignment of claims against sub-buyers.

Another point related to the fact that in *Romalpa* the claim was with respect to all resale proceeds, whereas here the buyers could keep the profits on resales. But we have seen from the preceding chapter that a *del credere* agency may entitle the buyer to resale profits.[42] According to Jessel M.R. in *Re Smith*[43] there was nothing to prevent the principal from remunerating the agent by a commission which varies dependent on the amount of profit procured by the sale. Further, Peter Gibson J. laid emphasis on the fact that counsel for Andrabell conceded that there was no obligation on Andrabell to keep separate from its own monies, the monies which it received from resales of the plaintiffs' travel bags. This seems a strange concession when it appears universally accepted that fiduciaries are under a "keep separate" duty even though this commitment may not have to be expressly stated.

Finally, the judge reasoned that the 45-day credit period meant that the plaintiff was free to use the resale proceeds in its business. In other words the provision of credit was irreconcilable with the equitable duty to account.

---

[40] *Ibid.* 414–415.
[41] See generally, for the grounds of distinction *ibid.* 415.
[42] See *supra*, Chap. 3, pp. 45–46.
[43] (1879) 10 Ch. 566, 570.

Professor Goode has persuasively argued, however, that this is not necessarily so. In his view[44]:

> "The sale agreement may, for example, be construed as providing that
> the buyer is to have 45 days' credit but subject to a duty to account for
> proceeds of sale on receipt, the transfer of such proceeds *pro tanto*
> reducing the buyer's price indebtedness. The duty to account thus cuts
> down the scope of the provision for credit but does not deprive it of
> effect, for the buyer remains entitled to avail himself of the full period
> of the credit except in so far as he receives proceeds of sale during that
> period."

Speaking at a high level of generality, the period since *Romalpa* up to the
decision of the Court of Appeal in *Clough Mill Ltd.* v. *Martin*[45] may be
described as one of retrenchment of the scope of reservation of title clauses.
In *Clough Mill*, however, a clause was upheld as not creating a registrable
charge even though its purpose may have been to secure payment of the
purchase price and performance of the other obligations under the sales
contract. This new found enthusiasm for *Romalpa* has not carried over to
tracing claims if the first instance judgments of Phillips J. in *E. Pfeiffer
Weinkellerei-Weineinkauf G.m.b.H. & Co.* v. *Arbuthnot Factors Ltd.*[46] and
Tatung (U.K.) Ltd. v. *Galex Telesure Ltd.*[47]

Pfeiffer is discussed at length in a later chapter.[48] Suffice it to say here that
wine was supplied by Pfeiffer to an English importer, Springfield, and then
resold on credit terms. The question arose as to the nature of the interest
which Pfeiffer had in the proceeds of the sub-sales.

Counsel on behalf of the plaintiffs forcefully contended that the plaintiff's
interest in the proceeds of sale of the wine did not constitute a charge over
property owned by the importer. Rather, it amounted to an absolute beneficial interest in the proceeds of sale, albeit that the plaintiff would come
under an implied contractual duty to account to Springfield to the extent that
proceeds of sale ultimately recovered by the plaintiff were in excess of the
debts owed by Springfield to it. The plaintiff's beneficial interest was not
created by Springfield. Instead it arose by operation of law as consequence
of a sale by Springfield of property owned by the plaintiff.[49] In support of this
submission, reliance was predictably placed on *Romalpa*.

Phillips J. found that this reliance was misplaced for two reasons. First of
all, in *Romalpa* counsel for the defendants conceded that the relationship of
the plaintiffs and defendants was that of bailor and bailee. Furthermore, the
latter part of clause 13 in *Romalpa* expressly described the buyers as "fiduci-

---

[44] Goode, *Proprietary Rights and Insolvency in Sales Transactions* (2nd ed., 1989), p. 100.
[45] [1985] 1 W.L.R. 111.
[46] [1988] 1 W.L.R. 150.
[47] (1989) 5 B.C.C. 325. See generally, on these two cases McCormack, "Reservation of
title—the controversy continues" [1989] L.M.C.L.Q. 198. See also, S. Wheeler (1989) 10 Co.
Law 151 and J. De Lacy (1989) 10 Co. Law 188.
[48] See *infra*, Chap. 9.
[49] [1988] 1 W.L.R. 150, 156.

ary owner" of mixed goods of which aluminium foil supplied by the plaintiffs formed part.

The judge opined that it was inappropriate to describe the relationship of a seller and a buyer in possession to whom title had not yet passed as that of bailor/bailee for it would not normally have the same incidents as the classic bailment relationship. This conclusion may be questioned. The feeling of inappropriateness was obviously not experienced by the Court of Appeal in *Romalpa*. Moreover, such feelings were equally alien to the court in another common law jurisdiction, namely New Zealand, where *Motor Mart Ltd.* v. *Webb*[50] is a case in point.

It is respectively submitted that Philips J. in *Pfeiffer* was guilty of over-simplification in dismissing the fiduciary relationship argument. He contented himself with the conclusion that there was no bailment in the present case but proceeded on the basis of a limited conception of the nature of bailment. The fact, however, that there is a bailment does not necessarily mean that there is a fiduciary relationship between the parties. In this particular case, nonetheless, the fiduciary relationship argument might be thought to have been strengthened by certain provisions in the contract between plaintiff and importer. The importer was subjected to a contractual obligation to separate the proceeds of cash sales from his other monies, book the sales accordingly, administer the funds until called for, notify the assignment of the seller's claim, and pass on all rights relating to the sub-sales to the seller.

The judgment of Phillips J. in *Tatung (U.K.) Ltd.* v. *Galex Telesure Ltd.* continues the process of distinguishing *Romalpa*. Indeed, the learned judge questioned the correctness of the conclusion that no registrable charge had been created on the facts of *Romalpa*. Here, the plaintiffs were manufacturers and suppliers of television, video and other electrical equipment and the defendants were in the business of reselling, "selling" on "hire-purchase" and renting goods supplied by the plaintiffs and other suppliers. The plaintiffs supplied goods to the defendants under two separate sets of conditions. The first set declared that the proceeds of resales of the goods belonged to the supplier absolutely. The second, and more elaborate, set of conditions obliged the defendants to keep the proceeds of resales in a separate account for the benefit of the plaintiffs. It was held that a charge had been created over the proceeds of sale.

Phillips J. noted that in *Tatung* the contracts made express provision for the interest that the plaintiffs were to have in the proceeds of dealing with the goods. In these circumstances he considered that the source of the plaintiffs' rights was the contractual agreement between the parties and not equitable principles that might have applied in the absence of such agreement. In other words, the plaintiffs are being penalised for precision in their supply contracts—a somewhat strange result to say the least.

[50] [1988] N.Z.L.R. 773. See generally, *supra*, Chap. 3, pp. 40–43.

After this survey of the authorities on tracing claims, one is tempted to set out certain principles which might appear to follow from the decided cases. But consistent conclusions are by no means easily stated. The authorities speak with forked tongues as it were. A seller who is contemplating the insertion of reservation of title clauses in his supply contracts has to steer between the Scylla of under-provision which proved fatal in *Andrabell* and *Hendy Lennox* and the Charybdis of over-elaboration which was the supplier's undoing in *Tatung*.[51] Some of these pitfalls are more elaborate than real, it is submitted. I would hazard the suggestion that Phillip J's reasoning in *Tatung* cannot be supported. Be that as it may, the following path through the thicket of competing principle is outlined. These serve as pointers towards acceptance of a tracing claim.[52]

First, the buyer should be required to store the goods in such a manner as to acknowledge the seller's ownership. It appears from *Romalpa* that separate storage as such is not essential, but rather the duty to store separately if so required by the seller. Moreover, the buyer should be designated a fiduciary. There might also be a declaration that the seller retains full ownership rights, subject to some contractual restrictions, and that the seller has the benefit of all claims against sub-buyers. In relation to resales, the buyer should be deemed an agent or fiduciary for the supplier with a duty to keep proceeds of resales apart from his own monies and to account to the seller in respect thereof. It is debateable whether the accounting obligation should extend to all resale proceeds or whether the buyer might safely be allowed to keep profits on resales.[53] It is submitted that the duty to account can be so restricted though it must be admitted that the authorities are not unanimous on this score.

Finally, there is no question of a credit period and the possibility of using resale monies in the buyer's business. One approach would be to make the purchase price immediately due but allowing a period of grace in practice. An even more laissez-faire approach would be to give the buyer liberty to use resale proceeds while its solvency was not in jeopardy but otherwise strictly to insist on segregation of assets and accounting. This course of action was deemed acceptable in *Romalpa* but has not cut much ice in subsequent cases. Perhaps the safest course is to oblige the buyer to pay the supplier the price of the goods at the end of the credit period irrespective of whether they have been resold or whether payment has been received from sub-buyers. The buyer might also be subjected to a duty to account for resale proceeds immediately on receipt. This is a provision which reduces the scope of the credit period.[54]

[51] (1989) 5 B.C.C. 325.
[52] See also, J. H. Farrar and Chiah Kim Chai [1985] J.B.L. 160, 164–165.
[53] In *Romalpa* [1976] 1 W.L.R. 676 the supplier was entitled under the terms of the reservation of title clause to keep resale profits whereas in *Re Andrabell* [1984] 3 All E.R. 407 the buyer was entitled to keep resale profits. This was taken as militating against a fiduciary relationship but *cf. Re Smith* (1879) 10 Ch.D. 566.
[54] See Goode, *Proprietary Rights and Insolvency in Sales Transactions* (2nd ed., 1989), p. 100.

Manufactured Goods

In *Romalpa* clause 13 of the supply contract provided that the seller should have title to any objects manufactured out of the goods supplied. It was not necessary to consider this aspect since the goods had been resold in their pristine form. The first case where "extended" reservation of title was really considered is *Borden (U.K.) Ltd. v. Scottish Timber Products Ltd.*[55] Here the plaintiffs supplied resin to the defendants which, as the plaintiffs well knew, was to be mixed with certain hardeners, wax emulsion and wood chippings so as to manufacture chipboard. The defendants went into receivership owing the plaintiffs some £318,000. The resin was supplied subject to the following reservation of title clause.

> "(2) *Risk and Property.* Goods supplied by the company shall be at the purchaser's risk immediately on delivery to the purchaser or into custody on the purchaser's behalf (whichever is the sooner) and the purchaser should therefore be insured accordingly. Property in goods supplied hereunder will pass to the customer when:
> (a) the goods the subject of this contract, and (b) all other goods the subject of any other contract between the company and the customer which, at the time of payment of the full price of the goods sold under this contract, have been delivered to the customer but not paid for in full, have been paid for in full."

The plaintiffs made a claim in respect of chipboard manufactured with their resin or any money or property representing the proceeds of sale of such chipboard. *Romalpa* was invoked in support of this contention but the incantation of that case proved unavailing. The Court of Appeal held that the plaintiffs' title to the resin disappeared once it was used in the manufacturing process.[56] The tracing remedy recognised in *Romalpa* did not apply where there was a mixture of heterogeneous goods in a manufacturing process wherein the original goods lost their character and what emerged was a wholly new product.[57]

Borden supports the distinction drawn in Chapter 3 between confusion or commingling without loss of physical identity and processing involving a loss of physical identity.[58] The cases referred to there are not however discussed in the judgments of the Court of Appeal. I have argued that co-ownership arises in cases of simple mixing but that the original supplier loses his title to goods where they form the constituents of a process of manufacture. The comments of Bridge L.J. are very much in line with this analysis. He suggested that a tracing argument might succeed where the goods mixed were all of a heterogenous character. The instance given was that of corn factor who mixes corn supplied to him as bailee with his own. This situation

---

[55] [1981] Ch. 25.
[56] *Ibid.* 41 *per* Bridge L.J. and 44 *per* Templeman L.J.
[57] See Bridge L.J. at 41.
[58] See *supra*, Chap. 3, pp. 51–58.

was conceived as leaving unaffected the bailor's rights, including the right to trace.

On the other hand, the process whereby resin was turned into chipboard was completely different. Bridge L.J. said what had happened in the manufacturing process here was much more akin to the process of consumption than to any simple process of admixture of goods. It was fairly analogous to the instances where cattle cake was sold to a farmer, or fuel to a steel manufacturer, in each case with a reservation of title clause, but on terms which permitted the farmer to feed the cattle cake to his herd and the steelmaker to fuel his furnaces, before paying the purchase price. It was universally agreed that the seller could not trace into the cattle or the steel. The learned Lord Justice suggested that if the seller wished to acquire rights over the finished product, he could only do so by express contractual stipulation.[59]

Templeman L.J. was of the same opinion. He said the following[60]:

"When the resin was incorporated in the chipboard, the resin ceased to exist, the plaintiff's title to the resin became meaningless and their security vanished. There was no provision in the contract for the defendants to provide substituted or additional security. The chipboard belonged to the defendants."

When is title to goods lost in the manufacturing process? This question is by no means easily answered. *Re Peachdart Ltd.*[61] demonstrates how prone the courts are to hold that title to goods has been lost in the reservation of title context. This is a case where Freudenberg Leath Co. Ltd. sold leather to a company which used it to manufacture handbags. The pertinent provision in the supply contract read:

"(b) ... the ownership of the products shall remain with the seller, which reserves the right to dispose of the products until payment in full for all the products has been received by it in accordance with the terms of this contract or until such time as the buyer sells the products to its customers by way of *bona fide* sale at full market value. If such payment is overdue in whole or in part the seller may (without prejudice to any of its other rights) recover or resell the products or any of them and may enter upon the buyer's premises by its servants or agents for that purpose. Such payment shall become due immediately upon the commencement of any act or proceeding in which the buyer's solvency is involved. If any of the products are incorporated in or used as material for other goods before such payment the property in the whole of such other goods shall be and remain with the seller until such payment has

---

[59] [1981] Ch. 25, 42.
[60] *Ibid.* 44.
[61] [1984] Ch. 131.

been made or the other goods have been sold as aforesaid and all the seller's rights hereunder in the products shall extend to those other goods. (c) Until the seller is paid in full for all the products the relationship of the buyer to the seller shall be fiduciary in respect of the products or other goods in which they are incorporated or used and if the same are sold by the buyer the seller shall have the right to trace the proceeds thereof according to the principles of *Hallett's Estate Re*. A like right for the seller shall apply where the buyer uses the products in any way so as to be entitled to payment from a third party."

Borden was invoked in support of the proposition that title to the leather vanished once the handbag-making operation was embarked upon. Counsel for Freudenbergs instanced the analogy of a sports person who having shot a rare animal takes the skin to a leather worker and instructs him to make it into a game bag. According to counsel's argument the property in the skin would remain with the sports person notwithstanding the fact that the skin would undergo many operations and would have thread and other material added to it. *Borden* was distinguished on the basis that resin was inevitably consumed and destroyed as a separate substance if used in the manufacture of chipboard.

Vinelott J. did not succumb to this line of reasoning. In his view the parties must have intended that, at least after a piece of leather had been appropriated to be manufactured into a handbag and work had started on it (when then the leather would cease to have any significant value as raw material), the leather would cease to be the exclusive property of Freudenbergs. Thereafter, Freudenbergs would have a charge on handbags in the course of manufacture and on the distinctive products which would come into existence at the end of the process of manufacture. The value of these products would be derived for the most part from the buyer's reputation and skill in design and the skill of its workforce.[62]

Some commentators would say that when a judge begins by saying what the parties must have intended, this is a sure sign that in reality he is substituting his own views for the views of the parties. *Peachdart* is nonetheless in line with the proposition advanced in Chapter 3 that where a party applies his own labour to another's raw materials in bringing out the formation of a new product, the worker, as it were becomes owner of the new product.[63]

The issue of admixture of goods did not really arise in *Clough Mill Ltd.* v. *Martin*.[64] There are suggestions, however, in the judgments of Robert Goff and Oliver L.JJ. that where a new product is made consisting of materials belonging to A and B, the parties are free to agree where title to the product shall lie. Where the seller's and buyer's goods are made into a new product

---

[62] *Ibid.* 142–143.
[63] See *supra*, Chap. 3, p. 58. See also, Goode, *op. cit.* p. 92 and references therein contained.
[64] [1985] 1 W.L.R. 111.

by the buyer, the problem with inserting a clause to this effect in a supply contract is that it gives the seller a large windfall profit.[65]

In the Irish case *Kruppstahl A. G.* v. *Quitmann Products Ltd.*[66] the draftsperson of the reservation of title clause dealt with this problem by providing that the seller and buyer were to hold the new product jointly in the ratio of the invoice value of the seller's goods to those of the buyer's goods. Gannon J. held that the provision constituted a registrable charge. The seller's interest was confined to securing the buyer's indebtedness in respect of the price of the goods supplied by the seller. The registration of charge point is discussed in more detail in Chapter 6.

In *Hendy Lennox (Industrial Engines) Ltd.* v. *Grahame Puttick Ltd.*[67] principles of accession discussed in Chapter 3 were applied in the reservation of title context. The facts of the case have been adumbrated earlier. It suffices to say here that the case concerned diesel engines which had been incorporated into generating sets. Staughton J. held that the proprietary rights of the sellers in the engines were not affected when the engines were wholly or partially incorporated into the generator sets.[68] The title of the original seller remained because the diesel engines could be removed without serious injury or to destruction of the whole so formed. The judge explained that the engines were not like the acrilan which became yarn and then carpet (*Bond Worth*), or the resin which became chipboard (*Borden*) or the leather which became handbags (*Peachdart*).

Tracing Claims to Proceeds of Sale of Mixed or Manufactured Goods

This matter can be dealt with in a relatively straightforward fashion. If the original supplier's title is still good, whether wholly or in part, then a tracing claim can be sustained to resale proceeds provided that the requisites of a valid tracing claim, discussed earlier in this chapter, are met. A case in point might be *Hendy Lennox.*

On the other hand, where the supplier's title is lost as a result of his goods being "consumed" in the manufacturing process, then he will not be able to maintain a claim to the proceeds of sale of the manufactured goods. *Borden (U.K.) Ltd.* v. *Scottish Timber Products Ltd.*[69] and *Peachdart Ltd. Re*[70] might be cited in this connection.

Conclusion

While it is dangerous to make broad generalisations the period since

[65] See generally, Goode, *op. cit.* pp. 98–99.
[66] [1982] I.L.R.M. 551.
[67] [1984] 1 W.L.R. 485.
[68] *Ibid.* 494. The action was tried at Winchester Crown Court. The judge regretted that the action was not transferred to the Commercial Court in London because it was not possible to obtain all the books that might have been desirable—*ibid.* 486–487.
[69] [1981] Ch. 25.
[70] [1984] Ch. 131.

Conclusion

Romalpa might be described as one of retrenchment and then regrowth. Initially the scope of reservation of title clauses was narrowed in decisions like *Re Bond Worth Ltd.*[71] and *Borden (U.K.) Ltd.* v. *Scottish Timber Products Ltd.* Latterly there has been some recapture of lost ground, particularly with the decision of the Court of Appeal in *Clough Mill Ltd.* v. *Martin.*[72] But these are quite sweeping statements. Reservation of title clauses are perhaps best considered under the particular individual heads dealt with in this chapter. Registration of charge points are taken in Chapter 6, while various strands are brought together in Chapter 14 of the book. This final chapter will provide pointers towards more effective drafting of reservation of title clauses having regard to the matters discussed in the book as a whole.

[71] [1980] Ch. 228.
[72] [1985] 1 W.L.R. 111.

CHAPTER 6

REGISTRATION OF COMPANY CHARGES AND
RESERVATION OF TITLE CLAUSES

In this chapter it is intended to examine the interaction between reservation of title clauses and the provisions relating to registration of company charges. First, it is appropriate to look at the general régime applicable in the case of company charge registration. Then we will turn our attention to particular types of registrable charge and finally to the various kinds of reservation of title clause to see whether they fall within any of the registrable categories.[1]

Charges Requiring Registration

Section 396(1) of the Companies Act 1985 as inserted by section 93 of the Companies Act 1989 sets out the various categories of registrable charge as follows:

(a) a charge on land or any interest in land, other than—
  (i) in England and Wales, a charge for rent or any other periodical sum issuing out of the land,
  (ii) in Scotland, a charge for any rent, ground, annual or other periodical sum payable in respect of the land;
(b) a charge on goods or any interest in goods, other than a charge under which the chargee is entitled to possession either of the goods or of a document of title to them,
(c) a charge on intangible movable property (in Scotland, incorporeal moveable property) of any of the following descriptions—
  (i) goodwill,
  (ii) intellectual property,
  (iii) book debts (whether book debts of the company or assigned to the company),
  (iv) uncalled share capital of the company or calls made but not paid,
(d) a charge for securing an issue of debentures, or
(e) a floating charge on the whole or part of the company's property.

This list is not all-extensive in that it does not embrace every type of

[1] Pt. XII of the Companies Act 1985 on the registration of charges has been completely overhauled by Pt. IV of the Companies Act 1985. The 1989 Act inserts new sections to replace the earlier Act. See generally statements of the D.T.I dated September 2, 1987, and July 7, 1988. See also Pt. III of Professor Aubrey Diamond's DTI commissioned *A Review of Security Interests in Property* (1989). Pt. IV of the Companies Act 1989 which contains the relevant provisions on registration of charges is set out in the appendix to this book as is Sched. 15, "Charges on Property of Oversea Companies."

financing transaction entered into by a company.[2] The Secretary of State, however, may by regulations add any description of charge to, or remove any description of charge from the list.[3]

In section 395(2) "charge" is defined as meaning any form of security interest (fixed or floating) over property, other than an interest arising by operation of law. Therefore, the expression includes a mortgage. As Slade J. explained in *Re Bond Worth Ltd.*[4] the technical difference between a "mortgage" and a "charge" lies in the fact that a mortgage involves a conveyance of property subject to a right of redemption, whereas a charge conveys nothing and merely gives the chargee certain rights over the property as security for the loan.[5] To repeat, a mortgage involves the transfer of rights of ownership whereas a charge entails merely a right of resort to the property for security purposes. In practice though the two terms are used interchangeably.

It is important to state that a charge arising by operation of law does not need to be registered.[6] An example is the unpaid vendor's lien. *London Cheshire Co. Ltd.* v. *Laplagrene Co. Ltd.*[7] might be referred to in this context. There Brightman J. pointed out that an unpaid vendor's lien was the creature of law, that it did not depend on contract but on the fact that the vendor had a right to specific performance of his contract. The lien is created on the formation of the contract of sale and the time of registration would expire 21 days thereafter. The lien is not discharged until the purchase money is paid on completion. If registration were necessary, every vendor selling to a company would be considerably inconvenienced in having to register the unpaid vendor's lien as a matter of course on the off chance that circumstances might arise in which it would be necessary to rely on the lien.

Consequences of Non-Registration

The primary obligation to register the particulars of charge is cast upon the company creating the charge but particulars of the charge may be delivered for registration by any person interested in the charge.[8] If registra-

---

[2] See in particular, the practice of block discounting of debts as made manifest in *Lloyd and Scottish Finance Ltd.* v. *Cyril Lord Ltd.* (1979) 129 N.L.J. 366. This case is commented upon by A. D. G. Giddins in "Block Discounting—Sale or Charge" (1980) 130 N.L.J. 207. See also, *Olds Discount Co. Ltd.* v. *John Playfair Ltd.* (1938) 1 All E.R. 275 and *Chow Yoong Hong* v. *Choong Fah Rubber Manufactury* [1962] A.C. 209.
[3] Subs. (4) of s. 396.
[4] [1980] Ch. 228.
[5] *Ibid.* 250.
[6] s. 395(2). So in the reservation of title context it might be argued in a particular case that a charge arises not from an agreement between the parties but rather by operation of law. For instance where traceable proceeds of sub-sales have been mixed with other funds equity will declare a charge on the mixed fund to secure the amount due.
[7] [1971] Ch. 499. See also, *Re Bernstein* [1925] Ch. 12 and *Capital Finance Co. Ltd.* v. *Stokes* [1969] 1 Ch. 261. See generally, Sunnucks [1970] 33 M.L.R. 131.
[8] According to s. 398(2) where particulars are delivered for registration by a person other than the company concerned, that person is entitled to recover from the company the amount of any fees paid by him to the registrar in connection with the registration.

tion is not accomplished within the 21-day period then the company and every officer of it who is in default is liable to a fine.[9]

In practice, registration is usually effected by the charge holder for the consequences of non-registration are very serious from his point of view. Section 399(1) states that if particulars are not delivered within the stipulated period, the charge is, so far as it confers any security over the company's property, void against:

(a) an administrator or liquidator of the company, and
(b) any person who for value acquires an interest in or right over property subject to the charge.

So the fundamental result of non-delivery of particulars is that the charge-holder loses his priority in an insolvency. Most notably in *Re Bond Worth Ltd.*[10] it was held that a particular reservation of title clause constituted a registrable charge. The consequences were disastrous for the supplier who was owed in excess of £500,000. £1.1 million was owed by the buyer to a debenture holder on its current bank account alone. It owed an additional £1 million in wages and salaries and had liabilities of over £12 million as guarantor. The registrability holding meant that the supplier was reduced to the level of an unsecured creditor with little prospect of recovering anything.

In *Re Bond Worth Ltd.* the non-registration point was taken by a receiver. The judgment has been criticised on this score for it is nowhere expressly stated that an unregistered, but registrable charge is void against a receiver appointed by a debenture holder. On this ground John Parris takes issue with the decision in *Re Bond Worth*.[11] His argument, however, ignores the first instance decision of Judge O'Donoghue in *Clough Mill Ltd.* v. *Martin*[12] who held that, since the receiver represented, as it were, the interests of the secured creditors who has appointed him, an unregistered charge was void against him. The decision of Judge O'Donoghue was reversed on appeal but no aspersions were cast on the decision in this respect.[13]

Section 44(1)(a) of the Insolvency Act 1986 deems an administrative receiver to be the company's agent provided that the company has not gone into liquidation. This statutory declaration merely confirms what is stated to be the position in most commercial debentures. It has been argued that the receiver, as agent of the company, is estopped from pleading the company's want to compliance with the statutory registration requirements. In *Independent Automatic Sales Ltd.* v. *Knowles and Foster*[14] Buckley J. noted that the statutory duty to register any registrable charge had been imposed upon the company. *Ex hypothesi*, where a charge had not been registered, the company was in default of the statutory obligation and in an action directed

[9] s. 398(3).
[10] [1980] Ch. 228.
[11] *Effective Retention of Title Clauses* (1986), p. 103.
[12] [1984] 1 W.L.R. 1067, 1081.
[13] [1985] 1 W.L.R. 111.
[14] [1962] 1 W.L.R. 974.

to avoiding such charge for non-registration must necessarily plead its own default. Buckley J. refused to allow it to do this.

Should the same position obtain in the case of a receiver who is appointed agent of the company? There is no reported judicial decision on the point save for *Clough Mill* which *sub silentio* rejects it. The better view, it is submitted, is to regard the receiver as being invested with the same capacity to plead lack of registration as the debenture holders who appointed him.

The revised form of statutory wording makes it clear that a subsequent purchaser of charged goods is empowered to plead non-registration.[15] So too is a factor of book debts.[16]

Late Delivery of Particulars

Particulars of a charge may be delivered for registration outside the 21-day period from the date of creation of the charge.[17] There is no need to apply to the court for permission for late delivery as was the case until the reform effected by section 91 of the Companies Act 1989.[18] Late delivery of particulars however, does not necessarily guarantee effectiveness.

The charge holder will rank after any person who prior to registration of the charge registered out of time, acquires for value an interest in or right over property subject to the charge.[19] Moreover, if the company at the date of delivery of the particulars is unable to pay its debts, or becomes unable to do so in consequence of the transaction under which the charge is created, and insolvency proceedings begin within a certain period from the date of delivery:

   (a) the charge is, so far as it confers any security over the company's property, void as against the administrator or liquidator; and

   (b) the whole of the money secured by it is repayable (together with any interest) on demand.[20]

---

[15] Under the old version of s. 395 of the 1985 Act an unregistered but registrable charge was void as against a liquidator, administrator and secured creditor of a company.

[16] Thus removing doubts about the decision in *E. Pfeiffer Weinkellerei Weineinkauf GmbH & Co.* v. *Arbuthnot Factors Ltd.* [1988] 1 W.L.R. 150: see McCormack, "Reservation of Title—the controversy continues" [1989] L.M.C.L.Q. 198, 211–212. For a detailed discussion of the new statutory regime in respect of registration of charges see McCormack [1990] L.M.C.L.Q. Further provision with respect to voidness of charges are contained in ss. 404–406, inserted by s. 99 of the Companies Act 1989.

[17] s. 400 of the Companies Act 1985 as inserted by s. 95 of the 1989 Act.

[18] See generally, McCormack, "Extension of time for Registration of Company Charges" [1986] J.B.L. 282. See also McCormack, "Late Registration—A Last Lament" [1989] J.B.L. 154.

[19] This is the combined effect of ss. 399 and 400. Registration out of time is worthless from the point of view of a chargee after

   (a) the presentation of a petition on which an administration order or winding-up order is made or

   (b) the passing of a resolution for voluntary winding up.

[20] s. 400(2).

The "certain period" is two years in the case of a floating charge given in favour of a person connected with the company, 12 months in respect of other floating charges and six months in any other case.

Correction of Particulars

Particulars submitted for registration may be inaccurate in some material particular. Up until the changes introduced by the Companies Act 1989 the original instrument of charge together with the requisite particulars had to be submitted to the Companies Registrar. He compared the charge document with the filed particulars and was required to issue a certificate of due registration.[21] This certificate was stated to be conclusive evidence that the requirements of the Act as to registration had been complied with.[22] The courts held the certificate effective even where a false date had been inserted on the charge,[23] where the amount secured was misstated[24] on the particulars and where the particulars did not accurately capture the full coverage of the charge.[25] Indeed, in judicial review proceedings the Court of Appeal held that the "conclusive evidence" formula precluded the reception of information to rebut the facts stated in the certificate.[26]

All this no longer holds good. There is no longer an obligation to provide the instrument of charge. The register maintained by the Registrar consists of the information supplied under Part XII of the Companies Act.[27] There is no provision for a certificate of due registration. Any person may, however, require the registrar to provide a certificate stating the date on which any specified particulars of, or other information relating to, a charge were delivered to him.[28] This certificate is conclusive evidence that the specified particulars or other information were delivered to the registrar not later than

[21] The Jenkins Company Law Committee of 1962 stated:

> "We understand that the Registrar has been advised that the effect of these provisions is to impose upon him an absolute duty to enter on the register the effect of every instrument of charge delivered to him under section 95 [of the Companies Act 1948]. Thus he may receive an instrument of charge which is extremely complicated or is obscurely drafted, but in fact creates both a specific charge on land and a floating charge over the remaining assets of the company, although the prescribed particulars furnished to him may mention only the fixed charge; if he fails to detect the existence of the floating charge and therefore omits any reference to it from his register, he may be liable to anyone who suffers loss in consequence of the omission." (Cmnd. 1749, para. 302).

[22] s. 401(2)(b) of the Companies Act 1985 as originally worded: see generally, McCormack, "Conclusiveness in the Company Charge Registration Procedure"(1989) 10 Co. Law 175.
[23] *Re Eric Holmes Ltd.* [1965] 1 Ch. 1052; *Re C.L. Nye Ltd.* [1971] 1 Ch. 442.
[24] *Re Mechanisations (Eaglescliffe) Ltd.* [1966] 1 Ch. 20.
[25] *National Provincial and Union Bank of England* v. *Charnley* [1924] 1 K.B. 431.
[26] *R.* v. *Registrar of Companies, ex parte Central Bank of India* [1986] Q.B. 1114.
[27] s. 397 as inserted by s. 94 of the Companies Act 1989. Diamond argues at para. 22.1.11 of his report that it is essential that the system of registering particulars of charges should be as fast and simple as possible. The registrar will be able to process registrations much more speedily if the process consists of little more than the filing of a document submitted to him.
[28] s. 397(3). The certificate is to be signed by the registrar or authenticated by his official seal.

the date stated in the certificate.[29] Given the importance for priority purposes of delivery of the particulars within the 21-day period, chargees are likely to insist on being supplied with a certificate by the registrar in almost all cases. This would help to ensure the marketability of debentures.[30]

Section 402 of the 1985 Act as inserted by section 97 of the Companies Act 1989 is an important provision designed to achieve accuracy in the particulars that have been delivered to the registrar. The charge is invalid to the extent that it confers rights in excess of those referred to on the particulars.[31] Invalidity operates as against:

(a) an administrator or liquidator of the company; and
(b) any person who for value acquires an interest in or right over property subject to the charge.

But there are a couple of qualifications to the principle of invalidation. Subsection (4) provides that the court may order that the charge is effective as against an administrator or liquidator of the company if it is satisfied:

(a) that the omission or error is not likely to have misled materially to his prejudice any unsecured creditor of the company; or
(b) that no person became an unsecured creditor of the company at a time when the particulars of charge were incomplete or inaccurate in a relevant respect.

Moreover, the court may order that the charge is effective as against a person acquiring an interest in or right over property subject to the charge if it is satisfied that he did not rely in connection with the acquisition, on particulars which were inaccurate or incomplete in a relevant respect.[32]

This section brings home the imperative of accuracy in the particulars submitted for registration. The previous section—section 401—allows for the correction of mistakes. Further particulars supplementing or varying the registered particulars may be delivered to the registrar for registration at any

---

[29] s. 397(5). Moreover, it is presumed unless the contrary is proved that they were not delivered earlier than that date.
[30] In *Re C.L. Nye Ltd.* [1971] 1 Ch. 442, 474 Russell L.J. stressed the marketability point in emphasising the conclusiveness of the certificate of due registration issued by the registrar pursuant to the original version of s. 401(2) of the 1985 Act. He said that the registration requirement should not sterilise a chargee in dealing with his charge. Therefore it was to be expected that the Act would provide in absolute terms for a marketable security which could not be achieved unless the certificate of the registrar was in every respect conclusive and unassailable.
[31] What if the particulars filed make excessive claims as to amount secured or property charged? Originally it was proposed that the presenter should be placed under a civil liability to any person (other than the debtor) who suffered a loss as a result of any inaccuracy in the particulars of a charge: see para. 2.9(ii) of the DTI statement of September 2, 1987, and also para. 22.3.3 of the Diamond Report. The proposal was later dropped however: see DTI statement of July 7, 1988.
[32] s. 402(5).

time. The further particulars must be signed by or on behalf of both the company and the chargee.[33]

If for instance, the amount secured by a charge has been increased since the date of creation of the charge, it appears from section 402 that the charge is generally not a good security for the excess amount. Therefore, to protect his position, the chargee should make the alteration in the amount secured known to the registrar pursuant to section 401.

Particulars Requiring Registration

In the case of a series of debentures the particulars which must be submitted for registration were specified in section 397(1) of the Companies Act 1985 as originally drafted. In any other event the particulars were set out in section 401. Now they are embodied in a statutory instrument. Basically these particulars cover the date of creation of a charge, the amount secured by the charge, short particulars of the property charged and the persons entitled to the charge.

Difficulties arise in relation to the phrase "date of creation." Take an aggregation clause for instance. Such a clause gives the seller rights with respect to goods manufactured out of the original goods supplied. After *Clough Mill* the general view is that straightforward retention of title clauses are not registrable. What if a contract for the sale of goods includes an aggregation clause as well as a "simple" reservation of title provision—is the "date of creation" the date of the making of the original supply contract or the date of manufacture? If the latter is the date of creation then it would be almost impossible for the seller to fulfil the registration requirements for he may not know the precise date when the goods supplied have become part of the process of manufacture. There may be other difficulties in meeting the letter of section 395 and succeeding sections. In practice goods may be delivered on reservation of title terms over a prolonged period. It has been asked whether the "date of creation" is every single invoice recording the delivery of goods subject to these conditions. If this is the case then the populace of Cardiff and its environs can expect a rapid diminution of their unemployment figures.[34] The point is that Part XII of the Companies Act on Registration of Charges is not structured to deal adequately with the reten-

---

[33] But if:

(a) the chargee refuses to sign or authorise a person to sign on his behalf, or cannot be found, or
(b) the company refuses to authorise a person to sign on its behalf,

the court may, on the application of the company or the chargee, or of any other person having a sufficient interest in the matter, order that further particulars be delivered without that signature (s. 417 as inserted by s. 103 of the Companies Act 1989).
[34] See Parris, *op. cit.* 129–130.

tion of title phenomenon. It is simply not feasible to expect a seller to register each contract of sale individually.[35]

Crucial Fact is the Submission of Particulars within the Prescribed Period

It must be stressed that the crucial occurrence is the submission of the relevant particulars to the Registrar of Companies within the 21-day period and not the fact of actual registration. It is immaterial from the point of view of the chargee whether notice of the charge does not appear on the company's file until some time after the 21-day period or indeed at all. The charge has escaped invalidation because of presentation of the requisite particulars within the time limit set down.

NV Slavenburg's Bank v. *Intercontinental Natural Resources Ltd.*[36] is of assistance in this area. The case relates to registration of charges by oversea companies. The course of judicial reasoning, however, bears more generally on the situation where the Registrar has declined to accept particulars of charge for registration. Lloyd J. insisted that the bank could have preserved the validity of its charge by delivering particulars within 21 days despite the unwillingness of the registrar to register the charge.

Categories of Registrable Charge

Having considered the general nature of the régime applicable in the context of the registration of company charges it is appropriate now to turn our attention to specific, individual categories of registrable charge. The list is set out in section 396(1) of the Companies Act 1985 and has been referred to earlier. Most relevant for our purposes are sub-headings (b), (c)(iii) and (e). We will look at each of these sub-headings and then at the different types of reservation of title clause to see whether they fall within any of the sub-headings.

A Charge on Goods—Section 396(1)(b)

Section 396(1)(b) makes registrable a charge on goods, or any interest in goods, other than a charge under which the chargee is entitled to possession

[35] Diamond, when suggesting that a supplier need only file one financing statement for each customer, was conscious of the burden even this requirement might impose. The work involved for a seller with thousands of customers would be enormous. See paras. 17.16 and 17.17 of the Report.

[36] [1980] 1 W.L.R. 1076. It should be noted that major changes in the law relating to registration of charges created by oversea companies have been made by s. 105 and Sched. 15 of the Companies Act 1989. These provisions insert a new Chap. III into Pt. XXIII of the Companies Act 1985. Under s. 691 of the 1985 Act when a company incorporated outside Great Britain establishes a place of business in Great Britain it must within a month of doing so deliver documents to the Registrar of Companies. In *Slavenburg* it was held that particulars of a charge created by an oversea company must be submitted for registration irrespective of whether the oversea company was in fact registered under s. 691. This decision was a cause of potential injustice to a chargee and has now been reversed. The 1989 Act ties the charge registration obligation to the fact of registration as an oversea company under s. 691 of the Companies Act 1985.

either of the goods or of a document of title to them.[37] This provision has been inserted into the Companies Act 1985 by section 93 of the Companies Act 1989.

In the original scheme of things section 396(1)(c) made registrable "a charge created or evidenced by an instrument which, if executed by an individual, would require registration as a bill of sale." The law on bills of sale is contained in the Bills of Sale Acts 1878–1882, as amended, and the Companies Act provision effectively incorporated into the Companies Code all the antique learning as to what constitutes a "bill of sale."[38] The Bills of Sale Acts are verbose and unclear to say the least, and in line with Professor Diamond's recommendation[39] the 1989 Act went for a more direct text.

The new verbal dispensation does not herald any major change in policy though in one respect the ambit of the registration obligation has been extended. Under the old régime charges on goods were registrable only if created or evidenced by an instrument. This limitation was the result of the restricted scope of the Bills of Sale legislation and has now been removed.[40]

A Charge on Books Debts Section 396(1)(c)(iii)

In the *locus classicus Shipley* v. *Marshall*[41] book debts were taken as meaning debts that could or would in the ordinary course of a business be entered in well-kept books relating to that business. Buckley J. in *Independent Automatic Sales Ltd.* v. *Knowles and Foster*[42] supplied, or attempted to supply, a working definition of "book debts." He said that a debt arising in the course of business and due or growing due to the proprietor of that business could properly be called a book debt. This was so whether in fact the debt was entered in the books of the business or not. Basically, this accords with the interpretation of the phrase in *Shipley* v. *Marshall.*

A controversy has arisen over whether section 396(1)(c)(iii) catches future book debts. John Parris, for instance, suggests that the provision relates only to existing book debts, *i.e.* money that is due to the company at the date when the charge is created by an instrument of some sort.[43] It is submitted that this view is not well founded.

The leading case is *Independent Automatic Sales Ltd.* v. *Knowles and Foster.* Here a company which carried on the business of manufacturing and dealing in automatic machines from time to time entered into hire-purchase agreements for the disposal of its machines. Subsequently, the company

---

[37] s. 396(2)(c) provides that a charge is not excluded from s. 396(1)(b) merely because the chargee is entitled to take possession on default or on the occurrence of some other event.
[38] See generally, on bills of sale, Chap. 8 *infra*. The bills of sale legislation is still relevant where goods have been supplied subject to a reservation of title clause to an individual or partnership.
[39] Para. 23.9.14 of the Diamond Report.
[40] See para. 23.9.19 of the Diamond Report.
[41] (1863) 14 C.B.N.S. 566.
[42] [1962] 1 W.L.R. 974, on which see W. J. Gough, *Company Charges* (London 1978), p. 293.
[43] Parris, *op. cit.*, 114. See generally, on this area McCormack [1989] L.M.C.L.Q. 198, 206–209.

opened an account with the defendants with a view to obtaining finance for its business. It also signed a letter of hypothecation in favour of the defendants. This letter reflected an agreement that all bills of exchange and other documents, securities and property whatsoever belonging to the company then or thereafter deposited with the defendants by the company and the proceeds thereof should be and remain pledged to the defendants as continuing security for due payment to the defendants of all moneys and satisfaction of all liabilities for which the company were then or might at any time thereafter be indebted or liable to the defendants. Buckley J. held that the agreement constituted a charge and was void against the liquidator of the company for non-registration.

It was contended that section 95 of the Companies Act 1948 did not, on its true construction, require a charge on future book debts to be registered and that "book debts" meant only existing book debts. Buckley J. had two answers to this argument. His first point was that the hirer became liable immediately upon the agreement coming into operation to the extent of his minimum liability under it notwithstanding that some part of that liability was to be discharged by future payments and that the debts so constituted were existing book debts at the date of the deposit. Secondly, he said that a charge on future book debts of a company was registrable under the section[44]:

> "That is competent for anyone to whom book-debts may accrue in the future to create an equitable charge upon those book-debts which will attach to them as soon as they come into existence is not disputed (see *Tailby* v. *Official Receiver*).[45] That such a charge can accurately be described as a charge on book-debts does not appear to me to be open to question. . . . A charge of book-debts, present and future, is not an unusual form of security in the commercial world, and it would seem to me strange if such a charge were registrable (as it undoubtedly is) and a charge confined to future book-debts were not. I find nothing in the language of section 95 requiring me to read sub-section (2)(e) in so restricted a way as to confine it to a charge on existing book-debts."

Paul and Frank Ltd. v. *Discount Bank (Overseas) Ltd.*[46] is often mustered in support of a non-registration point of view although that case appears distinguishable. There it was held that a letter of authority authorising the payment of the proceeds of an insurance policy to the defendant did not create a registrable charge.

There were two grounds for this decision. First of all, Pennycuick J. said that, in order to ascertain whether any particular charge was a charge on book debts within the meaning of the section, one had to look at the items of property which formed the subject-matter of the charge at the date of its

[44] [1962] 1 W.L.R. 974, 985.
[45] [1888] 13 A.C. 523.
[46] [1967] Ch. 348.

creation and to consider whether any of those items was a book debt. Where the item of property was the benefit of a contract and at the date of the charge the benefit of the contract did not comprehend any book debt, the contract could not be brought within the section merely by reason that the contract might ultimately result in a book debt. Hence the insurance policy did not comprehend any book debt at the date of the letter of authority.[47]

Secondly, the test for book debts was whether they should be entered into the books of a company as an ordinary matter of accountancy practice. The accountancy evidence indicated that the insurance policy would not, as a matter of practice, be entered as a book debt even after the admission of liability and the ascertainment of the amount.[48]

Pennycuick J. proceeded to distinguish *Independent Automatic Sales Ltd.* v. *Knowles and Foster.* He said[49]:

> "If a charge upon its proper construction covers future debts, in the sense of debts under a future contract which, when that contract comes to be made, will constitute book-debts, *e.g.* an ordinary contract for the sale of goods on credit, I see no reason why paragraph (e) should not be fairly applicable to the charge."

In the writer's opinion the position has been summarized admirably[50]:

> "(i) Registrability is tested at the date of creation of the charge.
> (ii) If, at the date of creation of the charge, what is charged is a contract which does not of itself constitute a book debt, the charge will not be registrable even if a book debt may arise out of the contract at some future date.
> (iii) If, however, on its true construction the charge is over book debts arising in the future, the fact that the debts are not in existence when the charge is created does not preclude the charge from registration."

A Floating Charge on the Company's Property or Undertaking

The *locus classicus* on the subject of floating charges is the judgment of Romer L.J. in *Re Yorkshire Woolcombers Association Ltd.*[51] The Lord Justice talked about the essential characteristics of a floating charge in the following manner[52]:

> "[I] certainly think that if a charge has the three characteristics that I am about to mention, it is a floating charge. (1) If it is a charge on a class of

---

[47] *Ibid.* 362.
[48] *Ibid.* It should be noted that Diamond at para. 23.5.4 of his Report has recommended that charges on insurance policies should become registrable charges.
[49] [1967] Ch. 348, 363.
[50] See Mark Lawson [1988] L.M.C.L.Q. 141 at 145.
[51] [1903] 2 Ch. 284. See generally, on the floating charge, Eilis Ferran [1988] C.L.J. 213.
[52] *Ibid.* 295.

assets of a company present and future; (2) if that class is one which, in the ordinary course of the business of the company, would be changing from time to time; and (3) if you find that by the charge it is contemplated that, until some future step is taken by or on behalf of those interested in the charge, the company may carry on its business in the ordinary way as far as concerns the particular class of assets I am dealing with."

However, it should be noted that Romer L.J. disclaimed any intention of saying that there could not be a floating charge within the meaning of the Companies Acts which did not contain all the three characteristics that he mentioned. Moreover, when the case went on appeal to the House of Lords, Lord Macnaughton drew a sharp distinction between a specific charge and a floating charge.[53] A specific charge without more fastened on ascertained and definite property or property capable of being ascertained and defined. A floating charge was ambulatory and shifting in its nature until some event occurred which caused it to fasten and settle on the subject of the charge within its reach and grasp.

The essence of a floating charge is that it permits the company to continue to carry on business in the normal way. This state of affairs continues until a "crystallising event" occurs which causes the floating charge to become fixed on the assets then in the ownership of the company which are within the coverage of the charge. Normally, crystallising events are specified in the instrument creating the charge but crystallisation occurs as a matter of general law on the commencement of winding up, on the cessation of the company's business and where the charge holder has appointed a receiver of the company's property subject to the charge.[54]

It would be extremely unusual for all goods in the possession of the company to have been acquired on retention of title terms from a single supplier. Does this fact, of itself, exclude the application of section 396(1)(e) of the Companies Act on the ground that any floating charge which might have been created does not cover the whole of the company's property or undertaking? The simple answer is "no." A floating charge over part of the company's property or undertaking comes within the provision.[55]

Some commentators have suggested that it is inapt to describe any charge created by a purported reservation of title clause as a floating charge—the refrain being that the goods supplied are not in any sense indeterminate.[56] It is suggested, however, that the property subject to a floating charge need

---

[53] *Illingsworth* v. *Houldsworth* [1904] A.C. 355, 358.
[54] On crystallisation, see J. H. Farrar (1976) 40 Conv. (N.S.) 397, A. J. Boyle [1979] J.B.L. 231. See also, *Re Woodroffes (Musical Instruments) Ltd.* [1986] Ch. 366, noted by Sealy [1986] C.L.J. 25.
[55] The new wording makes explicit what was held to be the position in *Mercantile Bank of India* v. *Chartered Bank of India, Australia and China* [1937] 1 All E.R. 231.
[56] Parris, *op. cit.* 113–114, *cf. Tettenborn* [1981] J.B.L. 173, 175. Compare too, Slade J. in *Re Bond Worth Ltd.* [1980] Ch. 228 and Bridge L.J. in *Borden* v. *Scottish Timber Products Ltd.* [1981] Ch. 25, 42 with Buckley and Templeman L.J.J. in *Borden* [1981] Ch. 25, 47 and 45.

not be indeterminate. The element of indeterminacy relates rather to the time when the floating charge fastens and settles on the assets within its reach and grasp. Therefore, assuming that a purported retention of title provision, amounts in reality to a charge, the view is presented that there is no logical *a priori* reason why the charge should not be a floating charge. After all, it is envisaged that a company to whom goods have been sent on reservation of title conditions should have considerable latitude in dealing with those goods and proceeds and products thereof.

Simple Retention of Title Clause

There is no doubt that it is legally efficacious to include in a contract for the sale of goods a provision that title shall not pass to the buyer until the goods, the subject-matter of the contract of sale, have been paid for. The goods belong to the seller at all times. Therefore, no charge over them has been created by the buyer requiring registration under Part XII of the Companies Act 1986. The effectiveness of a clause to this effect was affirmed by the Court of Appeal in *Clough Mill Ltd.* v. *Martin*. Moreover, it makes no difference that the buyer has been given a power of resale over the goods or a right to consume the goods in a process of manufacture. Robert Goff L.J. was adamant on this point. He said[57]:

> "I see nothing objectionable in an agreement under which A, the owner of goods, gives possession of those goods to B, at the same time conferring on B a power of sale and a promise to consume the goods in manufacture, though A will remain the owner of goods until they are either sold or consumed."

Furthermore, the fact that certain provisions of the contract of sale could only operate by way of charge did not warrant the conclusion that all efforts by the seller to obtain security for payment of goods must necessarily be by way of charge.

In *Clough Mill* the plaintiff agreed to supply yarn on credit terms to a company which intended to use it for the manufacture of fabrics. The company fell into financial difficulties and a receiver was appointed over its assets by debenture holders. The receiver permitted the company to use the yarn without paying the plaintiff. The plaintiff brought an action in conversion against the receiver who defended by saying that clause 12 of the contract of sale created a charge which was void for non-registration. Clause 12 is of such importance to the litigation that it deserves to be set out almost in full:

> "However the ownership of the material shall remain with the seller, which reserves the right to dispose of the material until payment in full for all the material shall have been received by it in accordance with the

[57] [1985] 1 W.L.R. 111, 116.

terms of this contract or until such time as the Buyer sells the material to its customers by way of bona-fide sale at full market value. If such payment is overdue in whole or in part the seller may (without prejudice to any of its other rights) recover or re-sell the material or any of it and may enter upon the buyer's premises . . . for that purpose. Such payments shall become due immediately upon the commencement of any act or proceeding in which the Buyer's solvency is involved. If any of the material is incorporated in or used as material for other goods before such payment the property in the whole of such goods shall be and remain with the seller until such payment has been made or the other goods shall have been sold as aforesaid, and all the seller's rights hereunder in the material shall extend to those other goods."

At first instance, Judge O'Donoghue opined that in construing a retention of title clause such as clause 12 in the present case, the court had to establish its true effect by looking at the purpose for which it had been inserted in the contract.[58] The judge believed that the sole purpose of clause 12 was to provide security for the payment of the purchase price. Furthermore, since the rights conferred on the plaintiff were for that limited purpose only the contract took effect as a contract for the sale of goods whereby the property in the goods passed to the company on delivery and a charge over the yarn in favour of the plaintiff was created by the company by way of security for payment of the purchase price. The conclusion followed that a charge has been created by the company which was invalid for want of registration though Judge O'Donoghue did not specify the precise sub-head under which any such charge was registrable. He cited with approval the following passage from the judgment of Slade J. in *Re Bond Worth Ltd.*[59]:

"... any contract which, by way of security for the payment of a debt confers an interest in property defeasible or destructible on payment of such debt . . . must necessarily be regarded as creating a mortgage or charge as the case may be."

The Court of Appeal laid to rest this notion. The Lord Justices fired two salvos at the first instance judgment. First of all, they emphasised that effect must be given to the ordinary meaning of the words of the contract if they were plain and unambiguous. Robert Goff L.J. recognised that the effect of the retention of title clause in the first sentence of clause 12 was very similar to that of a charge on goods created by the buyer in favour of the seller. He went on[60]:

"But the simple fact is that, under the first sentence of the condition, the buyer does not in fact confer a charge on his goods in favour of the

---

[58] The first instance decision is reported [1984] 1 W.L.R. 1067.
[59] [1980] Ch. 228, 248.
[60] [1985] 1 W.L.R. 111, 121.

seller; on the contrary, the seller retains his title in his goods for the purpose of providing himself with security. I can see no reason in law why a seller of goods should not adopt this course, and if the relevant contractual term is effective to achieve that result, I can see no reason why the law should not give effect to it in accordance with its terms."

Oliver L.J. was of a similar view. He did not accept the need to do violence to the language of the opening sentence which was, on its face, plain and unambiguous.[61] In any event Oliver L.J. doubted whether the whole purpose of the clause was to provide security for the purchase price.[62]

Thus the purposive approach has been firmly laid to rest in England although it is arguable that it retains some vitality north of the border in Scotland. In *Emerald Stainless Steel Ltd.* v. *South Side Distribution Ltd.*[63] the contract of sale provided that: "Title to each item of good sold or agreed to be sold shall remain vested in the Company until the full purchase price and all additional charges relating to that item and any other moneys for the time being owed by the customer to the Company . . ." shall have been paid.

Lord Ross was of the opinion that this condition was truly an attempt to create a security without possession. He believed that it would be contrary to Scottish legal principle that a seller should be able to obtain security in this way.[64] The view adopted by Lord Ross is clearly in accord with the first instance decision of Judge O'Donoghue in *Clough Mill*. However, it is no longer good law, at least in the English jurisdiction, following the Court of Appeal ruling in *Clough Mill*; and probably also in Scotland after dicta in *Armour* v. *Thyssen Edelstahlwerke A.G.*[65]

We have seen the wording of the clause that was effective to create a legally valid and efficacious straight forward retention of title clause in *Clough Mill*. Now let us see different wordings which have been held effective in other cases. In *Hendy Lennox (Industrial Engines) Ltd.* v.

---

[61] *Ibid.* 124.

[62] *Ibid.* 122.

[63] 1983 S.L.T. 162. It might be argued that the decision is only a decision against the validity of "all-liabilities" reservation of title clauses. In *Deutz Engines Ltd.* v. *Terex Ltd.* 1984 S.L.T. 273, Lord Ross accepted that property in a contract of sale need not pass until the expiry of a certain time period or the occurrence of a particular event. He concluded, however, that the reservation of title clause in this case fell outside that category by the stipulation that title to the goods was to remain vested in the buyer until all the moneys due from the buyer either relating to the goods or otherwise were paid. Moreover, in *Armour* v. *Thyssen Edelstahlwerke A.G.* Court of Session (Inner Session) 1989 S.L.T. 182 upheld a "simple" retention of title clause as effective in Scots law. Lord Wylie said the seller is doing no more than withholding performance of is primary obligation under the contract, namely the transfer of propery until the buyer fulfils his primary obligation, namely to make payment of the purchase price. In his view this illustrated the principle of mutuality of contractual obligations in contracts of sale of goods. See also *Hammer & Sohne* v. *H.W.T. Realisations Ltd.* 1988 S.L.T. 21.

[64] For commentary on the Scottish cases see Reid and Gretton, "Retention of Title in Romalpa Clauses" 1983 S.L.T. (News) 77, 175; Gretton, "Romalpa in Scotland" [1983] J.B.L. 334; Smith, "Retention of Title, Lord Watson's Legacy" 1983 S.L.T. (News) 105; Wilson, "Romalpa and Trust" 1983 S.L.T. (News) 106; and Thompson, "The Scottish Approach to Retention of Title" (1984) 5 B.L.R. 267, 316.

[65] 1989 S.L.T. 182.

Grahame Puttick Ltd.,[66] for instance, it was provided that "all goods . . . shall be and remain the property of the [plaintiffs] until the full purchase price thereof shall be paid" and that the plaintiffs had the right to retake possession in the event of default. Staughton J. referred to sections 16 and 17 of the Sale of Goods Act 1979 which stipulated basically that property passed when it was intended to pass. He could not see why the plain words of the contract should not mean what they say. The sellers retained the full rights of ownership, subject to contractual terms limiting the exercise of those rights and regulating how they might be transferred to others. The buyers did not "confer" any proprietary rights in the goods to the seller, rather it was the sellers who retained proprietary rights.

A cautionary tale from *Re Bond Worth Ltd.*,[67] however, is to avoid the use of terminology which purports to reserve only "equitable and beneficial ownership." In that case fibre was sold subject to a "retention of title" clause which contained those words. Slade J. concluded after an in-depth review of the authorities, that the proper manner of construing the reservation of title clause, together with all the other relevant provisions of the contracts of sale read as a whole, was to regard them as effecting a sale in which the entire property in the raw fibre passed to the buyer, Bond Worth, followed by a security, *eo instanti*, given back by Bond Worth to the seller Monsanto. The sellers argued that all they had passed to the purchasers was the shell of legal ownership from which the crabmeat of equitable ownership had been skilfully extracted. He said[68]:

> "However, no authority has been cited which satisfies me that on the transfer of the legal property in land or chattels, it is competent to a vendor expressly to except from the grant in favour of himself on equitable mortgage or charge thereon to secure the unpaid purchase price (in addition to or in substitution for any lien which may arise by operation of law), in such manner that the exception will take effect without any express or implied grant back of a mortgage or charge in the vendor's favour by the purchaser."

The judge distinguished *Re Connolly Bros. Ltd. (No. 2)*[69] upon which counsel for the sellers placed reliance. The *Connolly* case involved a situation where A, the purchaser of the relevant property from B, had before completion entered into a contract for good consideration to grant a charge over the property in favour of C. This meant that the very moment that A acquired the legal estate in the property, A held it in trust to give effect in

---

[66] [1984] 1 W.L.R. 485. It should be noted too that in *Re Peachdart Ltd.* [1984] Ch. 131 counsel for the receiver conceded that the seller had validly reserved title to unused leather sold to the company and that the receiver must therefore repay to the seller the sum of money obtained through reselling it under an implied authority to do so (£1400). The relevant clause of the contract in *Re Peachdart Ltd.* (clause 11(b)) was identical to condition 12 in *Clough Mill* save that the word "products" was substituted for "material."
[67] [1980] Ch. 228. See also, *Coburn* v. *Collins* (1887) 35 C.P.D. 373.
[68] *Ibid.* 253.
[69] [1912] 2 Ch. 25.

equity to C's rights, by virtue of the pre-existing contract between A and C. Slade J. said that notwithstanding the arrangements made between A and C, the transaction as between A and B remained throughout one for the sale of the entire legal and beneficial interest in the property. However, Cozens-Hardy M.R. in *Re Connolly Bros. Ltd.* put a different slant on A's right. He said that the court would be shutting its eyes to the real transaction if it were to hold that the unincumbered fee simple in the property was ever in A.[70]

Viewed in this light there is a very definite analogy between *Re Connolly Bros Ltd. (No. 2)* and *Re Bond Worth Ltd.* The point becomes clearer when one considers *Wilson* v. *Kelland*.[71] In the latter case an unpaid vendor relinquished his lien over property he had agreed to sell to a company in return for a contractual promise that he would be granted an equitable charge over the property. The interests of the vendor were held to prevail over an earlier created and registered floating chargee over all the assets present or future of the company. The reason for this conclusion was that the vendor retained a paramount equity in the property even after conveyance. Accordingly, he took priority over any charge to persons claiming through the company.

Wilson v. *Kelland* was cited to Slade J. in *Re Bond Worth Ltd.* but is not referred to in the judgment. It is respectfully submitted that despite an exhaustive and considered analysis, Slade J. probably came to the wrong conclusion, at least on "equitable and beneficial ownership." His decision however receives some support from the course of events across the Irish sea. A clause reserving simply equitable ownership was held effective by McWilliam J. in *Re Stokes and McKiernan Ltd.*[72] In *Frigoscandia (Contracting) Ltd.* v. *Continental Irish Meat Ltd.*[73] the same judge indicated, however, that his decision was made without the benefit of the decision in *Re Bond Worth* and would have to be reassessed in the light of that case.

Even though *Re Bond Worth Ltd.* may have misinterpreted the authorities on "equitable and beneficial ownership" the moral of the story is clear—one should, *ex abundanti cautela*, avoid use of the expression "equitable and beneficial ownership" in a reservation of title clause.

Current Account Clauses

Clauses which attempt to reserve ownership of the goods supplied in the seller until *all* obligations owed to the *seller* by the buyer have been discharged and not just those flowing from the contract of sale are slightly more problematic. The argument is that withholding ownership until a long overdue debt has been paid is creating something over and above what was in

[70] *Ibid.* 31.
[71] [1910] 2 Ch. 306.
[72] High Court, unreported, December 12, 1978.
[73] [1982] I.L.R.M. 396. See generally, on the Irish cases, R. A. Pearce, "Reservation of Title on the Sale of Goods in Ireland" (1985) 20 Ir.Jur. (n.s.) 264.

existence when the clause was first incorporated, unless it simply replaces another security right already provided for. Thus it is more difficult to disguise as something other than the creation of a security interest.

In *Romalpa* itself, an "all-monies" or "current account" clause had been inserted by the supplier. The clause provided that "the ownership of the material to be delivered . . . will only be transferred to the purchaser when he has met all that is owing" to the plaintiffs. The matter, however, occasioned no comment in the judgments.

What appears to have been an "all-monies" clause was upheld in *John Snow and Co. Ltd.* v. *D.B.G. Woodcroft and Co. Ltd.*[74] as not requiring registration under the Companies Act. The conditions of sale provided: "The property in the goods agreed to be sold will only pass to the purchaser when the purchaser has met all the indebtedness to the seller. . . ." It has been suggested that in the absence of words expressly providing that indebtedness included indebtedness under other contracts it is arguable that "all indebtedness" was limited to that under the particular contract and that the clause was in fact a single contract reservation of title clause. Boreham J. however treated it as an all liabilities clause and gave it the judicial *imprimatur* as such.[75]

In *Clough Mill Ltd.* v. *Martin* the Court of Appeal were faced with a contract to be performed in stages rather than an "all-monies" clause *stricto sensu*. Nevertheless an example proferred by Robert Goff L.J. brings home some of the difficulties in this area. He said[76]:

> "Suppose that the seller agrees to sell 1000 tons of material to the buyer at £10 a ton. He delivers 500 tons. Of those 500 tons, only 250 tons are paid for by the buyer. So £2500 has been paid and another £2500 is due and outstanding. The buyer becomes insolvent and is unable further to perform the contract. The seller accepts the repudiation. Of the 500 tons delivered, 300 tons are still at the buyer's premises, unsold and unused, now worth £4000 instead of £3000 as they were at the time of the contract of sale. Can the seller resell the whole 300 tons? And, if he can and does so, does he have to account to the buyer for that part of the price already paid which cannot be appropriated to the 200 tons already used by the buyer in manufacture and so must be appropriated to part of the 300 tons, *i.e.* £500? And must the seller account to the buyer for the profit element of £1000 obtainable on the resale (no doubt allowing for any expense of the resale)?"

The learned Lord Justice suggested a way out of the difficulties. He said that during the subsistence of the contract the seller could only resell such amount of the material as was needed to discharge the balance of the

---

[74] [1985] B.C.L.C. 54. See generally, on this area, McCormack [1989] Conv. 92.
[75] *Ibid.* 62.
[76] [1985] 1 W.L.R. 111, 117.

outstanding purchase price. If he sold more, then he was accountable to the buyer for the surplus. On the other hand, once the contract had been determined by the seller's acceptance of the buyer's repudiation, the seller had his rights as owner uninhibited by any contractual restrictions. However, any part of the purchase price received by the seller and attributable to the material so resold was recoverable by the buyer on the basis of total failure of consideration. The right of recovery was subject to any set off arising from a cross-claim by the seller for damages for the buyer's repudiation.

In the "acceptance of repudiation" situation there is no duty on the seller to account to the buyer for any excess value obtained through repossessing or reselling the property, for the simple reason that the property is all along the seller's. That is why, as Oliver L.J. pointed out in the same case, it is wrong to assume that the whole purpose of a reservation of title clause is to give the seller security for the payment of the purchase price.

Sir John Donaldson M.R. went about the matter in a slightly different way. He said[77]:

> "I am inclined to think that the word 'until' in the phrase reserves the right to dispose of the material until payment in full for all the material has been received connotes not only a temporal but also a quantative limitation. In other words, the appellants can go on selling [the fabric] hank by hank until they have been paid in full, but, if thereafter they continue to sell they are accountable to the buyers for having sold goods which, on full payment having been achieved, became the buyers' goods."

The difficulty with this view is that it seems to pre-suppose that the contract between the parties is still in existence, which of course will rarely be the case. If it has been discharged (through the seller's acceptance of the buyer's repudiatory breach) clauses can "live on" only if they concern dispute-settling matters (*e.g.* arbitration clauses, exemption clause, or liquidated damages clauses), not if they are part and parcel of the primary contractual obligations.[78]

In *Clough Mill* there is implied support for the validity of an "all liabilities" reservation of title clause. The judges in the Court of Appeal appeared to be of opinion that a clause reserving title to the seller was necessarily inconsistent with the creation of a charge by the buyer. This train of thought became manifest when the judges were faced with particular observations of Slade J. in *Bond Worth*. In that case Slade J. said[79]:

> ". . . any contract which, by way of security for the payment of a debt, confers an interest in property defeasible or destructible upon payment of such debt, or appropriates such property for the discharge of the

[77] *Ibid.* 126.
[78] See *Photo Productions Ltd.* v. *Securicor Transport Ltd.* [1980] A.C. 827.
[79] [1980] Ch. 228, 248.

debt, must necessarily be regarded as creating a mortgage or charge, as the case may be . . . ."

Oliver L.J. dealt with this passage in the following way[80]:

"The operative word, here, however, is 'confers' and the whole of Slade J.'s judgment in that case was based upon the fact, as he found, that the legal title to the goods had passed to the buyer. That was in the context of a clause which, in terms, sought to reserve only to the seller the 'beneficial' interest and to seek to apply it to the clause now under consideration is to assume the very thing that is sought to be proved. Of course, where the legal title has passed, security can be provided by a charge created by a new legal owner. But it is not a necessary incident of the seller's security his position that he should pass the legal title. The whole question is how has his position been secured? If in fact he has retained the legal title to the goods, then by definition the buyer cannot have charged them in his favour."

William Goodhart Q.C. in a comment on the *Clough Mill* case, argues that there is no apparent reason why a reservation of the legal title should be inconsistent with the grant by the buyer of a charge over the beneficial interest in the goods.[81] He suggests that in the case of an all liabilities reservation of title clause this is necessarily what happens. The argument is that if a true beneficial interest is reserved in goods supplied it must follow that if after payment of the full purchase price of those goods the supplier recovers possession of them because of non-discharge of some other liability, the supplier must refund the purchase price to the customer on the ground of total failure of consideration. This would of course defeat the object of the clause. In almost all instances it would be the intention of the supplier that he should be entitled to recover the goods and resell them elsewhere without having to refund the purchase price. Goodhart submits that this can only be done if the clause is construed as creating a security for the payment of the customer's debts to the supplier and not as a condition suspensive of the transfer of title.[82]

The argument is founded on the assumption that in the above situation a seller would be liable to refund the purchase price on grounds of total failure of consideration. It may be suggested, however, that there is not a total failure of consideration. After all, the buyer has had use of the goods for a certain time. Furthermore, in return for the buyer agreeing to a contract of sale which includes an "all liabilities" reservation of title clause, the seller may have desisted from enforcing certain other obligations owed by the buyer.

---

[80] [1985] 1 W.L.R. 111, 123.
[81] [1986] 49 M.L.R. 96.
[82] See also, the article by William Goodhart and Professor Gareth Jones, "The Infiltration of Equitable Doctrine into English Commercial Law" (1980) 43 M.L.R. 489, 508. The Goodhart view has been supported by J. R. Bradgate [1987] Conv. 434.

The law relating to recovery of money on the basis of total failure of consideration is considered in detail by Goff and Jones in their seminal work on *The Law of Restitution*.[83] The burden of their perception is that money is recoverable only if there is a total failure of consideration.[84]

A case in point is *Yeoman Credit Ltd.* v. *Apps*.[85] The defendant agreed to take a car on hire-purchase from the plaintiffs. The car suffered from unroadworthiness when delivered but the agreement excluded all liability for the condition of the car. The defendant complained about the defects but nevertheless kept the car and paid three hire instalments. The defendant eventually gave up and failed to pay the instalments. The plaintiffs put the hiring to an end and towed the car away. They then claimed damages and arrears of instalments to which the defendant responded by a counterclaim seeking the return of the deposit and instalments paid, on the basis of total failure of consideration. It was held that the defendant could reject the car as the plaintiffs were in fundamental breach of contract and so could not rely on the exemption clause. The counter claim did not succeed, however. Holroyd Pearce L.J. put the matter thus[86]:

> "This was not a case where title was lacking, and the defendant never had lawful possession. Here the defendant had the possession of the car and its use, such as it was. . . . Admittedly, the use was of little (if any) value, but in my view that use, coupled with possession, and his continuance of the hiring agreement with the intention of keeping the car and getting Goodbody [the dealers] to pay half the repairs, debars the defendant from saying that there was a total failure of consideration."

Similarly, in the reservation of title context the buyer has had use of the goods and this should weigh against a claim based on total failure of consideration. Moreover, the hands of the buyer are not completely clean. The controversy arises only because the buyer has failed to meet obligations owed under other contracts.

There have been cases where payments have been recovered although the consideration had not totally failed. Relevant cases include *Butterworth* v. *Kingsway Motors*[87] and *Warman* v. *Southern Counties Car Finance Corporation*.[88] In the latter case it was held that a hirer under a hire-purchase agreement could bring the agreement to an end for a defect of title on the

---

[83] (3rd ed., London 1986), pp. 458–465. See also, Professor Peter Birks, *An Introduction to the Law of Restitution* (Oxford 1985), 242–248. See too, Pottage, "Restitution and Enjoyment of Land" [1988] Conv. 333 for a discussion of the relevant principles in the context of a contract for the sale of land.

[84] *Ibid.* 54–55, 460.

[85] [1962] 2 Q.B. 508. See also, *Hunt* v. *Silk* (1804) 5 East 449 and *Lombard Banking Co.* v. *Kelly* [1959] 1 W.L.R. 41.

[86] [1962] 2 Q.B. 508, 521.

[87] [1954] 1 W.L.R. 1286.

[88] [1949] 2 K.B. 576. See also, *Karflex Ltd.* v. *Poole* [1933] 2 K.B. 251 and *Linz* v. *Electric Wire Co. of Palestine* [1948] A.C. 371. The Law Commission in Working Paper No. 65, para. 65 suggested that the buyer, upon recovering the price on the ground of failure of consideration, should make allowance for the period of possession.

part of the seller and also recover the whole of his deposit and all his hire-purchase instalments, despite his use of the chattel in the meantime. The buyer enjoyed part of the bargained-for exchange as represented by the use of the car. The seller nonetheless was not denied the use of a car to which he had title.

The principle of these cases does not have any application in the reservation of title context for there the seller clearly has title. To sum up it is suggested that an all-monies retention of title clause does not create a registrable charge.

The Scottish Court of Session has however, ruled against "all-liabilities" reservation of titles clauses by reference to section 62(4) of the Sale of Goods Act. The subsection states that the provisions of the Act concerning contracts of sale do not apply to a transaction in the form of a sale which is intended to operate by way of mortgage, pledge, charge or other security. It has never been relied upon in any of the English reservation of title cases. The subsection it seems was designed to deal with a different category of case, namely the "sham sale."[89] In this situation a debtor "sells" to his creditor for the purpose of conferring a security interest. In other words we have a debtor-creditor "sale" rather than the creditor-debtor transaction that arises in the *Romalpa* case.

Nevertheless, the Court of Session in *Armour* v. *Thyssen Edelstahlwerke A.G.*[90] ruled that section 62(4) invalidated all-monies reservation of title clauses. In the words of Lord Wylie where a provision goes beyond retention of title until payment of the price the result is an attempt to create a right in security which, without possession, is ineffectual in Scots law, the recognised forms of legal hypothec apart.[91]

The decision in the case has been criticised on the basis that section 62(4) merely excludes the application of the Sale of Goods Act.[92] Even if that section applies, it simply means that a particular reservation of title clause must be adjudicated upon apart from the Act and there is nothing in the common law of Scotland to prevent wide conditions suspensive of the passing of property.

Proceeds of Sale Clauses

An equitable trading right arising by operation of law is not registrable. That much is clear. The reason is that the rights arise by operation of law and

---

[89] See Gretton [1989] J.B.L. 260, 261.
[90] 1989 S.L.T. 182.
[91] *Ibid.* 192. *Clough Mill Ltd.* v. *Martin* [1985] 1 W.L.R. 111 was cited to the court but was distinguished as being a simple retention of title case. The House of Lords decision in the Scottish case *Michelin Tyre Co. Ltd.* v. *Macfarlane (Glasgow) Ltd.* 1916 2 S.L.T. 221 was similarly distinguished.
[92] Gretton [1989] J.B.L. 260–262. The argument in the case centred around s. 62 of the Sale of Goods Act because up until the enactment of the Companies Act 1989 security interests over goods in Scotland have not been registrable.

have not been conferred or created by the buyer company. Where traceable funds are mingled with other funds in a bank account equity may declare a charge on the mixed fund.[93] Again, since this charge has not been created by the buyer company it is not registrable under Part XII of the Companies Act 1985. So far the law is relatively straightforward. The big debate is over the precise circumstances which give rise to an equitable right to trace. This controversy has been plumbed to its depths elsewhere.[94]

Another issue is assuming that the prerequisites of an equitable tracing right have not been fulfilled and that a charge is held to have been created, under what precise category is this charge registrable? The matter was discussed in *Pfeiffer* where Phillips J. held that the charge was registrable as a charge on book debts. The facts of that case are quite complex and there is no need to set them out in detail here. Suffice it to say that a German company sold wine to an English importer on credit terms, on conditions which included a purported reservation of title clause. The contract, however, permitted the importer to resell. It also provided, in not very idiomatic English, that all rights arising from sub-sales would be passed on to the German company. Phillips J. decided that this "proceeds of sale" clause constituted a charge over book debts.

It may also be suggested that the charge was registrable as a floating charge.[95] Against this argument one might point to other provisions in the contract between plaintiff and wine importer. The importer was obliged to

---

[93] See *Re Diplock* [1848] Ch. 465; *Re Hallett's Estate* [1879] 13 Ch.D. 696; *Re Oatway* [1903] 2 Ch. 356; *James Roscoe (Bolton) Ltd.* v. *Winder* [1915] 1 Ch. 62; *Re Tilley's Will Trusts* [1967] Ch. 1179. For commentary see, generally, Birks, *An Introduction to the Law of Restitution* (Oxford 1985), pp. 363–370.

[94] See *supra*, Chap. 5, pp. 74–82. The boundaries of the *Romalpa* case have been charted in three relatively recent first instance decisions *Hendy Lennox (Industrial Engines) Ltd* v. *Graham Puttick Ltd.* [1984] 1 W.L.R. 485; *Re Andrabell Ltd.* [1984] 2 All E.R. 407 and *Pfeiffer Weinkellerei-Weineinkauf GmbH Co.* v. *Arbuthnot Factors Ltd.* [1988] 1 W.L.R. 150. J. H. Farrar and Chiah Kim Chai suggest ([1985] J.B.L. 160) that the following points should be borne in mind in drafting a proceeds of sale clause.

    (1) The buyer should be obliged to store the goods in a manner which manifests the seller's ownership.

    (2) There should be reference to the seller as "fiduciary" in respect of the goods. Further, that the seller retains full ownership rights over the goods although subject to some contractual restrictions. Also, that the seller should obtain the benefit of all claims against sub-buyers.

    (3) There should be an obligation to keep the proceeds of sub-sales in a separate account.

    (4) The contract should spell out that so long as the purchase price remains unpaid, any sub-sales by the buyer would be on the seller's behalf as agent.

    (5) The contract should provide for immediate payment of the price upon delivery but that the seller may at its discretion not enforce it for a stated period.

    (6) It should be provided that so long as the purchase moneys remain unpaid the proceeds of any resale should be held by the buyer as trustee for the seller.

[95] In the *Annangel Glory* [1988] 1 Lloyd's Rep. 45 Saville J. was not prepared to accept the proposition that a charge could not be registrable both as a charge over book debts and as a floating charge. For discussion of the floating charge see pp. 98–100, *supra*.

separate the proceeds of cash sub-sales from his other monies and to "book" and "administer" the funds accordingly. He was also under an obligation to administer the fund "until called for."

These provisions imposed some manner of restriction on dealing with the book debts and the proceeds thereof but were they enough to constitute any charge created a fixed rather than a floating charge? In recent times, much energy has been expended in endeavouring to ascertain whether and in what circumstances it is possible to create a fixed charge over future book debts of a company. Since *Siebe Gorman and Co. Ltd.* v. *Barclay's Bank Ltd.*[96] the answer to the "whether" question is clearly in the affirmative. Attention now focuses on the "when" part of the inquiry.

Before a charge over future book debts can be regarded as a fixed charge then the company must be limited in the manner in which it can deal with the debts. It is necessary for the proceeds of the debts to be segregated from the company's general assets. Payment into a special bank account maintained by the company with the charge holder points towards a fixed charge but this degree of sequestration of assets does not appear to be essential. In *Siebe Gorman* a fixed charge was held to have been created. A debenture was granted in favour of a bank. This debenture not only prohibited the company from selling or charging its book debts but required that they be paid into the company's account with the bank. Slade J. decided that on construction the bank would not have been obliged to allow the company to draw on the account at a time when it still owed the bank money under the debenture. The company was not at liberty to deal with the debts or their proceeds in the ordinary course of its business. Every debt as it accrued to the company could be said to be the subject of an equitable fixed charge.

The facts in the Irish case of *Re Keenan Bros. Ltd.*[97] were even stronger than those of *Siebe Gorman*. Once more a debenture was created in favour of a bank. On this occasion the company was obliged to pay the proceeds of all debtors into a designated account with the bank and not without the prior written consent of the bank to make any withdrawals or direct any payments from the said account. A fixed charge rather than a floating charge was the outcome of the court's characterisation of the nature of the security.[98]

On balance, though, it is suggested that the restrictions in *Pfeiffer* do not seem sufficiently extensive to convert what might outwardly appear as a floating charge into a fixed charge. The importer was free to assign or charge any book debts arising from sub-sales of the wine. Moreover, the courts have manifested a considerable reluctance to acknowledge the creation of a fixed charge over future book debts of a company.

---

[96] [1979] 2 Lloyd's Rep. 142; on which see Thomlinson (1978) 75 Law Soc. Gaz. 1177.
[97] [1986] B.C.L.C. 242.
[98] Other relevant cases are *Re Lakeglen Construction Ltd.* [1980] I.R. 347; *Re Armagh Shoes Ltd.* [1984] B.C.L.C. 405 and *Re Brightlife Ltd.* [1987] Ch. 200. See further, Pennington (1985) 6 Co. Law 9; McCormack (1987) 8 Co. Law 3; Pearce [1987] J.B.L. 18. See also, Byrne and Tomkin (1985) 135 N.L.J. 443.

Hitherto, the discussion has been limited to cases of sub-sales of the original goods supplied. The same principle obtains, however, where the original goods have been transformed into a new product or been mixed with other goods. In circumstances where it is possible to "reserve" title to mixed goods without creating a registrable charge, it is possible to transfer the entitlements to the proceeds of sale of those goods, provided that there are appropriate provisions governing segregation of the proceeds.

Aggregation Clauses and Commingling without Loss of Physical Identity

Where the supplier's goods have been mixed up with those of somebody else so as not to affect the physical characteristics of the commingled goods, the separate owners became tenants in common of the mass in accordance with their respective contribution.[99] This state of affairs arises by operation of law. No charge, never mind a registrable charge, comes into existence.

Cases where one chattel has been added to a more substantial chattel are discussed under the rubric of accession. The position appears to be that the accessories continue to belong to their original owner unless it is shown that as a matter of practicability they cannot be identified or if identified they have been incorporated to such an extent that they cannot be detached from the more substantial chattel without occasioning serious damage to it. If the accession test is satisfied and the goods attached cease to belong to their original owner this result has been brought about by overriding principles of law and not by agreement between the parties. Therefore, no registrable charge comes into being.

The doctrine of accession does not rear its head very often in the courts for the practical reason that it is common to include in a hire-purchase agreement a clause to the effect that any accessories or goods supplied with or for or attached to, or repairs executed to the hired goods shall become part of the hired goods. A supplier who includes a clause to this effect is not claiming something which was his at the outset and the something "extra", it might be said, is being claimed to ensure payment of a debt. Does this arrangement not look suspiciously like a registrable charge? Two categories of registrable charge suggest themselves. First, a charge on goods. Secondly, the arrangement might amount to a floating charge. The buyer is giving up what is his own property. The seller is taking this property to ensure payment of a debt. The buyer's property remains identifiably separate although not detachable from the seller's property without causing substantial damage to it. The buyer is free to resell this former asset, however, until some event occurs which causes the seller to intervene. The whole affair smacks of the creation of a security interest and "floating charge" may be the most appropriate designation.

[99] See generally, *Indian Oil Corp. Ltd.* v. *Greenstone Shipping S.A. (Panama)* [1988] 1 Q.B. 345; on which see Stein (1987) 46 C.L.J. 369 and Brown [1987] L.M.C.L.Q. 286. See also, Matthews [1981] C.L.P. 159 and *supra*, Chap. 3.

Loss of Physical Identity and Aggregation Clauses

A seller may have, by express contractual stipulation, conferred on himself rights in the product formed partly of the goods that he has supplied. Does such a stipulation constitute a charge? Robert Goff L.J. considered the point in *Clough Mill Ltd.* v. *Martin* a case where yarn was supplied for manufacture into fabrics. He said[1]:

> "Now it is no doubt true that, where A's material is lawfully used by B to create new goods, whether or not B incorporated other material of his own, property in the new goods will generally rest in B, at least where the goods are not reducible to the original materials (see *Blackstone's Commentaries* (17th ed., 1830), Vol. 2, pp. 404–405). But it is difficult to see why, if the parties agree that the property in the goods shall vest in A, that agreement should not be given effect to. On this analysis the buyer does not confer on the seller an interest in property defeasible upon the payment of the debt; on the contrary, when the new goods come into existence the property in them *ipso facto* vests in the seller, and he thereafter retains his ownership in them, in the same way and on the same terms as he retains his ownership in the unused material."

Oliver L.J. was of the same opinion. He failed to see any reason in principle why the original legal title in a newly manufactured article composed of materials belonging to A and B should not lie where A and B had agreed that it should lie.[2] Sir John Donaldson was more tentative. He said that if the incorporation of the yarn in, or its use as material for, other goods, left the yarn in a separate and identifiable state, there was no reason why the sellers should not be able to retain title in it. On the other hand, if the incorporation of the yarn created a situation in which it ceased to be identifiable, and a new product was created consisting of the yarn and the other material, it would be necessary to determine who owned that product. He made no pronouncement on the issue.[3]

The fourth condition of the reservation of title clause in *Clough Mill* provided that if any of the material supplied was incorporated in or used as material for other goods before payment the property in the whole of such goods shall be and remain with the seller until such payment had been made. It was not strictly unnecessary to decide whether this condition created a

---

[1] [1985] 1 W.L.R. 111, 119.
[2] *Ibid.* 124. Oliver L.J. also adopted the words of Lord Moulton in *Sandeman & Sons* v. *Tyzack & Branfoot Steamship Co.* [1913] A.C. 680, 695 that "the whole matter is far from being within the domain of settled law." It might also be argued that A and B should be free to apportion ownership of any newly manufactured article. In *Kruppstahl A.G.* v. *Quitmann Products Ltd.* [1982] I.L.R.M. 551 a reservation of title clause provided that the seller and buyer were to hold new products jointly in the ratio of the invoice value of the seller's goods to those of the buyers. The Irish High Court, however, construed the agreement as limiting the accountability of the buyers to the amount of their indebtedness on the original sales contract. The agreement was struck down as creating a registrable charge. See generally, *supra*, Chap. 5, pp. 85–86 and *infra*, Chap. 14, pp. 227–228.
[3] *Ibid.* 125.

registrable charge but nevertheless both Robert Goff L.J. and Oliver L.J. stated that it did.[4] This expression of opinion is quite surprising in light of the acknowledgement that where a new product had been formed consisting of material belonging to both A and B the parties could agree on the location of the title to the product. Robert Goff L.J. adduced two reasons for refusing fully to effectuate the logical consequences of his earlier argument.

First, he found it impossible to believe that it was the intention of the parties that the seller would thereby gain the windfall of the full value of the new product. The new product might derive not merely from the labour of the buyer but also from materials that were his. There did not appear to be any duty to account to the buyer for any surplus of the proceeds of sale above the outstanding balance of the price due by him to the seller.

There are two answers to this. Surely, the course of action available to the buyer in a situation like this is simple? He should sell the goods that incorporate his own materials or the value of his labour and use the proceeds to pay off the seller. Alternatively, it might be argued that an obligation to account arises from a general principle that no one should be unjustly enriched at another's expense. Lord Goff himself, in his capacity as co-author of one of Britain's leading textbooks on restitution, has contended that the time is now right for judges to recognise the existence of such a principle and its consequences.[5]

Secondly, he talked about the prospect of two lots of material, supplied by different sellers, each subject to a *Romalpa clause* which vests in the seller the legal title in a product manufactured from both lots of material. Agreed, the scenario is not at all sensible but an easy answer is to hold that a charge has been created in this situation. This conclusion does not affect the view that no charge arises where an agreement vests title to a product composed of material belonging to the seller and buyer in the seller. A "split" result like this, after all, corresponds to the Court of Appeal's conclusions in *Clough Mill*. It was held that the fact that condition four of the retention of title clause might constitute a charge did not mean that condition one was also a charge.

Robert Goff L.J. had Oliver L.J. on his side in suggesting that condition 4 amounted to a charge though Oliver L.J. had not anything additional to say in support of the charge conclusion. Robert Goff L.J. was also able to deploy the judgment of Vinelott J. in *Re Peachdart Ltd.*[6] to reinforce his line of reasoning.

In *Re Peachdart Ltd.* leather was supplied to a company which used it to manufacture handbags. The relevant part of the sales contract read:

> "(b) ... the ownership of the products shall remain with the seller, which reserves the right to dispose of the products until payment in full

---

[4] *Ibid.* 120, 124.
[5] (3rd ed., London 1986). For a strong affirmation of the principle of unjust enrichment, see pp. 12–13.
[6] [1984] Ch. 131.

for all the products has been received by it in accordance with the terms of this contract or until such time as the buyer sells the products to its customers by way of *bona fide* sale at full market value. . . . If any of the products are incorporated in or used as material for other goods before such payment the property in the whole of such other goods shall be and remain with the seller until such payment has been made or the other goods have been sold as aforesaid and all the seller's rights hereunder in the products shall extend to those other goods."

Vinelott J. came down in favour of a charge construction without much in the way of detailed analysis. He simply said that the parties must have intended that at least after a piece of leather had been appropriated to be manufactured into a handbag and work had started on it the leather would cease to be the exclusive property of the sellers.

The sellers, thereafter, would have a charge on handbags in the course of manufacture and on the distinctive products which would come into existence at the end of the process of manufacture. The value of the products would, for the most part, be derived from the buyer's reputation and the skills of its workforce. There is force in the view that the judge substituted for the actual agreement between the parties, an agreement which he thought they should have arrived at.[7]

Peachdart does bring home the necessity to make crystal clear the parties intentions that the seller should become owner of the resultant product. It is very desirable to incorporate provisions in the contract of sale requiring the buyer to segregate the goods from his own goods. Another provision that should be inserted is one obliging the buyer to pay the proceeds of sale into a separate interest bearing account and to keep them apart from their other moneys and not employ them in the trade. Vinelott J. commented on the absence of these features in *Re Peachdart Ltd.*

To sum up a clause vesting ownership in the buyer in products formed with materials belonging to seller and buyer should not be held to create a charge. The parties' intentions should be made manifest, however, by clauses requiring the buyer to keep the products apart from his own goods and also to keep proceeds of sale of the products in a separate account. On the other hand, a charge is created where a clause purports to vest the seller with title to a product partly consisting of goods supplied by a third party or parties.

Having held that a charge had been created, Vinelott J. in *Peachdart* held that the charge was registrable. This further conclusion seems well-nigh inevitable. The charge may be registrable as a floating charge or as a charge on goods.

Conclusion

After a long chapter of this nature it is tempting to essay some conclusions, however question-begging they might appear at first glance. What

---

[7] For criticism, see Parris, *op. cit.* p. 101.

follows is a terse summary that might seem all too bare without the benefit of the analysis in the preceding text:

(1) A "simple reservation" of title clause does not create a registrable charge. One should, however, avoid the use of phrases which purport to reserve only "equitable and beneficial ownership." The pitfalls of *Re Bond Worth Ltd.* are obvious.

(2) An "all-monies" or "all-liabilities" reservation of title clause does not create a registrable charge.

(3) A "proceeds of sale" does not amount to a registrable charge provided that the prerequisites of an equitable tracing action have been met. This statement seems most question-begging. If the necessary conditions have not been fulfilled then the purported proceeds clause may be regarded as constituting a floating charge or a charge over book debts.

(4) A charge confined to future book debts of a company is registrable.

(5) Where commingling of goods has been occasioned without loss of physical identity the separate owners become tenants in common of the mass in accordance with their respective contributions. Since this state of affairs arises by operation of law no charge, never mind a registrable charge, has been created by act of the parties.

(6) A clause in a contract of sale to the effect that any accessories to or goods attached to or repairs executed to the supplied goods shall become part of the supplied goods constitutes a registrable charge. The supplier is not claiming something which was his at the outset and the "extra" is being claimed to ensure payment of a debt. The agreement may be viewed as the creation of a charge over goods or a floating charge.

(7) A clause vesting ownership in the seller in products formed with materials belonging to buyer and seller does not constitute a charge.

(8) Where, however, the aggregation clause purports to vest title in the seller to products formed partly of materials belonging to third parties, it amounts to a charge over the products. This charge is registrable as a floating charge or as a charge on goods.

CHAPTER 7

RESTRICTIONS ON RESERVATION OF TITLE CLAUSES IN THE INSOLVENCY ACT 1986

The law relating to reservation of title clauses was discussed extensively by the Department of Trade Review Committee on Insolvency Law and Practice, chaired by Sir Kenneth Cork, which reported in 1982.[1] The Committee concluded that the absence of any provisions requiring disclosure of reservation of title clauses was unsatisfactory and should be remedied as soon as possible. As well as recommending the introduction of a registration requirement the Committee favoured a moratorium on the enforcement of reservation of title clauses.[2] They recommended[3]:

(a) During a period of 12 months from the commencement of a receivership or administration a seller should be prevented from exercising rights and remedies flowing from a reservation of title clause in a contract for the sale of goods and a receiver or administrator should be allowed to deal with the goods in a manner inconsistent with the title of the supplier.

(b) If the receiver or administrator sells the goods he should be obliged to account to the supplier for the proceeds of sale up to the amount secured by the reservation clause.

(c) If the receiver or administrator uses the goods in the manufacture of some product the proceeds of sale of the product should be applied in or towards the repayment of sums secured on reservation of title clauses affecting any of the constituent parts of the product.

(d) In the event of the proceeds being insufficient to pay all suppliers of goods under reservation of title clauses, the claim of each supplier should abate proportionately to the respective costs to the company of acquiring the goods incorporated in the product.

While the Cork Committee recommendations on reservation of title were not accepted, *in toto*, by the Government in the Insolvency Act reforms, the idea of a moratorium on the enforcement of claims was borrowed and fashioned somewhat. In particular, a moratorium on the enforcement of claims was imposed during the currency in office of the administrator, a new creature who came into being following the insolvency legislation. The procedure surrounding this new office and the effect on reservation of title clauses will now be considered.

[1] Cmnd. 8558.
[2] At para. 1650.
[3] *Ibid.* An earlier draft of what follows relating to the effect of the Insolvency Act 1986 on reservation of title clauses appeared in the form of an article by the author at (1990) 11 Co. Law.

The Administration Order Procedure

A company, any of its directors or indeed any creditor of the company can apply to the court for the making of an administration order.[4] Notice of the presentation of a petition must be given to any person who has appointed, or is or may be entitled to appoint, an administrative receiver, and to such other persons as may be prescribed.[5] An "administrative receiver" may be taken as meaning a receiver or manager of the whole (or substantially the whole) of a company's property or undertaking appointed by debenture-holders secured by a charge which, as created, was a floating charge or by such a charge and one or more other securities.[6] In *Re a Company (No. 00175 of 1987)*[7] Vinelott J. considered that the legislature must have intended that a person with power to appoint an administrative receiver should have adequate opportunity of considering whether or not to exercise his power before it is extinguished. In effect, sections 9 and 10 of the Insolvency Act give the holder of such a floating charge a practical veto on the appointment of an administrator. Neither the Insolvency Act nor the Insolvency Rules impose an obligation to notify creditors generally of the making of an administration order application whether or not they have the benefit of a reservation of title clause.

Administration Orders—the Powers of the Court

An administration order directs that during the subsistence in force of the order, the affairs, business and property of the company shall be managed by a person appointed by the court.[8] Section 8 of the Insolvency Act sets out the circumstances in which the court may make an administration order. The court is required to be satisfied that the company is or is likely to become unable to pay its debts. Secondly, it has to be of the view that the making of an order would be likely to achieve one or more of the following purposes:

(a) the survival of the company, and the whole or any part of its under-taking, as a going concern;
(b) the approval of a voluntary arrangement under the Insolvency Act;
(c) the sanctioning of a scheme of arrangement under section 425 of the Companies Act 1985;
(d) more advantageous realisation of the company's assets than would be effected on a winding-up.

It is of course open to any creditor, including a retention of title claimant, to oppose the making of an administration order. He may not hear of the

---

[4] s. 9(1) of the Insolvency Act 1986.
[5] s. 9(2).
[6] ss. 29(2) and 251.
[7] [1987] B.C.L.C. 467.
[8] s. 8(2). Pt. II of the Insolvency Act 1986 on "Administration Orders" is set out in the appendix to the book as is the definition of "retention of title agreement" in s. 251.

application, however, until it is heard. Moreover he is unlikely to have sufficiently detailed knowledge of the company's affairs to oppose an order, even if forewarned.

Some judicial disagreement has occurred in relation to the conditions to be satisfied before an administration order may be made. The first case in point is *Re Consumer and Industrial Press Ltd.*[9] Here Peter Gibson J. held that the court must be satisfied on the evidence before it that at least one of the purposes in section 8(3) is likely to be achieved if it is to make an administration order. The judge went on to say[10]:

> "That does not mean that it is merely possible that such purpose will be achieved; the evidence must go further than that to enable the court to hold that the purpose in question will more probably than not be achieved. Further, the court has to specify in the order the purpose which it is satisfied will be achieved. It is not a question of being satisfied that one purpose is likely to be achieved, and then adding to the order one or more of the other purposes which might perhaps be achieved but in respect of which the evidence is less compelling."

Hoffman J. ventured a different view on the degree of likelihood required in *Re Harris Simons Construction Ltd.*[11] He said that the court has to be satisfied that there is a real prospect that one or more of the stated purposes may be achieved but it is not necessary for the evidence to establish that the purpose in question will more probably than not be achieved.

He also suggested that it was not unlikely that the legislature intended to set a modest threshold of probability to found jurisdiction and to rely on the court's discretion not to make orders in cases in which, weighing all the circumstances, it seemed inappropriate to do so. Moreover the judge offered an analogy that is calculated to appeal to those with an equine streak. It was not a misuse of language to say that something is likely without intending to suggest that the probability of its happening exceeds 0.5 as in "I think that the favourite Golden Spurs at 5–1 is likely to win the Derby."[12]

In *Re Primlaks (UK) Ltd.*[13] Vinelott J. also favoured a test of whether there was a "real prospect" of the purposes being achieved. The controversy now appears to have been cleared up by the decision of Peter Gibson J. in *Re S.C.L. Building Services Ltd.*[14] Here, in deference to his brother judges, he decided not to follow the "more probable than not" formulation that he himself had propounded in *Re Consumer and Industrial Press Ltd.* and instead opted for a "real prospect" test.

[9] [1988] B.C.L.C. 177.
[10] *Ibid.* 178.
[11] [1989] B.C.L.C. 202.
[12] Hoffman J., in addition, referred to the fact that s. 8 requires the court to be "satisfied" of the company's actual or likely insolvency but only to "consider" that the order would be likely to achieve one of the stated purposes. Reference was also made to para. 508 of the Cork Report.
[13] [1989] B.C.L.C. 734.
[14] (1989) 4 B.C.C. 746.

Effect of Administration Order Application

Section 10 of the Insolvency Act 1986 sets out the consequences which follow from the presentation of a petition for the making of an administration order. In general, the effect is to freeze claims against the company although:

(a) a winding-up petition can be presented (but not advertised or heard).
(b) a debenture holder can appoint an administrative receiver (the result of which is to frustrate completely the administration petition).

Section 10(1)(b) relates specifically to retention of title clauses. The section provides that "no steps may be taken . . . to repossess goods in the company's possession under any hire purchase agreement except with the leave of the court and subject to such terms as the court may impose." A hire-purchase agreement is given an expansive meaning by section 10(4) so as to include retention of title agreements. The last expression is defined in section 251 as:

> "an agreement for the sale of goods to a company being an agreement—(a) which does not constitute a charge on the goods; but (b) under which, if the seller is not paid and the company is wound up, the seller will have priority over all other creditors of the company as respects the goods or any property representing the goods."

A "hire-purchase agreement" may be an inapt way of describing a contract for the sale of goods subject to a reservation of title clause.[15] However, the effect of the section is clear: upon presentation of a petition seeking the appointment of an administrator, a person who has sold goods subject to a reservation of title clause is prevented from recovering possession of those goods without the leave of the court. Moreover, this state of affairs continues if an administration order is made. Indeed, the embargo on action becomes stronger in that it is no longer possible to appoint an administrative receiver.[16] It is provided though that the administrator may consent to the recovery of goods supplied on reservation of title terms. The court may also permit such recovery subject to such terms as it may impose.[17]

After the presentation of an administration petition, no "other proceedings" may be commenced or continued against the company or its property. In the period prior to the making of an administration order the ban may be relaxed by leave of the court.[18] After an administration order has been made, the administrator as well as the court may permit such proceedings.[19]

Sellers who wish to escape the clutches of the moratorium may wish to look more closely at the definition of "retention of title" agreements. To

[15] See Parris, *Effective Retention of Title Clauses* (1986), p. 151.
[16] s. 11(3)(b).
[17] s. 11(3)(d).
[18] s. 10(1)(c).
[19] s. 11(3)(d).

come within the definition an agreement must have the effect that if the seller "is not paid," he will have priority over all other creditors of the company as respects the goods or any property representing the goods. It has been suggested that if the transfer of property under the agreement is not referable to payment to the seller but is referable to the performance of some other obligation then the agreement escapes control.[20] The definition, however, refers not to the ostensible object of the agreement but to its true effect. If the effect is to afford priority where the buyer becomes insolvent then it is within the scope of the definition.

Potentially a more profitable method of seeking to evade sections 10 and 11 of the Insolvency Act 1986 is to provide in the contract of sale that payment should be made by the buyer not to the seller but to an associated company.[21] It is arguable that the contract is not within the definition of "retention of title agreement" as there is no stipulation for payment to the seller. Whether the courts will accede to the argument is not entirely clear. There is no judicial guidance yet on this matter. The decision of Peter Gibson J. in *Royal Trust Bank* v. *Buchler*[22] suggests, however, that the courts will not readily allow a retention of title claimant to repossess goods in the company's possession.

The prohibition on the enforcement of claims against the company covers a security holder. In *Buchler*, the judge opined that the onus was on the secured creditor seeking leave under section 11(3) of the Act of 1986 to enforce his security to show that it was a proper case for leave to be given. But it was not essential to show some criticism of the administrator's conduct before the court would exercise its discretion to grant such leave. Such discretion would be exercised in the light of all the circumstances.

Sections 10(3) and 11(3) talk about a claim "to repossess goods in the company's possession." The phrase "repossess" is apposite to describe a situation where a seller seeks to recover the goods which he has supplied. There is more difficulty, however, in applying the word "repossess" to cover a situation where a new product has been manufactured out of the goods supplied. In *Clough Mill Ltd.* v. *Martin*[23] Robert Goff L.J. stated that if A's material is lawfully used by B to create new goods and the parties agree that the property in the goods should vest in A, that agreement might be effective. Furthermore, as one commentator puts it[24]:

> "If a supplier succeeds in establishing that his retention of title agreement confers upon him the ownership of any new goods he can scarcely be said to "repossess" them if he exercises his proprietary rights, because the possession of those goods by the buyer will never have been preceded by any possession on the part of the supplier."

[20] See Hamish Anderson, *Administrators* (1987), p. 55.
[21] Anderson, *op. cit.* pp. 55–56.
[22] [1989] B.C.L.C. 130.
[23] [1985] 1 W.L.R. 11.
[24] Anderson, *op. cit.* p. 59.

What if possession of the new products is not yielded to the retention of title claimant and resort to litigation is necessary? No "other" proceedings against the company may be commenced, except by leave of the court and subject to such terms as the court may impose.[25] In *Air Ecosse Ltd.* v. *Civil Aviation Authority*[26] it was held that the moratorium embraces only claims which could be made by creditors and not, for example, disputes between the company and a competitor as to which is entitled to a government or other public contract or privilege. Similarly, in our example, it might be argued that the supplier is not invoking a claim as creditor but rather relying on his rights as proprietor of the goods in question. This argument, however, is not a particularly convincing one.

A related argument is founded on the existence in a sale of goods contract of a provision enabling the seller to recover possession of the goods upon the presentation or intended presentation of an administration order petition. It might be argued that this automatic termination clause discharges the original contract and that the buyer is not in possession under a conditional sale agreement so that the restrictions imposed by the Insolvency Act 1986 do not apply.[27] It is doubtful, however, whether this contention would succeed given the undoubted fact that the goods have been in the buyer company's possession under a reservation of title agreement.

Power to Deal with Property Subject to Reservation of Title

The administrator may use goods which have been supplied with reservation of title conditions in the course of his management of the business of the company. In addition, he is empowered to sell the goods if he can persuade the court that disposal would be likely to promote one or more of the purposes specified in the administration order (section 15(2)). It is a condition of such orders that:

(a) the net proceeds of the disposal, and
(b) where those proceeds are less than such amount as may be determined by the court to be the net amount which would be realised on a

---

[25] ss. 10(1)(c) and 11(3)(d).

[26] (1987) 3 B.C.C. 492. See also, *Re Barrow Borough Transport Ltd.* [1989] B.C.L.C. 653 where it was held that an application to the court for an extension of time for registration of a charge could not be described as "proceedings against the company or its property" within s. 11(3)(d) of the Insolvency Act 1986. In *Re Paramount Airways Ltd.*, *Financial Times*, January 10, 1990, the Court of Appeal held that the detention of aircraft pursuant to the provisions of the Civil Aviation Act 1982 to secure the payment of monies owed was the taking of steps to enforce a security within s. 11(3)(c) of the Insolvency Act 1986.

[27] See de Lacy, "Administrative caution" [1989] L.M.C.L.Q. 506, 509 who refers to the hire-purchase case *Re Apex Supply Co. Ltd.* [1942] 1 Ch. 108 in this connection.

sale of the property or goods in the open market by a willing vendor, such sums as may be acquired to make good the deficiency shall be appropriated towards discharging the sums payable under the reservation of title agreement (section 15(5)).

These safeguards are by no means a panacea for suppliers. First, the market price of the goods may be below the agreed contractual price. If this be so, the supplier is then left with an unsecured claim for the balance. Secondly, there is the possibility that a supplier may have to resort to expensive litigation in order to establish a sale at an undervalue. It may be that before the court permits the administrator to dispose of the goods, it will specify the market price for the goods on the open market, if sold by a willing vendor. In this eventuality, there is no need for a supplier to apply *ex post facto* for a ruling that a sale has been effected at an undervalue. Presumably, however, if market conditions have altered between the time when a sale has been authorised and when it is actually made, the administrator might apply to the court under section 14(4). This is a general provision which enables the administrator to apply to the court for directions in relation to any particular matter arising in connection with the performance of his functions.

Section 15 of the Insolvency Act was construed by Knox J. in *Re A.R.V. Aviation Ltd.*[28] He held that in exercising its discretion under section 15 the court had to perform a balancing exercise between the prejudice that would be felt by the secured creditor if the order is made and the prejudice that would be felt by those interested in the promotion of the purposes set out in the administration order. He also said that the phrase "sums secured by the security" in section 15(5) covers not only the capital sum secured by the security and interest payable thereon but also any costs which the holder of the security was entitled to either under the general law or the terms of the security.

Rule 2.51 of the Insolvency Rules 1987 lays down detailed procedure to govern the case where an administrator applies under section 15(2). The court is charged with the task of fixing a time and place for hearing and the administrator is then to notify those claiming under reservation of title clauses. Rule 7.4(5) stipulates that the application must be served at least 14 days before the date fixed for the hearing. Rule 7.4(6) deals with cases of urgency where the full notice would frustrate the purposes for which an administration order was made. In such instances the court may:

(a) hear the application immediately, either with or without notice to, or the attendance of, other parties; or
(b) authorise a shorter period of notice.

The terms of sections 15(2) and 15(5) beg consideration of the phrases "open market" and "willing vendor." These phrases are often employed in

[28] [1989] B.C.L.C. 664.

taxation legislation.[29] Lord Reid in *Lynall* v. *I.R.C.*[30] proffered the following account of an open market sale:

> "No doubt sale in the open market may take many forms. But it appears to me that the idea behind this provision is the classical theory that the best way to determine the value in exchange of any property is to let the price be determined by economic forces—by throwing the sale open to competition when the highest price will be the highest that anyone offers. That implies that there has been adequate publicity or advertisement before the sale, and the nature of the property must determine what is adequate publicity. Goods may be exposed for sale in a market place or place to which buyers resort. Property may be put up to auction. Competitive tenders may be invited."

Lord Morris expressed himself in the following terms[31]:

> "There may be different markets or types of markets for differing varieties of property but ... the market which must be contemplated whatever its form, must be an "open" market in which the property is offered for sale to the world at large so that all potential purchasers have an equal opportunity to make an offer as a result of its being openly known what it is that is being offered for sale. Mere private deals on a confidential basis are not the equivalent of open market transactions. ..."

Attention must also be focused on the concept of the "willing vendor" mentioned in section 15(5). The Court of Appeal in *I.R.C.* v. *Clay*[32] breathed some life into this hypothetical character. Cozens-Hardy M.R. opined that a willing seller is a person who is a free agent and cannot be required by virtue of compulsory powers to sell.[33] Pickford L.J. suggested that the phrase meant a vendor who was prepared to sell provided a fair price was obtained under all the circumstances of the case. To put it another way, it did not mean an anxious vendor.[34]

Clay is concerned with a matter that has occasioned particular difficulty, namely, the situation where one prospective purchaser, because of peculiar circumstances, is prepared to pay more for the property than others. The case related to a house of which the value to anyone except certain trustees was no more than £750. The trustees were the proprietors of a nurses' home which adjoined the house and they desired to extend the premises. Accordingly, they purchased the property for £1,000 and the Court of Appeal held this was its value to a willing vendor. Cozens Hardy M.R. said[35]:

[29] See Foster, *Capital Taxes Encyclopedia*, Pt. H.
[30] [1972] A.C. 680, 695.
[31] *Ibid.* 699.
[32] [1914] 3 K.B. 466.
[33] *Ibid.* 473.
[34] *Ibid.* 478.
[35] *Ibid.* 472.

"To say that a small farm in the middle of a wealthy landowner's estate is to be valued without reference to the fact that he will probably be willing to pay a large price, but solely with reference to its ordinary agricultural value, seems to me absurd. If the landowner does not at the moment buy, land brokers or speculators will give more than its purely agricultural value with a view to reselling it at a profit to the landowner."

Swinfen-Eady L.J. developed the same theme. He said that not only is the probable buyer a competitor in the market but other persons, such as property brokers, compete in the market for what they know another person wants, with a view to a resale to him at an enhanced price, so as to realise a profit.[36]

I.R.C. v. *Clay* was approved of by the Privy Council in *Gajapatiraju* v. *Revenue Divisional Officer, Vizagapatam.*[37] Lord Romer expressed himself thus[38]:

"The disinclination of the vendor to part with his land and the urgent necessity of the purchaser to buy must alike be disregarded. Neither must be considered as acting under compulsion. But this does not mean that the fact that some particular purchaser might desire the land more than others is to be disregarded. The wish to a particular purchaser, though not his compulsion, must always be taken into consideration for what it is worth."

There are however, authorities which, if applied in the context of section 15(5) of the Insolvency Act 1986, are less favourable to a reservation of title claimant.[39] For example, in *Duke of Buccleuch* v. *I.R.C.*[40] Lord Morris said that open market value does not entail an assumption that the highest possible price will be realised. An estimate must be made of the price which would be realised under the reasonably competitive conditions of an open market on a particular date.[41]

Protection of Interests of Creditors

Section 27 is an important provision designed for the protection of a creditor or member of a company during the period when the company is in administration. The court is given power to intervene where a member or creditor complains that the company's affairs have been managed in a way unfairly prejudicial to the interests of its creditors or members generally, or

[36] *Ibid.* 475. See also, *Glass* v. *I.R.C.* 1915 S.C. 449.
[37] [1939] A.C. 302.
[38] *Ibid.* 312. See also, *Robinson Bros. (Brewers) Ltd.* v. *Durham County Assessment Committee* [1938] A.C. 321.
[39] See *I.R.C.* v. *Crossman* [1937] A.C. 26.
[40] [1937] A.C. 506.
[41] *Ibid.* 537.

of some part of its creditors or members (including at least himself) or that any actual or proposed act or omission of the administrator is or would be so prejudicial.[42] The court may grant such relief as it thinks fit and, in particular, may:

(a) regulate the future management by the administrator of the company's affairs, business and property;

(b) require the administrator to refrain from doing or continuing an act complained of by the petitioner, or to do an act which the petitioner has complained of or omitted to do;

(c) discharge the administration order and make such consequential provision as the court thinks fit.

The "unfairly prejudicial" criterion has been taken from section 459 of the Companies Act 1985 and decisions on the interpretation of that section are relevant to section 27 of the Insolvency Act. The Companies Act section, however, is confined to applications by members and the cases thereon cannot afford anything other than generalised guidance.

One thing is clear, however, about section 27—there is no need to prove that the petitioner was less fairly treated than other members or creditors. Section 459, as originally drafted, was not worded similarly and Vinelott J. in *Re Carrington Viyella plc*[43] appeared to insist upon the necessity for discrimination where an application was brought under that section. He said that even if the directors in that case had acted in breach of their fiduciary duties the breach would have affected all shareholders equally and as such would not have been within section 459.

The same principle was applied by Harman J. in *Re a Company (No. 00370 of 1987), ex parte Glossop*.[44] He said that relief under section 459 could only be granted where the conduct complained of was unfairly prejudicial to some part of the members. Accordingly, a section 459 petition could not be founded on conduct which had an equal effect on all of the members and which was not intended to discriminate between members. As a failure to declare a proper dividend affected all the members equally, it would not ground a petition.

The test for "unfairly prejudicial conduct is objective—it is the result of the conduct complained of and not the motive behind it that is the decisive factor." Nourse J. so stated in *Re Noble and Sons (Clothing) Ltd*.[45] He said that the issue was not whether the respondent intended to harm the petitioner but whether a reasonable bystander observing the consequences of

---

[42] See generally, on s. 459, Hannigan [1988] L.M.C.L.Q. 60.

[43] (1983) 1 B.C.C. 98, 951.

[44] [1988] B.C.L.C. 570. Peter Gibson J. refused to follow *Glossop* in *Re Sam Weller & Sons Limited*, July 13, 1989. S. 459 has recently been amended by s. 145 and Sched. 19, para. 11 of the Companies Act 1989 which removes the requirement that prejudice be suffered by some part of the members.

[45] [1983] B.C.L.C. 273.

the conduct would regard it as having unfairly prejudiced the petitioner's interests.

Subsection 3 of section 27 spells out limitations on the petition procedure. No such application shall prejudice a voluntary arrangement or, if made more than 28 days after proposals by an administrator have been approved, the implementation of those proposals.

Getting in the Company's Property

Section 234 stipulates that where an administrator disposes of property which is not property of the company, he is not liable to the true owner if at the time of seizure or disposal he believes and has reasonable grounds to believe that he is entitled to seize or dispose of the goods. Liability arises only in so far as any loss or damage was caused by his own negligence. Furthermore the administrator has a lien on the property or the proceeds of its sale for such expenses as were incurred in connection with the seizure or disposal.

The section has the result that if an administrator sells goods completely ignorant of the fact that they may be subject to a reservation of title claim he cannot be found liable in conversion where he is not negligent. Rights to trace the proceeds of sale remain, however. Section 234 and the exemption from liability therein contained applies not only to an administrator but also to an administrative receiver, a liquidator and a provisional liquidator. Section 14(6) should also be borne in mind, in this context. It provides that a person dealing with the administrator in good faith and for value is not concerned to inquire whether the administrator is acting within his powers.

Discharge of an Administrator

Section 18 empowers an administrator to apply to the court for an administration order to be discharged or to be varied so as to specify an additional purpose. Familiarity with the affairs of the company may persuade the administrator that it is advantageous to apply to the court for a purpose to be included that was not specified in the original order.[46] Furthermore, the administrator is obliged to make an application if it appears to him that the purpose of each of the purposes specified in the Order either has been achieved or is incapable of achievement.[47] Where an administrator has been appointed to secure rehabilitation of the company's fortunes discharge may represent either success or failure. In the event of success, management of the company's affairs will be restored to its directors and shareholders. If the

[46] s. 18(1).
[47] s. 18(2). It has been said that the gap between the administrator's power and duty under this section is a small one in that there are few occasions when he wishes to make an application for discharge or variation of the order when he will not also be obliged to do so. Rajak, *Company Liquidations* (1988), p. 59.

goal of rehabilitation proves unattainable, then liquidation will probably follow the discharge of an administration order. It has been decided, however, that there is no power to make a winding-up order immediately upon discharge unless a winding-up petition has already been presented.[48] Once the period of administration has come to an end, retention of title claimants may seek to recover their goods, that is, if they have not already been disposed of.

Section 20 of the Insolvency Act deals with release of an administrator from liability. A past administrator may be released at such time as the court may determine. The release equals a discharge from all liability both in respect of his acts or omissions in the administration and otherwise in relation to his conduct as administrator. Reservation of title claimants should therefore be on their guard to ensure that the administrator does not obtain his release where they are unhappy with his conduct of the administration. There is one exception to the release from liability. Nothing in the section affects the operation of section 212. The latter section affords a summary remedy in the course of a winding-up against a variety of persons who have been officers of or who have acted as liquidator, administrator, or administrative receiver of a company and in that capacity have misapplied or retained or otherwise dealt improperly with any money or other property of the company. The section 212 remedy, however, may be invoked against an administrator who has obtained a discharge only with the consent of the court.

Receivers and Reservation of Title Clauses

Section 43 of the Insolvency Act 1986 gives the administrative receiver power to dispose of property subject to the prior charge if the court is satisfied that such a sale is likely to promote a more advantageous realisation of the assets. The section talks about the disposal of property which is subject to a security. The word "security" is defined in section 248(b) as meaning "any mortgage, charge, lien or other security." Section 43 does not appear to permit the sale of assets which are the subject of a valid retention of title clause. This conclusion is strengthened by a distinction drawn in section 15 in the context of administrators between "any property of the company subject to a security" on the one hand and "any goods under a hire-purchase agreement" on the other hand.[49]

---

[48] See *Re Brooke Marine Ltd.* [1988] B.C.L.C. 546.
[49] See generally, Lightman and Moss, *The Law of Receivers of Companies* (1986), p. 147. S. 43 of the Insolvency Act 1986 as well as s. 15 may be found in the appendix.

CHAPTER 8

RESERVATION OF TITLE AND THE NON-CORPORATE BUYER

In the vast majority of cases, goods which have been sold subject to a reservation of title clause will be supplied to a company registered under the Companies Acts. In certain cases, however, the buyer may be an individual or partnership. Most of the matters which have been discussed in the context of corporate buyers apply equally here. The seller must show that the reservation of title clause has been incorporated into the contract of sale. He must also demonstrate that the contract, on a true construction, confers on him the rights to which he lays claim. The reservation of title provisions, though, cannot be attacked on the ground that they constitute a charge created by a company which, being unregistered, is void against the liquidator and creditors. There are, however, three issues peculiar to the position of a non-corporate buyer of which mention must be made.[1] These are:

   (a)   Bills of sale legislation.
   (b)   Reputed ownership doctrine.
   (c)   General assignment of book debts and section 344 of the Insolvency Act 1986.

Bills of Sale Acts

The legislation governing bills of sale is contained in the Bills of Sale Act 1878 and the Bills of Sale Act (1878) Amendment Act 1882.[2] The Acts extend only to documents and do not embrace oral transactions. Bills of sale which fall within the legislation are of two kinds. Firstly, there are those which constitute absolute assurances of chattels and secondly, there are bills of sale given by way of security. The former are regulated by the 1878 Act whereas the latter are affected both by the 1878 and 1882 Acts. Before delving further into these Acts it is appropriate to talk about the statutory definition of a bill of sale.

Section 3 of the Bills of Sale Act 1878 lays down that the Act shall apply to "every bill of sale . . . whereby the holder or grantee has power . . . to seize or take possession of any personal chattels." Section 4 of the same Act sets out three categories of bill of sale:

---

[1] See generally, *Benjamin's Sale of Goods* (3rd ed., 1987), paras. 389–392.
[2] See also the Bills of Sale Acts 1890 and 1891 which exempt certain letters of hypothecation from the operation of the Bills of Sale Act. For accounts of the bills of sale legislation see A. G. Guest, *The Law of Hire Purchase* (London 1966), Chap. 4; R. M. Goode, *Hire Purchase Law and Practice* (2nd ed., London 1970), Chap. 4 and the section on bills of sale in *Halsbury's Laws of England* (4th ed., 1973), Vol. 4 by R. M. Goode. The 1878 and 1882 Acts are set out in the appendix.

(1) assignments, transfers, declarations of trust without transfer, inventories of goods with receipt thereto attached, or receipts for purchase moneys of goods, and other assurances of personal chattels;

(2) powers of attorney, authorities or licences to take possession of personal chattels as security for any debt;

(3) agreements by which a right in equity to any personal chattels or to any charge or security thereon shall be conferred.

Section 4 goes on to set out a list of documents that are specifically exempted from the definition of "bill of sale." The exceptions include transfer of goods in the ordinary course of any trade or calling. The expression "bill of sale" is accorded the same meaning in the Act of 1882.[3]

Purpose of the Acts

The 1878 Act has the long title "An Act to consolidate and amend the law for preventing frauds upon creditors by secret Bills of Sale of Personal Chattels." The *raison d'être* of this Act and of the Act of 1882 was explained lucidly and concisely by Lord Herschell in *Manchester, Sheffield and Lincolnshire Railway Co.* v. *North Wagon Railway Co.*[4] He said the former enactment was designed for the protection of creditors, and to prevent their rights being affected by secret assurances of chattels which were permitted to remain in the ostensible possession of a person who had parted with the property in them.[5] The statutory scheme of protection is for a bill of sale to be attested and to be registered in a public register within seven days. Failure to comply with the registration requirement renders the bill void but only as against creditors or their representatives.[6] As between the parties thereto, an unregistered bill of sale remains perfectly valid.

The rationale of the Bills of Sale Act 1882 was expounded by Lord Herschell in the following terms[7]:

> "It was to prevent needy persons being entrapped into signing complicated documents which they might often be unable to comprehend and so being subjected by their creditors to the enforcement of harsh and unreasonable provisions. A form was accordingly provided to which bills of sale were to conform, and the result of non-compliance with the statute was to render the bill of sale void even as between the parties to it. But this being the object, the enactment is, as we have seen, limited to bills of sale given 'by way of security for the payment of money by the grantor thereof.' "

[3] s. 3 1982 Act.
[4] [1880] 13 A.C. 554.
[5] *Ibid.* 560.
[6] s. 8.
[7] [1880] 13 A.C. 554, 560–561.

Statutory Form of Bills of Sale

So the Bills of Sale Act (1878) Amendment Act 1882 makes provision for a form of bill of sale in respect of security bills. The reason behind the requirement is to ensure that the nature and terms of the loan and security are clearly marked out. The insistence on the statutory form has the consequence that certain categories of security cannot be employed as they are by nature incompatible with the statutory form. *Re Townsend, ex p. Parsons*[8] may be cited in this connection.

In this case the Court of Appeal held that a document giving a licence to take immediate possession of goods as security for a debt was a bill of sale within section 4 of the 1878 Act and was therefore within the 1882 Bills of Sale Act as well. The court also affirmed that such a licence was void under section 9 of the 1882 Act as substantially deviating from the prescribed form. This was so notwithstanding the fact that, from its nature, it was impossible that such a document should be made in the prescribed form. Lord Esher M.R. spoke thus[9]:

> "It seems to me that the words of s.9 strike at all documents which give a security upon goods for the payment of money, and I take it the legislature intended to say, if you cannot make your agreement by a document in the form specified in the schedule, you shall not be able to make it by any document at all."

Lopes L.J. spoke in a similar vein. He said[10]:

> "I say without any hesitation that by the Act of 1882 the legislature intended to enact and did enact that all documents giving security upon goods for the payment of money (other than those excepted) should loyally follow the form prescribed in the schedule; and that, if they did not in substance comply with that form they should be void."

Moreover, the court laid down that the grantee's position could not be improved by virtue of having taken possession under a document which was not in accordance with the statutory form.

Permitted Departures from Statutory Form

It is clear from observations in the House of Lords case of *Thomas* v. *Kelly*[11] that a literal conformity with the statutory form of a bill of sale is not necessary. Lord Macnaghten, for instance, said that section 9 does not require a bill of sale to be a verbal and literal transcript of the statutory form.[12] Lord Halsbury said the section was elastic.[13] It did not make every

[8] [1886] 16 Q.B. 532.
[9] *Ibid*. 545. He disapproved of the *ratio* in *Ex p. Close* [1884] 14 Q.B.D. 386 and *Re Cunningham* (1880) 28 Ch.D. 682.
[10] *Ibid*. 547.
[11] [1880] 13 A.C. 506.
[12] *Ibid*. 520.
[13] *Ibid*. 511. See also Lord FitzGerald at 516.

word imperative but provides that no form shall be permitted except one made "in accordance with the form in the schedule." He acknowledged however, that the degree of latitude involved in these words would be difficult, perhaps impossible, to define.

Some attempt at definition has been provided by Professor Goode who suggests that a bill of sale must possess the following 14 characteristics if it is to accord with the statutory form[14]:

"(1) the date of the bill;
(2) the names and addresses of the parties;
(3) a statement of the consideration;
(4) an acknowledgment of receipt, if the advance is a present advance;
(5) an assignment by way of security of personal chattels capable of specific description;
(6) exclusion of any description of the chattels from the body of the bill and relegation of such description to the schedule;
(7) the securing of a monetary obligation, as opposed to some other form of obligation;
(8) a statement of the sum secured, the rate of interest and the instalments by which repayment is to be made;
(9) any agreed terms for the maintenance or defeasance of the security;
(10) a proviso limiting the grounds of seizure to those specified in section 7 of the 1882 Act;
(11) signature and sealing by the grantor;
(12) an attestation clause;
(13) the name, address, and description of the attesting witness;
(14) a schedule in which a reference is made to chattels comprised in the bill."

Consequences of Non-compliance with Statutory Form

As we have seen section 9 of the Bills of Sale Act 1882 renders invalid a security bill of sale not in accordance with the statutory form.[15] The implications of this edict were spelled out by the Court of Appeal in *Smith* v. *Whiteman*.[16] It was held that derogation from the statutory form avoided a bill even as regards the grantor's personal covenant contained in the bill to repay the principal lent and interest thereon. The money advanced together with reasonable interest is recoverable in a quasi-contractual action for money had and received.[17]

---

[14] *Halsbury's Laws of England* (4th ed., 1973), Vol. 4 by R. M. Goode, para. 680.
[15] The statutory form is set out in a schedule to the Act of 1882 and may be located in the appendix.
[16] [1909] 2 K.B. 437. See also, *Davies* v. *Rees* [1886] 17 Q.B.D. 408; *Smith* v. *Whiteman* [1909] 2 K.B. 437 and *Bradford Advance Co. Ltd.* v. *Ayers* [1924] W.N. 152.
[17] See *North Central Wagon and Finance Co. Ltd.* v. *Brailsford* [1962] 1 All E.R. 502. See also, *Bradford Advance Co. Ltd.* v. *Ayers* [1924] W.N. 152.

Section 9 of the 1882 Act should be contrasted with section 8 of the Bills of Sale Act 1878. That section states the effect of non-registration of a bill of sale. It applies to both absolute and security bills of sale. Non-registration renders the bill void only as against the following classes of person: trustees or assignees in the grantor's bankruptcy, or under any assignment for the benefit of his creditors, sheriffs' officers and other persons seizing chattels comprised in the bill of sale under execution against the grantor, and every person on whose behalf such process shall have been issued.

Furthermore, the bill is not avoided by the filing of a bankruptcy petition within the seven days allowed for registration. In addition, if the grantee takes possession before the filing of a bankruptcy petition against the grantor, it is irrelevant whether the bill has been registered or not.[18] The grantee's title is good against the whole world. In *Re Tooth*,[19] Luxmoore J. made it clear that if the grantee obtains possession before the bankruptcy of the grantor this possession is trumps against all.

Application of Bills of Sale Acts to the Reservation of Title Scenario

Before venturing further it is to be noted that the application of the bills of sale legislation in the reservation of title context assumes the transfer of ownership from seller to buyer and the transfer back of some security interest to the seller. The House of Lords in *McEntire* v. *Crossley Bros Ltd.*[20] made it clear that a document is only a bill of sale if the owner of goods confers a right to possession on another person. In the classic conditional sale situation it is the owner himself who is invested with the right to recover possession.

Bills of Sale and Aggregation Clauses

It is fairly common to include in a contract for the sale of goods a provision to the effect that the property in additions or accessories to the goods supplied passes to the seller. Is a clause of this nature capable of constituting a bill of sale?

The position is complicated by the fact that the first two categories of bills of sale—transfer of ownership and right to possession as security—only apply to property which the grantor owns at the time the document is executed.[21] A little legislative history is appropriate at this stage. The first statute on the subject of bills of sale was enacted in 1854 with the Bills of Sale Act of that year. The Act was designed to prevent secret transfers. The

---

[18] As well as the filing of a bankruptcy petition, s. 8 refers also to the execution of any assignment for the benefit of creditors, or the execution of process of any court authorising the seizure of the chattels.

[19] [1934] Ch. 616. See also *Marples* v. *Hartley* (1861) 3 E. & E. 610.

[20] [1985] A.C. 457.

[21] See Allcock, "Romalpa Clauses and Bills of Sale" (1981) 131 New L.J. 842.

definition of "bill of sale" therein covered the first two limbs and in *Branton* v. *Griffits*[22] a document assigning future goods was held not to constitute an assurance of goods capable of complete transfer by delivery. Because of this decision it was necessary to add a third limb to the statutory definition of bill of sale in order to encompass agreements conferring a right in equity over after-acquired goods.

Be that as it may and let us take it that the buyer owns the goods added at the time when the contract of sale is made. The property in the annexed goods passes to the seller.[23] It would seem, therefore, that the contract is both an instrument transferring legal ownership and also an instrument conferring a right to take possession by way of security and hence a bill of sale.

Two arguments have been mounted against this conclusion. First, it might be argued that property passes to the seller, not by virtue of the sales contract but by virtue of the doctrine of accession. The principles relating to accession have been discussed in detail elsewhere.[24] The preponderance of authority supports an "injurious removal" test. This means that goods annexed are regarded as an accession and so forming part of the goods supplied where they cannot be removed without causing substantial damage to the latter goods.

Even if the test for accession is not satisfied it has been suggested that it is not the sale of goods contract which creates rights in the seller but rather the independent act of attachment. Professor Goode cites *Akron Tyre Co. Pty Ltd*. v. *Kittson*[25] in this connection but it is suggested that the case does not really support the proposition for which it is cited.[26] Here a vehicle was let on hire-purchase by the plaintiffs under an agreement which provided that: "Any accessories or goods supplied with or for or attached to or repairs executed to the goods shall become part of the goods." Some tyres were fitted to the vehicle by the hirer. He subsequently removed them, however, and sold them to the defendant who declined to deliver them up to the plaintiffs. The defendant was sued in conversion by the plaintiffs.

[22] (1877) 2 C.P.D. 212.
[23] See generally, Goode, *Proprietary Rights and Insolvency in Sale Transactions* (2nd ed., London 1989), p. 90.
[24] See generally, *supra*, Chap. 3, pp. 47–51; Goode, *Hire Purchase Law and Practice* (2nd ed., 1970), Chap. 33, and A. G. Guest, "Accession and Confusion in the Law of Hire-Purchase" (1964) 27 M.L.R. 505. See also *Rendell* v. *Associated Finance Pty Ltd*. [1957] V.R. 604 and *Thomas* v. *Robinson* [1977] 1 N.Z.L.R. 385. Three other tests have been suggested for determining whether goods have become an accession. A second test is one of separate existence. This asks whether the chattel which has been incorporated in another chattel has ceased to exist as a separate chattel. A third test, wider than that of injurious removal, is one of destruction of utility. It asks whether the removal of the article annexed would destroy the practical usability of the principal chattel. A fourth and final test analogises with fixtures to land and looks at the degree and purpose of annexation.
[25] (1951) 82 C.L.R. 477.
[26] See Goode, *Hire Purchase Law and Practice* (2nd ed., 1970), p. 752 and *Proprietary Rights and Insolvency in Sales Transactions* (2nd ed., 1989), p. 90. See also Guest, "Accession and Confusion in the Law of Hire Purchase" (1964) 27 M.L.R. 505, 510.

The plaintiffs were successful in the action. Goode understands the case to hold, *inter alia*, that the hire-purchase agreement did not constitute a bill of sale of the tyres since the document did not of its own force pass the property in them. That did not come about until an external act had taken place, namely the placing of the tyres on the vehicle. It is submitted, however, that the case was decided on the basis that under the law of Victoria a document affecting after-acquired property is not a bill of sale. There were two judgments delivered in the High Court of Australia, one by Latham C.J. and the other by Williams and Kitto JJ. Latham C.J. referred to the decision of Cussen A.C.J. in *King* v. *Greig*[27] as authority for the proposition that a provision in a document providing transfer of property in after-acquired goods was valid without registration under the Victorian Bills of Sale Act.[28] Williams and Kitto JJ. also referred approvingly to *King* v. *Greig*. They cited that case in support of the view that an agreement for the assignment of after-acquired property was not an assignment or other assurance of personal chattels within the meaning of the Act.[29]

This analysis leaves us somewhat bereft of authority on the point whether the seller's rights are to be regarded as deriving from the sales contract or the independent act of attachment. The matter must await a firm judicial ruling. In the interim period, there is much to be said for the view that in the situation under consideration the seller's rights are derived from the contract of sale, even though an additional act by the buyer is necessary. It is suggested that the document might amount to a bill of sale.[30]

As we have seen, a different situation obtains where the buyer did not own the additions at the time of the sale contract but subsequently acquired them. A document concerning after-acquired property is only a bill of sale if it comes within the third limb of the definition, *i.e.* an agreement conferring a right in equity to chattels or to any charge or security thereon. The precise scope of this third category of bill of sale came to be considered in *Reeves* v. *Barlow*.[31] In this case a clause in a building contract whereby all building and other materials brought by the builder upon the land should become the property of the landowner was held not to constitute a bill of sale within section 4 of the Bills of Sale Act 1878. It was held that the builder's agreement was at no time an equitable assignment of anything but a mere legal contract that, upon the happening of a particular event, the property in law should pass in certain chattels. An agreement creating a legal right over future goods, without any preceding equitable right, was not caught by the section.

Generally, it is true to say that an assignment of future property is binding in equity only in accordance with the principle of *Holroyd* v. *Marshall*.[32] This

[27] [1931] V.L.R. 413.
[28] (1951) 82 C.L.R. 477, 487.
[29] *Ibid.* 495.
[30] (1981) 131 New L.J. 842, 843.
[31] [1884] 12 Q.B.D. 436.
[32] (1862) 10 H.L. cas. 191.

principle lays down that an assignment of future property operates in equity by way of assignment, binding the conscience of the assignor, and so binding the property from the moment when the contract becomes capable of being performed on the principle that equity regards as done that which ought to be done. A legal interest may pass however if the grantor is required to perform some new act manifesting an intention to pass the property. This whole area was considered by the High Court of Australia in *Akron Tyre Co. Pty Ltd.* v. *Kittson*. The placing of tyres on a hired vehicle was accepted as an act sufficient to pass the property at law and in equity from the hirer to the plaintiff company. As Williams and Kitto JJ. said:

> "No intervention of a court of equity was required to give full effect to the bargain. Nothing was left upon which any equity as distinct from law could attach and no further performance of the contract was necessary or could be enforced."[33]

The foregoing exegesis leads to the conclusion that a contract conferring a right to additions to the goods supplied will not amount to a bill of sale if those additions were acquired by the buyer after the conclusion of the contract.

Bills of Sale and New Products

In *Borden* v. *Scottish Timber Products Ltd.*[34] both Templeman and Buckley JJ. were of opinion that a seller's rights in products manufactured out of the original materials supplied must be based on express contractual stipulation. They further believed that a provision conferring such rights operated by way of security and was registrable as a bill of sale. Leaving aside for a moment the contentious question whether such rights necessarily operate by way of security, there remains the question, assuming the former to be the case, that the rights amount to a bill of sale.

The stipulations relating to the new product will constitute a bill of sale only if they fall within the third limb of the definition provided by section 4 of the Bills of Sale Act 1878. It has been argued that the seller should claim ownership of the product after a new act has been performed by the buyer.[35] If the legal title is held to pass, the document will not then be a bill of sale. There follows the difficult question of laying bare the meaning of the phrase "new act."

According to Tindal C.J. in *Lunn* v. *Thornton*[36] the act must be done for "the avowed object and with the view of carrying the former grant or disposition into effect." The *Akron* case and *Reeves* v. *Barlow* supply examples of "new acts" sufficient to satisfy the doctrine. In *Akron* the

---

[33] (1951) 82 C.L.R. 477, 493.
[34] [1981] Ch. 25, 42, 44–45.
[35] See Alexander Hill-Smith, "Updating the Romalpa Clause" (1980) 130 New L.J. 529.
[36] (1845) 1 C.B. 379.

attachment of goods on to property which belonged to the transferee was held to be a "new act" and in *Reeves* v. *Barlow* the taking of possession of goods by the transferee was held to be of equivalent status. Neither option is likely in practice to be available to a seller where new products have been manufactured out of the materials he supplied.

One commentator has suggested the insertion in a sale of goods contract of a clause requiring separate storage. In his view separate storage would constitute the "new act" at which point property would pass to sellers. The existence of such a new act would permit property to pass at common law with all the problems bound up with the Bills of Sale Act having been circumvented.[37] Others are sceptical about the courts acceding to this argument.[38] Presumably one should insist that the new products be separated from the buyer's own goods. The courts, however, may not take the view that such separation is effected in the words of Tindal C.J. "for the avowed object and with the view of carrying the former grant or disposition into effect."

Dicta in *Holroyd* v. *Marshall* have been referred to in support of the proposition that the submission of an account by the buyer to the seller specifying new products made and acknowledging that they belong to the seller constitutes a new act.[39] If this be so, then a relatively carefree way of avoiding Bills of Sale complications is at hand. It is doubtful whether the court would look with favour on a new act manufactured out of such circumstances. One might predict a degree of judicial hostility to the new act principle.

Transfer of Goods in the Ordinary Course of any Trade or Calling

Section 4 of the 1878 Act exempts from the category of "bills of sale" transfers of goods made in the ordinary course of any trade or calling. At first, it appears a little incongruous to imagine how this provision might apply in a reservation of title context. The exemption presupposes first of all the transfer of title to the goods to the buyer, contrary to the express purpose of the reservation of title clause and secondly the retransfer of rights back to the seller in the ordinary course of a trade or calling. In 1977 the view was expressed that *Romalpa* clauses were not then sufficiently common to fall within this exemption if reliance needed to be placed thereon to escape the bills of sale legislation.[40] It has been suggested that there seems no reason not to apply the exception to *Romalpa* clauses.[41] The decided cases so far have covered letters of hypothecation and lien over trading stock executed by traders in need of short-term finance. The object, however, is the same in

---

[37] See Hill-Smith, *op. cit.*
[38] See (1981) 131 New L.J. 843.
[39] *Ibid.* [1922] 2 Ch. 211.
[40] See Farrar and Furey, "Reservation of Ownership and Tracing in a Commercial Context" (1977) 36 C.L.J. 27.
[41] [1981] J.B.L. 173, 175.

this situation and the reservation of title context: the regular use of trading stock as security for recurring obligations.

The leading case on the exception is *Re Young, Hamilton and Co., ex p. Carter*.[42] The case concerned a Manchester textile partnership which shipped goods to India. The firm was desirous of obtaining a loan from its bank. To facilitate this course it gave in accordance with its business practice letters of equitable charge or hypothecation over goods in its possession or in possession of its bailees. The partnership went bankrupt and the trustee in bankruptcy claimed that the letters constituted bills of sale and, being unregistered, were void as against him. Bigham J., at first instance, rejected this contention on the grounds, *inter alia*, that the letters amounted to a transfer of goods in the ordinary course of business. The Court of Appeal, however, managed to avoid making any definitive pronouncement on this particular issue.

How far the exception extends at the present time is largely a matter of conjecture, and in particular, whether reservation of title clauses fall within the exception. Perhaps there is an analogy with the doctrine of reputed ownership which applied in individual bankruptcy until it was swept away by the Insolvency Act reforms of 1985–1986.[43] Under the doctrine where a bankrupt had in his possession, at the time of bankruptcy, goods whereof he was reputed owner, the court had power to order that such goods be held for the benefit of his creditors. The custom of obtaining on hire-purchase practically every article employed in trade and businesses, however, made it virtually impossible to establish a right in the trustee in bankruptcy to goods belonging to other parties.[44] The reputed ownership doctrine before its abolition became more a nuisance than anything else. Perhaps the prevalence of reservation of title clauses in the modern business world has done the same to the bills of sale legislation at least in so far as it impinges on this area.

Reputed Ownership Doctrine

Where goods were supplied to an individual trader or partnership prior to the repeal of the reputed ownership doctrine by the Insolvency Act 1985, it was problematic whether a reservation of title clause was effective. Under section 38(a) of the Bankruptcy Act 1914 the property of the bankrupt included "all goods being, at the commencement of the bankruptcy, in the possession, order, and disposition of the bankrupt, in his trade and business, by the consent and permission of the true owner, under such circumstances that he is the reputed owner thereof." The purpose behind the provision was to preclude a trader from obtaining false credit by the apparent possession

---

[42] [1905] 2 K.B. 772. See also, *Re Slee, ex p. North Western Bank* (1872) L.R. 15 Eq. 69.
[43] For a consideration of the reputed ownership doctrine in the context of reservation of title clauses, see Allcock, "Romalpa Clauses and Reputed Ownership" (1981) 131 New L.J. 942.
[44] See the Cork Committee (Cmnd. 8558), para. 1088.

and ostensible ownership of property in the form of trade goods which in reality belonged to other people.[45]

Lord Blackburn in *Colonial Bank* v. *Whinney*[46] made it clear that it is a question of fact whether or not the circumstances are such as to create the reputation of ownership. Furthermore, the reputation of ownership was capable of being rebutted, by proving the existence of a notorious custom that goods of the particular description are in the possession of persons who are not the owners.[47] The Blagden Committee in 1957 were of opinion that the practice described above of procuring on hire-purchase almost every article used in trades and businesses made it very difficult for the trustee in bankruptcy to claim goods belonging to other parties.[48] Moreover, the Committee drew attention to the non-existent perils of a creditor being induced to give credit by an assumption that all goods in the possession of the debtor were his own property.[49]

In the retention of title context it has been suggested that the simplest method of overriding the effect of the law on reputed ownership was for the seller to require the buyer to indorse a memorandum on his or her accounts stating the seller's rights over the goods and proceeds of sale.[50] The efficacy of this device was never tested. The reputed ownership doctrine never applied to companies.[51] It was laid to rest completely by the Insolvency Act reforms of 1985–1986.[52]

General Assignment of Book Debts

Choses in action are outside the ambit of the Bills of Sale Acts.[53] Section 344 of the Insolvency Act 1986, however, invalidates general assignments of existing or future book debts by a trader in certain circumstances.[54] The section applies whenever a person engaged in any business makes a general assignment to another person of his existing or future book debts, or any class of them and is subsequently adjudged bankrupt. Such an assignment is void against the trustee of the bankrupt's estate as regards book debts which were not paid before the presentation of the bankruptcy petition, unless the

---

[45] See the comments of James L.J. in *ex p. Wingfield* (1879) 10 Ch.D. 591, 594:

> "It has always been construed as meaning this: that if goods are in a man's possession, or disposition, under such circumstances as to enable him by means of them to obtain false credit, then the owner of the goods who has permitted him to obtain that false credit is to suffer the penalty of losing his goods for the benefit of those who had given the credit."

[46] [1886] 11 A.C. 426.
[47] See Cork Report, *op. cit.* para. 1087.
[48] Cmnd. 221, para. 110.
[49] The Committee considered that the doctrine had become obsolete and served no useful purpose.
[50] See Allcock, "Romalpa Clauses and Reputed Ownership" (1981) 131 New L.J. 941.
[51] *Gorringe* v. *Irwell India Rubber and Gutta Percha Works* (1886) 34 Ch.D. 128.
[52] See now Insolvency Act 1986, s. 283; see also, Insolvency Act 1985, s. 130.
[53] s. 4 of the Bills of Sale Act 1878.
[54] The section replaces, with minor terminological changes, s. 43 of the Bankruptcy Act 1914.

assignment has been registered under the Bills of Sale Act. The expression "assignment" includes an assignment by way of security or charge on book debts.

It has been argued that an assignment under a *Romalpa* clause, by the buyer to the seller of existing or future debts due to the buyer from sub-purchasers of the goods, would be caught by this provision.[55] There are two escape routes from this conclusion. First, it might be contended that the seller's interest in proceeds of sub-sales is not created by the buyer. Instead it arises by operation of law in consequence of a sale by the buyer of property owned by the original seller.

Secondly, one might delve deeper into the wording of section 344. The section covers general assignments of existing or future book debts or any class of them. To make up a class of book debts it appears that some community of interest, or common characteristic or generic name must be discernible to identify the members of the alleged class.[56] In addition it is stated in section 344(3)(b) that "general assignment" does not include:

(1) an assignment of book debts due at the date of the assignment from specified debtors or of debts becoming due under specified contracts; or

(2) an assignment of book debts included either in a transfer of a business made in good faith and for value or in an assignment of assets for the benefit of creditors generally.

There has not been, though, a great deal of judicial guidance.[57] In the reservation of title context the crucial words are likely to be "becoming due under specified contracts." Note that the word is "specified" not "specific." In one textbook the matter is stated thus[58]:

"For debtors or contracts to be "specified" within this provision it would seem that the fact that the debts are identifiable from some document recording the transaction is insufficient: what the expression means, however, is not clear."

---

[55] *Benjamin's Sale of Goods, op. cit.* para. 392.
[56] See *Williams on Bankruptcy* (19th ed., 1979), p. 344 where reference is made to *Re Cornish, ex p. First County Finance Ltd.* v. *Trustee*, Divisional Court, December 21, 1955.
[57] But see *Re Cornish, supra,* and *Blakey* v. *Pendlebury Property Trustees* [1931] 2 Ch. 255.
[58] Fridman, Hicks and Johnson, *Bankruptcy Law and Practice* (1970), p. 188.

CHAPTER 9

RESERVATION OF TITLE AND PRIORITIES

One of the interesting and important issues thrown up by the *Romalpa* decision[1] lies in its potential effect on the practices of factoring companies. It was argued before the Cork Committee[2] that the proliferation of reservation of title clauses could strike at the system of credit. A major volume of the credit made available to industry is dependent upon the factoring of book debts. It may be that the claim of supply creditors to the book debts into which the goods supplied would, in the course of business, have been converted, would prevail over the claim of the factor who had bought the debts. If this were so, the flow of funds from factors could cease.[3] The effect of tracing rights arising from reservation of title clauses on factoring arrangements has generated considerable debate. To set the matter in context, it is necessary to state some of the background surrounding assignment of book debts.[4]

Assignment of Book Debts

A book debt is an item of incorporeal property—a chose in action as opposed to a chose in possession. It is incapable of physical possession. A chose in possession is a tangible thing. In general the common law sets its face against assignments of choses in action without the consent of the debtor, though there were certain exceptions to this opposition.[5] According to Coke assignments would be " . . . the occasion of multiplying of contentions and suits, of great oppression of the people . . . and the subversion of the due and equal execution of justice."[6]

Equity took a different view however. It permitted the assignment of both legal and equitable choses in action as well as possibilities.[7] In the case of an assignment in equity, if the assignee was seeking to sue the debtor he was

[1] [1976] 1 W.L.R. 676.
[2] Cmnd. 8558 (1982).
[3] *Ibid.* para. 1602.
[4] See generally, Marshall, *The Assignment of Choses in Action* (1950); Keeton and Sheridan, *Equity* (2nd ed., 1976), pp. 197–223; *Crossley Vaines' Personal Property* (5th ed., 1973), pp. 262–279.
[5] See generally, Marshall, *op. cit.* Chap. 2. He discusses the exceptions to the non-assignability rule at pp. 61–71.
[6] *Lampet's Case* (1613) 10 Co.Rep. 46b, 48a. There was also the objection that the relationship between obligor and obligee was too personal to permit the substitution of any other party: see generally, Spence, *Equitable Jurisdiction of the Court of Chancery*, Vol. 11, p. 850; Winfield (1919) 35 L.Q.R. 143.
[7] See Marshall, *op. cit.* Chap. 3.

faced with the hurdle of persuading the assignor to lend his name to the action. If such persuasion failed, the alternative was to bring a chancery action compelling the assignee to co-operate.[8] The Common Law Procedure Act 1854 had the effect of altering the procedure somewhat.[9] The modern practice was stated by Warrington J. in *Bowden's Patents Syndicate Ltd*. v. *Herbert Smith & Co.*[10]:

> "Now what is the general rule with regard to an action brought by an equitable owner of property? The common case with which we are most familiar is an action relating to some debt in respect of which the provisions of the Judicature Act have not been complied with. In that case . . . the well-accepted practice of this Court is that the legal owner of the property in question must be a party to the action either as plaintiff or defendant. He is the proper person to bring the action. If he does not bring the action then the course which the plaintiff adopts is that of proving that fact and making him a defendant."

Viscount Cave L.C. said much the same in *Performing Right Society Ltd*. v. *London Theatre of Varieties Ltd*. observing[11]:

> "That an equitable owner may commence proceedings alone, and may obtain interim protection in the form of an interlocutory injunction is not in doubt, but it was always the rule of the Court of Chancery, and is, I think, the rule of the Supreme Court that in general when a plaintiff has only an equitable right in the thing demanded the person having the legal right to demand it must in due course be made a party to the action."

Section 25(6) of the Supreme Court of Judicature Act 1873 allowed legal assignment of choses in action and permitted the assignor to sue in his own name. That subsection was re-enacted, with minor changes in terminology, by section 136(1) of the Law of Property Act 1925 but it does not appear any difference in result was intended. Section 136(1) provides:

> "Any absolute assignment by writing under the hand of the assignor (not purporting to be by way of charge only) of any debt or other legal chose in action of which express notice in writing has been given to the debtor, trustee or other person from whom the assignor would have been entitled to claim such debt or thing in action, is effectual in law (subject to equities having priority over the right of the assignee) to pass and transfer from the date of such notice
> (a) the legal right to such debt or thing in action;
> (b) all legal and other remedies for the same; and

---

[8] *Hammond* v. *Messenger* (1838) 9 Sim. 327; *Bolton* v. *Powell* (1851) 14 Beav. 275.
[9] s. 85.
[10] [1904] 2 Ch. 86, 91. See also Lord Macnaghten in *William Brandt's Sons & Co.* v. *Dunlop Rubber Co.* [1905] A.C. 454, 462.
[11] [1924] A.C. 1, 14. See also, *Williams* v. *Atlantic Assurance Co.* [1933] 1 K.B. 81; *Re Steel Wing Co.* [1921] 1 Ch. 349.

(c) the power to give a good discharge for the same without the concurrence of the assignor.

Provided that, if the debtor, trustee or other person liable in respect of such debt or thing in action has notice—

(a) that the assignment is disputed by the assignor or any person claiming under him; or

(b) of any other opposing or conflicting claims to such debt or thing in action;

he may, if he thinks fit, either call upon the persons making claim thereto to interplead concerning the same, or pay the debt or other thing in action into court under the provisions of the Trustee Act 1925."

Subject to Equities

The crucial phrase, for our purposes, is "subject to equities." Do these words include a prior equitable interest such as a seller's right to trace?[12] Most of the discussion in the cases has centred on defences that the debtor might have against the assignor. A leading authority is *Roxburghe* v. *Cox*.[13] Here James L.J. said that an assignee of a chose in action takes subject to all rights of set-off and other defences which were available against the assignor. This principle was subject to the exception that after notice of an assignment of a chose in action the debtor could not, by payment or otherwise, do anything to take away or diminish the rights of the assignee as they stood at the time of notice.[14]

The "subject to equities" principle was discussed at length and distinguished by the Court of Appeal in *Stoddart* v. *Union Trust Ltd.*[15] The defendants contracted to purchase a newspaper for £1,000, of which £200 was paid on completion of the contract and £800 was payable by certain instalments. The defendants were induced to enter into the contract by fraudulent representations made to them by the vendor. The latter assigned the £800 debt to the plaintiffs who were ignorant of the fraud. The plaintiffs communicated notice of the assignments to the defendants. Upon being sued by the plaintiffs, the defendants claimed that they had sustained damage in excess of £800 by reason of the fraud and that no money was due from them. The Court of Appeal held, however, that this claim to damages could not be set off against the plaintiff assignees.

Vaughan Williams L.J. referred to cases like *Young* v. *Kitchin*[16] and *Government of Newfoundland* v. *Newfoundland Ry, Co.*[17] They supported

---

[12] See generally, R. M. Goode, "The Right to Trace and its Impact in Commercial Transactions—II" (1976) 92 L.Q.R. 528, 556; *Commercial Law* (1982), pp. 872–873; D. W. McLauchlan, "Priorities—Equitable Tracing Rights and Assignment of Book Debts" (1980) 96 L.Q.R. 90.

[13] (1881) 17 Ch.D. 520.

[14] *Ibid.* 526. See also, *Re Knapman* (1881) 18 Ch.D. 300 and *Re Pain* [1919] 1 Ch. 38.

[15] [1912] 1 K.B. 181. Compare *Lawrence* v. *Hayes* [1927] 2 K.B. 111.

[16] (1878) 3 Ex.D. 127.

[17] [1888] 13 A.C. 199.

the proposition that matters flowing out of, and inseparably connected with, the contract which gave rise to the chose in action assigned may be set up by way of defence as against an assignee suing in respect thereof.[18] But this principle had no application to the facts of the case.

Kennedy C.J. subscribed to the same view. He said that the defendants were claiming damages for the fraud which induced them to enter into the contract on the footing that they were liable under it. At the same time they were seeking to repudiate their obligations under the contract. The claim for damages was a personal claim against the wrongdoer *dehors* the contract.[19]

The defendants had recovered on a counterclaim against the assignor but both claim and counterclaim had been tried contemporaneously when the action was first heard. Nothing had accrued under the counterclaim before notice of the assignment. Kennedy C.J. added that if the case had been one in which the defendants were entitled to elect and had elected, on the ground of fraud, to cancel and rescind the contract, and treat it as void, a different situation might have arisen.[20]

Seller's Right to Trace Proceeds of Sale as an Equity

As we have seen, it is well-settled that an assignment is subject to equities of the debtor against the assignor. The question remains to what extent he is bound by equities of third parties *vis-à-vis* the assignor. On this issue, academic debate has raged between Professor Goode and D.W. McLauchlan. According to the latter commentator the phrase "equities" in section 136 should be read as a convenient compendious phrase for equitable remedies and rights, personal and proprietary, thus encompassing equitable interests held by third parties.[21] This exegesis meant that in determining priorities one was thrown back on the general law.

Professor Goode's view at first was that while the *Romalpa* seller being prior in time had initial priority, this could be displaced if the factor got in the legal title, having advanced his money without notice of the seller's rights.[22] To put it another way, the bona fide purchaser for value without notice rule operated. That rule was conveniently summed up by James L.J. in *Pilcher* v. *Rawlins*.[23] While that was a case involving realty the statement of general principle still holds good. He said[24]:

---

[18] [1912] 1 K.B. 181, 189.
[19] *Ibid*. 194.
[20] *Ibid*. 194–195.
[21] McLauchlan, *op. cit.* 92.
[22] (1976) 92 L.Q.R. 528, 556. Goode's view was criticised by Donaldson (1977) 93 L.Q.R. 342. Donaldson argued that the *tabula in naufragio* permitted by the bona fide purchaser doctrine did not apply where an assignor disposed of assets in breach of trust. Moreover, a conditional buyer, who was accountable for proceeds of sub-sales took them as constructive trustee. For Goode's reply to this line of argument see (1977) 93 L.Q.R. 487. In essence, Professor Goode responded by saying that the exception alluded to by Donaldson was confined to express trusts. See generally, *Bailey* v. *Barnes* [1894] 1 Ch. 25; *Taylor* v. *Russell* [1892] A.C. 244.
[23] (1872) 7 Ch.App. 259.
[24] *Ibid*. 268, 269.

> "... a ... plea of purchase for valuable consideration without notice is an absolute, unqualified, unanswerable defence. ... Such a purchaser may be interrogated and tested to any extent as to the valuable consideration which he has given in order to show the *bona fides* or *mala fides* of his purchase, and also the presence or absence of notice, but when once he has gone through that ordeal, and has satisfied the terms of the plea of purchase for valuable consideration without notice then ... this Court has no jurisdiction whatever to do anything more than let him depart in possession of that legal estate, that legal right, that legal advantage which he has obtained, whatever it may be. In such a case, a purchaser is entitled to hold that which, without breach of duty, he has had conveyed to him."

In fact, there is authority supporting the application of the bona fide purchaser rule in the context of statutory assignments of book debts. This authority comes in the shape of dicta in the House of Lords case of *Performing Right Society Ltd.* v. *London Theatre of Varieties Ltd.*[25] The facts of that case are not relevant for present purposes. Suffice it to say that Viscount Finlay envisaged a situation where a person who had made an equitable assignment might by a subsequent assignment have transferred the legal interest in the same work to a purchaser for value without notice. The latter's title, he said, would prevail over the merely equitable right.[26]

In *E. Pfeiffer-Weinkellerei-Weineinkauf G.m.b.H. & Co.* v. *Arbuthnot Factors Ltd.*[27] however, Phillips J. ruled out application of the bona fide purchaser doctrine. Given the potential importance of *Pfeiffer* it is appropriate to discuss the case in detail.

Pfeiffer—the Facts and Result

In this case the plaintiff was a German company which carried on business as an exporter of wines. The company sold wine to an English importer on terms which included a property reservation clause. That clause lost some grammatical elegance after translation from the German. Basically, however, it provided that the goods remained the plaintiff's property until they had been paid for. In addition, the clause permitted the importer to resell the goods. The following is a verbatim transcription of further provisions in the clause with all oddities included:

---

[25] [1924] A.C. 1.
[26] *Ibid.* 19. See also, Viscount Cave at 14 and Lord Sumner at 28. See generally, Biscoe, *Law and Practice of Credit Factoring* (1975), pp. 132–139. Oditah (1989) 9 O.J.L.S. 521 argues strongly for the application of the bona fide purchaser rule. In addition to *Performing Rights Society Ltd.* v. *London Theatre of Varieties Ltd.* [1924] A.C. 1 he cites dicta of Lord Macnaghten in *Ward* v. *Duncombe* [1893] A.C. 369, 392 and Robert Goff L.J. in *Ellerman Lines Ltd.* v. *Lancaster Maritime Co. Ltd.* [1980] 2 Lloyd's Rep. 497, 503 in support of the bona fide purchaser rule. Oditah concedes however, that the opinion he is propounding may appear to some as a minority view, *op. cit.* at 527.
[27] [1988] 1 W.L.R. 150. For a detailed account and analysis of the case see McCormack [1989] L.M.C.L.Q. 198. See also Lawson [1988] L.M.C.L.Q. 141.

"All claims that [the importer] gets from the sale ... with all rights including his profit amounting to his obligation towards [Pfeiffer], will be passed on to [Pfeiffer]. On demand the [importer] is obliged to notify the assignment of the claim to give [Pfeiffer] in written all necessary information concerning the assertion of [Pfeiffer's] claims. ... In case of cash sales, the money that has come from a third person immediately becomes [Pfeiffer's] ... this money has to be separated from other money, it must be booked correspondingly, and must be administered until called for."

As was its wont, the English importer, Springfield, sub-sold the wine on credit terms. Then Springfield entered into a factoring agreement whereby it agreed to assign to the defendant Arbuthnot Factors Ltd. absolutely debts owed to the importer by sub-purchasers. The agreement included a term by virtue of which Springfield warranted that "no reservation of title by any third party will apply to all or any part of the goods sold" by the importer.

Assignments were effected in accordance with the terms of the agreement. Notice of assignments were given to the sub-purchasers both by the factor and by Springfield. This helped satisfy the requirements of section 136 of the Law of Property Act 1925 so as to vest in the defendant a legal title to the debts. Arbuthnot were paid by the sub-purchasers in compliance with the terms of the notice of assignment. Springfield did not pay Pfeiffer all the sums due to it. Consequently Pfeiffer instituted proceedings in which it claimed (a) to be the beneficial owner of the proceeds of each sub-sale and (b) that Arbuthnot's title to the debts assigned under the factoring agreement ranked after Pfeiffer's prior equitable title. The plaintiffs accordingly sought an order that Arbuthnot account to it for, and pay over, the moneys received under the assignments made pursuant to the factoring agreement. By its defence Arbuthnot claimed that (a) any interest which Pfeiffer had in the proceeds of the sub-sales was in the nature of a charge on the importer's property.

The learned judge took the view that clause 5 of the supply contract constituted an agreement by Springfield to assign to the plaintiff future choses in action, namely future debts owed by sub-purchasers to Springfield to the plaintiff. In so far as debts came into existence falling within that agreement, the agreement was held to create an equitable assignment of the debts. Phillips J. stated that the agreement was by way of security, and the assignments under it were capable of being redeemed by payment by Springfield of the outstanding indebtedness. The consequence of this line of reasoning was that by agreeing to the provisions of clause 5 Springfield created a charge by way of security over certain of its assets, namely book debts, which being unregistered was rendered void as against Springfield's creditors by sections 395(1) and 396(1)(e) of the Companies Act 1985.

Phillip J.'s conclusions on the registration issue were enough to dispose of the case in favour of Arbuthnot. If the reservation of title clause created a charge over the assets of Springfield and this charge was void against

Arbuthnot for want of registration, then *Pfeiffer* were relegated to the position of unsecured creditors *vis-à-vis* Arbuthnot. He went on though to consider the question of priorities in the event of his being wrong on the registration point. He held that the priority of interests as between the plaintiff and the defendant depended on the order in which notice of their respective interests had been given to the sub-purchaser. Arbuthnot Factors had been the first to give such notice and therefore they enjoyed priority over the interest of *Pfeiffer*. A *Romalpa* supplier may however take a crumb of comfort from the case in that Phillips J. discounted the bona fide purchaser doctrine in the context of section 136 of the Law of Property Act.

The learned judge looked at the legislative history of section 136. The section succeeded section 25(6) of the Judicature Act 1873. That subsection contained an even clearer expression of the "subject to equities" exception. An assignment that went through the hoops of the statutory procedure was deemed effectual in law "subject to all equities which would have been entitled to priority over the right of the assignee if this Act had not been passed. . . ."

According to Phillips J. the submission that "subject to equities" included the equitable interests of a third party was more soundly based upon the natural meaning of the statutory wording.[28] One might also refer to the aim of the subsection which was to amend procedure.[29] Further than that, it was not intended to do so. For instance, witness the statement of Channell J. in *Torkington* v. *Magee*[30] where he said[31]:

> "[T]his subsection is merely machinery, it enables an action to be brought by the assignee in his own name in cases where previously he would have sued in the assignor's name but only where he could so sue."

Even stronger is the opinion of Lord Macnaghten in *William Brandt's Sons & Co.* v. *Dunlop Rubber Co.*[32] He said that the statute "does not forbid or destroy equitable assignments or impair their efficacy in the slightest degree."[33] It is relatively easy to multiply examples but the point appears already made. The provision for statutory assignment of book debts did not signify a new departure in substantive policy; rather it shortened and simplified the procedure. There was no intention to introduce a new set of priority rules but what exactly did the section leave in place? Is priority to be accorded to the first in time or does the rule in *Dearle* v. *Hall*[34] apply?

[28] He referred to *Marchant* v. *Morton, Down & Co.* [1901] 2 K.B. 829, 832 and also to *Halsbury's Statutes of England* (3rd ed., 1971), Vol. 27, p. 549 as well as *Snell's Principles of Equity* (28th ed., 1982), p. 82.
[29] See Sargant J. in *Re Westerton* [1919] 2 Ch. 104.
[30] [1902] 2 K.B. 427.
[31] *Ibid.* 435. See also the observations of Lord Lindley in *Tolhurst* v. *Associated Portland Cement Manufacturers (1900) Ltd.* [1903] A.C. 414, 424 that it "has not made contracts assignable which were not assignable in equity before, but it has enabled assigns of assignable contracts to sue upon them in their own names without joining the assignor."
[32] [1905] A.C. 454.
[33] *Ibid.* 461.
[34] (1828) 3 Russ. 1. In the Canadian case *Harding Carpets Ltd.* v. *Royal Bank of Canada* [1980] 4 W.W.R. 149 it was held that the rule in *Dearle* v. *Hall* applied to determine priorities so that a

Rule in *Dearle* v. *Hall*

As Phillips J. explained in *Pfeiffer* the rule in *Dearle* v. *Hall* is an exception to the general principle that equitable interests take priority in the order in which they are created. The effect of the rule is that priority turns upon the order in which notice of the interest created by the dealing is given to the person affected by it, *i.e.* in the case of assignments of a debt, the debtor.[35]

Dearle v. *Hall* is a case where a person had a beneficial interest in a sum of money invested in the name of trustees. He assigned it for valuable consideration to A but no notice of the assignment was given to the trustees. Afterwards, the same person proposed to sell his interest to B. The latter made inquiry of the trustees as to the nature of the vendor's title, and the amount of his interest. He received no intimation of the existence of any prior incumbrance. This being so B completed the purchase and gave the trustees notice. It was held that B had a better equity than A to the possession of the fund. The assignment to B, though posterior in terms of time, was to be preferred to the assignment to A.

There are two justifications for the rule in *Dearle* v. *Hall* both of which derive a measure of support from that case itself. The first view is that notice to the legal holder of the fund is a must to perfect the transfer of a chose in action. Plumer M.R. observed[36]:

> "Notice, then, is necessary to perfect the title—to give a complete right *in rem*, and not merely a right as against him who conveys his interest . . . these are principles on which I think to be very old law, that possession, or what is tantamount to possession, is the criterion of perfect title to personal chattels, and that he who does not obtain such possession must take his chance."

This rationale was stated to be the true reason for the rule by Shadwell V.-C. in *Jones* v. *Jones*.[37] There is another principle, however, namely prevention of fraud, that also lies at the basis of the rule. In *Dearle* v. *Hall*, Plumer M.R. opined that the omission to give notice enabled the assignor to "carry the same security repeatedly into the market" and thereby to induce "third persons to advance money upon it in the erroneous belief that it continues to belong to him absolutely, free from encumbrance." In short, some scrutiny of the conduct of the competing assignees was appropriate. One had to decide whether a subsequent assignee had been misled by receiving no intimation of the earlier incumbrance upon making inquiries of the trustees.

specific legal assignment prevailed over a prior general assignment because notice of it was given to the debtor before notice of the earlier general equitable assignment. The result would have been the same, however, had the bona fide purchaser rule been applied.

[35] [1988] 1 W.L.R. 150, 163.

[36] (1828) 3 Russ 1, 24. See generally, Firth, "The Rule in Dearle v. Hall" (1985) 11 L.Q.R. 337.

[37] (1838) 8 Sim. 633. See also Wigram V.-C. in *Meux* v. *Bell* (1841) 1 Hare 73; Jessel M.R. in *Re Freshfield's Trusts* (1879) 11 Ch.D. 202 and Kay L.J. in *Arden* v. *Arden* (1885) 29 Ch.D. 708.

The House of Lords decided in *Foster* v. *Cockerell*[38] though that the absence of inquiries was immaterial. Priority simply depends upon being the first to give notice to the trustees, subject to the proviso that the subsequent assignee does not have actual or constructive notice of the earlier assignment at the time when he takes his security.[39] So we have the application of a mechanical rule of thumb.[40]

In *Gorringe* v. *Irwell India Rubber and Gutta Percha Works*,[41] it was assumed that this rule of thumb applied to competing assignments of debts. Assumption became an actual decision in *Marchant* v. *Morton Down & Co.*[42] Here, a debt due to a firm was assigned by one partner to the defendants by writing. It was later assigned by the other partners to the plaintiff by deed. The plaintiff gave the debtor notice of assignment before the defendants. Channell J. held that the plaintiff's notice was good, and being prior to that of the defendants, had the effect of displacing them.

In *Pfeiffer*, counsel on behalf of the defendant conceded that if the rights being asserted by the plaintiff were rights accruing from an equitable assignment, then *Dearle* v. *Hall* must apply. Phillips J. had already reached the conclusion that clause 5 of the agreement between plaintiff and wine importer constituted an equitable assignment of future book debts in favour of the plaintiff. From this followed the conclusion that *Dearle* v. *Hall* applied and that the defendants had priority in that they were the first to give notice to sub-purchasers of the goods supplied. The judge appears to have left unresolved the priority issue if an equitable tracing right arising by operation of law from a fiduciary relationship competes against an equitable assignment.[43]

Exceptions to the Application of *Dearle* v. *Hall*

A number of reasons have been adduced for not applying *Dearle* v. *Hall* to determine priorities where a *Romalpa* supplier is pitted against an assignee of debts arising from sub-sales.[44] First, there is support for the view that the rule should not be extended to "novel" situations. In *Ward* v. *Duncombe*[45] Lord Macnaghten spoke about the undesirability of doing anything to

---

[38] (1835) 9 Bl.N.S. 332. In *Re Lake ex p. Cavendish* [1903] 1 K.B. 151, 154 Wright J. said that in modern times the court only asked which assignee was the first to protect his security by notice.
[39] See *Spencer* v. *Clarke* (1878) 9 Ch.D. 137; *Mutual Life Assurance Society* v. *Langley* (1886) 32 Ch.D. 460 and *English and Scottish Investment Trust* v. *Brunton* [1892] 2 Q.B. 1. *Rhodes* v. *Allied Dunbar Pension Services Ltd.* [1987] 1 W.L.R. 1703 (H.C.); [1989] 1 W.L.R. 800 (C.A.).
[40] For an example of the apparent injustice of such application see *Re Dallas* [1904] 2 Ch. 385. Oditah, *op. cit.* 525–527, advances eight considerations in support of the notion that the rule is harsh, hard to justify and decidedly inconvenient. He concludes by suggesting that there is no convincing argument of principle or policy why it should be extended to a contest between a prior equitable assignment and a subsequent bona fide legal assignee.
[41] (1886) 34 Ch.D. 128.
[42] [1901] 2 K.B. 829.
[43] [1988] 1 W.L.R. 150, 163.
[44] See McLauchlan, *op. cit.* 95–100.
[45] [1893] A.C. 369.

extend that doctrine to cases which are not already covered by it. Secondly, the rule is reckoned to be an unsatisfactory determinant of priority in situations of stock-in-trade and receivables financing.[46] We have the opinion of the Crowther Committee on Consumer Credit to that effect.[47]

The third reason argues by analogy from two judicial decisions. The first in point of time, but lesser in status, is *Hill* v. *Peters*.[48]

Here, it was held that *Dearle* v. *Hall* had no application where a declaration of trust was ranged against a subsequent mortgage. The title of the *cestui que trust* under the declaration of trust did not require to be perfected by notice according to Eve J. Consequently, the defendant, as beneficiary under the declaration, was entitled to priority over the subsequent mortgagees who had given notice. He endorsed the observations of Lord Macnaghten in *Ward* v. *Duncombe* about the disadvantages of applying *Dearle* v. *Hall* and went on to say[49]:

> "The principle on which the rule in *Dearle* v. *Hall* is founded, which regards the giving of notice by the assignee as the nearest approach to the taking of possession, has no application in my opinion, to the beneficiary who has no right to possession himself, and who can only assert his claim to receive through his trustee."

Hill v. *Peters* has been subjected to searching criticism. For instance, Peter Biscoe in *Law and Practice of Credit Factoring*[50] contends that the decision paves the way for fraud. If no requirement of notice is cast upon a *cestui que trust*, then third parties may be unable to ascertain the existence of a trust. In his view[51]:

> "It is an example of a case where the Court paid too much attention to the form of the instrument which created the security. If the attention had been focused on effect rather than on form, it would have been seen that the object of a trust by way of security is the same as the object of an agreement by way of security."

The second case to be mentioned is the House of Lords decision in *B.S. Lyle Ltd.* v. *Rosher*.[52] The facts are somewhat complicated and for our purposes there is no need for a detailed investigation. Two strands are discernible in the judgments. On the one hand we have Lord Reid who accepted the correctness of *Hill* v. *Peters*. His Lordship suggested that to use *Dearle* v. *Hall* as a trump card to defeat the rights of a *cestui que trust* would

---

[46] See Ziegel, "The Legal Problems of Wholesale Financing of Durable Goods in Canada" (1963) 41 *Canadian Bar Review* 54, 109–110; and Goode (1976) 92 L.Q.R. 528, 566. See also, Oditah, *op. cit.* 525–527.
[47] Cmnd. 4596, Vol. 2, p. 579.
[48] [1918] 2 Ch. 273.
[49] *Ibid.* 279.
[50] Butterworths, London 1975.
[51] *Ibid.* 138.
[52] [1959] 1 W.L.R. 8.

introduce an exception to the general law. The rights of a *cestui que trust* were different from those of an assignee. To apply the rule would be to amplify its application at variance with the edict expressed in a number of cases.[53] Lord Reid's judgment has been criticised on the score that it does not clarify an arbitrary rule but rather introduces an arbitrary exception to it.[54]

The majority did not rely on *Hill* v. *Peters*. Instead they invoked a second ground of decision that may afford another means of escaping the effect of the rule in the *Romalpa* context. Viscount Kilmuir L.C. said the doctrine had never been used without there being someone who had at one time a beneficial interest. He further stated[55]:

> "I do not think that the rule would be restricted beyond its intendment or present effect if it were held to apply only where, at the time of the assignment, the assignor had a beneficial interest or had no beneficial interest only because he had voluntarily divested himself of it."

Lord Cohen ventured the same view holding that it would be an extension of the rule to say that the creator of incumbrances could give to a second incumbrance a larger equitable right than he himself had.[56]

But Lord Reid for one was unimpressed. He was unable to appreciate the significance of the distinction between an "assignor" who never had an interest and one who had parted with the whole of it.[57] Moreover, there are certain cases not cited in *Lyle Ltd.* v. *Rosher* that point towards a different conclusion than that taken by the majority.[58]

One case in point is *English and Scottish Mercantile Investment Trust* v. *Brunton*.[59] Here a company issued debentures creating a floating charge over all its property, present and future. The debenture also contained a restrictive clause restraining the company from creating any charge in priority to the debentures. Subsequently, after the company had become entitled to money under an insurance policy, it purported to mortgage the money due to it. The mortgagee gave notice to the insurance company before the debenture holders.

Charles J. took the view that the mortgagee had priority to the debenture holders. In his opinion, it was the giving of notice which creates the priority. If the former assignee was prevented from giving notice, either by contract with the assignor, as might often be the case, or by the nature of the charge

---

[53] *Ibid*. 22. Lord Reid also referred to *Shropshire Union Railways & Canal Co.* v. *R.* (1875) L.R. 7 H.L. 496.

[54] See Keeton and Sheridan, *op. cit.* 208.

[55] [1959] 1 W.L.R. 8, 14.

[56] *Ibid*. 24.

[57] *Ibid*. 19–20. See also, Lord Keith at 25.

[58] The decision has been criticised by Elphinstone, "The Mischief of Secret Trusts" (1961) 77 L.Q.R. 69. See also, McLauchlan, *op. cit.* 96 who suggests that the *ratio* in *Lyle* may be limited to situations where the assignor had neither legal nor beneficial ownership.

[59] [1892] 2 Q.B. 1. See also, *Meux* v. *Bell* (1841) 1 Hare 73; *Hallows* v. *Lloyd* (1888) 39 Ch.D. 686.

which he holds, the same result should follow as in a case where a prior assignee had negligently omitted to give notice which he might have given.[60]

This case suggests that the rule in *Dearle* v. *Hall* may apply, notwithstanding the fact that the assignor never has the totality of the beneficial interest in a fund when it comes into existence.

Be that as it may, the cases do not seem to provide a conclusive indicator, one way or the other. Most commentators agree though, that the *Romalpa* seller versus factor situation falls within the spirit of the rule.[61] Further, that purely theoretical distinctions like that between an equitable assignment and a trust by way of security ought to have no influence on priorities.

As Professor Goode suggests, there is a strong case for using the rule in *Dearle* v. *Hall* to regulate the priority conflict.[62] Although an equitable tracing right in the situation of a *Romalpa* sale will arise, in appropriate cases, as a matter of law, the supplier chooses the form of his interest by laying down an accounting obligation in the sales contract. He has left himself with an equitable interest in debts arising from sub-sales, knowing full well that they may be disposed of to a bona fide purchaser. Therefore, his complaints carry little sympathy if the rule is applied to relegate him in the priority stakes where the purchaser of the book debts is the first to give notice to the debtor.

Perhaps there is an element of tautology in this argument for no reasons are put forward for applying *Dearle* v. *Hall* other than broad considerations of justice and equity. It may be said however, that the courts have narrowed the operation of reservation of title clauses. With this background in mind, the use of "normal" priority principles, *i.e. Dearle* v. *Hall* hardly strikes one as an unduly severe restriction on the reservation of title clause.

If the rule applies in this particular priority conflict, then the factor should enjoy the spoils of victory in the bulk of cases. He is conditioned to providing notices of assignment whereas this practice is foreign to the seller of goods subject to a reservation of title clause.

Actual Receipt of the Debts as a Priority Point

In *Pfeiffer* Phillips J. mentioned, though without adjudicating upon, a point that arose late in argument. Assuming that the plaintiff's equitable interest in the debts owed by the sub-purchasers had priority to that of the defendant as statutory assignee the question was raised whether the fact that the defendant had actually been paid the debts entitled it to claim precedence as a bona fide purchaser for value of the legal title in the payments received.[63] *Taylor* v. *Blakelock*[64] was cited to justify an affirmative answer to that question.

[60] *Ibid.* 8.
[61] See McLauchlan, *op. cit.* 98; Ziegel, *op. cit.* 110.
[62] *Commercial Law* (1982) 873.
[63] [1988] 1 W.L.R. 150, 163.
[64] (1886) 32 Ch.D. 560.

To generalise the debate, we are inquiring whether priority may be awarded to him who collects the debt provided that he has no notice that another assignee has been the first to give notice to the debtor. The debate is conducted on the assumption that *Dearle* v. *Hall* normally governs priorities. *Taylor* v. *Blakelock* would indeed appear to warrant an affirmative response to that query.

It was a case where one C was a co-trustee of two funds. He misappropriated moneys from one fund (Fund B). Later he used a sum from the other Fund (Fund A) to purchase stock which was transferred into the name of Fund B. It was held that Fund B could not be compelled to transfer the stock to Fund A. The defendant, who was a co-trustee of Fund B, had by accepting the transfer of the stock given up his right to sue C for his debt to Fund B. He was entitled to be treated as a purchaser for value without notice, and consequently to retain the stock as part of Fund B.

Bowen L.J. said bluntly that the defendant had a legal right to this property and why on earth was it to be taken away from him.[65] It could only be divested on the basis of some breach of trust which affects it. If he had notice of the breach of trust, his legal title would be swept aside. If he was a volunteer he could not stand in a better position than the person who conveyed to him but not being a volunteer his position was impregnable in the circumstances.

Cotton L.J. cited *Thorndike* v. *Hunt*[66] which lends tacit support to the position adopted in *Taylor* v. *Blakelock*. *Thorndike* v. *Hunt* is concerned with payments into court which were affected with a breach of trust. The Appeal Court took up a stance in line with the notion that the position of a bona fide purchaser for value of the legal title in payments received is unassailable. Turner C.J. opined that if the position were otherwise he could not see how any person could be safe in getting funds out of court which had been paid in for his benefit, without having made inquiry to whom the funds originally belonged.[67]

Conclusion

By way of conclusion, it is suggested that the following propositions apply with respect to priorities where a seller of goods subject to a reservation of title clause is competing against a factor of book debts.

(1) A statutory assignment of book debts is no more effectual than an equitable assignment. The phrase "subject to equities" in section 136(1) of the Law of Property Act 1925 includes equitable interests of third parties.

(2) Where a provision in a *Romalpa* clause relating to book debts arising

[65] *Ibid*. 569.
[66] (1859) 44 E.R. 1386.
[67] *Ibid*. 1389. There is also American authority for the *Taylor* v. *Blakelock* viewpoint. See Williston, *Contracts* (revised ed.), Vol. 3, p. 225, para. 435, where reference is made to *Judson* v. *Corcoran* 17 How (U.S.) 612, a decision of the American Supreme Court.

from sub-sales amounts to no more than an equitable assignment, then the seller will be postponed to a subsequent assignee of the book debts if the latter is the first to give notice to the debtors. In other words, the rule in *Dearle* v. *Hall* applies to determine priorities.

(3) More controversially, an equitable tracing right which derives from an accounting obligation in a *Romalpa* clause is subject to the rule in *Dearle* v. *Hall* so a subsequent factor will gain priority over a *Romalpa* supplier if he affords the debtor notice of his rights before the supplier.

(4) Irrespective of the rule in *Dearle* v. *Hall*, a person who is paid by the debtor is entitled to retain the payment if he is a bona fide purchaser for value without notice of any other assignment.

CHAPTER 10

RESALE OF GOODS SOLD
SUBJECT TO A RESERVATION OF TITLE CLAUSE

It may happen that a person who has agreed to buy goods subject to a reservation of title clause passes them on to a third party. The question arises as to the rights of the original seller in relation to the goods. Denning L.J. explained in *Bishopsgate Motor Finance Corporation Ltd.* v. *Transport Brakes Ltd.*[1] that in the development of our commercial law two principles have striven for mastery. The first is for the protection of property; no one can give a better title than he himself possesses. The second is for the protection of commercial transactions; the person who takes in good faith and for value without notice should get a good title.

The general rule is *nemo dat quod non habet.* This principle is encapsulated in section 21(1) of the Sale of Goods Act 1979. The provision reads as follows:

> "Subject to the provisions of this Act, where goods are sold by a person who is not the owner thereof, and who does not sell them under the authority, or with the consent of the owner, the buyer acquires no better title to the goods than the seller had, unless the owner of the goods is by his conduct precluded from denying the seller's authority to sell."

This statement of the general rule incorporates a couple of exceptions thereto; namely sale under the authority or with the consent of the owner and estoppel. There is also another exception relevant to the position of a purchaser of goods subject to a reservation of title clause. This is the situation of a disposition of goods by the buyer in possession.

Sales under the Authority or with the Consent of the Owner

If a sale is effected under the authority or with the consent of the true owner of the goods the latter will lose all his rights *in rem* in relation to the goods.

In many retention of title cases, the buyer is expressly given the right to sell goods that form the subject-matter of a retention of title clause. In many other instances, a power of resale can be implied. For example, a reservation of title clause may provide that the seller is to retain ownership of the goods until they shall have been resold by the purchaser in which case the seller's

---

[1] [1949] 1 All E.R. 37, 46.

155

rights shall attach to the proceeds of sale. In other cases the implication of an authority to resell is slightly more difficult but nevertheless a power of resale has been inferred. As an illustration one might cite the first of the relatively recent English cases on retention of title, *Aluminium Industrie Vaassen B.V. v. Romalpa Aluminium Ltd.*[2] In this case Roskill L.J. said[3]:

> "It was common ground at the trial and during argument in this court that some implication had to be made into the first part of cl. 13 [the reservation of title clause]: since otherwise the defendants could not lawfully sell the unmanufactured goods in their possession, at least until they were paid for—for, as already pointed out, they were the plaintiffs' and not the defendants' goods. To hold otherwise, as I think both parties accepted, would be to stultify the whole business purpose of these transactions."

The Lord Justice regarded the original buyer of the goods as occupying a curious hybrid position. The buyer was envisaged as selling as principal rather than as agent for the seller, although accounting as agent to the original seller for the proceeds of sale. *Romalpa* permits a party to appear as principal in his own right, while under an obligation to account to the original seller, in like manner as an agent being obliged to account to its principal for sale proceeds. The consequence of this duality of functions was that the sub-buyer could not sue the original seller for damages for breach of the statutory conditions of sale implied by sections 13–15 of the Sale of Goods Act 1979.[4]

The implication point also arose in *Four Point Garage Ltd.* v. *Carter.*[5] In this case the contractual nexus was between two commercial garages and the dispute related to a motor car. The vehicle was sold subject to the following clause: "The buyer is advised that title to the goods contained in this invoice remains with the seller until such goods are fully paid." The suppliers believed that the buyers did not sell motor cars but rather leased or hired them but the buyers were unaware of the sellers' misapprehension. Unlike in *Romalpa*, the goods were not being supplied for incorporation within a manufacturing process.

Simon Brown J., however, concluded that the *Romalpa* principle of implied authorisation to sub-sell could not be distinguished on the facts of the case. The totality of the circumstances warranted the implication of a term authorising the garage which buys from reselling the goods if that is in fact in the ordinary course of its business and if it is unaware that the selling garage believes otherwise.[6]

---

[2] [1976] 1 W.L.R. 676.
[3] *Ibid.* 689. See also, *Re Bond Worth Ltd.* [1980] Ch. 228, 246; *Archivent Sales and Developments* v. *Strathclyde R.C.* [1984] 27 Build L.R. 98.
[4] *Ibid.* 690. See *infra.*
[5] [1985] 3 All E.R. 12.
[6] *Ibid.* 16.

The supplier of goods may seek to negative the buyer's authority to sell by including a clause to this effect in the contract and also by including what the Germans call a *weitergeleitete eigensvorbeholsbetstimmung* (a "continuing retention of title clause").[7] A clause of this nature purports to retain in the seller ownership of the goods delivered as against the buyer and any sub-buyer until the full purchase price for those goods has been paid or until all debts owed by the buyer to the seller have been discharged. Such clauses are largely ineffective because of (1) possibly the principles of estoppel and (2) principally because of section 25(1) of the Sale of Goods Act 1979 and section 9 of the Factors Act 1889.

Estoppel

Section 21 of the Sale of Goods Act 1979 talks about situations where the owner of goods is by his conduct precluded from denying the seller's authority to sell. The nature of the estoppel arising by virtue of the section was discussed by Devlin J. in the Court of Appeal in *Eastern Distributors Ltd.* v. *Goldring*.[8] Reference was made to the view that an estoppel cannot affect the reality of the transaction. As Brett L.J. put it in *Simm* v. *Anglo-American Telegraph Co.*,[9] an estoppel assumes that the reality is contrary to that which the person is estopped from denying and the estoppel has no effect at all upon the reality of the circumstances.

An estoppel binds the representor and his privies but at the least it is doubtful whether a purchaser for value without notice is bound.[10] It was plain however, from the wording of section 21 that if the owner of the goods is precluded from denying authority the buyer will in fact acquire a better title than the seller. The effect of its application was to transfer a real title, and not merely a metaphorical title, by estoppel.

The basis of this form of estoppel was explored by Denning L.J. in *Central Newbury Car Auctions Ltd.* v. *Unity Finance Ltd.*[11] He said estoppel could arise from a representation made by a person which he was not allowed to controvert. But conduct was also a recognised head of estoppel. So we have two heads of estoppel; estoppel by representation and estoppel by conduct which could be viewed, alternatively, as estoppel by negligence. Sometimes the two forms of estoppel are run together. In *Mercantile Bank of India Ltd.*

[7] See generally, for an analysis of the continental position, Pennington (1978) 27 I.C.L.Q. 277.
[8] [1957] 2 Q.B. 600.
[9] [1875] 5 Q.B.D. 188, 206.
[10] Devlin J. refers to Ewart on *Estoppel by Misrepresentation* (1900), pp. 199–203, where the author concludes that a purchaser for value without notice is not bound. See generally, on estoppel, Spencer Bower and Turner, *Estoppel by Representation* (3rd ed., 1977). In *McIlkenny* v. *Chief Constable of the West Midlands* [1980] Q.B. 283, 317 Lord Denning explained that the word estoppel was derived from the old French word "estoupail" by which was meant a bung or cork that stopped something from coming out.
[11] [1957] 1 Q.B. 371. Reference was made to two Australian cases, *Thompson* v. *Palmer* (1933) 49 C.L.R. 507, 547 and *Grundt* v. *Great Boulder Proprietary Mines Ltd.* (1937) 59 C.L.R. 641, 675.

v. *Central Bank of India Ltd.*,[12] the Privy Council talked about, as apparent synonyms, estoppel by negligence, or by conduct, or by representation, or by a holding out of ostensible authority.

The Privy Council in the *Mercantile Bank of India* case also poured scorn on the wide words of Ashurst J. in *Lickbarrow* v. *Mason* "that wherever one of two innocent persons must suffer by the acts of a third, he who has enabled such third person to occasion the loss must sustain it."[13] Lord Wright said that this statement was too broad to be accepted without qualification.[14] Also he referred to the dicta of Cockburn C.J. in *Johnson* v. *Credit Lyonnais*[15] that the mere delivery of possession did not produce an estoppel. If it were otherwise, the specific statutory "buyer in possession" exception to the *nemo dat* rule would have been unnecessary.

A plea of estoppel by representation succeeded in *Henderson* v. *Williams*.[16] This was a case where the owner commanded that goods in the possession of a warehouseman be transferred to the order of another. The latter purported to sell them as owner and the true owner was held to be precluded from refuting the permission to sell. Lord Halsbury put the matter thus[17]:

"[The] question here is whether the true owner of the goods has so invested the person dealing with them with the *indicia* of property as that when an innocent person entered into negotiations with the person to whom these things have been entrusted with the *indicia* of property the true owner of the goods cannot afterwards complain that there was no authority to make such a bargain."

The "something more" necessary to constitute estoppel by representation was discussed in *Eastern Distributors Ltd.* v. *Goldring*.[18] Here, X, who was the owner of a Bedford van sought to purchase a Chrysler car from Y, a dealer but was not able to pay the necessary deposit. To surmount this hurdle, Y devised a scheme whereby X would sign proposal forms and memoranda for hire-purchase agreements on both vehicles. X also signed a delivery note stating that he had taken delivery of the Bedford from Y. Y completed the documentation and furnished the materials to the plaintiff hire-purchase company. The latter, oblivious to any sharp practice, accepted the proposal in respect of the Bedford but rejected that in relation to the Chrysler. Y had no authority to proceed in respect of the Bedford unless the transaction with the Chrysler also went ahead. Nonetheless he

[12] [1938] A.C. 287, 297. See generally, on title by estoppel in the context of sale of goods contracts, *Benjamin's Sale of Goods* (3rd ed., 1987), paras. 456–466.
[13] (1793) 2 T.R. 63, 70.
[14] [1938] A.C. 287, 298. In support of this view he mentioned *R.E. Jones Ltd.* v. *Waring and Gillow Ltd.* [1926] A.C. 670, 693 and *London Joint Stock Bank* v. *Macmillan* [1918] A.C. 777, 836.
[15] (1877) 3 C.P.D. 32, 36.
[16] [1895] 1 Q.B. 521. See also, *Pickering* v. *Busk* (1812) 15 East 38.
[17] *Ibid.* 525. See also, *Farquharson Bros. & Co.* v. *King & Co.* [1902] A.C. 35; *cf. Commonwealth Trust Ltd.* v. *Akotey* [1926] A.C. 72.
[18] [1957] 2 Q.B. 600.

purported to sell the Bedford to the plaintiffs. The plaintiffs completed the agreement and sent a counterpart to X. X later purported to sell the Bedford van which at all material times was in his possession to the defendant. The plaintiffs claimed the van from the defendant.

It was held that X was precluded from denying Y's authority to sell. Consequently, X had no title to pass to the defendant and the plaintiffs were entitled to succeed in their action. There was no transfer of possession of the van to Y but nonetheless he was invested with apparent authority to sell. He was armed with some *indicia*, namely the proposal forms and memoranda for hire-purchase agreements, which made it appear that he was either the owner or had the right to sell. The doctrine of estoppel or apparent authority applied to any form of representation or holding out of apparent ownership or the right to sell.[19]

So in *Goldring* estoppel operated despite the fact that the party estopped retained possession of both the motor vehicle and the car's registration book. Yet in *Central Newbury Car Auctions Ltd.* v. *Unity Finance Ltd.*[20] where both the vehicle and the logbook came into the hands of the purported seller an estoppel was held not to apply.

In the *Newbury* case it was agreed that the plaintiffs should sell a car to a finance company who would let it on hire-purchase to one "C." C signed proposal forms that were to be submitted to the finance company. Contrary to the agreement obtaining between the plaintiffs and the finance company, he was permitted to take away the car and its registration book. The car, a Morris, at that time was registered in the name of one A who had not signed the registration book. The book, however, stated: "The person in whose name a vehicle is registered may or may not be the legal owner of the vehicle." Later, a mystery stranger who had assumed the identity of and was presumably C, offered the car for sale to a third party, the purported signature of A being then in the book. The car later found its way into the hands of the defendants by means of a sale transaction and the plaintiff sought damages for conversion.

The action was unsuccessful in the Court of Appeal. Hodson and Morris L.J., who formed the majority, declared that by entrusting the car to C, together with a document which clearly stated that it did not prove legal ownership, the plaintiffs were not making any representation that C was entitled to deal with the car as his own. Therefore, they were not estopped from asserting their own title.[21] Morris L.J. said it cannot be assumed that

[19] *Ibid.* 610. *Goldring* has been followed in *Spencer* v. *North County Finance Co. Ltd.* [1963] C.L.Y. 212; *Stoneleigh Finance Ltd.* v. *Phillips* [1965] 2 Q.B. 537 and *Snook* v. *London and West Riding Investments Ltd.* [1967] 2 Q.B. 786. See also, *Shaw* v. *Commissioner of Police of the Metropolis (Natalegawa, claimant)* [1987] 1 W.L.R. 1332. Here the Court of Appeal said *obiter* that the signing of a notification of sale or transfer slip and a document stating in so many words that the owner had sold the car, was the clearest possible representation that the ownership had been transferred.

[20] [1957] 1 Q.B. 371.

[21] Hodson L.J. at 387–388 referred to *Joblin* v. *Watkins and Roseveare Motors Ltd.* (1948) 64 T.L.R. 464 as authority for the proposition that a car registration book was not a document of title within s.1(4) of the Factors Act 1889. He accepted, however, that since the keeper of a car

the person in possession of a car and its registration book is the owner of the car. The absence of a registration book when a car is being sold will occasion much inquiry. The presence of one, however, in the hands of the seller did not displace all need for inquiry and did not prove legal ownership.[22]

Representation by Omission

In the circumstances of a particular case, an omission to correct some impression may generate the necessary representation to constitute an estoppel. The matter arose in *Spiro* v. *Lintern*.

This was a case where the first defendant wished to sell his house. He left his wife, the second defendant, to go about making the arrangements to find a purchaser. However, he gave her no authority to sell. The wife, through estate agents, agreed to a sale of the property to the plaintiff. Moreover, a written agreement was entered into purporting to be an agreement for the sale of the property by the wife to the plaintiff. After that, the husband neither indicated that his wife had acted without authority nor stated that he was not willing for the sale to proceed. Furthermore the plaintiff was permitted by the husband to carry out certain repairs to the property.

It was held that the plaintiff was estopped from asserting that the contract for sale was entered into without his authority. Knowing of the plaintiff's misconception as to the true state of play he had allowed the latter to act to his detriment. The situation imposed an obligation to disclose the wife's lack of actual authority.[23]

Estoppel by Negligence

The true owner may be estopped, by his conduct, from denying the seller's authority to sell where he has been guilty of negligence. In *Wilson* v. *Meeson and Pickering*,[24] it was suggested that the doctrine of estoppel by negligence was confined to negotiable instruments. However, there is a body of cases to the contrary collected in *Mercantile Credit Co. Ltd.* v. *Hamblin*.[25] The case suggests that three ingredients have to be established before estoppel by negligence can be made out. First, it is necessary for the third party to show that the true owner owed him a duty to be careful. The second requirement is that in breach of this duty the true owner failed to take reasonable care. The third condition is that the negligence of the true owner was the proximate and real cause of the third party being induced to part with the purchase price of the goods to the seller.

is specifically instructed to keep the book in a safe place not in his car, a stolen car will not normally be accompanied by the registration book. In *Pearson* v. *Rose and Young Ltd.* [1951] 1 K.B. 275 it was held that a mercantile agent dealing with a car, without the book, was not dealing in the ordinary course of business.

[22] [1957] 1 Q.B. 398.
[23] [1973] 1 W.L.R. 1002.
[24] [1946] K.B. 422.
[25] [1965] 2 Q.B. 242.

The claim fell in *Mercantile Credit Co. Ltd.* v. *Hamblin*, on the second and third heads the person who sold the goods to the third party was guilty of fraud. *Apropos* the third head Sellers and Pearson L.JJ. took the view that the effective cause of the third party's loss was this fraud and not any negligence on the part of the owner.

The facts in *Hamblin* bear some relationship to those in *Eastern Distributors Ltd.* v. *Goldring*. We had the owner of a motor vehicle signing hire-purchase documents which allowed the dealer to misrepresent to the finance company that he was the owner of the vehicle. *Goldring*, however, was distinguished by all the judges. Sellers L.J. said in that case there was a misrepresentation to which both the dealer and true owner of the vehicle were parties. In the present case, although the defendant signed blank forms, she was not in any way a party to the dealer's fraudulent conduct.[26] Pearson L.J. noted that in *Goldring* the owner of the vehicle concerned—a Bedford van, signed the documents and agreed that they should be presented to the finance company and agreed that the dealer should pretend to be the owner of the car. That, therefore, was a clear case of ostensible authority by holding out.[27]

Salmon L.J. said much the same. In the present case, unlike *Goldring's* case, the dealer had no authority to fill in the hire-purchase documents or to put them forward on the defendant's behalf. Moreover, in *Goldring* the true owner expressly agreed to the dealer misrepresenting to the finance house that the Bedford van was the dealer's property.[28]

Much of the argument in the decided cases has centred on the second requirement, namely the existence of a duty of care on the part of the owner of the goods and owed to the person who will suffer loss if the goods are restored to the owner's possession. In *Swan* v. *North British Australasian Co. Ltd.*,[29] Blackburn J. said there must not merely be neglect of what would be prudent in respect to the party himself, or even of some duty owing to third persons with whom those seeking to set up the estoppel are not privy.[30]

The duty of care point was discussed by Simon Brown J. in the recent case of *Debs* v. *Sibec Developments Ltd.*[31] This was a case where a Mercedes-Benz motor car was taken from an owner by robbers who forced him to sign a purported receipt for its sale price. It was held that the owner owed no duty of care to subsequent bona fide purchasers or hirers of the motor vehicle, so as to estop him from claiming to recover it from them. In particular he owed them no duty promptly to report the robbery to the police.

A dealer to whom the vehicle had been offered by the thieves a day after the robbery checked with Hire-Purchase Information Ltd. (HPI) that the

---

[26] *Ibid.* 266.
[27] *Ibid.* 276.
[28] *Ibid.* 277–278. The judge thought the present case approximated more closely to *Campbell Discount Co. Ltd.* v. *Gall* [1961] 1 Q.B. 431.
[29] (1863) 2 H. & C. 175.
[30] *Ibid.* 181. See also, Parke B. in *Freeman* v. *Cooke* (1848) 2 Exch. 654, 663, 664.
[31] *The Times*, May 19, 1989.

car was not registered as stolen or on hire-purchase but of course the inquiry revealed nothing. It took between three and four weeks for a reported theft to reach HPI's records. Therefore, the submission was made that there should be a duty of care towards each in a chain of purchasers. This had the surprising result that protection would, or would not be gained according to when an inquiry of HPI would reveal the theft.

Simon Brown J., after stating the facts, opined that the scope of the doctrine of estoppel by negligence was relatively narrow. In support of this proposition he referred to two House of Lords cases. In *Farquharson Bros. & Co.* v. *King & Co.*,[32] the speeches made it plain that the true owner's rights in a chattel were not prejudiced or affected by his own carelessness resulting in the robbery of the chattel. The judge said that if an owner owed nobody a duty of care to prevent his loss in the first place, it would be surprising if such a duty should, after such loss, spring up towards others.

Reference was also made to *Moorgate Mercantile Co. Ltd.* v. *Twitchings*.[33] Here, a car dealer who was a member of HPI was offered a car for sale by X who told him that it was free of all hire-purchase liability. The dealer was also informed by HPI that their files contained no recorded hire-purchase agreement in respect of the car. Thereupon he bought the car from M. The car in fact was subject to a hire-purchase agreement made with the plaintiffs, a finance company, also a member of HPI. The plaintiffs discovered what had happened and brought an action against the dealer claiming damages for conversion. The dealer, in his defence, claimed that by failing to record the agreement with HPI the finance company were estopped from claiming damages for conversion by reason of their own negligence.

The estoppel plea failed in the House of Lords. It was held that the finance company's conduct in not registering the hire-purchase agreement with M was, at worst, careless in respect of the finance company's own property. There was no breach of any duty owed to other parties.[34] Moreover, the mere fact that both plaintiff and defendant were members of HPI did not make them neighbours in the legal sense of that term as expounded in *Donoghue* v. *Stevenson*.[35] Lord Edmund-Davies distinguished a situation where the owner of goods is precluded from asserting his title because he has deliberately caused another to believe in the existence of a certain state of things from the other type of cases where the preclusion arises from a merely negligent act or omission. In the former instance, the owner is *ex hypothesi* unable to deny his intention that others should act as they did. In the latter

[32] [1902] A.C. 325, 336—Lord Macnaghten said that if a person leaves a watch or a ring on a seat in the park or on a table at a cafe and it ultimately gets into the hands of a bona fide purchaser, it is no answer to the true owner to say that it was his carelessness and nothing else that enabled the finder to pass it off as his own.

[33] [1977] A.C. 890.

[34] Lords Edmund-Davies, Fraser and Russell formed the majority. Lords Wilberforce and Salmon dissented.

[35] [1932] A.C. 562.

case, on the other hand, it was common ground that the preclusion was based on the existence of a duty of care that had been violated by the negligent act or omission complained of.[36]

To return to *Debs* v. *Sibec Developments Ltd.*, Simon Brown J. concluded that the plaintiff's position must *a fortiori* be that of *Moorgate Mercantile Ltd.* so that the defence based on estoppel by negligence failed. One might conclude from *Debs* that a plea of estoppel by negligence will not succeed against a supplier in the reservation of title context. The supplier owes no duty to sub-buyers to keep the goods in his possession.

Disposition by a Buyer in Possession

Section 9 of the Factors Act 1889 provides as follows:

> "Where a person having bought or agreed to buy goods obtains, with the consent of seller, possession of the goods or the documents of title to the goods, the delivery or transfer by that person or by a mercantile agent acting for him, of the goods or documents of title, under any sale, pledge or other disposition thereof [or under any agreement for sale, pledge or other disposition thereof], to any person receiving the same in good faith and without notice of any lien or other right of the original seller in respect of the goods shall have the same effect as if the person making the delivery or transfer were a mercantile agent in possession of the goods or documents of title with the consent of the owner."

Section 25(1) of the Sale of Goods Act 1979 is an identikit version of the same, save for the fact that the words in square brackets are absent.

Bought or Agreed to Buy

Technically speaking, a person who has taken goods subject to a reservation of title clause has agreed to buy rather than bought the goods. Under the Sale of Goods Act an "agreement to sell" arises where there is a contract of sale but the transfer of the property in the goods to the buyer is to occur at a future time or subject to some condition thereafter to be fulfilled.

The distinction makes no difference for the purpose of the sections for the position of the two is equated. A buyer to whom the property in goods has passed under a contract of sale will be able to confer a good title on a third-party purchaser by virtue of his property in the goods without relying on any of the exceptions to the *nemo dat* rule. The section has its relevance, however, where the buyer obtains something less than full unincumbered ownership. Examples are a voidable title or ownership subject to a charge or lien in favour of a third party.[37]

---

[36] [1977] A.C. 890, 919. To support his finding of no duty of care in this particular case, Lord Edmund-Davies referred to *Cambridge Finance Co. Ltd.* v. *Union Transport Ltd.*, County Court, June 22, 1973, and *United Dominions Trust (Commercial) Ltd.* v. *Cartwright*, March 21, 1961; Bar Library Transcript No. 124 of 1961, Court of Appeal.

[37] See generally, *Benjamin's Sale of Goods* (3rd ed., 1987), paras. 521–536.

Notice

The sections apply only in a situation where the sub-purchaser is ". . . receiving the same in good faith and without notice of any lien or other rights of the original sellers."

The notice and good faith issues came up in the Irish case of *Re Interview Ltd.*[38] In this case the company, which was in voluntary liquidation, had been carrying on the retail trade of selling domestic electrical goods. Early in 1972 it had become the agent for the distribution in Ireland of television and radio sets manufactured by a West German company, Telefunken GmbH, a wholly-owned subsidiary of another West German electrical company, AEG GmbH. Part of Interview Ltd.'s stock was acquired directly from an associated Irish company which up until then had been acting as the sole Irish distributor of AEG's goods, and the rest was to be supplied directly by Telefunken. All the goods supplied by the German companies were supplied subject to reservation of title clauses.

Kenny J. held that Interview Ltd. was not entitled to claim ownership of the goods originally supplied to the associated company by virtue of any exception to the *nemo dat* rule contained in the Factors Act or the Sale of Goods Act. Interview Ltd. knew of the reservation of title clause in the conditions of sale and thus had notice within the meaning of the relevant provisions.

It seems that actual and not constructive notice is required before the *nemo dat* exception is negatived. Constructive notice refers to situations where the inquiries which ought reasonably to have been made are not made. It is correlative with a duty to inquire. The courts have frowned upon the application of the doctrine of constructive notice to commercial transactions.

In *Manchester Trust* v. *Furness*[39] Lindley L.J. said:

". . . as regards the extension of the equitable doctrines of constructive notice to commercial transactions, the Courts have always set their faces resolutely against. The equitable doctrines of constructive notice are common enough in dealing with land and estates, with which the Court is familiar; but there have been repeated protests against the introduction into commercial transactions of anything like an extension of those doctrines, and the protest is founded on perfect good sense. In dealing with estates in land title is everything, and it can be leisurely investigated; in commercial transactions possession is everything and there is no time to investigate title; and if we were to extend the doctrine of constructive notice to commercial transactions we should be doing infinite mischief and paralysing the trade of the country."

This passage received the approval of the Court of Appeal in *Greer* v. *Downs Supply Co. Ltd.*[40] and also that of the Irish Supreme Court in *Bank of*

[38] [1975] I.R. 382.
[39] [1895] 2 Q.B. 539, 545.
[40] [1927] 2 K.B. 28.

Ireland Ltd. v. *Rockfield Ltd.*[41] Lord Denning summed up the matter well in *Worcester Works Finance Ltd.* v. *Cooden Engineering Co. Ltd.*[42] He said that the word "notice" in this context means actual notice, that is to say, knowledge of the sale or deliberately turning a blind eye to it. Our commercial law did not like constructive notice and would have nothing to do with it.[43]

Significance of Reference to Mercantile Agent

The sections state the delivery or transfer has "the same effect as if the person making the delivery or transfer were a mercantile agent in possession of the goods or documents of title with the consent of the owner." This is a somewhat obscure provision to say the least and opinions differ as to its meaning. Section 2(1) of the Factors Act 1889 states the position in the case of an actual mercantile agent. That subsection stipulates that a sale, pledge or other disposition of the goods will only be validated if it is made by him/her when acting in the ordinary course of business of a mercantile agent.

The point to be made is that if the buyer in possession is not a mercantile agent, how then can he be regarded as acting in the ordinary course of business of a mercantile agent? Up until 1964 the view abroad was that this requirement was inapplicable. The way in which the goods were disposed of went to the issue of bona fides and nothing more. However, in *Newtons of Wembley Ltd.* v. *Williams*[44] the English Court of Appeal struck a different vein. Pearson L.J. stated the law in the following manner[45]:

> "I suppose it follows that when one is applying the hypothesis in section 2 one assumes that he is a mercantile agent; if he has a business it is assumed to be the business of a mercantile agent; or the other way of putting it is that the transaction will be validated if this buyer is doing something which would constitute acting in the ordinary course of business if he were a mercantile agent."

It seems to follow therefore, from dicta of Buckley L.J. in *Oppenheimer* v. *Attenborough & Son*,[46] that the transaction between buyer and disponee must take place at a proper place of business within business hours and in other respects the transaction must accord with the ordinary way in which a mercantile agent would act. In *Newtons'* case Sellers L.J. suggested that, in some cases, what is in "the ordinary course of business" of a mercantile agent may call for some special investigation but it envisaged a transaction by a mercantile agent and was to be derived from such data as was either known to the court or established by evidence as to what would be the

[41] [1979] I.R. 21, 38, *per* Kenny J.
[42] [1972] 1 Q.B. 210.
[43] *Ibid.* 579–580.
[44] [1965] 1 Q.B. 560.
[45] *Ibid.* 579–580.
[46] [1908] 1 K.B. 221, 230, 231. See also, Lord Alverstone C.J. at 226, 227.

ordinary course of business.[47] *Newtons of Wembley Ltd.* v. *Williams* was followed by Lord Lowry C.J. in the Northern Ireland case of *R.F. Martin Ltd.* v. *Duffy (Cooper, Third Party)*.[48] In that case the plaintiff seller had delivered catering equipment to a restaurateur, who later sold both his business and the equipment to the defendant before having paid the plaintiff. The plaintiff sued the defendant for the return of the equipment and relied upon a term in the original contract whereby property in the goods was not to pass to the restaurateur until the price had been paid in full. The defendant sought to rely on section 9 of the Factors Act 1889 and section 25(1) of the Sale of Goods Act 1979. The judge held that these sections could not avail the defendant because the resale to him did not bear the slightest resemblance to a sale of goods by a mercantile agent; it was, in effect, a transfer of goods merely as an adjunct to a sale of leased land.

Possession with the Consent of the Owner

The statutory language provides that where "a person having . . . agreed to buy goods obtains with the consent of the seller possession of the goods" the delivery or transfer by that person of the goods under a sale to a person receiving them in good faith "shall have the same effect as if the person making the delivery or transfer were a mercantile agent in possession of the goods . . . with the consent of the owner."

At first sight, the section would seem to suggest that, if a person who had stolen goods from the owner sold or agreed to sell the goods and delivered possession of them to a buyer (bona fide or not), the buyer could pass a good title to a person purchasing the goods from him.[49] The section appears to equate the consent of the thief with the consent of the true owner. This contention, however, was rejected by the House of Lords in the recent case of *National Employers Mutual General Insurance Association Ltd.* v. *Jones*.[50] Lord Goff conducted a detailed review of the legislative history of the Factors Acts. With this background in mind he concluded that section 9 of the Factors Act 1889 must be read as providing that the delivery or transfer given by the intermediate transferor, B, shall have the same effect as if he was a mercantile agent in possession of the goods or documents of title with the consent of the owner, A, who entrusted them to him.[51] This conclusion was fortified by reference to section 2 of the 1889 Act which went no further than to divest the title of an owner if he entrusted the goods or documents of title to a mercantile agent who sold them.[52]

---

[47] (1985) 11 N.I.J.B. 80.
[48] *Ibid.* 575.
[49] See Powles (1974) 37 M.L.R. 213, (1975) 38 M.L.R. 83; also Benjamin, *op. cit.* para. 533.
[50] [1988] 2 W.L.R. 952.
[51] *Ibid.* 962.
[52] Lord Goff also referred to *Cahn* v. *Pockett's Bristol Channel Steam Packet Co. Ltd.* [1899] 1 Q.B. 643, 658–659, *per* Collins L.J. and *Folkes* v. *King* [1923] 1 K.B. 282, 305–306, *per* Scrutton L.J. as well as *Central Newbury Car Auctions Ltd.* v. *Unity Finance Ltd.* [1957] 1 Q.B. 371; *Butterworth* v. *Kingsway Motors Ltd.* [1954] 1 W.L.R. 1286; *Elwin* v. *O'Regan and Maxwell*

The possession issue arose in another relatively recent case *Four Point Garage Ltd.* v. *Carter*.[53] Here Simon Brown J. held that for the purposes of section 25(1) of the 1979 Act there was no distinction between a delivery of goods direct to a sub-purchaser by the seller and a delivery of goods by the seller to a buyer who then delivered the goods to the sub-purchaser. In either case there was an effective delivery of goods to the sub-purchaser for the purpose of passing title to the sub-purchaser under section 25. In the case of delivery direct to the sub-purchaser by the seller the buyer was deemed to take constructive delivery of the goods and the seller was deemed to act as the buyer's agent when making delivery to the sub-purchaser.

For section 9 of the Factors Act and section 25(1) of the Sale of Goods Act to operate, possession and the disposition must be simultaneous. In *Beverley Acceptances Ltd.* v. *Oakley*,[54] Donaldson and Slade L.JJ. saw no room for reading in some such words as "or has within a reasonable time before the relevant disposition been. ..." Slade L.J. suggested that any such super-added condition would in any event be of such uncertain import that it would be very difficult to apply in practice.[55] Moreover, there was no support for the view that the provisions might apply if the mercantile agent was in possession at the time when he made representations which led to the sale. That circumstance could enable the recipient of the disposition to invoke common law estoppel but did not justify reliance on the statutory provisions.[56]

"Possession with consent for the purpose of the provisions arises even if the consent has been procured by fraud." In *Du Jardin* v. *Beadman Bros. Ltd.*[57] Sellers J. said there was no reason to interpret the word "consent" in section 9 of the Factors Act 1889 in such a way as to bring it into harmony with the criminal law. The operation of the Act was not affected by the fact that an agent or buyer was guilty of larceny.[58]

Delivery or Transfer under a Sale, Pledge or Other Disposition

The question arises whether a receiver, administrator or liquidator may be able to defeat the claims of a supplier who has sold goods subject to a reservation of title by relying on section 9 of the Factors Act 1889 or section

[1971] N.Z.L.R. 1124; *Brandon* v. *Leckie* (1972) 29 D.L.R. (3d) 633. Atiyah's *The Sale of Goods* (7th ed., 1985), pp. 302–303 was mentioned in addition.
[53] [1985] 3 All E.R. 12.
[54] [1982] R.T.R. 417.
[55] *Ibid.* 438.
[56] *Ibid.* 425. Lord Denning, on the other hand, argued that the "disposition" need not be at the very time of the "possession." To hold that it must be simultaneous, he said, would be far too narrow and legalistic an interpretation.
[57] [1952] 2 Q.B. 712.
[58] See also, on "consent," *Lloyds Bank Ltd.* v. *Bank of America* [1938] 2 K.B. 147, which has been interpreted as holding that where goods are admixed with others, s.25(1) will only apply if the "consent" with which the sub-purchaser is in possession of the goods is the consent of all the owners: see Parris, *Effective Retention of Title Clauses* (1986), p. 18.

25(1) of the Sale of Goods Act 1889. "Sale," "pledge" or other "disposition" are the crucial words in the sections as well as "transfer" and "delivery." The Factors Act 1889 may be ruled out of reckoning straightaway from the point of view of a receiver, administrator or liquidator.

Section 5 of the 1889 Act stipulates that the consideration necessary for the validity of a sale, pledge or other disposition of goods in pursuance of the Act may be either a payment in cash, or the delivery or transfer of other goods, or of a document of title to goods, or of a negotiable security, or any other valuable consideration. In *Thomas Graham & Sons Ltd.* v. *Glenrothes Development Corporation,*[59] Lord President Clyde said that under the Factors Act any sale made by a mercantile agent must be for valuable consideration.

The situation under the Sale of Goods Act is slightly more problematic. Section 61 of the Sale of Goods Act 1979 states that "delivery" means voluntary transfer of possession from one person to another. On the other hand, it might be argued that when a receiver, administrator or liquidator is appointed to a company there is no voluntary transfer of goods which at that time are in the company's possession. Even in a voluntary winding-up the liquidator is obliged to distribute the assets of the company for the benefit of its creditors (see section 107 of the Insolvency Act 1986). Therefore, there is a compulsory element involved in the transfer of possession.[60]

Exclusion of Buyer under a Conditional Agreement

It is provided that a buyer in possession under a conditional sale agreement is not to be regarded as a person who has bought or agreed to buy goods for the purposes of sections 9 and 25(1) of the Factors Act and the Sale of Goods Act respectively.[61] From the point of view of the exclusion, "conditional sale agreement" means an agreement for the sale of goods which is a consumer credit agreement within the meaning of the Consumer Credit Act 1974. Further conditions are that the purchase price or part of it is payable by instalments, and the property in the goods is to remain in the seller (notwithstanding that the buyer is to be in possession of the goods) until such conditions as to the payment of instalments or otherwise as may be specified in the agreement are fulfilled. The definition of "consumer credit agreement" is contained in section 8 of the Consumer Credit Act 1974. The buyer must be an individual and the amount of credit provided under the consumer credit agreement must not exceed £15,000, a figure increased from the original £5,000 by the Consumer Credit (Increase of Monetary

[59] 1968 S.L.T. 2. See also, *Worcester Works Finance Ltd.* v. *Cooden Engineering Co. Ltd.* [1972] 1 Q.B. 210.
[60] When a company goes into liquidation the unsecured creditors acquire rights against the property of the company: see *Re Spiral Globe Ltd.* [1902] 1 Ch. 396; *Re S. Abrahams & Sons Ltd.* [1902] 1 Ch. 695; *Re Anglo-Oriental Carpet Manufacturing Co. Ltd.* [1903] 1 Ch. 914, and *Re Ehrmann Bros. Ltd.* [1906] 2 Ch. 697.
[61] s. 25(2) of the Sale of Goods Act 1979.

Limits) Order 1983. Basically conditional sale agreements falling within these financial and other limitations are treated as hire-purchase agreements for the purpose of the application of consumer credit legislation. Section 9 of the Factors Act and section 25(1) of the Sale of Goods Act 1979 never applied to hire-purchase agreements.[62] At first sight, this might seem a retrogressive move having regard to the increasing exceptions to the *nemo dat* rule. Conditional sale agreements of this ilk, though, are rarely met as a method of consumer finance. It may have been considered desirable to assimilate hire-purchase and conditional sales so as to curb evasion of consumer credit legislation and for simplicity's sake.

Moreover, the practical effect of the statutory assimilation is offset to a certain extent by Part III of the Hire-Purchase Act 1964. Under this legislation, which is still in force,[63] a disposition of a motor vehicle by a hirer under a hire-purchase agreement or a buyer under a conditional sale agreement, if made to a bona fide private purchaser without notice of the agreement, is effective to transfer to the purchaser the title of the person who had let the vehicle on hire-purchase or agreed to sell it on conditional sale.

Liability of Original Seller to Sub-buyer

In *Romalpa,* Roskill L.J. suggested that *vis-à-vis* a sub-buyer, the buyer of goods under a retention of title clause sold as principal. Notwithstanding that fact, he occupied an agency relationship with respect to the original seller. The latter, however, was not amenable to any action by the sub-buyer in relation to the quality of the goods or arising from any other breach of the sub-sale contract.[64] One distinguished commentator has suggested though that the original seller may be liable to a sub-buyer as an undisclosed principal.[65] This argument involves some consideration of the nature of the liability of an undisclosed principal.[66]

In *Cathay* v. *Fennel*[67] the concept of the undisclosed principal was expounded in the following terms[68]:

> "If an agent makes a contract in his own name, the principal may sue and be sued upon it; for it is a general rule that, whenever an express contract is made, an action is maintainable upon it, either in the name of the person with whom it was actually made, or in the name of the person with whom in point of law it was made."

The doctrine runs counter to the notion of privity of contract under which

---

[62] *Helby* v. *Matthews* [1895] A.C. 471. See also, *Lee* v. *Butler* [1893] 2 Q.B. 318 and *Marten* v. *Whale* [1917] 2 K.B. 480.
[63] Re-enacted in Sched. 4 to the Consumer Credit Act 1974 as amended by s. 63 of and Sched. 2, para. 4 to the Sale of Goods Act 1979.
[64] [1976] 1 W.L.R. 676, 690.
[65] See F. B. Reynolds (1978) 94 L.Q.R. 223, 238.
[66] See generally, *Benjamin's Sale of Goods* (3rd ed., 1987), paras. 2251–2259; Bowstead, *Agency* (14th ed.), pp. 257 *et seq.*; *Fridman's Law of Agency* (5th ed., 1983), pp. 223–236.
[67] (1830) 109 E.R. 599.
[68] *Ibid.* 600.

only a party to a contract may sue upon it.[69] One author has described the idea of the undisclosed principal as an anomaly, "introduced into and accepted by the common law for reasons of mercantile convenience, and rigorously controlled by the law, so far as its scope and effects are concerned, lest this unusual relaxation of the strict attitude of the common law with regard to personal contracts be allowed to cause undue subversion."[70] In particular, the liability of the undisclosed principal to be sued has been questioned and this is very relevant for the purposes of the present discussion. But first let us look at how the doctrine of the undisclosed principal may be cut down by other rules. These are fivefold and may be summarised thus:

(1) No ratification.
(2) Contractual exclusion of undisclosed principal.
(3) Personality.
(4) Effect of judgment against agent.
(5) Election.

(1) *No ratification*

The House of Lords in *Keighley Maxsted & Co.* v. *Durant*[71] laid down firmly that a contract can only be ratified by the person on whose behalf it was purportedly made. An undisclosed principal could not ratify. To repeat the same point in slightly different language, a contract made by a person intending to contract on behalf of a third party, but without his authority, cannot be ratified by the third party, where the person who made the contract did not profess at the time of making it to be acting on behalf of a principal.

(2) *Contractual exclusion of undisclosed principals*

The principles governing contractual exclusion of undisclosed principals were discussed by the House of Lords in *Fred Drughorn Ltd.* v. *Frederiaktiebolaget Transatlantic*.[72] Viscount Haldane said that if B contracts with C prima facie that is a contract between these two only, but if at the time B entered into the contract he was really acting as agent for A, then evidence is generally admissible to show that A was the principal, and A can take advantage of the contract as if it had been actually made between himself and C. However, he went on to say that evidence of the existence of an outside principal is not admissible, if to give such evidence would be to contradict some term in the contract itself.[73]

---

[69] *Dunlop Pneumatic Tyre Co. Ltd.* v. *Selfridge and Co. Ltd.* [1915] A.C. 847.
[70] See Fridman, *op. cit.* 223. This sentence was cited and relied upon by Lander L.J.S.C. in the British Columbia case of *Vancouver Equipment Corp.* v. *Sun Valley Contracting Ltd.* (1979) 16 B.C.L.R. 362, 367.
[71] [1901] A.C. 240.
[72] [1919] A.C. 203.
[73] *Ibid.* 206–207.

Reference was made to two cases in support of this proposition. For instance, in *Humble* v. *Hunter*[74] it was held that where a charterer dealt with someone described as the owner, evidence was inadmissible to show that some other person was the owner. Secondly, in *Formby Brothers* v. *Formby*,[75] the expression "proprietor" was invested by the Court of Appeal with the same significance as the word "owner" in excluding intervention on the part of an undisclosed principal. The House of Lords held, however, that the term "charterer" did not have the same magic. A description in a charterparty of one of the contracting parties as "charterer" did not, of itself, designate him as the only party capable of filling that position.

It is relatively easy to multiply examples on the matter though it must be said that recent cases tend to run against implied contractual exclusion of the undisclosed principal. In *Danziger* v. *Thompson*,[76] a person was described in a tenancy agreement as the "tenant" of the premises. Lawrence J. received oral evidence to prove that the person entered into the agreement as the agent or nominee of another.

In *Epps* v. *Rothnie*,[77] the same view was taken of the expression "landlord" at least by Scott L.J. He went so far as to say that *Humble* v. *Hunter* and *Formby Brothers* v. *Formby* could no longer be regarded as good law,[78] but it was not really necessary to express a concluded view of the matter for the purpose of the decision in the case. In fact Lawrence J. was far more cautious. He said the only words in the agreement capable of being contradicted by proof of agency were the words "hereinafter called the landlord." These words were not necessarily incompatible with the fact of the person so called being the agent for an undisclosed principal.[79]

The authorities were reviewed in *O/Y Wasa SS. Co.* v. *Newspaper Pulp and Wood Export Ltd.*,[80] by Morris J. He reached the conclusion that the phrase "disponent owner" did not preclude the admission of oral evidence to demonstrate the existence of an undisclosed principal.[81]

(3) *Personality*

The question arises whether the personality of an agent is so important that intervention or liability of an undisclosed principal would be uncalled for. Scrutton L.J. addressed the issue in *Greer* v. *Downs Supply Co.*[82] where he said[83]:

[74] [1848] 12 Q.B. 310.
[75] (1910) 102 L.T. 116. It should be noted that Lord Shaw did not express any opinion about the correctness of the decisions in *Humble* v. *Hunter* or *Formby Bros.* v. *Formby*.
[76] [1944] 1 K.B. 654.
[77] [1945] 1 K.B. 562.
[78] *Ibid.* 565.
[79] *Ibid.* 566.
[80] [1949] 82 Lloyd's Law Rep. 936. See also, *Finzel Berry & Co.* v. *Eastcheap Dried Fruit Co.* [1962] 1 Lloyd's Rep. 370, 375 (affirmed [1962] 2 Lloyd's Rep. 11); *Murphy* v. *Rae* [1967] N.Z.L.R. 103.
[81] *Ibid.* 953.
[82] [1927] 2 K.B. 28.
[83] *Ibid.* 35.

"When a person claims as an undisclosed principal the question some-times arises whether the contract was made with the agent for reasons personal to the agent which induced the other party to contract with the agent to the exclusion of his principal or any one else."

The case most often cited in this connection is *Said* v. *Butt*.[84] Here it was held that an undisclosed principal was not entitled to sue in respect of a denial of admission to a theatre first night. The principal arrived with a ticket bought by his agent but in the view of the theatre management this was not sufficient to secure admission. Their stance was vindicated by the court.

Sometimes, personality is so significant that intervention by an undis-closed principal is excluded, whether expressly or impliedly by the terms of the contract. This is clearly an application of general principle. Apart from that, it has been argued that the undisclosed principal cannot intervene where the benefit of the contract is unassignable or its burden could not be vicariously performed[85]—*Said* v. *Butt* perhaps fits into this scheme of analy-sis in that it could be contended that first-night theatre tickets should not be regarded as assignable.

(4) *Effect of judgment against agent*

A plaintiff cannot after recovering judgment against the agent proceed against the principal. The justification for the rule was stated by Lord Cairns L.C. in *Kendall* v. *Hamilton*.[86] He said[87]:

"[If] an action were brought and judgment recovered against the agent, he, the agent, would have a right of action for indemnity against his principal, while, if the principal were liable also to be sued, he would be vexed with a double action. Further than this, if actions could be brought and judgments recovered, first against the agent and after-wards against the principal, you would have two judgments in existence for the same debt or cause of action; they might not necessarily be for the same amounts, and there might be recoveries had, or liens and charges created, by means of both, and there would be no mode upon the face of the judgments or by any means short of a fresh proceeding, of showing that the two judgments were really for the same debt or cause of action; and that satisfaction of one was, or would be, satis-faction of both."

(5) *Election*

Where both principal and agent are liable, it seems clear from *Clarkson, Booker Ltd.* v. *Andjel*,[88] that the third party may lose his rights against one

---

[84] [1920] 3 K.B. 497.
[85] Goodhart and Hamson (1932) 4 C.L.J. 320; *Benjamin's Sale of Goods* (3rd ed., 1987), para. 2253.
[86] [1879] 4 A.C. 504.
[87] *Ibid.* 515. See also, Scrutton L.J. in *Moore* v. *Flanagan* [1920] 1 K.B. 919, 926.
[88] [1964] 3 All E.R. 260. See also, *Calder* v. *Dobell* (1871) L.R. 6 C.P. 486 and *Curtis* v. *Williamson* (1874) L.R. 10 Q.B. 57.

by reason of an unequivocal election to sue the other short of obtaining final judgment. Russell L.J. stated the situation thus[89]:

> "The defendant having contracted as agent for an undisclosed principal, the plaintiffs were entitled to enforce the contract either against the defendant on the footing that he was contracting and liable as principal or against the principal on the footing that the defendant was not liable, being merely an agent. The plaintiffs could not enforce the contract against both. Their right against the defendant and their right against the principal were inconsistent rights. At some stage the plaintiffs had to elect to avail themselves of one of those inconsistent rights and to abandon the other."

In *Clarkson* the Court of Appeal confirmed that to constitute a conclusive election which will bar subsequent proceedings against the agent or undisclosed principal, as the case may be, the decision must be shown (a) to have been taken with a full knowledge of all the relevant facts and (b) to have been a truly unequivocal act. The determination of the latter question had to be based on a review of all the circumstances. In this particular case the commencement of proceedings against one party by the issue of a writ did not amount to a final election.[90] The "knowledge of all the relevant facts" criterion means that the third party is not free to elect so long as the principal remains undisclosed.[91]

Liability of an Undisclosed Principal to be Sued

It has been suggested by some commentators that while an undisclosed principal should be entitled to sue, he should not be answerable in an action brought by the third party. In favour of liability one might argue that by giving his authority to the middleman the principal is to a certain extent an indirect actor who causes the loss to the third-party contractor.[92] On the other hand, the third party is unaware of the existence of the undisclosed principal and if he is wrong about the creditworthiness of the person with whom he deals he should shoulder the loss himself.[93] Also against liability is the consideration that our law should not be obsessed with neat symmetry. Lord Halsbury put the point well in *Keighley-Maxsted & Co.* v. *Durant* when he said[94]:

> "If [this] is an anomaly, it certainly is not the only one in our law, and if it were sought to make our laws harmonious by deciding that any

---

[89] *Ibid.* 267.
[90] Though according to Wilmer L.J. at 267 the case was very near the borderline.
[91] See Fridman, *op. cit.* 230. In Benjamin, *op. cit.* para. 258 the doctrine of election is questioned. The vast majority of cases refer to it only to rule that there has been no election.
[92] See generally, Muller-Frienfels, "The Undisclosed Principal" (1953) 16 M.L.R. 299.
[93] See Zweigert and Kotz, *An Introduction to Comparative Law* (1977), Vol. 11, p. 108.
[94] [1901] A.C. 240, 244.

proposition which our laws establish involves as a necessary consequence the establishment of everything that is analogous to it, the result would be very perplexing indeed."

In arguing against liability of an undisclosed principal in a sale of goods/ reservation of title situation one commentator has pointed to the device of the trust receipt.[95] Basically, this refers to a document which permits a pledgee to release goods to his pledgor as agent for sale and trustee of the proceeds and at the same time maintaining his pledge interest.

The device received the sanctification of the House of Lords in *North Western Bank Ltd.* v. *Poynter, Son and Macdonalds*.[96] It was held that a pledgee may redeliver the goods to the pledgor for a limited purpose without thereby losing his rights under the contract of pledge. Pledgees of a bill of lading representing a specific cargo returned the bill of lading to the pledgors to obtain delivery of the merchandise and sell on the pledgees' behalf and account for the proceeds towards satisfaction of the debt. The House of Lords took the view that the pledgees' security was not affected and that they were entitled to the proceeds of the cargo as against the general creditors of the pledgors.

The same principle was applied in *Re David Allester Ltd*.[97] Here a company pledged bills of lading with a bank to secure an overdraft. When it was time to sell the goods the company, in accordance with long-standing mercantile practice, obtained the bills of lading from the bank. Realisation was on the terms stated in the usual letter of trust given by the company to the bank, *i.e.* that the company received the bills of lading in trust on the bank's account and undertook to hold the goods when received and the proceeds when sold as the bank's trustees and to remit the entire net proceeds as realised. Astbury J. held that the bank's previous rights as pledgee remained unaffected by this common and convenient mode of realisation.

Even closer to the reservation of title and resale scenario are cases concerned with buying agents. Certain of these cases appear to uphold the direct passage of property from third party to principal without giving rise to a contractual connection between them.[98] Statements to that effect are often associated with Blackburn J. However, his most-cited pronouncement on the subject occurs in his dissenting judgment in *Robinson* v. *Mollett*[99] where he said[1]:

"Any person, if he chooses, may give an order to an agent to buy as his agent, not only with an express dispensation from any obligation to establish privity of contract between him and the person from whom the

---

[95] See Reynolds (1978) 94 L.Q.R. 223, 237.
[96] [1895] A.C. 56.
[97] [1922] 2 Ch. 211.
[98] See generally, the articles by D. J. Hill (1968) 31 M.L.R. 623; [1964] J.B.L. 304; [1967] J.B.L. 122 as well as Geva (1979) 25 McGill L.J. 32.
[99] (1874) L.R. 7 H.L. 802.
[1] *Ibid.* 809–810. See also, *Ireland* v. *Livingston* (1872) L.R. 5 H.L. 395; *Cassaboglou* v. *Gibb* [1883] 11 Q.B.D. 797; *Bolus & Co.* v. *Inglis* [1924] N.Z.L.R. 164.

agent buys, but even expressly refusing authority to the agent to establish such privity. ... This, however, in no way interferes with the existence of a fiduciary relation, or the consequent obligation on the agent not to put his own interest in conflict with that of his principal".

More modern authority may be cited in the form of Donaldson J.'s judgment in *Tehran-Europe Co. Ltd.* v. *S.T. Belton (Tractors) Ltd.*[2] He said that one of the ways in which an agent can conclude a contract on behalf of his principal is by creating privity of contract between himself and the third party, but no such privity between the third party and his principal. To put it another way, in relation to the third party he is a principal but as regards his principal he is an agent. Shades of Roskill L.J.'s judgment in *Romalpa* one might say.

Conclusion

To conclude this part of the chapter, it is suggested that a *Romalpa* seller is not liable to sub-buyers for breach of the conditions of sale implied by the Sale of Goods Act or for other breaches of the sub-sale contract. While this liability may appear to be the logical corollary of the entitlement of the supplier under a suitably drafted *Romalpa* clause to resale proceeds, the life of the law, to use a well-worn expression, has not been logic but experience. The identity and existence of the supplier may be unknown to a sub-buyer and to afford the latter a right of action against the supplier is to provide an undeserved and unbargained-for benefit. In any event, even if a *Romalpa* seller is liable to be sued as an undisclosed principal, then his potential liability is cut down by the other doctrines discussed in this chapter, such as contractual exclusion of an undisclosed principal.

---

[2] [1968] 1 Q.B. 54, 60. For the C.A. judgment see [1968] 2 Q.B. 545.

CHAPTER 11

RESERVATION OF TITLE AND REAL PROPERTY

Goods supplied subject to a reservation of title clause may have become so attached to land as to form part of the land. In this case the supplier is in danger of having the purpose sought by the inclusion of the clause defeated. The statutory definition of land in section 62 of the Law of Property Act 1925 includes fixtures attached to the land. The section amounts to a statutory confirmation of the maxim *quidquid plantatur solo, solo cedit* (whatever is affixed to the ground, becomes part of it). Notwithstanding the fact that goods have become part of the realty, all is not lost for the *Romalpa* supplier. He may be able to enter and remove the same. The matter is one of some complexity and in the following pages an attempt will be made to thread a path through the thicket of competing principles. The cases have tended to discuss the applicable principles, with reference to hire-purchase agreements but similar considerations obtain in the case of reservation of title.

Fixtures versus Chattels[1]

As Lord James pointed out in *Reynolds* v. *Ashby & Sons* the authorities controlling the questions respecting the difference between fixtures and chattels are very numerous and have arisen between different parties.[2] The rights of landlord or tenant, of mortgagor or mortgagee, have all brought this question to a legal issue for the determination of the courts. An oft-cited statement on the topic is that of Blackburn J. in *Holland* v. *Hodgson*.[3] He said[4]:

> "Perhaps the true rule is, that articles not otherwise attached to the land than by their own weight are not to be considered as part of the land, unless the circumstances are such as to show that they were intended to be part of the land, the onus of showing that they were so intended lying on those who assert that they have ceased to be chattels, and that, on the contrary, an article which is affixed to the land even slightly is to be considered as part of the land, unless the circumstances are such as to

---

[1] See generally, the leading article by Guest and Lever, "Hire-Purchase, Equipment Leases and Fixtures" (1963) 27 Conv. 30. A version of this chapter appears in the form of an article by the present author at (1990) 44 Conv.
[2] [1904] A.C. 466, 471. See generally, Megarry and Wade, *The Law of Real Property* (5th ed., 1984), pp. 730–738; Gray, *Elements of Land Law* (1987), pp. 20–25.
[3] (1872) L.R. 7 C.P. 328.
[4] *Ibid.* 335.

show that it was intended all along to continue a chattel, the onus lying on those who contend that it is a chattel."

The learned judge went on to instance the case of blocks of stone placed one on top of another without any mortar or cement for the purpose of forming a dry stone wall. These would become part of the land, although the same stones, if deposited in a builder's yard and for convenience sake stacked on top of each other in the form of a wall, would remain chattels.

The applicable test is usually talked of in terms of the degree and purpose of the annexation. Over the years the importance ascribed by the courts to the purpose part of the test has increased. As Lord Macnaghten put it in *Leigh* v. *Taylor*,[5] "its relative importance is probably not what it was in ruder or simpler times." In those days anything substantially attached to the realty became part of the realty. Nowadays, the test appears to be whether chattels are affixed for the more convenient use and enjoyment of the chattel as a chattel, or to enhance the enjoyment of the realty as realty. *Leigh* v. *Taylor* was concerned with valuable tapestries which were fairly firmly affixed to the walls of a mansion house. The House of Lords held that the tapestries never ceased to be chattels, since affixing them to the walls of the mansion house was necessary for their enjoyment as items of personalty.[6]

The existence of a hire-purchase or conditional sale agreement does not prevent a chattel affixed to realty from becoming a fixture. A case in point is *Hobson* v. *Gorringe*.[7] The case concerned a gas engine which was let out on hire-purchase. The hirer affixed the engine to his freehold land by bolts and screws to prevent it from rocking, and it was used by him for the purpose of his trade. The Court of Appeal held that the engine was sufficiently annexed to the land to become a fixture. Moreover, any intention to be inferred from the terms of the hiring agreement that it should remain a chattel did not prevent it from becoming a fixture.

Tenants' Fixtures

As well as holding that the purpose and also the degree of annexation is relevant in determing whether an object of personalty has become a fixture, the courts have permitted a tenant to remove a fixture if it has been affixed to the land for particular purposes. As Lord Chelmsford pointed out in *Bain* v. *Brand*[8] an exception has long been established in favour of a tenant erecting fixtures for the purposes of trade, allowing him the privilege of removing them during the continuance of the term.

---

[5] [1902] A.C. 157, 162.
[6] The Court of Appeal took the view that the tapestries had become fixtures but that the tenant for life had power to remove them. The Court of Appeal decision is reported *sub nom. Re De Falbe* [1901] 1 Ch. 533. As Megarry and Wade point out (*op. cit.* p. 733) it is remarkable that in the House of Lords none of the numerous authorities on fixtures were discussed.
[7] [1897] 1 Ch. 182.
[8] [1876] 1 A.C. 762.

"When he brings any chattel to be used in his trade and affixes it to the ground it becomes a part of the freehold, but with a power as between himself and his landlord of bringing it back to the state of a chattel again by severing it from the soil."[9]

In theory this right of removal situation should be distinguished sharply from a case where objects annexed to realty have not become fixtures because of the purpose of annexation. In the one instance, the items have become part of the realty but with a right of removal; in the other case the objects have never ceased to be chattels. In practice, however, the two instances tend to run together.[10]

So there is a right to remove tenants' trade fixtures. The same principle applies with respect to ornamental fixtures, though here the exception is more limited and covers only chattels complete in themselves which can be removed without substantial injury to the building.[11]

When a term comes to an end, a tenant's right to remove fixtures normally comes to an end with it. The operative word here is "normally." A tenant's right to remove fixtures does not automatically come to an end on determination of the term. The matter was discussed thoroughly by the Court of Appeal in *New Zealand Government Property Corp.* v. *H.M. & S. Ltd.*[12] where the conflicting authorities were reviewed. Lord Denning referred to the observations of Alderson B. in *Weeton* v. *Woodcock* who said[13]:

"The rule to be collected from the several cases on this subject seems to be this, that the tenant's right to remove fixtures continues during his original term, and during such further period of possession by him, as he holds the premises under a right still to consider himself as tenant."

The Court of Appeal in *Ex p. Brook*,[14] however, experienced some difficulty in stating the exact limits of the principle enunciated in *Weeton* v. *Woodcock*. Moreover, the waters were muddied even further by two first instance decisions. In *Leschallas* v. *Woolf*[15] Parker J. held that if a tenant surrenders his lease, albeit with the view to the grant of a new lease and does not reserve the right to remove tenant's fixtures, he loses that right altogether, even though he remains in possession as a tenant. This decision was followed by Scrutton J. in *Slough Picture Hall Co. Ltd.* v. *Wade*.[16]

[9] *Ibid.* 772.
[10] Gray, *op. cit.* p. 24 suggests that it can be argued quite cogently that the case law concerning "tenant's fixtures" merely comprises instances where the courts, by engaging in a more benevolent interpretation of the purpose of the annexation, have been more difficult to convince that the object attached to the land has lost its chattel character.
[11] Megarry and Wade, *op. cit.* p. 736 citing *Martin* v. *Roe* (1857) 7 E. & B. 237, 244 and *Spyer* v. *Phillipson* [1931] 2 Ch. 183.
[12] [1982] 1 Q.B. 1145.
[13] (1840) 7 M. & W. 14, 19.
[14] (1878) 10 Ch.D. 100.
[15] [1988] 1 Ch. 641.
[16] (1916) 32 T.L.R. 542. See also, the dictum of Warrington L.J. in *Pale-Carew* v. *Western Counties and General Manure Co. Ltd.* [1920] 2 Ch. 97, 122, *cf.* Lord Sterndale M.R. at 119 and Younger L.J. at 123; also the Court of Appeal decision in *Ex p. Baroness Willoughby D'Eresby* (1881) 44 L.T. 781.

In the *New Zealand Govt. Corp.* case, Dunn L.J. stated the true rule at common law to be that a tenant has the right to remove tenant's fixtures so long as he is in possession as a tenant, whether by holding over, or as a statutory tenant under the Rent Acts, or upon an extension of a lease of business premises under Part II of the Landlord and Tenant Act 1954.[17] This statement of principle appears to have been assented to by the other members of the Court of Appeal.[18]

Agricultural Fixtures

As Fox L.J. pointed out in *New Zealand Govt. Corp.* v. *H.M. & S. Ltd.*[19] agricultural tenants never had the right at common law to remove tenant's fixtures. This deficiency has been removed by successive pieces of legislation on agricultural tenancies. The relevant provisions are now found in section 10 of the Agricultural Holdings Act 1986.[20] The section gives the tenant of an agricultural holding the right to remove fixtures at any time during the continuance of the term or within two months of its determination. The fixtures remain the tenant's property so long as he has a right to remove them. The right of removal is conditional on the following factors being fulfilled:

(1) a month's written notice must be given to the landlord before both the exercise of the right and the determination of the tenancy;
(2) the landlord may serve a written counter-notice thereby triggering a right to purchase the fixtures at their fair value to an incoming tenant;
(3) the tenant must have paid the rent and satifisfed his other obligations under the tenancy;
(4) the tenant is required to make good any damage done in the removal and to refrain from causing avoidable damage.

The Owner's Right to Remove Chattel

A *Romalpa* seller or the owner of chattels which have been let under a hire-purchase agreement should reserve to himself in the contract a right to enter premises to which the chattels have been affixed and to remove the same. A clause of this nature will not prevent the chattel from becoming a fixture. Nevertheless, it strengthens the hand of the owner enormously. The agreement is good *vis-à-vis* hirers or conditional buyers and it may prevail against third parties.

It has been held that the right to re-enter and repossess chattels is not dependent on an express clause in the agreement between the parties. This

[17] [1982] 1 Q.B. 1145, 1161.
[18] *Ibid.* 1160, *per* Lord Denning M.R. and 1165, *per* Fox L.J.
[19] *Ibid.* 1161 citing *Elwes* v. *Maw* (1802) 3 East. 38.
[20] This section replaces s. 13 of the Agricultural Holdings Act 1948.

was so held by Keane J. in the Irish case *Re Galway Concrete Ltd.*[21] The case is interesting, not least because it appears to be the first case in these islands in which the law relating to fixtures was discussed in the modern context of reservation of title clauses.

A company ordered a batching plant consisting, *inter alia*, of two cement silos and two cement screw conveyors and installed it in its factory premises. The premises were held under an informal lease. Title to the plant had been reserved by the supplier until the full purchase price had been paid. The company went into liquidation leaving the supplier unpaid. The liquidator contended that the plant, having been substantially incorporated in the company's premises, became part thereof under the maxim *quidquid planta-tur solo, solo cedit*. Accordingly, he suggested that the reservation of title agreement was ineffective.

The judge held that the plant had become so affixed to the land as to become part of it. Since, on the facts, however, this was for the purposes of the company's trade it was in the nature of a tenant's fixture which could be removed by the tenant.[22] Keane J. also took the view that the owner of chattels under a conditional sale or hire-purchase agreement was entitled at common law to require the tenant to sever the chattels (where they had become tenant's fixtures) or to avail himself of the right of the tenant to enter and sever them.[23] More controversially, the judge affirmed that this right was not conditional on a clause expressly conferring on the owner the remedy of repossession where it was clearly intended that the owner should have such a right.[24]

It must be said this decision adopts a view which is very favourable to the *Romalpa* seller. In the main, the tendency of judges has been to narrow the effect to reservation of title clauses. The owner of goods would be wise to include an express clause in the hire-purchase or conditional sale agreement rather than to rely on judicial inference.

Section 92 of the Consumer Credit Act 1974 should also be borne in mind in this context. This section provides that except under an order of the court, the creditor or owner shall not be entitled to enter any premises to take possession of goods subject to a regulated hire-purchase agreement, regulated conditional sale agreement or regulated consumer hire agreement. In the vast majority of cases however, contracts for the sale of goods fall outside the scope of the legislation because of the definitions of "regulated agreement" and "conditional sale agreement" contained in sections 16 and 189 of the Act.

Right of Repossession as a Property Right

Heretofore, the discussion has centred on the relationship between the

[21] [1983] I.L.R.M. 402.
[22] *Ibid.* 405.
[23] *Ibid.* 405–406 citing *Crossley Bros. Ltd.* v. *Lee* [1908] 1 K.B. 86.
[24] *Ibid.* The judge makes reference to *Becker* v. *Riebold* (1913) 30 T.L.R. 142.

owner of chattels on the one hand, and the hirer/conditional buyer on the other. It remains to be considered to what extent a right to re-enter and repossess chattels affects third parties. Important in this connection is the potential application of the Land Charges Act 1925 where the land is unregistered and the Land Registration Act 1925 with respect to land title to which has been registered in the Land Registry.

To answer the questions posed it is necessary to analyse the precise nature of the right. Judicial pronouncements have not elucidated matters greatly. In *Hobson* v. *Gorringe*[25] A. L. Smith L.J. said simply: "But this right was not an easement created by deed, nor was it conferred by a covenant running with the land." Whatever the nature of the right it is clear that after the 1925 reforms, it must be equitable in character. Section 1(2)(a) of the Law of Property Act 1925 provides that any easement, right or privilege in or over land can only subsist at law for an interest equivalent to an estate in fee simple or a term of years absolute.

It has been suggested that a right of re-entry to repossess chattels is registrable as a Class D(iii) land charge: "any easement, right or privilege over or affecting land . . . being merely an equitable interest."[26] This suggestion was scotched, however, by Cross J. in *Poster* v. *Slough Estates Ltd.*[27] though he expressed some diffidence in reaching this conclusion.

The judge said it was always a moot point what rights were encompassed in the notion of "equitable easements" in section 2(3) of the Law of Property Act 1925 and Class D(iii) of the Land Charges Act.[28] Two cases were referred to in support of the proposition that the express grant of a right to enter on land in the possession of another for the purpose of removing a fixture was not registrable as an "equitable easement." The first case mentioned by Cross J. was *Lewisham Borough Council* v. *Maloney*.[29] There it was decided that a right conferred on a local authority by the defence regulations to requisition property was not an equitable easement. But, as Cross J. recognised, this case was not really in point, for a right of the kind therein contained was not at all analogous to an incorporeal right such as an easement or profit.

The second case was *E.R. Ives Investment Ltd.* v. *High*.[30] Here the Court of Appeal (Lord Denning M.R., Danckwerts and Winn L.JJ.) took the view that equities arising out of the principle that "he who takes the benefit must accept the burden" and equities arising out of acquiescence were not registrable as equitable easements. What was most relevant for present purposes however, was the view propounded by Lord Denning that "equitable easements" comprised only those equitable interests which, before 1926, could have subsisted as legal estates in easements or profits.[31]

[25] [1897] 1 Ch. 182, 192.
[26] See, for instance, Megarry and Wade, *Law of Real Property* (3rd ed., 1966), p. 723.
[27] [1968] 1 W.L.R. 1515.
[28] *Ibid.* 1520.
[29] [1948] 1 K.B. 50.
[30] [1967] 2 Q.B. 379.
[31] Thus adopting the view advocated by C. V. Davidge (1937) 53 L.Q.R. 259.

It was on this broader principle deduced from *Ives Investments Ltd.* v. *High* that Cross J. held that a right to repossess chattels did not come within the statutory definition of an equitable easement. Reference might now be made also to *Shiloh Spinners Ltd.* v. *Harding*[32] where it was held by the House of Lords that an equitable right of entry for breach of a leasehold covenant was not registrable as an equitable easement.

The consequence of the non-registrability holding means that the effect of the equitable interest of the owner of the chattel affixed on purchasers of the land is dependent on the doctrine of notice. Where a person acquires the legal estate, bona fide, for value and without notice of the hire or conditional sale agreement, then his interest prevails over that of the owner of the chattels. We will now explore traditional priority principles a little further in so far as they apply in relation to mortgages.

Mortgages of Unregistered Land and Priorities

Where the land to which chattels are affixed is mortgaged, a question of priority arises between the mortgagee and the chattel owner who has retained a right to repossess. The priorities are settled by application of the maxim—where the equities are equal the first in time prevails. Where the owner of the land grants an equitable mortgage after the chattels have been attached, the equitable mortgagee is postponed to the prior equitable right of the owner of the chattels. A case in point is the Court of Appeal decision in *Re Morrison, Jones and Taylor Ltd.*[33] The case concerned a hire-purchase agreement in respect of an automatic sprinkler. The sprinkler was installed in premises that later formed the subject-matter of a floating security. The hire-purchase agreement provided that in the event of default the owner might enter upon the premises and remove the installation. It was held that the owner of the chattels took precedence over the debenture-holders. Cozens-Hardy M.R. cited with approval the dicta of Parker J. in the earlier case *Re Samuel Allen & Sons Ltd.*[34]:

> "I think that those agreements ... do create an equitable interest by which a subsequent mortgagee who does not get the legal estate is bound, and that, applying the ordinary principles of priorities as between the interest of the hirer under the hiring agreement and the interest created by the equitable mortgage, the interest created by the hiring agreement takes precedence."

Where an equitable mortgage already exists in relation to land to which chattels have been attached, the equitable mortgagee should prevail over the interest of the owner of the chattels by reason of being first in time.[35] This

[32] [1973] A.C. 691.
[33] [1914] 1 Ch. 50.
[34] [1907] 1 Ch. 575, 582.
[35] See *Meux* v. *Jacobs* (1875) L.R. 7 H.L. 481.

is subject to two qualifications, one concerning registration of the mortgage as a land charge and the other concerning trade fixtures, on which more anon.

Legal Mortgages

A legal mortgage executed after attachment of chattels to land will rank ahead of the interest of the owner under a conditional sale or hire agreement unless the mortgage was taken with notice of the prior equitable right. In other words, the legal mortgagee comes first in the priority stakes if he is without notice, actual or constructive, of the earlier equitable right. The attractions of being "Equity's Darling," *i.e.* a bona fide purchaser of the legal estate for value without notice of earlier equitable claims, are no less significant in this context than in the law generally. As A. L. Smith L.J. put it in *Hobson* v. *Gorringe*[36]:

> "Neither could the right [to remove the chattels] be enforced in equity against any purchaser of the land without notice of the right, and the defendant Gorringe is such a purchaser."

Gorringe was a mortgagee who had the legal estate.

If the legal mortgage is prior in point of time to the attachment of the chattels, then it has a double claim to precedence—temporal considerations and also the superiority of the legal estate. This priority, however, is subject to the exceptions discussed under the next two heads.

Registration

The discussion so far has been premised on the assumption that the mortgage is protected by deposit of title deeds. If the mortgage is not protected by deposit of title deeds different considerations apply. The mortgage is registrable under the Land Charges Act if legal as a puisne mortgage, and if equitable as a general equitable charge.[37] Failure to register where appropriate results in a loss of precedence. Section 4(5) of the Land Charges Act 1972 stipulates that a puisne mortgage or general equitable charge shall be "void against a purchaser of the land charged therewith, or of any interest in such land, unless the land charge is registered in the appropriate register before the completion of the purchase."

Is the owner of chattels affixed to land a "purchaser" for this purpose? It appears that he is. The expression is defined as meaning "any person (including a mortgagee or lessee) who, for valuable consideration, takes any interest in land or in a charge on land."[38]

---

[36] [1897] 1 Ch. 182, 192. See also *Gough* v. *Wood & Co.* [1894] 1 Q.B. 713, 717, 722; *Re Samuel Allen & Sons Ltd.* [1907] 1 Ch. 575, 51 and *Re Morrison, Jones and Taylor Ltd.* [1914] 1 Ch. 50, 59.
[37] Land Charges Act 1972, s. 2(4).
[38] Land Charges Act 1972, s. 17(1).

Trade Fixtures

By leaving a mortgagor in possession a mortgagee impliedly gives permission that the mortgagor may fix and unfix chattels to the premises. According to Lindly L.J. in *Gough* v. *Wood & Co.*[39] a mortgagor is impliedly authorised while in possession to hire and bring and fix other fixtures necessary for his business and to agree with their owner that he shall be at liberty to remove them at the end of the term for which they are hired. The specific instance mentioned by the Lord Justice does not exhaust the situations where a right of removal exists. Thus a *Romalpa* seller would be able to enter and remove trade fixtures even though the premises to which they have been attached has been mortgaged.

The Court of Appeal in *Ellis* v. *Glover & Hobson Ltd.*[40] made it clear that this right of removal is subject to two important qualifications. First, it applies only in the absence of an express stipulation to the contrary in the mortgage. Secondly, the right of removal ceases when possession is taken by the mortgagee.[41]

Registered Land

According to the principle enshrined in the Land Registration Acts, a purchaser of registered land takes free from unregistered rights which are not overriding interests. Section 20(1) of the 1925 Act provides that a disposition for valuable consideration of a legal estate in registered land (whether freehold or leasehold) confers that estate upon the transferee or grantee subject only "to the incumbrances and other entries, if any, appearing on the register . . . and . . . to the overriding interests, if any, affecting the estate transferred or created." The title of the new proprietor is "free from all other estates and interests whatsoever." Elsewhere it is declared that:

> ". . . a purchaser acquiring title under a registered disposition shall not be concerned with any . . . document, matter or claim (not being an overiding interest . . .) which is not protected by a caution or other entry on the register, whether he has or has not notice thereof express, implied or constructive."[42]

In *Poster* v. *Slough Estates Ltd.*[43] Cross J. opined that a right to repossess chattels was not an overriding interest. He also suggested that the result of holding that it was not registrable as an equitable easement may, in the case of registered land, be that there was no way of making it bind a purchaser.[44]

---

[39] [1894] 1 Q.B. 713, 720.
[40] [1908] 1 K.B. 388.
[41] For discussion of the priority principles, where a landlord has mortgaged property and the *Romalpa* seller is dealing with the tenant, see Guest and Lever (1963) 27 Conv.(N.S.) 30, 40–41.
[42] Land Registration Act 1925, s. 59(b).
[43] [1968] 1 W.L.R. 1515.
[44] *Ibid*. 1521.

A. G. Guest and Jeremy Lever in their seminal article "Hire-Purchase, Equipment Leases and Fixtures" had taken a different view. In their opinion, the right, while not an overriding interest nor protectible by notice, was protectible by restriction or caution.[45]

It is suggested that neither of these views are correct and that a right to repossess chattels is registrable in the form of a notice on registered land under section 49(1)(f) of the Land Registration Act 1925 which allows for the registration of creditors' notices and "any other right, interest or claim which it may be deemed expedient to protect by notice instead of by caution, inhibition or restriction." Any disposition by a registered proprietor takes effect subject to all estates, rights and claims which are protected by way of notice on the register at the date of registration or entry of notice of the disposition.[46] This is so, in so far as such estates, rights and claims are valid. Therefore, the owner of goods who has agreed to sell them subject to a reservation of title clause may make his interest binding on subequent purchasers or mortgagees of land to which the goods are affixed.

There is one potential drawback, however. A notice may be entered on the register only on production of the land certificate.[47] Therefore, registration is possible only with the assistance of the registered proprietor or where the land certificate happens to be in the registry. The seller of goods in the contract of sale should make provision for securing the co-operation of the conditional buyer in effecting registration of the seller's rights by way of notice.

As an alternative to protection by notice the owner of chattels may seek the entry of a restriction or caution on the register. The entry of a restriction has the effect of precluding further dealings with the registered title unless in the manner expressly indicated by the restriction. To enter a restriction it is normally necessary however to lodge the land certificate with the Registrar.[48] The paradigmatic case of the entry of a restriction involves the protection of equitable interests arising under a trust for sale or strict settlement. The restriction states that no further transaction with the title shall be registered by the Registrar unless capital monies are paid to at least two trustees or to a trust corporation.

Another possibility for the owner of chattels is to register a caution against further dealings. Such an entry has the result that no dealing with the land to which the caution relates is to be registered until notice has been served on the cautioner. The main advantage of the caution is the facility for unilateral action. There is no need for the registered proprietor to co-operate in the procedure by making his land certificate available. A caution is a form of temporary protection. A cautioner may be "warned off" the register unless

[45] *Op. cit.* 43.
[46] Land Registration Act 1925, s. 52.
[47] Land Registration Act 1925, s. 64(1)(c).
[48] But see, however, Land Registration Act 1925, s. 58(5) which provides that rules may be made to enable applications to be made for the entry of restrictions by persons other than the proprietors.

he makes good his claim within 14 days notice of potential adverse action in relation to the land being served upon him. The Registrar has broad discretionary powers and he may order the entry of a notice on the register to protect the interest which was previously safeguarded only by caution. So the ultimate form of protection is the entry of a notice.[49]

If the owner of chattels protects his equitable interest by entry of a notice, restriction or caution on the register, his interest prevails against that of a subsequent purchaser or mortgagee of the land.[50] Any earlier-registered rights but not subsequently registered rights should prevail against him. It has been held, however, that a caution lodged pursuant to section 54 of the Land Registration Act 1925 does not affect the issue of priorities.[51] Therefore a mortgagee has a superior claim to the interest of a person protected by caution even though the mortgage was not registered until after entry of the caution. While the mortgage remained unregistered both interests were minor interests which took effect in equity, and the mortgage, being first in time, enjoyed priority.

Conclusion

After somewhat dense argument it is useful to state a number of points by way of conclusion. The following exposition sums up the points discussed in the chapter.

(1) A clause in a conditional sale agreement forbidding the attachment of goods to land without the consent of the owner will not prevent the courts from holding that the goods constitute fixtures and consequently form part of the land. The test for fixtures turns on the degree and purpose of the annexation so a clause of the kind described above may provide evidence as to the purpose of annexation.

(2) A conditional sale agreement may contain a clause that confers on the seller a right to enter premises to which the goods have been attached and to remove the same. Even without such an express clause the courts have been prepared to imply a right of entry and removal.

(3) A provision of this nature invests the owner with an equitable interest in the land to which the goods have been attached.

(4) This right is not registrable under the Land Charges Act 1972 as an "equitable easement" or in any other category of land charge. Conse-

---

[49] See generally, on cautions, the Land Registration Act 1925, ss. 49 and 50.
[50] Land Registration Act 1925, ss. 20(1) and 59(b).
[51] *Barclays Bank Ltd.* v. *Taylor* [1974] 1 Ch. 137. See also *E. S. Schwab & Co. Ltd.* v. *McCarthy* (1975) 31 P. & C.R. 196; *Watts* v. *Waller* [1973] Q.B. 153. The Law Commission has recommended that the existing rules as to the priority of minor interests should be altered so that priority henceforth should depend on the order of appearance on the register (Law Comm. Working Paper No. 158, para. 4.98).

quently its effect on subsequent purchasers or mortgagees of unregistered land is determined by traditional equitable principles, namely where the equities are equal the first in time prevails.

(5) Where a mortgage protected by deposit of title deeds antedates the attachment of chattels, the mortgagee, whether legal or equitable, takes priority since he is first in time.

(6) If the mortgage is not protected by deposit of the title deeds then it must be registered under the Land Charges Act. If not so registered, the equitable interest of the owner of the chattels ranks ahead of the mortgagees.

(7) A mortgagor in possession is impliedly authorised to affix and remove trade fixtures during the currency of the term. The same right of removal inheres in the owner of the chattels. The right of removal, however, may be ousted by a contrary agreement between mortgagor and mortgagee and in any event comes to an end upon the mortgagee entering into possession.

(8) In the case of registered land, the equitable interest of the owner of chattels attached to land does not constitute a overriding interest which affects subsequent disponees without registration.

(9) The interest is, however, protectible by notice in the register. A subsequent purchaser or mortgagee will not be affected by the interest if not entered on the register but if the interest has been protected by notice it will bind subsequent purchasers, etc.

(10) The equitable interest of the owner of chattels may also be protected by a caution or restriction.

CHAPTER 12

RESERVATION OF TITLE AND THE LAW OF TORT

One of the functions of the law of tort is to protect proprietary and possessory interests in goods. Reservation of title clauses may give rise to a variety of problems which impinge upon that area of law. Some of these have been discussed in passing in previous chapters.[1] For instance, in Chapter 3 on tracing and admixture of goods there is a discussion of the question whether one co-owner can maintain an action in conversion against another.[2]

If a company buys goods that are subject to a reservation of title clause and it later goes into liquidation, receivership or administration, the relevant insolvency practitioner will need to know whether he is entitled to deal with the goods as if they belonged to the company. If they still belong to the suppliers, the liquidator, receiver or administrator may well be liable for the torts of trespass or conversion if he interferes with their interest. *Clough Mill Ltd.* v. *Martin*,[3] for example, involved an action in conversion. A receiver permitted the buyers to use yarn which had been supplied subject to a reservation of title clause, without paying the suppliers. The latter instituted proceedings against the receiver claiming damages for wrongfully depriving them of possession of the yarn and converting it to his own use. The action proved successful in the Court of Appeal.

Even if the purchasing company has not gone into liquidation the goods may be damaged or destroyed by a third party. The question would then arise as to who is entitled to sue for wrongful interference with the goods or under the tort of negligence. Does the supplier and/or the buyer have the requisite type of interest to be able to sue? Again, if the suppliers wish to enforce the reservation of title clause, are they entitled to go on to the land where the goods happen to be and to remove the same? Each of these issues shall be considered in turn.

Interference with Goods

The law on "chattel torts" is notoriously complicated and the Torts (Interference with Goods) Act 1977 did not do much to simplify it.[4] The Act

[1] See in particular, *supra*, Chap. 11.
[2] See *supra*, pp. 55–56.
[3] [1985] 1 W.L.R. 111.
[4] Clerk and Lindsell, *The Law of Torts* (16th ed., 1989), Chap. 22; *Halsbury's Laws of England* (4th ed.), Vol. 45; Rogers, *Winfield and Jolowicz on Tort* (13th ed., 1989), Chap. 17; Brazier, *Street On Torts* (8th ed., 1988), Chap. 4. For an account of the 1977 Act, see Palmer, *Bailment* (1979), pp. 1014–1034. S.234 of the Insolvency Act 1986 should also be borne in mind in this context. The section provides that where an administrator, administrative receiver, liquidator

abolished the old tort known as detinue but maintained the distinction between conversion of goods and trespass to goods. Detinue was committed when a person who was in possession of another's goods refused to give them up. Section 2 of the 1977 Act makes it clear that such refusal can now constitute conversion, at least in the preponderance of cases.[5] Section 2(2) provides as follows:

> "An action lies in conversion for loss or destruction of goods which a bailee has allowed to happen in breach of his duty to the bailor (that is to say it lies in a case which is not otherwise conversion, but would have been detinue before detinue was abolished)."

Conversion may be described succinctly as an intentional dealing with goods which is seriously inconsistent with the possession or right to immediate possession of another person.[6] Trespass to goods on the other hand, involves an intentional or negligent interference with goods in the possession of the plaintiff provided that the interference is direct.[7] I shall look more closely at the precise forms of conduct which constitute conversion or trespass before delving into the questions of entitlement to sue and the measure of damages recoverable. Most attention will be directed at conversion, since this tort has more significance in the reservation of title context.

Conversion nowadays is a bit like ancient Gaul which as Caesar said, was divided into three parts.[8] The first form of conversion and the classic conception, entails dealing with goods in a manner incompatible with the right of the true owner, provided that in so doing the defendant intends to deny the owner's right or to assert a right inconsistent with it. Some amplification of this idea was provided by Lord Porter in *Caxton Publishing Co. Ltd.* v. *Sutherland Publishing Co.*[9] He said[10]:

> "Another way of reaching the same conclusion would be to say that conversion consists in an act intentionally done inconsistent with the owner's right, though the doer may not know of or intend to challenge the property or possession of the true owner."

In *Penfolds Wines Pty. Ltd.* v. *Elliott*[11] Dixon J. investigated in some detail the actions which may amount to conversion. He said that conversion may

or provisional liquidator disposes of property which is not property of the company, he is not liable to the true owner if at the time of seizure or disposal he believes and has reasonable cause to believe that he is entitled to seize or dispose of the goods. Rights to trace the proceeds of sale remain with the true owner: see generally, *supra*, p. 127.

[5] In *Howard E. Perry & Co. Ltd.* v. *British Railways Board* [1908] 1 W.L.R. 1375, Megarry V.-C. observed that every act of detinue by adverse detention amounted also at common law to a conversion but it has been argued that this dictum was not necessary to the immediate decision and is too widely stated: see Palmer, "Title to Goods and Occupation of Land: A Conflict of Interests" (1980) 9 *Anglo-American Law Review* 279, 291.

[6] Brazier, *Street On Torts*, *ibid.* p. 36.

[7] *Ibid.* p. 59.

[8] *Gallic Wars* Book One, p. 1.

[9] [1939] A.C. 178. See also the statement of Atkin J. in *Lancashire & Yorkshire Railway Co.* v. *MacNicoll* (1918) 88 L.J.K.B. 601, 605.

[10] *Ibid.* 202.

[11] (1946) 74 C.L.R. 204, 228–230.

take the form of a disposal of the goods by way of sale, or pledge, or other intended transfer of an interest followed by delivery. Mere damage to the chattel however was not conversion; neither was use otherwise than for the purpose of affecting the immediate right to possession. Let us apply this statement of principle in the reservation of title context.

In many of the leading cases on *Romalpa* clauses there has been much discussion about the implied terms which must be read into a supply contract in order to give it business efficacy. The assumption is that unless the terms of the contract afford some justification for the buyer's (or liquidator, etc.'s) actions, the acts committed will amount to conversion. Using goods is, as we have seen, enough to constitute conversion. So is a resale or hiring out of the goods. But by section 21(1) of the Sale of Goods Act 1979 the owner of goods can be estopped by his own conduct from denying the seller's authority to sell. This is a specific statutory instance of a more general principle which can be applied to non-resale situations. Thus, if a seller has supplied goods subject to a reservation of title clause, and the clause is not just a "simple" clause but one which is linked to the payment of other debts owed by the buyer and/or purports to cover other goods which are wholly or partly manufactured out of the goods supplied, or the proceeds of any of those goods, then the supplier might be held to be estopped from denying that the buyer had the right to deal with the goods as if he were the owner.

The second form of conversion involves wrongful detention of goods by the defendant. The *locus classicus* here is *Howard E. Perry & Co. Ltd.* v. *British Railways Board.*[12] Here it was argued that a mere refusal in response to a demand was not itself a conversion, though it could be evidence of a conversion. The case concerned a supply of steel in the defendant's possession awaiting delivery to the plaintiffs which the defendants refused to allow the plaintiffs themselves to collect. Ordinarily the steel would have been delivered by members of the National Union of Railwaymen in the defendants' employ but these workers were instructed by their union to "black" the steel. British Rail feared an upsurge in industrial unrest if the plaintiffs were allowed to collect it.

The defendants denied conversion. Reference was made to the words of Bramwell B. in *Hiort* v. *Bott*[13] that a good description of what constituted a conversion was "where a man does an unauthorised act which deprives another of his property permanently or for an indefinite time. The defendants argued that "indefinite time" meant a period which was not only uncertain in length but also of substantial duration. In essence their contention was that the Torts (Interference with Goods) Act 1977 had blundered by removing from the sphere of tort some acts which previously were clearly tortious, without any apparent reason for doing so. Pre-1977, the defendants would have committed the tort of detinue by refusing to deliver the goods but it was argued that their conduct did not constitute conversion.

[12] [1980] 1 W.L.R. 1375.
[13] (1874) L.R. 9 Ex. 86, 89.

Megarry V.-C. would have none of this. He referred to the *Eighteenth Report of the Law Reform Committee*[14] for a statement of the pre-existing law. The report states at paragraph 8:

"The present position appears to be that conversion will lie in every case in which detinue would lie, save only that detinue lies, but conversion does not lie, against a bailee of goods who in breach of his duty has allowed them to be lost or destroyed."

Mention was also made of the Common Law Procedure Act 1852 where the course of action in conversion was stated as follows:

"That the defendant converted to his own use, or wrongfully deprived the plaintiff of the use and possession of the plaintiff's goods."

The judge said that the defendants here were denying the plaintiffs most of the rights of ownership for an indefinite period. He added that a denial of possession to the plaintiffs did not cease to be a denial merely because it was accompanied by a statement that the plaintiffs were entitled to the possession that was being denied to them.[15]

The third mode of conversion is that referred to in section (2) of the 1977 Act, namely an action for loss or destruction of goods which a bailee has allowed to happen in breach of his duty to the bailor. This form of liability fell within the concept of detinue before the reforms effected in 1977. Before 1977 liability in conversion presupposed a voluntary act by the alleged tortfeasor. As Maugham L.J. put it in *The Arpad*[16] if goods were by accident or carelessness lost or destroyed the possessor could not be sued for conversion. This state of affairs remains true today with the exception of the case alluded to in section 2(2) of the Act of 1977.

A couple of cases may be cited in support of the no liability in conversion for mere negligence point of view. For instance in *Heald* v. *Carey*[17] Maule J. stated straightforwardly that a negligent dealing with goods was not a conversion. A suit only lies where some dominion was asserted by the defendant over the chattel which was the subject of the action. Conversion can occur when goods are destroyed. This may take effect when a chattel is burnt or broken to pieces and also when it is so dealt with that its identity is dissipated subject to the qualification that there be a voluntary act. A case in point is *Simmons* v. *Lillystone*.[18] Here the defendant in the process of digging a sawpit had sawn through the plaintiff's timber embedded in the soil of the defendant's close. Later some of the timber was swept away by the Thames and it was held that no conversion had been committed. Parke B. put the matter thus[19]:

[14] Cmnd. 4774. The judge remarked that the report of the Committee was signed by a number of eminent judges (Lord Pearson, Lord Diplock, Buckley L.J. and Orr L.J.) as well as by himself.
[15] [1980] 1 W.L.R. 1375, 1380.
[16] [1934] P. 189, 232.
[17] (1852) 11 C.B. 762.
[18] (1853) 8 Ex. 430.
[19] *Ibid.* 442.

"In order to constitute a conversion, there must be an intention of the defendant to take to himself the property in the goods, or to deprive the plaintiff of it. If the entire article is destroyed, as for instance by burning it, that would be a taking of the property from the plaintiff and depriving him of it, although the defendant might not be considered as appropriating it to his own use. In this case nothing is done but cutting the timber, and by accident, it is washed away by the river—not purposely thrown by the defendant to be washed away; consequently, we think that does not amount to a conversion."

Trespass has been described as a wrong done to possession.[20] The essence of the action lies in the unlawful taking, damaging or removal of a personal chattel provided that the taking, etc., is direct.

Entitlement to Sue

As Ackner L.J. observed in *The Playa Larga*[21] the general rule is that the right to bring an action for conversion of goods belongs to the person who can prove that he had, at the time of conversion, either actual possession or the immediate right to possess. This statement is certainly in accord with the authorities. One might cite *Lord* v. *Price*.[22] Here it was held that the purchaser of goods which remain in the possession of the vendor subject to the vendor's lien for unpaid purchase money cannot maintain an action of conversion against the wrongdoer. Bramwell B. stated shortly that the action cannot be maintained without a right of present possession in the plaintiff. He said that here there was no evidence that the plaintiff had any right of possession. That right was in the vendor, who was entitled to retain possession of the goods until the balance of the purchase money was paid, and on non-payment, to resell the goods and recoup himself for any loss sustained on the resale.

Possession *per se* is relatively non-problematic. For there to be possession, the plaintiff must not only have factual control over the goods but also the intention to exercise control. It does not matter that the possession was unlawfully obtained in the first place, so even thieves can sue in conversion if the property they steal is later interfered with by a third party.[23] Of course, the need to have factual control over the goods does not mean that the plaintiff must at all times have them by his side. They may be miles away but left in such a state as to indicate that he is their possessor (*e.g.* under lock and key).[24]

---

[20] See, *e.g.* Dixon J. in *Penfolds Wines Pty. Ltd.* v. *Elliott* (1946) 74 C.L.R. 204 at 224. See also, *Gordon* v. *Harper* (1796) 7 Term Rep. 9.

[21] [1983] 2 Lloyd's Rep. 171, 187.

[22] (1874) L.R. 9 Ex. 54.

[23] Clerk and Lindsell, *op. cit.* para. 22.60, suggest quoting Winfield, *Tort* (9th ed.), pp. 308–309 that "even wrongful possession such as that acquired by a thief, will, in principle, be protected except against the owner of the thing stolen or someone acting lawfully on his behalf."

[24] For a discussion of what constitutes possession in the eyes of the law, see *Salmond on Jurisprudence* (12th ed., 1966), Chap. 9.

A Right to Immediate Possession

The right to immediate possession as the foundation of an action in conversion gives rise to a host of difficulties. This basis of the action is well established. A case often cited in the textbooks is *Rogers* v. *Kennay*.[25] Here Patteson J. quoted Parke B. in the earlier case of *Legg* v. *Evans*[26] that "any person having a right to the possession of goods may bring trover in respect of the conversion of them, and allege them to be his property."[27] A right of lien, as a right of immediate possession, was held to ground an action.

Although one of the usual concomitants of ownership is the right to immediate possession, this may be given up for a limited period by virtue of a contractual arrangement between the owner and another party. This contractual limitation proved fatal in the Australian High Court decision *Short* v. *City Bank of Sydney*.[28] The case concerned the storage of wheat. Isaacs J. opined that the construction of the owner's contract with the storage company, he had no right to resume possession of the wheat for eight months. On the assumption of an existing contact the owner had no right to have possession of the goods—at least in the absence of any unauthorised dealing with them by the society.[29] Therefore the action had to fail. *Lord* v. *Price*[30] was cited in this connection.

When goods are supplied subject to a reservation of title clause, the very least which the clause will say is that property in the goods is not to pass to the buyer until they are fully paid for. Does this leave the supplier with the requisite possession or right to possession for the purposes of suing in conversion? The answer is certainly "no" if the right to immediate possession still vests in the buyer under the terms of the contract but the supply contract may contain further or additional terms. The contract may provide that the supplier retains the right to possession as well as ownership, but that he may grant the buyer permission to have possession so long as any credit period remains unexpired. This is a pretty severe restriction on the buyer's right. A more common clause would be to invest the seller with a right to resume possession in certain specified circumstances. In *Re Peachdart Ltd.*,[31] for example, the reservation of title provision was drafted in the following terms:

> "(b) However, the ownership of the products shall remain with the seller which reserves the right to dispose of the products until payment in full for all the products has been received by it in accordance with the terms of this contract or until such time as the buyer sells the products to its customers by way of *bona fide* sale at full market value. If such

[25] [1846] 9 Q.B. 594.
[26] (1841) 6 M. & W. 36 at 41.
[27] [1846] 9 Q.B. 594 at 595–596.
[28] (1912) 15 C.L.R. 148.
[29] *Ibid.* 157.
[30] (1874) L.R. 9 Ex. 54.
[31] [1984] 1 Ch. 131.

payment is overdue in whole or in part the seller may (without prejudice to any of its other rights) recover or resell the products or any of them and may enter upon the buyer's premises by its servants or agents for that purpose. Such payment shall become due immediately upon the commencement of any act or proceeding in which the buyer's solvency is involved."

Controversy has often arisen in the context of hire-purchase agreements, which usually say that the agreement will terminate as soon as the hirer disposes of the goods or acts in a way which is repugnant to the terms of the agreement. In *Union Transport Finance Ltd.* v. *British Car Auctions Ltd.*[32] the owners of a car successfully sued a firm of auctioneers who had sold it on the instructions of a dishonest hire-purchaser. The Court of Appeal held that the owners had acquired the right to immediate possession as soon as the hire-purchaser instructed the auctioneers to sell the car, for the agreement had said that the hire-purchaser would not, without the owner's prior consent, part with possession or control of the car or sell it or offer it for sale. The hire-purchaser himself could also have been sued had any trace of him been discovered.

The auctioneers had contended that the plaintiffs could not maintain the action in conversion because, by the terms of the hire-purchase agreement, the plaintiffs had no right to immediate possession unless they served a notice of termination. The Court of Appeal however held that the hire-purchase contract on its true construction did not operate to prevent the plaintiffs from immediately terminating the agreement apart from its express provisions and thus claiming to be the persons entitled to immediate possession and thus to sue for conversion.[33] Roskill L.J. regarded it as axiomatic that the act of the bailee in doing something inconsistent with the terms of the contract terminates the bailment, causing the possessory title to revert to the bailor and entitling him to maintain an action in conversion.[34]

Bridge L.J. agreed. He also observed that it would be possible to introduce into a contract of bailment a term expressly limiting the manner in which the bailee's right to possession as against the bailor could be terminated.[35] The clearest terms however, were required to have that effect. A clause which merely gave a right to terminate by notice for any breach of the

---

[32] [1978] 2 All E.R. 385.

[33] *Ibid.* 389. Reference was made in this connection to the decision of the Court of Appeal in *North Central Wagon and Finance Co. Ltd.* v. *Graham* [1950] 2 K.B. 7, 15 where Cohen L.J. quoted Pollock and Wright's *Possession in the Common Law* (p. 132) to the following effect:

"Any act or disposition which is wholly repugnant to or as it were an absolute disclaimer of the holding as bailee re-vests the bailor's right to possession and therefore also his immediate right to maintain trover or detinue even where the bailment is for a term or is otherwise not revocable at will, and so *a fortiori* in a bailment determinable at will."

[34] *Ibid.* 390.

[35] *Ibid.* 391. The learned Lord Justice said that in the present case the clause could not possibly be construed as restricting the bailor's right to terminate the bailment without notice on the happening of a breach which was a repudiation.

contract of bailment could not possibly have that result. Its purpose was to enhance the bailor's right and not to restrict them. The object was to give a right to terminate for breach of any term of the bailment, not just for repudiatory breaches.

The lesson from *Union Transport Finance Ltd.* v. *British Car Auctions Ltd.* is that while the owner of goods may confer on himself a right to resume possession of the goods in a wide variety of circumstances, this does not necessarily exhaust his rights. Any act which is wholly repugnant to the status of a hirer or conditional buyer as bailee revests the bailor's right to possession. It remains to be determined what acts are of this precise character. It would not perhaps be sufficient if the buyer merely failed to store the goods in accordance with the terms of the contract or if the goods were put through some manufacturing process which was not expressly allowed by those terms. But if the contract were to prohibit the buyer from, say, offering the goods to a third party as security for a further loan, or from reselling the goods without giving the supplier notice of the resale, any breach of these terms might well automatically reinvest the right to immediate possession in the supplier and thereby justify a suit in conversion. The corollary, of course, is that if the right to immediate possession has not in the eyes of the law been reinstated in the supplier, any attempt to recover the goods may itself amount to conversion committed by the supplier of goods in the possession of the buyer.

The "deviation from the terms of a bailment" cases may provide some guidance in this context.[36] In *Lilley* v. *Doubleday*[37] the defendant contracted to warehouse certain goods at a particular place, but warehoused them at another place where, without any negligence on his part, they were destroyed. A successful action in conversion was mounted by the owner of the goods. Essentially the court held that by departing from the central tenets of the bailment, the defendant had forfeited his status as a bailee and thereby his immunity from liability on proof of reasonable care.

Where the plaintiff in an action in conversion relies on an immediate right to possession, this right must have a proprietary base. It is clear however that an equitable proprietary base suffices for this purpose. The leading case is *International Factors Ltd.* v. *Rodriquez*.[38] Here the plaintiff was the beneficiary under a trust created by a debt factoring agreement. The defendant had misapplied to his own use four cheques which constituted part of the subject-matter of the trust. It was held by the Court of Appeal that he could be sued in conversion by the plaintiff.

Sir Davin Cairns (with whom Bridge L.J. agreed) cited *Jarvis* v. *Williams*[39] as authority for the proposition that a contractual right to have goods

---

[36] See Palmer, *Bailment* (1979), Chap. 13. See also C. Debattista [1989] J.B.L. 22; C. Cashmore [1989] J.B.L. 492.

[37] [1881] 7 Q.B.D. 510.

[38] [1979] 1 Q.B. 351.

[39] [1955] 1 W.L.R. 71. Reference was made to the observations of Sir Raymond Evershed at 74.

handed to him by another person was not in itself sufficient to clothe the person who has that right with the freedom to sue in conversion. The position was different however where the plaintiff was the beneficiary under a trust. *Healey* v. *Healey*[40] was mentioned in this connection. According to the learned judge the policy favouring a right of action in the *cestui que trust* was a strong one since the fusion of law and equity.[41]

The decision of the Privy Council in *Maynegrain Pty. Ltd.* v. *Campafina Bank*[42] confirms that a person with an equitable proprietary interest—in that case the interest of an equitable pledgee—may maintain an action in conversion. It has been argued that the defendant's knowledge of the plaintiff's equitable interest is a necessary ingredient of liability.[43] This view derives some support from the observations of Sir David Cairns in *International Factors Ltd.* v. *Rodriquez* that the defendant "knew perfectly well that what he was doing was contrary to the agreement with the plaintiff"[44] which gave rise to the trust. The *Maynegrain* case does not explore this issue much further.

How may one relate this discussion back to the reservation of title context? In *Re Bond Worth Ltd.*[45] Slade J. held that where a seller purported to reserve "equitable and beneficial ownership" this operated as a transfer to the buyer followed by a transfer back to the seller. This retransfer was held to create a charge which was void for want of registration under the companies legislation. Since *Bond Worth* persons who draft supply contracts would be well advised to eschew use of the phrase "equitable and beneficial ownership." *Bond Worth* has been heavily criticised however.[46] The cases we have discussed justify the conclusion that if a seller purports to rely on equitable proprietorship he is not thereby deprived of rights of action in conversion.

Trespass—Entitlement to Sue

The better view appears to be that to mount an action in trespass the plaintiff must have had actual possession of the goods at the time that the alleged tort occurred.[47] A seminal case is *Ward* v. *Macaulay*.[48] Here Lord

---

[40] [1915] 1 K.B. 938.

[41] Professor Norman Palmer has questioned whether the Court's insistence upon an immediate right to possession which emanates from some proprietary right was securely grounded on existing authority: see "The Vindication of Commercial Security Over Commodities: equitable pledges and conversion" [1986] L.M.C.L.Q. 218. Reference is there made to *Bolwell Fibreglass Pty. Ltd.* v. *Foley* [1984] V.R. 97, 98–99, 117, *per* Young C.J. and Brooking J. respectively.

[42] [1984] 1 N.S.W.L.R. 258.

[43] See Palmer, *op. cit.* pp. 226–230. *But* it may be argued *contra* that English commercial law has set its face against any notion at least of constructive notice: see *Manchester Trust* v. *Furness* [1895] 2 Q.B. 539.

[44] [1979] 1 Q.B. 351, 355.

[45] [1980] 1 Ch. 228, 252–256.

[46] See *supra*, Chap. 1, pp. 9–10 and Chap. 6, pp. 103–104 for references therein contained.

[47] See *Halsbury's Laws of England* (4th ed.), Vol. 45, paras. 1494–1495; Clerk and Lindsell on Torts (16th ed., 1989), para. 22.120.

[48] (1791) 4 Term Rep. 489.

Kenyon C.J. said the distinction between actions of trespass and conversion is well settled: the former is founded on possession; the latter on property. There are suggestions in some of the authorities though that a right to immediate possession may form the basis of a trespass action. In the Australian High Court decision *Penfolds Wines Pty. Ltd.* v. *Elliott*[49] Dixon J. quoted Pollock and Wright's *Possession in the Common Law*[50] to the effect that the right to possession, as a title for maintaining trespass was a right in one person to sue for a trespass done to another's possession.

Measure of Damages Recoverable

It seems clear that a plaintiff who sues in conversion relying on actual possession or a right to immediate possession, may recover the full value of the goods converted. He is not confined to the value of his limited proprietary interest. The leading case is now the Privy Council decision in *The Jag Shakti*.[51] Lord Brandon who gave the opinion of the Board expressed himself in the following terms[52]:

> "It has been ... established by authority of long standing, that where one person, A, who has or is entitled to have possession of goods, is deprived of such possession by the tortious conduct of another person, B, whether such conduct consists in conversion or negligence the proper measure in law of the damages recoverable by A from B is the full market value for the goods at the time when and the place where possession of them should have been given. For this purpose it is irrelevant whether A has the general property in the goods as the outright owner of them, or only a special property in them as pledgee, or only possession or a right to possession of them as a bailee. Furthermore, the circumstance that if A recovers the full market value of the goods from B, he may be liable to account for the whole or part of what he has recovered to a third party, C, is also irrelevant, as being *res inter alias acta*."

The authority of long standing referred to by Lord Brandon is *The Winkfield*.[53] This is a case where the owners of a ship were sued for negligently causing the loss of another ship which was carrying mail in the custody of the Postmaster-General. The Court of Appeal held that the Postmaster-General should succeed in his claim as bailee even though he himself could not have been sued in respect of the lost mail by the bailors (the persons who

---

[49] (1946) 74 C.L.R. 204, 224–228. The meaning of this statement is not immediately apparent.
[50] At pp. 144–145.
[51] [1986] 1 A.C. 337.
[52] *Ibid*. 345.
[53] [1902] P. 42. See also *Swire* v. *Leach* (1865) 18 C.B.N.S. 479; *cf. Claridge* v. *South Staffordshire Tramway Co.* [1892] 1 Q.B. 422. See too, *Armory* v. *Delamire* (1721) 1 Stra. 504; *Burton* v. *Hughes* (1842) 2 Bins. 173; *Sutton* v. *Buck* (1810) 2 Taunt. 302 and *Turner* v. *Hardcastle* (1862) 11 C.B.N.S. 683.

had sent the letters). Collins M.R. cited other cases where finders, borrowers and pawnbrokers had all been allowed to sue regardless of their position *vis-à-vis* the owners of the goods in question. In a passage of considerable clarity and lucidity he summed up the matter thus[54]:

> "[t]he root principle of the whole discussion is that, as against a wrong-doer, possession is title. The chattel that has been converted or damaged is deemed to be the chattel of the possessor and of no other, and therefore its loss or deterioration is his loss, and to him, if he demands it, it must be recouped. His obligation to account to the bailor is really not *ad rem* in the discussion. It only comes in after he has carried his legal position to its logical consequence against a wrongdoer, and serves to soothe a mind disconcerted by the notion that a person who is not himself the complete owner should be entitled to receive back the full value of the chattel converted or destroyed. There is no inconsistency between the two positions; the one is the complement of the other. As between bailee and stranger possession gives title—that is, not a limited interest but absolute and complete ownership, and he is entitled to receive back a complete equivalent for the whole loss or deterioration of the thing itself. As between bailor and bailee the real interests of each must be inquired into, and, as the bailee has to account for the thing bailed, so he must account for that which has become its equivalent and now represents it. What he has received above his own interest he has received to the use of his bailor. The wrongdoer, having once paid full damages to the bailee, has an answer to any action by the bailor."

Statute has now intervened in this area. Section 8 of the Torts (Interference with Goods) Act 1977 permits a defendant in an action for wrongful interference with goods (which includes the tort of conversion) to show that a third party has a better right than the plaintiff as respects all or any part of the interest claimed by the plaintiff, or in right of which he sues. Any rule of law (the *ius tertii*) to the contrary is abolished. The aim of this exercise is that other interested parties be brought before the court so that a full and final determination may be made. The section has been fleshed out by rules of court made thereunder. The rules stipulate that, if a plaintiff is one of two or more persons having, or claiming any interest in the goods concerned, he must, save where he has the written authority of every other such person to sue on the latter's behalf, indorse his writ or originating summons with a statement giving particulars of his own title and identifying every other person who, to his knowledge, either has or claims any interest in the goods.[55]

Section 7 of the 1977 Act is designed to avoid a situation of double liability. The section applies whenever (a) two or more rights of action for

---

[54] *Ibid.* 60. See also, Palmer, *Bailment* (1979) Chap. 4.
[55] R.S.C., Ord. 15, r. 10A; C.C.R. 1981, Ord. 15, r. 4; *Clerk and Lindsell, op. cit.* para. 22.79.

wrongful interference are founded on a possessory title or (b) where the measure of damages in an action for wrongful interference founded on a proprietary title is or includes the entire value of the goods, although the interest is one of two or more interests in the goods. Where two or more claimants sue concurrently the relief awarded must be such as to avoid double liability. The matter is more troublesome if competing or cumulative claims are not made concurrently. A claimant will still recover the full value of the goods but an overcompensated claimant is liable to account to other potential claimants to such an extent as will avoid double liability on the part of the wrongdoer. Moreover, where as the result of enforcement of a double liability a claimant is unjustly enriched to any extent, he becomes liable to reimburse the wrongdoer to that extent.[56]

Section 3 of the 1977 Act deals with remedies. The section lays down that in proceedings for wrongful interference against a person who is in possession or in control of the goods, relief may take any of the following forms:

(a) an order for delivery of the goods, and for payment of any consequential damages; or

(b) an order for delivery of the goods, but giving the defendant the alternative of paying damages by reference to the value of the goods, together in either alternative with payment of any consequential damages; or

(c) damages *simpliciter*.

Relief under the first head is at the discretion of the court but the claimant himself may choose between (b) and (c).

Take a situation where goods have been sold subject to a reservation of title agreement. Say a tortfeasor has converted the goods to his own use. Assume also that the market value of the goods is less than the amount remaining due under the contract of sale. May the owner or conditional buyer recover this amount from the tortfeasor or is the claim limited to the market value of the goods at the time of the wrong? The Australian case *Miller* v. *Candy*[57] suggests that the cause of action is confined to the market value of the goods.

This case involved a motor vehicle supplied under a hire-purchase agreement. The hirer sought to recover from a tortfeasor the difference between the market value of the vehicle and the sum due pursuant to the hire-purchase agreement. The attempt failed. McGregor J. opined that the loss claimed flowed from a collateral matter. As far as the wrongdoer was concerned this loss was *res inter alios acta*.[58]

---

[56] s.7(4).

[57] (1981) 58 F.L.R. 145.

[58] See the extensive review of the mainly textbook authorities conducted at pp. 161–165. Counsels' research and the court's own investigation failed to discover any cases directly in point. Blackburn J. agreed with McGregor J. Franki J. dissented.

Trespass—Measure of Damages

In trespass, a plaintiff is entitled to recover for the destruction or deprecia-tion of goods suffered as a result of the tortious act.[59] The statutory rules in the Torts (Interference with Goods) Act 1977 in relation to avoidance of double liability, joinder of interested parties, etc., apply to trespass in the same way as they affect actions in conversion.

Protection of Reversionary Interests

A bailor of goods with no immediate right to possession may bring an action on the case for damage to his reversionary interest.[60] An example would be the supplier of goods subject to a reservation of title clause where the contract has been drafted so as to restrict his right to possession save in certain circumstances. The *locus classicus* on damage to reversionary inter-ests is *Mears* v. *London and South Western Ry. Co.*[61] Here it was held that the owner of a chattel—in this case a barge—which was out on hire for an unexpired term, might maintain an action against a third party for a perma-nent injury thereto.

There is not a great deal of analysis in the judgments. Erle C.J. referred to *Tancred* v. *Allgood*[62] where he suggested it was held by implication that an action for permanent injury done to a chattel while the owner's right to the possession is suspended, may be maintained.[63] Williams J. argued that though the owner cannot bring an action where there has been no perma-nent injury to the chattel, it has never been doubted, where there is a permanent injury, the owner may maintain an action against the person whose wrongful act has caused that injury.

In the Queensland case *Henry Berry and Co. Pty. Ltd.* v. *Rushton*,[64] Henchman J. applied this principle. He said that a person not in actual possession or entitled immediately to such possession could sue if he had been deprived, permanently or temporarily, of the benefit of his reversion-ary interest. The judge added[65]:

> "Thus he can sue if the chattel has been destroyed or if it has been so disposed of that a valid title to it has become vested in a third person, as by sale in market overt, or if after his reversionary interest has fallen into possession, he is prevented from obtaining possession by reason of the previous act of conversion."

Henchman J. went on to hold that damage was the gist of the action and

---

[59] See *Halsbury's Laws of England* section on DAMAGES (4th ed.), Vol. 12, paras. 1159, 1163–1167.
[60] See Palmer, *Bailment* (1979), pp. 153–155.
[61] (1862) 11 C.B.N.S. 850.
[62] (1859) 4 Hurlst. & N. 438.
[63] (1862) 11 C.B.N.S. 850 854.
[64] [1937] St.R.Qd. 109.
[65] *Ibid.* 117. Reference was made to *Donald* v. *Suckling* (1866) L.R. 1 Q.B. 585 and *Halliday* v. *Holgate* (1867) L.R. 3 Ex. 302–303.

the value of the chattel was not the measure of the damages. There are also the observations of Pollock C.B. in *Tancred* v. *Allgood*[66] along such lines. He said that in these situations the damage sustained by the plaintiff was the whole foundation of the action.

A somewhat discordant note was struck in another Australian case: *Dee Trading Co. Pty. Ltd.* v. *Baldwin*.[67] Here repair costs were recovered by the owner of a vehicle let on hire purchase from the defendant tortfeasor. According to Gavon Duffy J. these were probably recoverable from the hirer of the vehicle. Nevertheless he said that a wrongdoer could not minimise damages by proving that there was some other source from which the complainant might recoup its losses. *Tancred* v. *Allgood* and *Henry Berry & Co. Pty. Ltd.* v. *Rushton* are not discussed in the judgment however and it is best perhaps to regard the case as an aberration.

The action on the case for damage to a reversionary interest is brought within the new generic category of wrongful interference with goods by the Torts (Interference with Goods) Act 1977. That term is defined in section 1 as including, *inter alia*, "(c) negligence so far as it results in damage to goods or to an interest in goods." The legislation does not address the issue however of the quantum of damages recoverable.

Negligence

To succeed in an action for negligence, a plaintiff must show that the defendant owed him or her a duty of care and that the loss suffered was not too remote. In cases involving loss of or damage to goods, courts have held that the plaintiff must have the legal ownership of, or a possessory title to, the property in question at the time when the loss or damage occurred. Merely having contractual rights in relation to the property is not enough, even where they have been adversely affected by the loss or damage though a contractually derived right of possession may be enough to ground an action.

In the leading case of *Cattle* v. *Stockton Waterworks Co.*,[68] a contractor who was carrying out work on another's land was held to be unable to recover from a waterworks company the loss suffered as a result of that company's negligence in causing or permitting water to leak from a pipe laid and owned by it. This and intervening decisions were approved by the Privy Council in *Candlewood Navigation Corpn.* v. *Mitsui O.S.K. Lines Ltd.*,[69] on appeal from the Supreme Court of New South Wales. In that case, time charterers of a ship were held unable to sue the owners of another ship which had negligently collided with the chartered ship and caused economic loss to the charterers (by necessitating payment of further hire charges and entail-

---

[66] (1859) 4 Hurlst. & N. 438 444.
[67] [1938] V.L.R. 173.
[68] (1875) L.R. 10 Q.B. 453.
[69] [1986] A.C. 1, on which see Tettenborn [1986] C.L.J. 13 and Jones (1986) 102 L.Q.R. 13.

ing loss of profits). The reason given was that which is enshrined as part of the *ratio decidendi* of many earlier cases, namely, that in the case of a chattel the common law does not confer rights to sue in tort on persons whose only right is a contractual right to have the use of the chattel for purposes of making a profit or gain and who do not have possession of or property in the chattel.[70]

Within a year the House of Lords came to the same conclusion in a similar case. In *Leigh and Sillavan Ltd. v. Aliakmon Shipping Co. Ltd. (The Aliakmon)*[71] the buyers of steel coils which were being shipped c & f from South Korea to England attempted to sue the shipowners for their negligent stowing of the cargo on board. They were not permitted to do so. Although they had accepted the risk of goods being damaged, they had not yet become the holder of the bill of lading for the goods and had no other legal ownership in or possessory title to the goods at the time when the loss or damage occurred. The House approved the decision in *Margarine Union GmbH v. Cambay Prince Steamship Co. Ltd. (The Wear Breeze)*,[72] where c.i.f. buyers who had accepted four delivery orders for part of a bulk cargo of copra were held unable to sue the shipowners for loss caused by the improper fumigation of the cargo holds before the copra was loaded.

In answer to the argument put forward in *The Aliakmon* to the effect that under a c.i.f. or c & f contract the buyer immediately acquires equitable ownership of goods once they have been shipped, Lord Brandon cited with approval the *obiter dictum* of Atkin L.J. in *Re Wait*,[73] where he said that the Sale of Goods Act 1893 had codified "the total sum of legal relations" arising out of a contract for the sale of goods. In Atkin L.J.'s words[74]:

> "It would have been futile in a Code intended for commercial men to have created an elaborate structure of rules dealing with rights at law, if at the same time it was intended to leave, subsisting with the legal rights, equitable rights inconsistent with, more extensive, and coming into existence earlier than the rights so carefully set out in the various sections of the Code."

Lord Brandon also said that, even if the buyer were an equitable owner of the goods, he could not sue in his own name but only in the joint names of himself and the legal owner. Only if the buyer has a possessory title in addition to the equitable ownership could he himself sue in tort for negligence.[75]

---

[70] See, *e.g. Simpson & Co. v. Thompson* [1877] 3 A.C. 279; *S.A. de Remorquage a Helice v. Bennetts* [1911] 1 K.B. 243.
[71] [1986] 1 A.C. 785 on which see Reynolds [1986] L.M.C.L.Q.; Tettenborn [1987] J.B.L. 12; Powles, *ibid.* 313; Markesinis (1987) 103 L.Q.R. 354, 385 *et seq.*; Goode, *ibid.* 433, 453 *et seq.*
[72] [1969] 1 Q.B. 219. The first instance decision of Lloyd J. in *The Irene's Success* [1982] Q.B. 481 was overruled and a dictum of Sheen J. in *The Nea Tyhi* [1982] 1 Lloyd's Rep. 606 disapproved.
[73] [1927] 1 Ch. 606.
[74] *Ibid.* 635–636.
[75] [1986] 1 A.C. 785, 812.

The reasoning in *The Aliakmon* has since been applied to a sale of goods f.o.b. In *Mitsui and Co. Ltd.* v. *Flota Mercante Grancolombiana S.A.*[76] the buyers paid 80 per cent. of the contract price before the goods were shipped but were still held not to be entitled to sue the shipowners in negligence when the goods were damaged. Under section 19 of the Sale of Goods Act 1979, the Court of Appeal said, payment in full was presumed to be required before property in the goods—and with it the right to sue—could pass.

In *The Aliakmon* Lord Brandon opined that the persons who had a right to sue the shipowners for loss of or damage to the goods were the sellers.[77] The buyers should have made it a term that the sellers should exercise this right for their account or assign such right to them to exercise for themselves. The entitlement of the owners to sue in such circumstances was confirmed by Hobhouse J. in *The Sanix Ace.*[78] There is one subtle difference in wording from *The Aliakmon* however.

According to Lord Brandon in *The Aliakmon* legal ownership *per se* conferred a right to sue. Equitable ownership *per se* did not however. A person who was the equitable owner of certain goods could only sue if he had a possessory title to them. In such a situation moreover, it was the possessory title rather than the equitable ownership which bestowed a freedom to sue in tort for negligence without joining the legal owner as a party to the action.[79]

Hobhouse J. in *The Sanix Ace* took a slightly different approach. In his view, if a person was suing in tort, his claim might be defeated if his title was a bare proprietary one and did not include any right to possession of the goods.[80] In so far as this formulation intended to suggest that legal proprietorship of itself, is not enough to ground an action, then it seems impossible to reconcile with the statement of principle enunciated in *The Aliakmon*.

Be that as it may Hobhouse J. in *The Sanix Ace* went on to hold that in English law it was the claimants' property in the goods which gave a right to recover substantial damages. In tort, the title to sue and recovery of substantial damages were concurrent.[81]

What about the passing of risk? Section 20(1) of the Sale of Goods Act 1979 states, unless the parties to a contract for the sale of goods otherwise agree, "the goods remain at the seller's risk until the property in them is transferred to the buyer." As far as the seller is concerned, the advantage in transferring risk ahead of ownership and possession is that he can still take an action for the price of or for damages for non-acceptance even though the

---

[76] [1988] 1 W.L.R. 145.
[77] [1986] 1 A.C. 785, 819. Reference was made to *The Albazero* [1977] A.C. 774 in this connection.
[78] [1987] 1 Lloyd's Rep. 465.
[79] [1986] 1 A.C. 785, 812. Lord Brandon added that an equitable owner of goods could also sue if he joined the legal owner as a party to the action, either as co-plaintiff if he was willing or as co-defendant if he was not.
[80] [1987] 1 Lloyd's Rep. 465 468.
[81] *Ibid.* In the learned judge's view there was no such thing in the relevant context as a right to sue in tort for merely nominal damages. *The Charlotte* [1908] P. 206 and *R. & W. Paul Ltd.* v. *National Steamship Co. Ltd.* [1937] 59 Lloyd's Rep. 28 were cited on this point.

goods have been lost or destroyed. Naturally therefore, in order to avoid suffering a loss, the party who bears the risk at any particular time will usually want to insure the goods.

Does the fact that the owner no longer bears the risk affect his entitlement to sue or the measure of damages recoverable? According to Hobhouse J. in *The Sanix Ace* the answer is emphatically not. The fact that a plaintiff had contracts of sale which enabled him to collect the price from his buyer did not disentitle him from recovering full damages. *The Aliakmon*[82] was referred to. It was said to be fundamental to the reasoning in that case that the proprietary or possessory title in goods carried with it the right to recover substantial damages for the loss of or damage to the goods. The fact that the risk was in another merely affected the distinction of those damages.[83] Otherwise there would be a lacuna in English law.

Applying this reasoning in the reservation of title context, the seller should always be able to sue for negligently inflicted damage to the goods. Since *Re Bond Worth Ltd.*[84] it is standard practice for him to reserve legal ownership in the goods. The fact that the risk is in the buyer is irrelevant. The buyer, if he has possession of the goods, should also be able to sue in reliance upon a possessory title. Something of a question-mark hangs over the concept of a possessory title in this context however. As one commentator puts it[85]:

> "One suspects that considerable elucidation of the expression 'possessory title' (and particularly of the question as to whether such a title may consist merely of a contractually-derived right of possession) will be needed before the rule in *The Aliakmon* will begin to possess the measure of certainty attributed to it by Lord Brandon."

Trespass to Land

When a contingency occurs which, according to the contract, justifies the supplier in terminating the contract and in repossessing the goods, the practical difficulty which he or she may encounter is that the goods will be physically situated on premises to which the supplier normally has no right of access. Any attempt to repossess the goods will therefore be met with a claim for trespass to land. To sue for trespass a plaintiff does not have to be the owner of the land, only the person with possession, so if the buyer of the goods has stored them on premises occupied under a lease, or even if he or she is occupying the land only under a licence, there may still be an action. Exclusive occupation is the key to a plaintiff's entitlement to sue in trespass.[86] Even illegal occupation, such as that of a squatter, can found a right

---

[82] [1986] 1 A.C. 785.

[83] [1987] 1 Lloyd's Rep. 465 468–469.

[84] [1980] 1 Ch. 228.

[85] See section by Professor Palmer on "Commercial Law" in [1986] *All E.R. Annual Review*.

[86] *Street On Torts* (8th ed., 1988), pp. 70–71 citing Lord Upjohn in *National Provincial Bank Ltd.* v. *Ainsworth* [1965] A.C. 1175 and Megarry J. in *Hounslow L.B.C.* v. *Twickenham Garden Developments Ltd.* [1971] Ch. 233, 257. Clerk and Lindsell on Torts (16th ed., 1989),

to sue in trespass. An action of trespass will even lie against an owner of land, at any rate if the owner enters the land in breach of a contractual undertaking which he has given to the person in possession of it.

In order to counteract a claim for trespass to land, the supplier should include in the reservation of title clause a sub-clause to the effect that the buyer thereby agrees to confer upon the supplier a right of access to the goods whenever the supplier wishes to exercise the right to repossess them. Even if the buyer is a mere licensee of the premises where the goods are stored, this contractually conferred right of access will be valid and enforceable *vis-à-vis* the buyer. Unless the owner of the land is also owed money by the buyer (perhaps arrears of rent), he or she will not usually be concerned with the fate of the goods and will disclaim any interest in them, leaving the supplier with contractual right to go on to the land in order to take the goods away.

Rights of entry, over the above mere rights of repossession and removal, were expressly conferred in the cases of *Re Peachdart Ltd.*[87] and *Clough Mill Ltd.* v. *Martin*[88] and in neither did the judges make any adverse comments about the propriety of such sub-clauses. Nor did Keane J. object to a wider provision in the Irish case of *Re Galway Concrete Ltd.*,[89] where it read: "our personnel allowed free access to the site and plant at all times." The judge even said that the right to enter and repossess the goods is not dependent on an express clause to that effect in the supply contract. One could argue, however, that, the wider the wording of an express clause, the more likely a judge is to infer that the reservation of title was genuine and intended. Such reasoning gains support from the approach of Peter Gibson J. in *Re Andrabell Ltd.*[90] Among the reasons the learned judge listed for concluding that the relationship between the seller and the buyer was not a fiduciary one but an ordinary creditor/debtor one, was the absence of any sub-clause obliging the buyer-company to store the travel bags in a manner manifesting the seller's continued ownership of them. This suggests that the clearer the cause can be in indicating the seller's reserved rights—and what they mean in practice—the likelier it is that the law will adjudge it to be valid. The supply contract can just as easily provide defences against future claims in tort as it can defences to contract or even property actions.

The question arises as to how one might characterise the supplier's right to enter on the buyer's land. In the previous chapter it has been argued that it constitutes a species of equitable interest.[91] Another view might regard it as a licence coupled with an interest which is irrevocable so long as the interest

p. 1314: "The terms of an occupational licence may give the licensee such a degree of control over access as to entitle him to the protection of the law of trespass against intruders."
[87] [1984] 1 Ch. 131.
[88] [1985] 1 W.L.R. 111.
[89] [1983] I.L.R.M. 402; this case has already been discussed in connection with the distinction between fixtures and chattels: see *supra*, Chap. 11, pp. 179–180.
[90] [1984] 3 All E.R. 407.
[91] *Supra*, Chap. 11.

to which the licence relates subsists.[92] An alternative hypothesis is to conceive of it as a contractual licence. Contractual licences may be invoked only in accordance with the terms of the contract creating the licence and an injunction may be granted to restrain premature revocation.[93] Moreover, an order of specific performance may be made to secure performance of the agreement.[94]

Refusal to Hand Over the Goods

Say the buyer is not the owner of the land where the goods happen to be and the owner refuses the supplier access to where the goods happen to be. Has the supplier any remedy?[95] Perhaps the nature of the problem is best explained by looking at the facts of *Moffatt* v. *Kazana*.[96] This was a case where the purchaser of a bungalow employed a workman to install a boiler. The workman found a biscuit tin lodged in the chimney flue which contained some £1,987. The money passed into the hands of the purchaser's solicitors but the vendors successfully sought its return. Wrangham J. dismissed the contentions that the tin had been abandoned or that it and the money contents had passed to the purchaser by virtue of section 62 of the Law of Property Act 1925.[97] It was also argued that the law should imply a conveyance of the lost property in the circumstances which had arisen because otherwise a complete impasse might be reached. The point was made[98]:

> "[T]he result would be that there was property admittedly belonging to the plaintiffs which could not be reached by the plaintiffs, because the plaintiffs could have no right to trespass on the defendant's land and the defendant could be under no duty to bother himself to move the biscuit tin to the edge of his land. Why should he do anything? Still less could he be expected to incur the risk of perhaps some damage to the flue if by any chance the biscuit tin had become in some way attached, to the flue by the effluxion of time."

---

[92] See *Jones* v. *Earl of Tankerville* [1915] 1 Ch. *Jones & Sons Ltd.* v. *Tankerville* [1909] 2 Ch. 440.

[93] See *Hounslow L.B.C.* v. *Twickenham Garden Developments* [1971] Ch. 233 where Megarry V.-C. applied *Hurst* v. *Picture Theatres Ltd.* [1915] 1 K.B. 1 and *Winter Garden Theatre (London) Ltd.* v. *Millenium Productions Ltd.* [1948] A.C. 173. He confessed to feeling great difficulty about the grounds for the decision (though not about the decision itself) in *Thompson* v. *Park* [1944] K.B. 408, where an interlocutory injunction was granted to a schoolmaster to restrain his licensee from trespassing.

[94] See *Verrall* v. *Great Yarmouth B.C.* [1981] Q.B. 202. Here it was held that the temporary nature of a licence was no objection to the grant of specific relief.

[95] See generally, Palmer (1980) 9 *Anglo-American Law Review* who discusses extensively the New South Wales case *Fitzgerald* v. *Kellion Estates Pty. Ltd.* (unreported) December 16, 1977.

[96] [1969] 2 Q.B. 152 on which see Cretney (1969) 119 N.L.J. 356.

[97] This is a word-saving provision which deems a conveyance of land to include various rights ancillary thereto.

[98] [1969] 2 Q.B. 152, 156–157.

Wrangham J. was unmoved by these considerations preferring to leave the problems to be dealt with as and when they arose.

In this area the real question is whether the owner of the land is guilty of conversion in excluding the supplier from recovering possession of his goods. Does a mere refusal of access constitute conversion? Maule J. in *Wilde* v. *Waters*[99] seemed to suggest not. Speaking of a landlord-tenant scenario he said[1]:

> "The question in such a case, would be whether the jury could infer from the refusal that the new tenant exercised any dominion over the chattel. If it appeared that he had merely said: 'I don't want your chattel, but I shall not give myself any trouble over it; that would not give the owner an action for conversion.' "

Another case in point is *British Economical Lamp Co. Ltd.* v. *Empire Mile End Ltd.*[2] Here the defendant lessors re-entered theatre premises and determined the lease for non-payment of rent. The plaintiff was the owner of some filament lamps out on hire to the lessees of the theatre. These were attached to lamp brackets in the theatre at the time that the defendants entered. The King's Bench Division decided that the lamps did not amount to fixtures and that the plaintiffs had no cause of action in respect of the defendants' refusal of permission to enter. Lush J. put the matter thus[3]:

> "The plaintiffs had no cause of action against them for refusing to allow them to enter on the premises and remove the lamps or for themselves refusing to remove and restore them. If there had been . . . a dealing [with the lamps by the defendants as their property] I think that there would have been a conversion and . . . the plaintiffs would, in my opinion, on proving that fact have been entitled to damages."

So if the defendant does not intend to assert dominion over the chattels he is not guilty of conversion and our supplier refused access would appear to be without a remedy. The courts however might now be prepared to infer conversion from the slightest acts. *Howard E. Perry & Co. Ltd.* v. *British Railways Board*[4] is worth mentioning again in this context. There it was held that the detention of the plaintiffs' steel by the defendants for an indefinite period constituted conversion notwithstanding that this detention was motivated by a well-justified fear of reprisal by third parties. Megarry V.-C. observed[5]:

> "There is a detention of the steel which is consciously adverse to the

[99] (1855) 24 L.J.C.P. 193.
[1] *Ibid*. 195.
[2] (1913) 29 T.L.R. 386.
[3] *Ibid*. 387. See also, *De Voe* v. *Long* [1951] 1 D.L.R. 203 and *Phillips* v. *Murray* [1929] 3 D.L.R. 770.
[4] [1980] 1 W.L.R. 1375.
[5] *Ibid*. 1380.

plaintiffs' rights and this seems to me to be the essence of at least one form of conversion."

Admittedly that case may be distinguished on the ground that the possession by the defendants of the steel derived originally from a contract between themselves and the plaintiffs. The case does show however that the boundaries of the tort of conversion may be expanding.[6]

Conclusion

What follows is a brief resume of the points discussed in this chapter.

(1) An action in conversion lies where a defendant has purported to exercise dominion over goods belonging to another or converted them to his own use. Generally, negligence causing damage to or destruction of goods is not amenable in an action for conversion save in the situation of loss or destruction of goods which a bailee has allowed to happen in breach of his duty to his bailor.

(2) An action for trespass to goods lies for direct interference with goods in the possession of the plaintiff.

(3) A conversion action is maintainable at the suit of any person in actual possession of the goods or with a right to immediate possession. Where reliance is placed on a right to immediate possession as the foundation of the plaintiff's claim to litigate, this must be derived from a legal or equitable proprietary base.

(4) The seller in the reservation of title context may be given a right to immediate possession by the terms of the contract of sale. Also, where the buyer is guilty of a repudiatory breach of the bailment constituted by the reservation of title agreement, the right to immediate possession revests in the seller.

(5) Trespass is a wrong done to possession and as a general proposition a trespass suit may be instituted only at the instance of somebody in actual possession of the goods at the time that the alleged tort occurs.

(6) Where a conversion action is grounded destruction of or conversion by the defendant of the goods to his own use, the measure of damages recoverable is the full value of the chattel. The plaintiff is not confined to the value of his own limited interest, irrespective of whether

[6] Palmer (1980) 9 *Anglo-American Law Review* 279, 305 has contended that the law should be sensitive to the distinction between those occupiers whose refusal of access connotes an intention to arrogate to themselves the powers of an owner in relation to the goods and those whose refusal of access is motivated solely by an intention (however perverse) to treat their homes as their castles. An occupier in the second category, it is argued, should be under no greater duty than the duty to permit such recovery as does not cause sufficient inconvenience or annoyance to him to give rise to a reasonable expectation of compensation. He should be compensated for any greater inconvenience. Professor Palmer suggests that a duty in the latter category may not be tortiously enforceable. The *Perry* case [1980] 1 W.L.R. 1375 runs counter to the notion though that there is any gap in remedies.

he sues on the basis of actual possession or a right to immediate possession. To the extent that a plaintiff is over-compensated however, he must account to the other persons interested in the chattel.

(7) In a trespass action a plaintiff may recover for the damage or destruction of the goods occurring as a result of the tortious act.

(8) The owner of a reversionary interest in goods, such as a *Romalpa* supplier, with no immediate right to possession, may recover for permanent injury done to his reversionary interest.

(9) To succeed in a negligence claim, the plaintiff must have legal ownership of or a possessory title to, the property in question at the time when the loss or damage took place. Mere contractual rights in relation to the goods are not sufficient though a contractually-founded right of possession may be enough to maintain an action.

(10) The fact that the risk is in another does not affect entitlement to sue though it generates a duty to account to the persons actually damnified by the loss.

(11) An equitable owner of goods may sue if he joins the legal owner as a party to the action, either as co-plaintiff if he is willing or as co-defendant if he is not.

(12) A buyer may afford a reservation of title supplier a right of entry onto land for the purpose of recovering possession of the goods. Such a right of entry is good *vis-à-vis* the buyer and provides a defence to trespass actions maintained by the buyer.

(13) If the owner of the land who is not the buyer refuses the supplier access to the land to recover possession of the goods, then the question arises whether the supplier may institute proceedings for conversion against the owner of the land. Refusal of access, of itself, does not appear to constitute conversion. The courts however seem prepared to infer conversion from the slightest acts of control exercised over the goods by the owner.

CHAPTER 13

THE INTERNATIONAL DIMENSIONS

There are two important international aspects to the topic of reservation of title. One is the attempt to harmonise different systems of law so that conflicts of laws cannot arise. In this regard the United Kingdom has often looked at the United States law as a model to follow. Both the European Economic Community and the Council of Europe were active in the 1970s in drawing up international agreements but nothing further has been achieved by these bodies in more recent years. The other aspect is that of private international law, which is the collection of rules within each national legal system prescribing the country whose domestic laws are to be applied to the solution of disputes touching upon more than one country. We shall deal with each of these aspects separately.

National Reform and Regional Harmonisation

(a) *United Kingdom reforms*

In 1971 the Crowther Committee on Consumer Credit reported on how to reform the United Kingdom's law concerning borrowing by consumers.[1] One of its numerous recommendations was that even in consumer contracts it should be possible for sellers and suppliers to obtain some form of registered security over the goods they are transferring. The model which Crowther wanted England to follow was that of Article IX of the Uniform Commercial Code (1952), which has been incorporated into most of the state laws of the United States as well as into the laws of some Canadian provinces. Article IX requires a reservation of title clause to be treated as a provision creating a security interest: sellers can protect their rights—not only in goods sold but also in products and proceeds of sale—by registering a single one-page "financing statement" which indicates the types of goods over which the seller intends to take a security interest and is renewable every five years. The Crowther Committee recommended that an English version of Uniform Commercial Code Article IX should be included in a new Lending and Security Act. The government, however, in its reform package which led to the Consumer Credit Act 1974, did not act upon this particular recommendation.

Attention then turned to reservation of title clauses in non-consumer sales, especially in the context of company insolvencies. The Review Committee on Insolvency Law and Practice, chaired by Sir Kenneth Cork,[2] took

[1] Cmnd. 4596.
[2] Cmnd. 8558 (1982).

the same line as Crowther: clauses in non-consumer sales should be valid only if registered, and the precedent of Article IX of the Uniform Commercial Code was again regarded as helpful.[3] But the Committee wished to restrict the validity of reservation of title clauses to the price outstanding for the goods supplied: it thought that any attempt to secure the payment of monies in excess of that price should be made by means of a charge, whether fixed or floating.[4] Even "simple" clauses were to be enforceable only after one year had elapsed since the commencement of a receivership or administration. As explained in Chapter 8, the Cork Report's proposals were largely implemented by the Insolvency Act 1985,[5] which was almost immediately re-enacted in the consolidating Insolvency Act 1986.[6] This latter Act provides that a supplier cannot, except with the leave of and subject to such terms as are imposed by a court, enforce a retention of title agreement[7] against a company from the date of presentation of a petition for an administration order.[8] The unenforceability continues for the duration of the administration order itself, once it has been made.[9]

Having reformed the law in the context of insolvency, the government next appointed Professor Aubrey Diamond to examine the need in other contexts for alteration of the law on security over property other than land. His final report was published in 1989[10] and in it he endorses the Crowther view that simple retention of title clauses should be valid (and gain priority even over earlier clauses) provided they are registered.

(b) *The European Community*

Contemporaneously with the deliberations of the Crowther Committee in

[3] *Ibid.* paras. 1635–1641.
[4] *Ibid.* paras. 1644–1645. See also, Chap. 7, text accompanying nts. 2 and 3.
[5] This was preceded by the Department of Trade and Industry's response to the Cork Report: A Revised Framework for Insolvency Law (Cmnd. 9175; February 1984).
[6] In force from December 29, 1986.
[7] Defined in s. 251 as meaning "an agreement for the sale of goods to a company, being an agreement—(a) which does not constitute a charge on the goods, but (b) under which, if the seller is not paid and the company is wound up, the seller will have priority over all other creditors of the company as respects the goods or any property representing the goods." It is unclear whether this definition, when it refers to sellers having priority over all other creditors, intends to refer to the effect in law of the clause or to the import of the clause whether or not the law endorses it.
[8] ss. 10(1)(b) and 10(4).
[9] s. 11(3)(c). By s.15, provided the administrator obtains court approval, he or she may dispose of goods in the possession of the company under a retention of title agreement and the net proceeds of that disposal (together with such amount as may need to be added to these proceeds in order to bring up the amount to that which would have been realised on a sale in the open market by a willing vendor) are to be applied towards discharging the sums payable under the retention of title agreement. Strangely, there is no precise equivalent to this power as regards administrative receivers (the new name for receivers and managers): s. 43 makes no mention of retention of title agreements. The effect of the Insolvency Act 1986 on reservation of title clauses is discussed in detail in Chap. 7.
[10] Professor Diamond first issued a consultative paper in July 1986 to canvas ways in which the law might be improved. See Ziegel, "British Chattel Security Law: A New Deal?" (1987) 131 Sol.Jo. 209.

the United Kingdom, the Commission of the EEC was considering the feasibility of a Directive on the harmonisation of laws within the Member States relating to security over movable property. In 1973 it produced a draft Directive on the recognition of non-possessory securities and of retention of ownership clauses.[11] This proposed that reservation of ownership provisions should be recognised as valid by the laws of all the Member States provided they were evidenced in writing and were valid by the system of law which governed the contract of sale; they should be effective against the buyer's creditors and against sub-purchasers from the buyer and their creditors. No registration requirements were proposed. Security interests, on the other hand, should be recognised as valid, according to the draft Directive, provided they were registered either in a central register kept for the whole of the EEC or in a national register; they should rank for priority according to the law of the country where they were situated when the security was enforced. The draft did not specify precisely how a reservation of ownership provision was to be distinguished from a security interest: it seemed to let the form of the provision, rather than its substance, dictate the consequences.

Confined as it was to questions of inter-state recognition of clauses, and containing no provisions on the buyer's insolvency or on the status of a reservation to the seller of the right to the resale price, the 1973 draft Directive met with severe criticism and was allowed to lapse. After issuing a questionnaire on security interests in 1977,[12] the Commission published in 1979 a preliminary draft proposal for a new Council Directive[13] which dealt with reservation of title separately from security interests and provided that all forms of title retention clauses were to be treated as "simple clauses" which did not require to be registered or given any other kind of publicity: they merely had to be evidenced in writing.[14] By "simple" clauses the Commission meant clauses which merely postpone the passing of property from seller to buyer until the buyer has paid the purchase price of the goods in full[15]; anything more elaborate was presumably to be ineffectual. A 1980 draft of the same Directive[16] abandoned the attempt to give all clauses the effect of simple clauses, but maintained the stance that simple clauses required no publicity.

The provisions of the 1980 draft Directive were subjected to devastating criticism by Professor Goode.[17] He first of all observed that in view of the widespread use of extended reservation of title clauses, particularly in the Netherlands and West Germany, it was difficult to see what useful purpose was served by a Directive limited to simple reservation. He then noted that

[11] Doc. XI/466/73E.
[12] Working Paper III/767/77E.
[13] Working Paper III/872/79 Rev. 1.
[14] For further details of the 1979 draft proposal, see Phillips and Schuster, "Reservation of Title in the Commercial Laws of England" (1979–1980) D.U.L.J. 1, 9–13.
[15] Art. 1(1).
[16] Working Paper III/D/278/80.
[17] (1980) 1 Co. Law 185.

because English law laid down no formalities at all for the creation of simple reservation of title clauses, no English seller would be better off in Europe under the terms of the Directive than he or she would be in England. That the seller might be considerably worse off in Europe was clear from Articles 3(1) and 6, which said that, although the seller was entitled to retake possession of the goods on the buyer's default in payment, he or she must repay to the buyer all payments made by the latter (subject to the seller's cross-claim for loss caused through the buyer's default). At present in English law the seller cannot be sued for payments made by the buyer,[18] but instead can retain for his own use any deposit paid by the buyer and any profit made out of reselling the repossessed goods. So in this respect the draft Directive was more favourable to a buyer than domestic English law would be. Yet to allow even modest protection of the original seller's interest in the goods is, reasons Goode, too indulgent if there is no require-ment of registration. If registration is required for personal security inter-ests, why is it not also required (he argues) for reservation of title interests which, after all, are but a form of security interest in disguise? To allow the seller to enforce his or her interest against the buyer even in the event of the latter's bankruptcy or liquidation is to damage even further the justifiable claims of other unsecured creditors of the buyer.

For the time being, the work of the European Community on reservation of title has come to a standstill. The Commission has been waiting to see what, if any, progress can be made by the Council of Europe.

(c) *The Council of Europe*

The Council of Europe's European Committee on Legal Co-operation appointed a committee of experts on the rights of creditors in 1978. It first met in October 1979, when it decided that the only type of reservation of title clause about which delegates would be likely to reach agreement were, once again, "simple" clauses. Even this matter took two-and-a-half years to sort out, for the committee's draft Convention was not finalised until 1982[19] and was not presented to the Legal Co-operation Committee until June 1983. The draft does not contain a definition of a "simple" reservation of title clause, but it acknowledges the criticism directed at the EEC Commission's efforts in this respect. Bowing to pressure from Scandinavian delegates, the Committee agreed that the term should be taken to include situations where the unpaid seller has the right by contract or by law to repossess the goods, notwithstanding that ownership has already passed to the buyer. This would presumably embrace such rules of English law as that enshrined in section 48(4) of the Sale of Goods Act 1979, which provides that, where the seller resells in the exercise of an express power of resale in the contract, then the

---

[18] Though in *Clough Mills Ltd.* v. *Martin* [1985] 1 W.L.R. 111, 117H–118A Goff L.J. suggested that the seller would have to pay back the money already paid by the buyer "because such sum would be recoverable by the buyer on the ground of failure of consideration."
[19] C.D.C.J. (82) 15, Restricted. See Latham, [1983] J.B.L. 81.

original contract of sale is rescinded. Rescission, of course, revests in the seller any property already transferred to the buyer.

The Council of Europe's draft Convention goes on to repeat the EEC Commission's view that an oral agreement for simple retention of title should not be valid unless confirmed in writing before delivery of the goods, but that it should be valid whether or not registered or given any other form of publicity (except perhaps in the case of retention of title affecting motor vehicles). It is also to apply whether or not the buyer has become bankrupt or insolvent, and in cases of non-innocent acquisition of the goods by a third party. As a result of the draft's confinement to simple clauses, and again following the EEC precedent, no provision is made for the seller's rights over the proceeds of sale of any goods which are sold, but the draft does say that even a simple clause will be valid only so long as the goods to which it applies can be identified as such.

Unfortunately, the Council of Europe has been no more successful than the EEC Commission in gathering support for its proposed Convention. Developments are likely to take place on the domestic front long before any European initiative becomes law.

The Uniform Law

Reservation of title clauses in contracts for the sale of goods are not affected by the Uniform Law on the International Sale of Goods, which has been incorporated into the law of the United Kingdom by the Uniform Laws on International Sales Act 1967.[20] Article 8 of the Uniform Law says that the Convention is not concerned with the effect which the contract may have on the property in the goods sold, except as expressly otherwise provided—and there is no such express provision in the Uniform Law.

Nor is the Vienna Convention on International Sales Law of any relevance.[21] Although this United Nations-derived Convention looks set to gain more adherents than the earlier Hague Uniform Laws, it too specifically excludes "the effect which the contract may have on the property in the goods sold."[22] The exclusion is no doubt due to the fact that the passing of property affects legal issues over and above the law of contract.

Private International Law

The practice of reserving title to transferred property is a long established one on the Continent of Europe, especially in Austria, France, the Netherlands and West Germany. In French the relevant clause is called "*une clause*

---

[20] See Feltham (1967) 30 M.L.R. 670.
[21] See Feltham, [1981] J.B.L. 346 and Nicholas (1989) 105 L.Q.R. 201.
[22] Art. 4(b).

de réserve de propriété," in German it is an *"eigentumsvorbehaltsbestim-mung"* and in Dutch an *"eigendomvoorbehoudsclausul."* Ultimately, the reason for the institution's popularity in Europe lies in the rooting of European legal systems in Roman law, where the basic rule was that, even if a seller of goods had delivered them to the buyer, the ownership of the goods (*dominium*) remained with the seller until the full purchase price had been paid. This was an understandable enough rule for a society where making bargains on the basis of credit was not yet a common practice.[23] When such bargains did become commonplace, the Romans passed a law (the *lex commissoria*) whereby ownership passed to the buyer when the goods were delivered, but subject to what we would call a condition subsequent that, if the full purchase price was not paid, the owner could reclaim ownership by bringing a court action.[24] This was the version of Roman law which took hold in France and Germany.[25]

In the nineteenth century reservation of title clauses do not seem to have been employed very often in England because, buyers being able to borrow money from lending institutions, sellers were not obliged to sell on credit. If such clauses were used, they did not attract the attention either of the courts or of the textbook writers. In Germany, where the economic situation was less favourable, reservation of title clauses were common. And they came to be worded so as to provide for the *retention* of ownership, rather than just allowing ownership to be reclaimed if a condition was not fulfilled. This was because the first codification of Prussian law in 1794 had laid down the requirement that the latter type of clause could be operative only when the seller had first of all re-obtained possession of the goods. Such a restrictive condition made the "retention" of title a more attractive proposition.[26] Just three years after Sir Mackenzie Chalmers codified English law in the Sale of Goods Act 1893, the new *Bürgerliches Gesetzbuch* (which did not enter into force until 1900) put established German practice on to a proper legislative footing. By paragraph 455:

> "If the seller of a movable thing has withheld ownership until payment of the purchase price has been made, it is to be taken, in cases of doubt, that the transfer of ownership occurs only when the condition precedent of complete payment has been fulfilled, and that if the buyer delays in making payment the seller is justified in rescinding the contract."

French law has recognised the legality of clauses retaining title ever since the enactment of the Napoleonic Code in 1804 (articles 1181 and 1183) and again much advantage has been taken in practice of this particular aspect of the freedom of contract notion.

---

[23] See Pennington, "Retention of Title to the Sale of Goods under European Law" (1978) 27 I.C.L.Q. 277.
[24] Buckland, *A Textbook of Roman Law* (3rd ed., 1963), pp. 496–497.
[25] For a practical guide to the position in 19 national legislations, see *Retention of Title*, published by the International Chamber of Commerce (Paris, 1989).
[26] See Pennington, *supra*, n. 23.

It is the widespread use of retention of title clauses in European legal systems that explains their eventual appearance on the British scene.[27] The chances of encountering such a clause in a contract involving the supply of goods from Europe to Britain are considerable. The only reason why there was no judicial discussion of an international dimension in the seminal *Romalpa* case[28] was that none of the parties alluded to it. The dimension is most likely to manifest itself whenever the international contract contains a clause subjecting the contract to a foreign legal system: most systems of private international law, including the English, accord almost unlimited freedom to contracting parties to choose virtually any law they please as the one to govern their contract. In English private international law the only qualification to this is that the choice must be *"bona fide* and legal."[29] In the absence of an expressed or clearly inferred choice, the law applied by the court will be that of the legal system which has the closest connection with the contract.[30] Autonomy to choose the contract's so-called "proper" law extends also to the selection of laws to govern particular parts of the contract. It would be legal, therefore, in English private international law, for a contract as a whole to be subject to the law of England, but for the parties to stipulate that the validity and effect of a reservation of title clause within the contract are to be governed by some other law.

As far as suppliers are concerned, the law on reservation of title is in most respects more favourable in continental legal systems than in the United Kingdom. For that reason it might seem sensible to insert a clause in any contract where goods are being supplied to continental countries whereby the foreign legal system in question is to be taken as the law governing the validity and effect of the clause. Such a course is dangerous, however, unless the supplier has reliable information as to the precise state of the foreign legal system involved. As has been made clear,[31] German law is not the same as French law in this context and there remain some respects in which neither system is as helpful to a supplier as English law would be.

The main difficulty with including an express choice-of-law clause for reservation of title is that it cannot operate so as to alter the *proprietary* effects of the contract in the country where the clause is to be enforced. It is a rule of most systems of private international law that the proprietary effects of assignments are governed by the *lex situs*, that is, the law of the place where the things assigned are situated.[32] As the leading textbook puts it:

> "... it is for the *lex situs* to decide whether title has passed to the buyer or has been validly reserved by the seller and the proper law of the

[27] For further information about the law on this topic in West Germany, France, the Netherlands, Italy, Switzerland and Sweden, see Sauveplanne (ed), *Security Over Corporeal Movables* (1974).

[28] [1976] 1 W.L.R. 676.

[29] Dicey and Morris, *The Conflict of Laws* (11th ed., 1987), Vol. 2, pp. 1169–1176.

[30] *Ibid.* pp. 1190–1195.

[31] See Pennington, *supra*, n. 23.

[32] Dicey and Morris, *supra*, n. 29, pp. 942–946.

contract is relevant only to the extent that the *lex situs* takes account of it in determining whether title has or has not so passed. Similarly, the extent to which title has been validly retained should also be governed by the *lex situs*."[33]

The obvious rationale for this rule is that it is desirable for the country where the goods are physically controlled to have the final say as to who should be able to exercise that control. Of course, if that system would in turn refer the issue to another system of law, this "renvoi" should for the same reason be accepted.[34]

Two Irish cases illustrate the role of the *lex situs* very well,[35] for, although the German clauses were there held to be effective as regards the reservation of ownership in the very goods supplied, they were held unable to avoid the operation of the Irish law on registration of security interests in movable property. In *Re Interview Ltd.*,[36] for example, where an affidavit on German law was filed for the benefit of the Irish court and at the hearing itself oral evidence as to German law was given by a person other than the deponent of the affidavit, it was accepted that, under German law (which was the proper law of the contract), including German private international law, the effect of a sub-sale by the purchaser was governed by the law of the place where the goods were situated (the *lex loci rei sitae*), which in that case was Irish law.

It was with the aim of ensuring compliance with the *lex situs* that the German suppliers in *Re Interview Ltd.*[37] included the following sub-clause in the supply contracts:

"If the reservation of ownership in the foregoing form is not effective under the law of the country of destination, the purchaser must co-operate in establishing a similar security right complying with the provisions of his country, in favour of the supplier."

Similarly, in *Kruppstahl* v. *Quitmann*,[38] the sub-clause obliged the Irish buyer to "take all necessary steps to substantiate and protect" the German supplier's rights. But such stipulations can only increase the supplier's contractual entitlement *vis-à-vis* the buyer: if they are not complied with, the local law of property will still operate so as to override the supplier's foreign property rights *vis-à-vis* third parties. The policy reason for not giving effect to an agreement between contracting parties that a law other than the local law should govern the proprietary aspects of their transaction is that this could too easily operate to the prejudice of innocent third parties.

---

[33] *Ibid.* p. 1265. See also, *Benjamin's Sale of Goods* (3rd ed., 1987), paras. 2465 and 2486.
[34] For a discussion of whether the doctrine of *renvoi* applies in this context, see Cheshire and North, *Private International Law* (11th ed., 1987), pp. 796–798.
[35] *Re Interview Ltd.* [1975] I.R. 382, *Kruppstahl AG* v. *Quitmann Products Ltd. and Fitzgerald* [1982] I.L.R.M. 551.
[36] *Ibid.*
[37] *Ibid.*
[38] [1982] I.L.R.M. 551.

There is a reported decision in Scotland where the pre-eminence of the *lex situs* is confirmed. In *Hammer and Sohne* v. *H.W.T. Realisations Ltd.*[39] the pursuers were a German firm which had supplied jewellery to the defenders in Scotland. The proper law of this contract was West German law, and the pursuers argued that the retention of title clause it contained was enforceable in Scotland. The Sheriff held that Scottish law, which does not allow any non-possessory security interests to exist over movables,[40] must prevail. It is submitted that he did so primarily because Scottish law was the *lex situs*, for he accepted what was said in a leading textbook on Scottish private international law, *viz.* that it is a "well settled rule that the *lex situs* governs the creation of securities over movables."[41] The learned judge then went on to consider what the Scottish law on that topic was. He admitted that there were some statutory exceptions to the rule against non-possessory security interests over movables, but none which took away from the fundamental principle. He therefore seems to be applying Scottish law because it was the *lex situs*, not because, as the *lex fori*, it contained a fundamental principle which for public policy reasons could not be ignored. In 1985 another Scottish judge dealt with a similar case,[42] again involving German suppliers, by saying that contracting parties could expressly agree that the proper law of the contract should govern the question of accession (that is, the passing of title). With all due respect, it may be doubted whether the role of the *lex situs* should be allowed to be subverted in this manner. But at least the common starting point for any argument on the issue does seem to be that, according to the general rule, the governing law is the *lex situs*.[43]

A subsidiary problem is when should the *situs* of the goods be determined? The case law seems to favour the time when the alleged transfer of title takes place, though identifying when exactly that is may itself be difficult.[44] For goods in transit at that time it would be inappropriate to apply a *lex situs* that was fortuitously so. In this situation a better governing law would be the "proper law of the transfer," which has been defined as, "broadly speaking, the law having the 'closest and most real connection' with the transfer of property rights which takes place by virtue of the sale."[45] As regards the question whether title is retained by the seller even over goods manufactured out of the goods supplied, the relevant *situs* is the country where the manufacturing process takes place.

[39] 1985 S.L.T. 21 (Sh.Ct); Stewart 1985, S.L.T. 149; Sellar 1985. S.L.T. 313, where the Scottish private international law on the sale of book debts is also examined.
[40] On this Scottish principle, see the recommendations made in the Diamond Report, "A Review of Security Interests in Property" (HMSO, 1989).
[41] Anton, *Private International Law* (1967), p. 406.
[42] *Zahrad Fabrik Passau Gmbh* v. *Terex Ltd.* 1986 S.L.T. 84. See also the slightly earlier, but less helpful, case of *Armour* v. *Thyssen Edelstahlwerke A-G* 1986 S.L.T. 94, discussed in Cheshire and North, *supra*, n. 34, p. 796.
[43] For analogous Canadian authorities on the passing of title in cases involving conditional sales and chattel mortgages, see Castel, *Canadian Conflict of Laws* (2nd ed., 1986), Chap. 24.
[44] *Cammell* v. *Sewell* (1858) 3 H. & N. 617.
[45] Benjamin, *supra*, n. 33, para. 2468.

It would appear, therefore, that the only way in which a supplier can be sure of fully protecting his interest is by registering that interest in the prescribed form in the buyer's legal system. It is that system which governs the procedures to be followed in order to register the interest effectively and it would obviously be wise for the supplier to seek advice from a lawyer who has a sound knowledge of the registration requirements in the buyer's system. As far as English law is concerned, the registration provisions in the Companies Act 1985 apply to charges created by companies registered in England as well as to charges on property in England created by companies with an established place of business in England.[46]

Matters other than proprietary ones will not be governed by the *lex situs*. All aspects of the purely contractual position of the supplier and buyer will be governed by the contract's proper law. In particular, the extent of the buyer's right to deal with the goods supplied (*e.g.* by reselling them, hiring them out, mixing them with other goods, or affixing them to immovable property) will be determined by that law. The buyer's duty to account, and whether he is a bailee, an agent and/or a fiduciary, will be for that law to settle as well.[47] However, the right of the buyer to bring any sub-buyer into a relationship with the original seller (*e.g.* by assigning to the seller the price owed by the sub-buyer to the buyer) will be governed by the proper law of the sub-sale, not the proper law of the sale. The validity of the assignment itself will be determined by whatever is the proper law of the assignment (usually the same as the proper law of the original contract of sale).[48] The tortious liability of the buyer, or of a sub-buyer, will be governed by the double-barrelled rule in *Phillips* v. *Eyre*,[49] as modified by the House of Lords in *Boys* v. *Chaplin*,[50] although it is well to remember that no English court has ever applied a foreign law to a tort committed in England.[51] Issues relating purely to what would be the appropriate remedy in a particular case should be governed by English law in its capacity as the *lex fori*, except that in the case of tracing claims, which are as much substantive as procedural, a more appropriate *lex causae* would be the law governing the obligation to account in the first place.[52]

Summary

It seems clear that international attempts to harmonise different countries' laws on the validity of reservation of title clauses are unlikely to bear fruit in the next few years. In the absence of such harmonisation problems of conflicts of laws will continue to occur. Fortunately, there seems to be more

---

[46] s. 409.
[47] Benjamin, *supra*, n. 33, para. 2489.
[48] Dicey and Morris, *supra*, n. 29, pp. 1266–1267.
[49] (1874) L.R. 6 Q.B. 1.
[50] [1971] A.C. 356.
[51] Cheshire and North, *supra*, n. 34, pp. 537–538.
[52] Benjamin, *supra*, n. 33, para. 2489.

uniformity amongst nations at the level of private international law than there is at the level of domestic law. An almost universally accepted principle is that contractual obligations are to be governed by their "proper" law, which is usually the law which has the closest connection with the obligation in question. The parties themselves have virtually complete autonomy expressly or impliedly to designate the proper law. But the contract's effects in the law of property are *not* governed by that proper law. Instead, the generally accepted rule is that the governing law is that of the place where the goods are situated when the contract is made (the *lex situs*). In particular, the *lex situs* will determine whether, and how, the interest created by a reservation of title clause has to be registered. However, the scope of the *lex situs* will in turn be restricted in situations where there are good policy reasons for subjecting a specific issue to a different law.

CHAPTER 14

CONCLUSION

The law relating to reservation of title clauses has been described as "a maze if not a minefield."[1] The potential pitfalls become only too apparent if one is attempting to draft clauses that secure maximum protection for the seller. What follows is an effort to clear a path through the battlefield of strewn corpses that constitute unsuccessful attempts to reserve title. The best approach is perhaps to look at the drafting of the different types of clauses in ascending order of complexity.

"Simple" Reservation of Title

One way of going about the drafting of a "simple" reservation of title clause is to state succinctly that the "seller retains ownership of the goods the property in which shall not pass to the buyer until paid for." This should be enough to reserve a "right of disposal" within the meaning of section 17 of the Sale of Goods Act 1979. This is a legally efficacious reservation of title clause notwithstanding that the intention behind the clause is to provide security for payment of the purchase price of the goods.[2]

The decided cases provide examples of "simple" reservation of title clauses that have withheld judicial scrutiny. In *Hendy Lennox (Industrial Engines) Ltd.* v. *Grahame Puttick Ltd.*[3] the clause upheld by Staughton J. provided that "all goods . . . shall be and remain the property of the [the plaintiffs'] until the full purchase price thereof shall be paid." *Re Peachdart Ltd.*[4] was a case involving the supply of leather to a company which manufactured handbags. A receiver was appointed to the buyer company and it was held that a reservation of title clause in the supply contract was effective as regards unused leather in its possession at that time. The clause stipulated as follows:

> "[T]he ownership of the products shall remain with the seller which reserves the right to dispose of the products until payment in full for all the products has been received by it in accordance with the terms of this contract or until such time as the buyer sells the products to its customers by way of bona fide sale at full market value."

Re Andrabell Ltd.[5] was a somewhat similar case. It concerned the supply

---

[1] *Per* Staughton L.J. in *Hendy Lennox (Industrial Engines) Ltd.* v. *Grahame Puttick Ltd.* [1984] 1 W.L.R. 485.
[2] *Clough Mill Ltd.* v. *Martin* [1985] 1 W.L.R. 111.
[3] [1984] 1 W.L.R. 485.
[4] [1984] Ch. 131.
[5] [1984] 3 All E.R. 407.

221

of travel bags which were then resold. The buyer company went into liquidation but at that time all of the travel bags had been resold. The dispute in the case centred around a claim to the resale proceeds. It appears, however, that the reservation of title clause would have been effective as regards any travel bags still in the buyer company's possession at the commencement of liquidation. The clause contained the following provision:

> "It is a condition of sale that ownership of the goods shall not pass to The Company until The Company has paid to Airborne the total purchase price including VAT."

A lesson to be learned from *Re Bond Worth Ltd.*[6] is to avoid the use of words reserving only "equitable and beneficial ownership." While that decision has been criticised, clearly the safest course for a draftsperson is to steer clear of any possible controversy. In *Re Bond Worth Ltd.* the exact wording of the clause held ineffective was as follows:

> "The risk in the goods passes to the buyer upon delivery, but equitable and beneficial ownership shall remain with us until full payment has been received (each order being considered as a whole), or until prior resale in which case our beneficial entitlement shall attach to the proceeds of resale or to the claim for such proceeds."

Reservation of title clauses have been given the judicial *imprimatur* in the Republic of Ireland. The Irish cases provide further instances of clauses which are viewed as acceptable to reserve title:

> "The ownership of the sugar ... shall only be transferred to the purchaser when the full amount of the purchase price has been discharged." (*Sugar Distributors Ltd.* v. *Monaghan Cash and Carry Ltd.*)[7]

> "until all sums due to the seller shall have been fully paid to it, the plant, machinery and materials supplied by the seller herein shall remain the seller's personal property." (*Frigoscandia*)[8]

It is also desirable, though probably not essential, to include in a "simple" reservation of title clause a provision to the effect that the buyer shall hold the goods as bailee for and on behalf of the seller. This might be coupled with a clause that the buyer shall store the goods in a safe and proper manner and in such a way to ensure that they are readily identifiable as the property of the seller.

Authorisation to Enter Land

The seller should be empowered to enter upon any land of the buyer for

---

[6] [1980] Ch. 228.
[7] [1982] I.L.R.M. 399.
[8] *Frigoscandia Ltd.* v. *Continental Irish Meat Ltd.* [1982] I.L.R.M. 396. See generally, Pearce, "Reservation of Title on the Sale of Goods in Ireland" (1985) 20 Ir.Jur. (N.S.) 265, 270–273.

the purpose of repossessing the goods. Something along the lines of the following would be appropriate:

> "The Buyer hereby irrevocably authorises the representatives of the seller to enter upon the Buyer's premises where the goods are stored, or are thought by the seller to be stored for the purpose of repossessing them and subsequently reselling them."

If the goods are such as they might be attached to land by the buyer, the seller should consider including a term prohibiting the attachment of goods to land without the consent of the seller. As explained in Chapter 11 a clause of this kind will not prevent the courts from holding that the goods constitute fixtures and so form part of the land. The clause, however, provides evidence as to the purpose of annexation and the test for fixtures depends on the degree and purpose of annexation.

A clause conferring a right of entry in relation to premises to which the goods have been attached invests the seller with a species of equitable interest in the premises. In the case of unregistered land the interest is not registrable under the Land Charges Act. The position of registered land is somewhat different however. The interest of the seller is protectible by entry of a notice, caution or restriction under the Land Registration Act. This is necessary to ensure priority and effectiveness against subsequent transferees of the registered land. A problem from the point of view of the seller is that production of the land certificate is required to secure registration of a minor interest. The co-operation of the registered proprietor is therefore needed to effect registration. The seller should incorporate in the contract a provision stipulating that the buyer should make available to him the land certificate for the purpose of effecting an entry under the Land Registration legislation.

Right to Repossess—Effect of the Insolvency Act 1986

The generally accepted view is that the Insolvency Act 1986 imposes restrictions on the enforcement of reservation of title clauses after the presentation of a petition for the making of an administration order and during the subsistence of such an order. In the period between presentation of the petition and the making of an administration order, no steps may be taken to repossess goods in the company buyer's possession save with the leave of the court. After the making of an administration order the embargo on repossession continues except for the fact that, now, both the administrator and the court may permit the recovery of goods. An administration petition may be presented by the company, its directors, and creditors, separately or collectively.

Given these constraints on recovery of goods, a seller should consider the possibility of provisions designed to cater for an administration petition. The seller may not be aware of a petition being presented until it is too late. A buyer could be obliged to notify the seller if the buyer or its directors intends to present a petition for the making of an administration order or if it is aware of any such intention on the part of any of its creditors.

There are two methods suggested in Chapter 7 of circumventing the restrictions imposed by the Insolvency Act. One hinges on the definition of "retention of title agreement" in section 251 of the Act. The term is defined as meaning an agreement for the sale of goods to a company being an agreement:

> "(a) which does not constitute a charge on the goods, but
> (b) under which, if the seller is not paid and the company is wound up, the seller will have priority over all other creditors of the company as respects the goods or any property representing the goods. . . ."

The contract of sale might make the transfer of title turn not on payment of the price but rather on performance of some other obligation. It seems unlikely, however, that such an approach will save a clause from the clutches of the Act. The Insolvency Act refers to the effect of an agreement rather than its form. The result of any reservation of title agreement should be to give the seller priority in the event of the buyer's insolvency.

A more promising avenue of escape from the Act might be to provide for payment not to the seller but to an associated company. In terms of basic contractual doctrine, there does not seem to be anything heretical about such a provision. Consideration must move from a promisee but it need not necessarily move to the promisor. It does seem, though, a somewhat technical and artificial device and whether it will withstand judicial scrutiny is open to question.

Right to Possession

We have seen from Chapter 12 that the right to sue in conversion depends on the plaintiff having actual possession or an immediate right to possession of the goods. So the seller, in the reservation of title context, will have to make appropriate provision in the supply contract. If the buyer sues, however, he is entitled to recover the full value of the goods. Any surplus, over and above the value of his own possibly limited interest in the goods, must be held for the account of the seller. The seller may wish to have the option of instituting proceedings on his own behalf. In this eventuality he should retain an immediate right to possession in the sales contract while perhaps affording a facility to the buyer to obtain possession while any credit period remains unexpired. Alternatively, the buyer may be invested with the right to possession but the seller may reserve on entitlement to resume possession in a wide range of specified circumstances, or by service of a notice, or at any time.

Passing of Risk

From the seller's point of view it is obviously desirable to include a provision that the risk passes to the buyer on delivery. One might draft something like this:

"Risk in the goods shall pass to the buyer on delivery to the buyer or to its agent or other person to whom the seller has been authorised by the buyer to deliver the goods or immediately prior to loading where the goods are being collected by the buyer, its servant or agent from the seller's premises."

It is also common practice to require the buyer to insure the goods with an insurance office of repute. An example is provided by the conditions of sale in *Re Peachdart Ltd.*[9]:

"(a) The risk in the products shall pass to the buyer (i) when the seller delivers the products in accordance with the terms to the buyer or its agent or other person to whom the seller has been authorised by the buyer to deliver the products or (ii) if the products are appropriated to the buyer but kept at the seller's premises at the buyer's request and the seller shall have no responsibility in respect of the safety of the products thereafter and accordingly the buyer should insure the products thereafter against such risks (if any) as it thinks appropriate."

It is relatively easy to multiply examples. In *Borden (U.K.) Ltd.* v. *Scottish Timber Products Ltd.*[10] the relevant provisions were as follows:

"Goods supplied by the company shall be at the purchaser's risk immediately on delivery to the purchaser or into custody on the purchaser's behalf (whichever is the sooner) and the purchaser should therefore be insured accordingly."

Extended Reservation of Title Clauses

It has been argued in Chapter 6 that, contrary to suggestions from certain quarters, extended reservation of title clauses do not amount to registrable charges. By "extended reservation of title" are meant clauses that withhold the passing of property even though the goods that form the subject-matter of the particular contract of sale have been paid for. In *Romalpa*[11] itself the clause was in the following terms:

"The ownership of the material to be delivered by A.I.V. will only be transferred to purchaser when he has met all that is owing to A.I.V., no matter on what grounds."

This is an example of "all-liabilities" reservation of title; *John Snow & Co. Ltd.* v. *D.B.G. Woodcroft & Co. Ltd.*[12] supplies another example. There the clause stipulated:

---

[9] [1984] Ch. 131.
[10] [1981] Ch. 25.
[11] *Aluminium Industrie Vaassen BV* v. *Romalpa Aluminium Ltd.* [1976] 1 W.L.R. 676.
[12] [1985] B.C.L.C. 54.

"The property of the goods agreed to be sold will only pass to the purchaser when the purchaser has met all indebtedness to the seller . . . ."

Irish cases provide further examples of what might be described as extended reservation of title:

"the product supplied shall . . . remain the property of the supplier until all debts owing to the supplier . . . have been paid in full." (*Re Interview Ltd.*)[13]

"No property in any goods . . . shall pass until full payment for all goods supplied hereunder has been received by the seller and until such payment has been received by the seller the buyer shall hold the goods for the seller in a manner which enables them to be identified as the goods of the seller and the buyer shall immediately return the goods to the seller, should the seller so request." (*Re W. J. Hickey Ltd.*)[14]

Proceeds of Sale

The nature of the goods and the circumstances surrounding the transaction may be such that the goods have to be resold before the seller is paid. The seller should endeavour to ensure that the buyer is accountable for resale proceeds. He must also take care that he is not in any way liable to sub-buyers as an undisclosed principal. The buyer may be afforded a period of credit but to the extent that resale proceeds are received during the credit period they should be accounted for to the seller. The accounting obligation thus reduces the advantages afforded by the period of credit. The buyer may or may not be allowed to retain profits on resales. Resale proceeds should be payable into a separate bank account for the benefit of the seller. The counsel of prudence is not to allow the buyer to use proceeds from resales in the ordinary course of his business. The Court of Appeal in *Romalpa* seemed unperturbed that this permission was afforded. The subsequent course of judicial decisions suggests a stricter attitude, however. It would be unwise for any draftsperson of a reservation of title clause to assume a return to the halcyon days of *Romalpa*. What follows is a clause investing the seller with rights in relation to resale proceeds:

"The buyer shall be entitled to offer for sale and sell the goods at the best obtainable price in the ordinary course of its business as principal *vis-à-vis* sub-buyers and not as agent for the seller. The seller, however, shall be legally and beneficially entitled to the proceeds of sale and the

---

[13] [1975] I.R. 382.
[14] [1988] I.R. 126. See also, *Carroll Group Distributors Ltd.* v. *G. and J. F. Bourke Ltd.* (unreported) Irish High Court, 1989.

buyer shall pay such proceeds of sale into a separate account or otherwise shall ensure that all such proceeds of sale are kept by or on behalf of the buyer in a separate and identifiable form. In particular but without prejudice to the generality of the foregoing the buyer shall not pay the proceeds of sale into any bank account which is overdrawn. Further forthwith upon receipt of the proceeds of sale the buyer shall pay to the seller any of the aforesaid sums outstanding to the seller and shall not use or deal with the proceeds of sale in any way whatsoever until such sums shall have been paid."

The tracing clause might also include a statement to the effect that failure by the buyer to store the goods separately or to keep them in such a way that they remain identifiable as the property of the seller does not prejudice the claim of the seller to resale proceeds. Reservation of title provisions could include a clause obliging the buyer to pass on to the seller the proceeds of all claims against sub-buyers. The clause might be worded so as to state that the buyer holds any claims against sub-buyers on trust for the seller.

Products Clause

A not uncommon feature in the reservation of title context is a provision to the effect that the goods supplied should not be attached to other goods without the consent of the seller. The *raison d'être* of such a clause is easy to discern but it is difficult to see how it can achieve the desired effect. The purpose clearly is to prevent the supplier from losing title to the goods by virtue of the doctrine of accession. If the goods are attached, however, without the supplier's knowledge or consent, then he might have a personal action against the buyer for breach of contract but this personal claim does not involve any right to priority in the event of the buyer's insolvency. The whole object of the reservation of title phenomenon is of course to put the supplier ahead of the queue of creditors in the buyer's insolvency.

Another approach might be for the seller to state that any additions to the goods supplied become the seller's property. The danger in this attempt at drafting lies in the fact that if the additions are identifiably separate from the goods supplied, then the seller can only be regarded as transferring his own property to the buyer. If this is done for the purpose of ensuring payment of the purchase price then the arrangement will probably be viewed by the courts as creating a registrable charge. An object lesson in this regard is provided by the decision of the Court of Appeal in *Specialist Plant Services Ltd.* v. *Braithwaite Ltd.*[15] The relevant provision was in the following terms:

"(b) Further, it is hereby agreed that if the said goods and materials, or any part thereof supplied hereunder in any way whatsoever become a constituent of another article or other articles the company shall

[15] [1987] B.C.L.C. 1.

be given the ownership of this (these) new article(s) as surety of the full payment of what the customer owes the Company. . . .

(c) The word 'article' or 'articles' contained in clause (b) above shall mean and include and be deemed to mean and include any building or part thereof, any structure of whatever description or part thereof, any machinery or part thereof, or any other object, goods or article of whatever description."

The case concerned a contract for the repair of machinery. The repairer was claiming ownership of the entirety of the customer's machinery if any parts he supplied were incorporated therein. The provision was designed to afford security for payment of the repair bill. The Court of Appeal had no hesitation in holding that a charge had been created over the customer's assets which was void for want of registration.

A way out of the impasse was suggested by the Court of Appeal in *Clough Mill Ltd.* v. *Martin*.[16] There it was tentatively indicated by the court that if a new product is formed consisting of goods supplied by A and B, then A and B are free to agree between themselves where ownership of the new product shall lie.[17] In that case the relevant clause read as follows:

"If any of the material is incorporated in or used as material for other goods before such payment the property in the whole of such goods shall be and remain with the seller until such payment shall have been made, or the other goods have been sold as aforesaid and all the seller's rights hereunder in the material shall extend to those other goods."

The court, however, refused to give effect to the clause according to its terms largely because the parties were supposed not to have intended to confer a windfall on the seller as the clause would have done. But if this intention is made very explicit, the courts should hardly see fit to override it. Moreover, major difficulties arose where a new product was formed composed of materials belonging to the seller and a third party.

The general difficulties posited in *Clough Mill* may not be insoluble. If the parties are free to stipulate that title to a new product consisting of goods belonging to A and B shall lie with either A or B, they should be free to apportion ownership of the resultant product. An attempt at apportionment was made by a German supplier in the Irish case of *Kruppstahl AG* v. *Quitmann Products Ltd.*[18] It was provided in the sales contract that the seller and buyer were to hold the product jointly in the ratio of the invoice value of the seller's goods to those of the buyer's goods. Gannon J. interpreted the contract as meaning that the accountability of the buyers was limited to the extent of their indebtedness. In consequence the agreement was construed as conferring on the suppliers a means of security for the discharge of an

[16] [1985] 1 W.L.R. 111.
[17] *Ibid.* 119, *per* Robert Goff L.J. and at 124, *per* Oliver L.J.
[18] [1982] I.L.R.M. 551.

indebtedness. It may be that if accountability was not restricted to the amount of indebtedness on the original sales contract, the agreement would have been upheld.

The difficulties flowing from the rights of third parties adverted to in *Clough Mill* could be dealt with by a clause along the following lines:

"(1) If the buyer incorporates or mixes the goods with other equipment or products ('the new goods') in such a way that the goods are not a readily identifiable and removable part of the new goods the buyer shall store such new goods separately and shall notify the seller of the precise location and position thereof and the ownership of such new goods and the property therein shall vest in the seller.

(2) Upon any sale of any new goods falling within the scope of the foregoing provision by the seller, then if the proceeds of sale exceed the price or the balance of the price of the goods due to the seller from the buyer, the seller shall apply the balance of the proceeds of sale as follows:

(a) first, reimbursing the seller the cost and expense of the taking of possession and the sale of the new goods and any damages which the seller has suffered as a result of any repudiation of the contract by the buyer;

(b) secondly, paying any sums due and owing to other creditors of the buyer in respect of other items and materials used in connection with the manufacture of the new goods where the property in such items and materials has remained vested in such other creditors by reason of effective reservation of title clauses and the claims of such other creditors pursuant to such reservation of title clauses have been notified to the seller by the buyer or its liquidator, administrator or receiver or by such other creditors."

It is inadvisable to include a statement requiring the seller to pay any balance to the buyer. The danger is that this provision would taint the whole agreement with a charge construction.

If it is sought to establish a tracing claim to the proceeds of sale of products, then there should be provisions equivalent to those applying to proceeds of resales of the original goods. These would include stipulations requiring payment of proceeds into a separate bank account and prohibiting their use in the ordinary course of business of the supplier.

BILLS OF SALE ACT 1878
(c. 31)

ARRANGEMENT OF SECTIONS

SCHEDULES

An Act to consolidate and amend the Law for preventing Frauds upon Creditors by secret Bills of Sale of Personal Chattels

[July 22, 1878]

[*This Act should be read subject to the provisions of the Bills of Sale* (1878) *Amendment Act* 1882.]

1. Short title

This Act may be cited for all purposes as the Bills of Sale Act 1878.

2. Commencement

... on the first day of January one thousand eight hundred and seventy-nine is in this Act referred to as the commencement of this Act.

[*The words omitted were repealed by the Statute Law Revision Act* 1894.]

3. Application

This Act shall apply to every bill of sale executed on or after the first day of January one thousand eight hundred and seventy-nine (whether the same be absolute, or subject or not subject to any trust) whereby the holder or grantee has power, either with or without notice, and either immediately or at any future time, to seize or take possession of any personal chattels comprised in or made subject to such bill of sale.

4. Interpretation of terms

In this Act the following words and expressions shall have the meanings in this section assigned to them respectively, unless there be something in the subject or context repugnant to such construction; (that is to say),

The expression "bill of sale" shall include bills of sale, assignments, transfers, declarations of trust without transfer, inventories of goods with receipt thereto attached, or receipts for purchase moneys of goods, and other assurances of personal chattels, and also powers of attorney, authorities, or licenses to take possession of personal chattels as security for any debt, and also any agreement, whether intended or not to be followed by the execution of any other instrument by which a right in equity to any personal chattels, or to any charge or security thereon, shall be conferred, but shall not include the following documents; that is to say, assignments for the benefit of the creditors of the person making or giving the same, marriage settlements, transfers or assignments of any ship or vessel or any share thereof, transfers of goods in the ordinary course of business of any trade or calling, bills of sale of goods in foreign parts or at sea, bills of lading, India warrants, warehouse-keepers' certificates, warrants or orders for the delivery of goods, or any other documents used in the ordinary course of business as proof of the possession or control of goods, or authorising or purporting to authorise, either by indorsement or by delivery, the possessor of such document to transfer or receive goods thereby represented:

The expression "personal chattels" shall mean goods, furniture and other articles capable of complete transfer by delivery, and (when separately assigned or charged) fixtures and growing crops, but shall not include chattel interests in real estate, nor fixtures (except trade machinery as hereinafter defined), when assigned together with a freehold or leasehold interest in any land or building to which they are affixed, nor growing crops when assigned together with any interest in the land on which they grow, nor shares or interests in the stock, funds, or securities of any government, or in the capital or property of incorporated or joint stock companies, nor choses in action, nor any stock or produce upon any farm or lands which by virtue of any covenant or agreement or of the custom of the country ought not to be removed from any farm where the same are at the time of making or giving of such bill of sale:

Personal chattels shall be deemed to be in the "apparent possession" of the person making or giving a bill of sale, so long as they remain or are in or upon any house, mill, warehouse, building, works, yard, land, or other premises occupied by him, or are used and enjoyed by him in any place whatsoever, notwithstanding that formal possession thereof may have been taken by or given to any other person:

"Prescribed" means prescribed by rules made under the provisions of this Act.

5. Application of Act to trade machinery

From and after the commencement of this Act trade machinery shall, for the purposes of this Act, be deemed to be personal chattels, and any mode of disposition of trade machinery by the owner thereof which would be a bill of sale as to any other personal chattels shall be deemed to be a bill of sale within the meaning of this Act.
For the purposes of this Act—

"Trade machinery" means the machinery used in or attached to any factory or workshop;

1st   Exclusive of the fixed motive-powers, such as the water-wheels and steam-engines, and the steam-boilers, donkey-engines, and other fixed appurtenances of the said motive-powers; and

2nd   Exclusive of the fixed power machinery, such as the shafts, wheels, drums, and their fixed appurtenances, which transmit the action of the motive-powers to the other machinery, fixed and loose; and,

3rd   Exclusive of the pipes for steam gas and water in the factory or workshop.

The machinery or effects excluded by this section from the definition of trade machinery shall not be deemed to be personal chattels within the meaning of this Act.

"Factory or workshop" means any premises on which any manual labour is exercised by way of trade, or for purposes of gain, in or incidental to the following purposes or any of them; that is to say,

 (*a*) In or incidental to the making any article or part of an article; or
 (*b*) In or incidental to the altering, repairing, ornamenting, finishing of any article; or
 (*c*) In or incidental to the adapting for sale any article.

6. Certain instruments giving powers of distress to be subject to this Act

Every attornment instrument or agreement, not being a mining lease, whereby a power of distress is given or agreed to be given by any person to any other person by way of security for any present future or contingent debt or advance, and whereby any rent is reserved or made payable as a mode of providing for the payment of interest on such debt or advance, or otherwise for the purpose of such security only, shall be deemed to be a bill of sale, within the meaning of this Act, of any personal chattels which may be seized or taken under such power of distress.

Provided, that nothing in this section shall extend to any mortgage of any estate or interest in any land tenement or hereditament which the mortgagee, being in possession, shall have demised to the mortgagor as his tenant at a fair and reasonable rent.

7. Fixtures or growing crops not to be deemed separately assigned when the land passes by the same instrument

No fixtures or growing crops shall be deemed, under this Act, to be separately assigned or charged by reason only that they are assigned by separate words, or that power is given to sever them from the land or building to which they are affixed, or from the land on which they grow, without otherwise taking possession of or dealing with such land or building, or land, if by the same instrument any freehold or leasehold interest in the land or building to which such fixtures are affixed, or in the land on which such crops grow, is also conveyed or assigned to the same persons or person.

The same rule of construction shall be applied to all deeds or instruments, including fixtures or growing crops, executed before the commencement of this Act, and then subsisting and in force, in all questions arising under any bankruptcy liquidation assignment for the benefit of creditors, or execution of any process of any court, which shall take place or be issued after the commencement of this Act.

[*Section 8 was repealed by the Bills of Sale Act* (1878) *Amendment Act 1882, sections* 3 *and* 15 *in respect of bills of sale given by way of security for the payment of money.*]

9. Avoidance of certain duplicate bills of sale

Where a subsequent bill of sale is executed within or on the expiration of seven days after the execution of a prior unregistered bill of sale, and comprises all or any part of the personal chattels comprised in such prior bill of sale, then, if such subsequent bill of sale is given as a security for the same debt as is secured by the prior bill of sale, or for any part of such debt, it shall, to the extent to which it is a security for the same debt or part thereof, and so far as respects the personal chattels or part thereof comprised in the prior bill, be absolutely void, unless it is proved to the satisfaction of the court having cognizance of the case that the subsequent bill of sale was bona fide given for the purpose of correcting some material error in the prior bill of sale, and not for the purpose of evading this Act.

10. Mode of registering bills of sale

A bill of sale shall be attested and registered under this Act in the following manner:

(2) Such bill, with every schedule or inventory thereto annexed or therein referred to, and also a true copy of such bill and of every such schedule or inventory, and of every attestation of the execution of such bill of sale, together with an affidavit of the time of such bill of sale being made or given, and of its due execution and attestation, and a description of the residence and occupation of the person making or giving the same (or in case the same is made or given by any person under or in the execution of any process, then a description of the residence and occupation of the person against whom such process issued), and of every attesting witness to such bill of sale, shall be presenting to and the said copy and affidavit shall be filed with the registrar within seven clear days after the making or giving of such bill of sale, in like manner as a warrant of attorney in any personal action given by a trader is not by law required to be filed:

(3) If the bill of sale is made or given subject to any defeasance or condition, or declaration of trust not contained in the body thereof, such defeasance, condition, or declaration shall be deemed to be part of the bill, and shall be written on the same paper or parchment therewith before the registration, and shall be truly set forth in the copy filed under this Act therewith and as part thereof, otherwise the registration shall be void.

In case two or more bills of sale are given, comprising in whole or in part any of the same chattels, they shall have priority in the order of the date of their registration respectively as regards such chattels.

A transfer of assignment of a registered bill of sale need not be registered.

[Subsection (1) was repealed by the Bills of Sale Act (1878) Amendment Act 1882, sections 3 and 10, in respect of bills of sale given by way of security for the payment of money. This section should be read subject to the Administration of Justice Act 1925, section 23(2), which provides:—

(2) Section ten of the Bills of Sale Act, 1878, shall have effect as though it required the presentation to the registrar on the registration of a bill of sale, in addition to the copy of the bill of sale mentioned in paragraph (2) of that section, of such number of copies of the bill and every schedule and inventory annexed thereto as the registrar may deem to be necessary for the purpose of carrying out the requirements of the said section eleven as amended by this section.]

11. Renewal of registration

The registration of a bill of sale, whether executed before or after the commencement of this Act, must be renewed once at least every five years, and if a period of five years elapses from the registration or renewed registration of a bill of sale without a renewal or further renewal (as the case may be), the registration shall become void.

The renewal of a registration shall be effected by filing with the registrar an affidavit stating the date of the bill of sale and of the last registration thereof, and the names, residence, and occupations of the parties thereto as stated therein, and that the bill of sale is still a subsisting security.

Every such affidavit may be in the form set forth in the Schedule (A) to this Act annexed.

A renewal of registration shall not become necessary by reason only of a transfer or assignment of a bill of sale.

12. Form of register

The registrar shall keep a book (in this Act called "the register") for the purposes of this Act, and shall, upon the filing of any bill of sale or copy under this Act, enter therein in the form set forth in the second schedule (B) to this Act annexed, or in any other prescribed form, the name, residence and occupation of the person by whom the bill was made or given (or in case the same was made or given by any person under or in the execution of process, then the name, residence and occupation of the person against whom such process was issued, and also the name of the person or persons to whom or in whose favour the bill was given), and the other particulars shown in the said schedule or to be prescribed under this Act, and shall number all such bills registered in each year consecutively, according to the respective dates of their registration.

Upon the registration of any affidavit of renewal the like entry shall be made, with the addition of the date and number of the last previous entry relating to the same bill, and the bill of sale or copy originally filed shall be thereupon marked with the number affixed to such affidavit of renewal.

The register shall also keep an index of the names of the grantors of registered bills of sale with reference to entries in the register of the bills of sale given by each such grantor.

Such index shall be arranged in divisions corresponding with the letters of the alphabet, so that all grantors whose surnames begin with the same letter (and no others) shall be comprised in one division, but the arrangement within each such division need not be strictly alphabetical.

13. The registrar

The masters of the Supreme Court of Judicature attached to the Queen's Bench Division of the High Court of Justice, or such other officers as may for the time being be assigned for this purpose under the provisions of the Supreme Court of Judicature Acts, 1873 and 1875, shall be the registrar for the purposes of this Act, and any one of the said masters may perform all or any of the duties of the registrar.

14. Rectification of register

Any judge of the High Court of Justice on being satisfied that the omission to register a bill of sale or an affidavit or renewal thereof within the time prescribed by this Act, or the omission or mis-statement of the name, residence or occupation of any person, was accidental or due to inadvertence, may in his discretion order such omission or mis-statement to be rectified by the insertion in the register of the true name, residence or occupation, or by extending the time for such registration on such terms and conditions (if any) as to security, notice by advertisement or otherwise, or as to any other matter, as he thinks fit to direct.

15. Entry of satisfaction

Subject to and in accordance with any rules to be made under and for the purposes of this Act, the registrar may order a memorandum of satisfaction to be written upon any registered copy of a bill of sale, upon the prescribed evidence being given that the debt (if any) for which such bill of sale was made or given has been satisfied or discharged.

16. Copies may be taken, etc.

Any person shall be entitled to have an office copy or extract of any registered bill of sale, and affidavit of execution filed therewith, or copy thereof, and of any affidavit filed therewith, if any, or registered affidavit of renewal, upon paying for the same at the like rate as for office copies of judgments of the High Court of Justice, and any copy of a registered bill of sale, and affidavit purporting to be an office copy thereof, shall in all courts, and before all arbitrators or other persons, be admitted as prima facie evidence thereof, and of the fact and date of registration as shown thereon. ...

[The words omitted were repealed by the Bills of Sale Act (1878) Amendment Act 1882, section 16.]

17. Affidavits

Every affidavit required by or for the purposes of this Act may be sworn before a master of any division of the High Court of Justice, or before any commissioner empowered to take affidavits in the Supreme Court of Judicature. . . .

[The words omitted were repealed by the Perjury Act 1911, section 17 and schedule.]

[Section 18 was repealed by the Statute Law Revision Act 1950.]

19. Collection of fees under 38 & 39 Vict, c.77, s.26

Section twenty-six of the Supreme Court of Judicature Act, 1875, and any enactments for the time being in force amending or substituted for that section, shall apply to fees under this Act, and an order under that section may, if need be, be made in relation to such fees accordingly.

[See the Supreme Court Fees Order 1980 (S.I. 1980 No. 821), items 21 and 24.]

[Section 20 was repealed by the Bills of Sale Act (1878) Amendment Act 1882, sections 3 and 15, in respect of bills of sale given by way of security for the payment of money.]

21. Rules

Rules for the purposes of this Act may be made and altered from time to time by the like persons and in the like manner in which rules and regulations may be made under and for the purposes of the Supreme Court of Judicature Acts, 1873 and 1875.

[See Rules of the Supreme Court, Order 95.]

22. Time for registration

When the time for registering a bill of sale expires on a Sunday, or other day on which the registrar's office is closed, the registration shall be valid if made on the next following day on which the office is open.

23. As to bills of sale and under repealed Acts

. . . Provided that (except as is herein expressly mentioned with respect to construction and with respect to renewal of registration) nothing in this Act shall affect any bill of sale executed before the commencement of this Act, and as regards bills of sale so executed the Acts hereby repealed shall continue in force.

Any renewal after the commencement of this Act of the registration of a bill of sale executed before the commencement of this Act, and registered under the Acts hereby repealed, shall be made under this Act in the same manner as the renewal of a registration made under this Act.

[*The words omitted were repealed by the Statute Law Revision Act 1894.*]

24. Extent of Act

This Act shall not extend to Scotland or to Ireland.

Appendix

Schedule A

I [*A.B.*]   *of*   *do swear that a bill of sale, bearing*
date the   *day of*   *18*   [*insert the date of the*
bill], and made between [*insert the names and descriptions of the parties in the*
original bill of sale] and which said bill of sale [*or*, and a copy of which said
bill of sale, *as the case may be*] was registered on the   day
of   18   [*insert date of registration*], is still a subsisting
security.

Sworn, &c.

Schedule B

Satisfaction entered.	No.	By whom given (or against whom process issued).			To whom given.	Nature of Instrument.	Date.	Date of Registration.	Date of Registration of affidavit of renewal.
		Name.	Residence.	Occupation.					

240

BILLS OF SALE ACT (1878) AMENDMENT ACT 1882
(c. 43)

ARRANGEMENT OF SECTIONS

SCHEDULES

An Act to amend the Bills of Sale Act, 1878

1. Short title

This Act may be cited for all purposes as the Bills of Sale Act (1878) Amendment Act 1882; and this Act and the Bills of Sale Act, 1878, may be cited together as the Bills of Sale Acts, 1878 and 1882.

2. Commencement of Act

This Act shall come into operation on the first day of November one thousand eight hundred and eighty-two, which date is hereinafter referred to as the commencement of this Act.

3. Construction of Act

The Bills of Sale Act, 1878, is hereinafter referred to as "the principal Act," and this Act shall, so far as is consistent with the tenor thereof, be construed as one with the principal Act; but unless the context otherwise requires shall not apply to any bill of sale duly registered before the commencement of this Act so long as the registration thereof is not avoided by non-renewal or otherwise.

The expression "bill of sale," and other expressions in this Act, have the same meaning as in the principal Act, except as to bills of sale or other documents mentioned in section four of the principal Act, which may be given otherwise than by way of security for the payment of money, to which last-mentioned bills of sale and other documents this Act shall not apply.

4. Bill of sale to have schedule of property attached thereto

Every bill of sale shall have annexed thereto or written thereon a schedule containing an inventory of the personal chattels comprised in the bill of sale; and such bill of sale, save as hereinafter mentioned, shall have effect only in respect of the personal chattels specifically described in the said schedule; and shall be void, except as against the grantor, in respect of any personal chattels not so specifically described.

5. Bill of sale not to affect after-acquired property

Save as hereinafter mentioned, a bill of sale shall be void, except as against the grantor, in respect of any personal chattels specifically described in the schedule thereto of which the grantor was not the true owner at the time of the execution of the bill of sale.

6. Exception as to certain things

Nothing contained in the foregoing sections of this Act shall render a bill of sale void in respect of any of the following things; (that is to say,)

(1) Any growing crops separately assigned or charged where such crops were actually growing at the time when the bill of sale was executed.

(2) Any fixtures separately assigned or charged, and any plant, or trade machinery where such fixtures, plant, or trade machinery are used in, attached to, or brought upon any land, farm, factory, workshop, shop, house, warehouse, or other place in substitution for any of the like fixtures, plant, or trade machinery specifically described in the schedule to such bill of sale.

7. Bill of sale with power to seize except in certain events to be void

Personal chattels assigned under a bill of sale shall not be liable to be seized or taken possession of by the grantee for any other than the following causes:

(1) If the grantor shall make default in payment of the sum or sums of money thereby secured at the time therein provided for payment, or in the

performance of any covenant or agreement contained in the bill of sale and necessary for maintaining the security;

(2) If the grantor shall become a bankrupt, or suffer the said goods or any of them to be distrained for rent, rates, or taxes;

(3) If the grantor shall fraudulently either remove or suffer the said goods, or any of them, to be removed from the premises;

(4) If the grantor shall not, without reasonable excuse, upon demand in writing by the grantee, produce to him his last receipts for rent, rates, and taxes;

(5) If execution shall have been levied against the goods of the grantor under any judgement at law;

Provided that the grantor may within five days from the seizure of taking possession of any chattels on account of any of the above-mentioned causes, apply to High Court, or to a judge thereof in chambers, and such court or judge, if satisfied that by payment of money or otherwise the said cause of seizure no longer exists, may restrain the grantee from removing or selling the said chattels, or may make such other order as may seem just.

7A. Defaults under consumer credit agreements

(1) Paragraph (1) of section 7 of this Act does not apply to a default relating to a bill of sale given by way of security for the payment of money under a regulated agreement to which section 87(1) of the Consumer Credit Act 1974 applies—

 (*a*) unless the restriction imposed by section 88(2) of that Act has ceased to apply to the bill of sale; or

 (*b*) if, by virtue of section 89 of that Act, the default is to be treated as not having occurred.

(2) Where paragraph (1) of section 7 of this Act does apply in relation to a bill of sale such as is mentioned in subsection (1) of this section, the proviso to that section shall have effect with the substitution of "county court" for "High Court."

[*Section 7A was inserted by the Consumer Credit Act 1974, section 192(3) (a), and Schedule 4, Part I, paragraph 1.*]

8. Bill of sale to be void unless attested and registered

Every bill of sale shall be duly attested, and shall be registered under the principal Act within seven clear days after the execution thereof, or if it is executed in any place out of England then within seven clear days after the time at which it would in the ordinary course of post arrive in England if posted immediately after the execution thereof; and shall truly set forth the consideration for which it was given; otherwise such bill of sale shall be void in respect of the personal chattels comprised therein.

9. Form of bill of sale

A bill of sale made or given by way of security for the payment of money by the grantor shall be void unless made in accordance with the form in the schedule to this Act annexed.

[*This section should be read subject to the Bills of Sale Act 1890, section 1 as amended by the Bills of Sale Act 1891, which provides*:

> **1.** An instrument charging or creating any security on or declaring trusts of imported goods given or executed at any time prior to their deposit in a warehouse, factory, or store, or to their being reshipped for export, or delivered to a purchaser not being the person giving or executing such instrument, shall not be deemed a bill of sale within the meaning of the Bills of Sale Acts 1878 and 1882.]

10. Attestation

The execution of every bill of sale by the grantor shall be attested by one or more credible witness or witnesses, not being a party or parties thereto . . . .

[*The words omitted were repealed by the Statute Law Revision Act 1898*]

11. Local registration of contents of bills of sale

Where the affidavit (which under section ten of the principal Act is required to accompany a bill of sale when presented for registration) describes the residence of the person making or giving the same or of the person against whom the process is issued to be in some place outside [the London insolvency district] or where the bill of sales describes the chattels enumerated therein as being in some place outside [the London insolvency district], the registrar under the principal Act shall forthwith and within three clear days after registration in the principal registry, and in accordance with the prescribed directions, transmit an abstract in the prescribed form of the contents of such bill of sale to the county court registrar in whose district such places are situate, and if such places are in the districts of different registrars to each such registrar.

Every abstract so transmitted shall be filed, kept, and indexed by the registrar of the county court in the prescribed manner, and any person may search, inspect, make extracts from, and obtain copies of the abstract so registered in the like manner and upon the like terms as to payment or otherwise as near as may be as in the case of bills of sale registered by the registrar under the principal Act.

[*The words in square brackets were substituted by the Insolvency Act 1985, Schedule 8.*]

[*This section should be read subject to the Administration of Justice Act 1925, section 23(1) which provides*:

23.—(1) Section eleven of the Bills of Sale Act (1878) Amendment Act, 1882 (which makes provision for the local registration of the contents of bills of sale), shall have effect as if it required the registrar of bills of sale to transmit to county court registrar's copies of the bills instead of abstracts of the contents of the bills, and references in that section to the abstract transmitted and the abstract registered shall be construed accordingly.]

12. Bill of sale under £30 to be void

Every bill of sale made or given in consideration of any sum under thirty pounds shall be void.

13. Chattels not to be removed or sold

All personal chattels seized or of which possession is taken . . . under or by virtue of any bill of sale (whether registered before or after the commencement of this Act), shall remain on the premises where they were so seized or so taken possession of, and shall not be removed or sold until after the expiration of five clear days from the day they were so seized or so taken possession of.

[*The words omitted were repealed by the Statute Law Revision Act 1898.*]

14. Bill of sale not to protect chattels against poor and parochial rates

A bill of sale to which this Act applies shall be no protection in respect of personal chattels included in such bill of sale which but for such bill of sale would have been liable to distress under a warrant for the recovery of taxes and poor and other parochial rates.

15. Repeal of part of Bills of Sale Act 1878

. . . all . . . enactments contained in the principal Act which are inconsistent with this Act are repealed. . . .

[*The words omitted were repealed by the Statute Law Revision Act 1898.*]

16. Inspection of registered bills of sale

. . . any person shall be entitled at all reasonable times to search the register, on payment of a fee of one shilling, or such other fee as may be prescribed, and subject to such regulations as may be prescribed, and shall be entitled at all reasonable times to inspect, examine, and make extracts from any and every registered bill of sale without being required to make a written application, or to specify any particulars in reference thereto, upon payment of one shilling for each bill of sale inspected, and such payment shall be made by a judicature stamp. Provided that the said extracts shall be limited to the dates of execution, registration, renewal of registration, and satisfaction, to the names, addresses, and occupations of the parties, to the amount of the consideration, and to any further prescribed particulars.

[*The words omitted were repealed by the Statute Law Revision Act* 1898.]

17. Debentures to which Act not to apply

Nothing in this Act shall apply to any debentures issued by any mortgage, loan, or other incorporated company, and secured upon the capital stock or goods, chattels, and effects of such company.

18. Extent of Act

This Act shall not extend to Scotland or Ireland.

SCHEDULE

FORM OF BILL OF SALE

This Indenture made the   day of   between *A.B.* of   of the one part and *C.D.* of   of the other part, witnesseth that in consideration of the sum of £   now paid to *A.B.* by *C.D.*, the receipt of which the said *A.B.* hereby acknowledges [*or whatever else the consideration may be*], he the said *A.B.* doth hereby assign unto *C.D.*, his executors, administrators, and assigns, all and singular the several chattels and things specifically described in the schedule hereto annexed by way of security for the payment of the sum of £   , and interest thereon at the rate of   per cent per annum [*or whatever else may be the rate*]. And the said *A.B.* doth further agree and declare that he will duly pay to the said *C.D.* the principal sum aforesaid, together with the interest then due, by equal   payments of £   on the   day of   [*or whatever else may be the stipulated times or time of payment*]. And the said *A.B.* doth also agree with the said *C.D.* that he will [*here insert terms as to insurance, payment of rent, or otherwise, which the parties may agree to for the maintenance or defeasance of the security*].

Provided always, that the chattels hereby assigned shall not be liable to seizure or to be taken possession of by the said *C.D.* for any cause other than those specified in section seven of the Bills of Sale Act (1878) Amendment Act 1882.

In witness, &c.

Signed and sealed by the said *A.B.* in the presence of me *E.F.* [*add witness's name, address, and description*].

SALE OF GOODS ACT 1979
(c. 54)

16. Goods must be ascertained

Where there is a contract for the sale of unascertained goods no property in the goods is transferred to the buyer unless and until the goods are ascertained.

17. Property passes when intended to pass

(1) Where there is a contract for the sale of specific or ascertained goods the property in them is transferred to the buyer at such time as the parties to the contract intend it to be transferred.

(2) For the purpose of ascertaining the intention of the parties regard shall be had to the terms of the contract, the conduct of the parties and the circumstances of the case.

18. Rules for ascertaining intention

Unless a different intention appears, the following are rules for ascertaining the intention of the parties as to the time at which the property in the goods is to pass to the buyer.

Rule 1—Where there is an unconditional contract for the sale of specific goods in a deliverable state the property in the goods passes to the buyer when the contract is made, and it is immaterial whether the time of payment or the time of delivery, or both, be postponed.

Rule 2—Where there is a contract for the sale of specific goods and the seller is bound to do something to the goods for the purpose of putting them into a deliverable state, the property does not pass until the thing is done and the buyer has notice that it has been done.

Rule 3—Where there is a contract for the sale of specific goods in a deliverable state but the seller is bound to weigh, measure, test, or do some other act or thing with reference to the goods for the purpose of ascertaining the price, the property does not pass until the act or thing is done and the buyer has notice that it has been done.

Rule 4—When goods are delivered to the buyer on approval or on sale or return or other similar terms the property in the goods passes to the buyer:

(*a*) when he signifies his approval or acceptance to the seller or does any other act adopting the transaction.

(*b*) if he does not signify his approval or acceptance to the seller but retains the goods without giving notice of rejection, then, if a time has been fixed for the return of the goods, on the expiration of that time, and, if no time has been fixed, on the expiration of a reasonable time.

Rule 5—(1) Where there is a contract for the sale of unascertained or future goods by description, and goods of that description and in a deliverable state are unconditionally appropriated to the contract, either by the seller with the assent of the buyer or by the buyer with the assent of the seller, the property in the goods then passes to the buyer, and the assent may be express or implied, and may be given either before or after the appropriation is made.

(2) Where, in pursuance of the contract, the seller delivers the goods to the buyer or to a carrier or other bailee or custodier (whether named by the buyer or not) for the purpose of transmission to the buyer, and does not reserve the right of disposal, he is to be taken to have unconditionally appropriated the goods to the contract.

19. Reservation of right of disposal

(1) Where there is a contract for the sale of specific goods or where goods are subsequently appropriated to the contract, the seller may, by the terms of the contract or appropriation, reserve the right of disposal of the goods until certain conditions are fulfilled; and in such a case, notwithstanding the delivery of the goods to the buyer, or to a carrier or other bailee or custodier for the purpose of transmission to the buyer, the property in the goods does not pass to the buyer until the conditions imposed by the seller are fulfilled.

(2) Where goods are shipped, and by the bill of lading the goods are deliverable to the order of the seller or his agent, the seller is prima facie to be taken to reserve the right of disposal.

(3) Where the seller of goods draws on the buyer for the price, and transmits the bill of exchange and bill of lading to the buyer together to secure acceptance or payment of the bill of exchange, the buyer is bound to return the bill of lading if he does not honour the bill of exchange, and if he wrongfully retains the bill of lading the property in the goods does not pass to him.

20. Risk prima facie passes with property

(1) Unless otherwise agreed, the goods remain at the seller's risk until the property in them is transferred to the buyer, but when the property in them is transferred to the buyer the goods are at the buyer's risk whether delivery has been made or not.

(2) But where delivery has been delayed through the fault of either buyer or seller the goods are at the risk of the party at fault as regards any loss which might not have occurred but for such fault.

(3) Nothing in this section affects the duties or liabilities of either seller or buyer as a bailee or custodier of the goods of the other party.

Transfer of title

21. Sale by person not the owner

(1) Subject to this Act, where goods are sold by a person who is not their owner, and who does not sell them under the authority or with the consent of the owner, the buyer acquires no better title to the goods than the seller had, unless the owner of the goods is by his conduct precluded from denying the seller's authority to sell.

(2) Nothing in this Act affects—

(*a*) the provisions of the Factors Acts or any enactment enabling the apparent owner of goods to dispose of them as if he were their true owner;

(*b*) the validity of any contract of sale under any special common law or statutory power of sale or under the order of a court of competent jurisdiction.

22. Market overt

(1) Where goods are sold in market overt, according to the usage of the market, the buyer acquires a good title to the goods, provided he buys them in good faith and without notice of any defect or want of title on the part of the seller.

(2) This section does not apply to Scotland.

(3) Paragraph 8 of Schedule 1 below applies in relation to a contract under

which goods were sold before 1 January 1968 or (in the application of this Act to Northern Ireland) 29 August 1967.

23. Sale under voidable title

Where the seller of goods has a voidable title to them, but his title has not been avoided at the time of the sale, the buyer acquires a good title to the goods, provided he buys them in good faith and without notice of the seller's defect of title.

24. Seller in possession after sale

Where a person having sold goods continues or is in possession of the goods, or of the documents of title to the goods, the delivery or transfer by that person, or by a mercantile agent acting for him, of the goods or documents of title under any sale, pledge, or other disposition thereof, to any person receiving the same in good faith and without notice of the previous sale, has the same effect as if the person making the delivery or transfer were expressly authorised by the owner of the goods to make the same.

25. Buyer in possession after sale

(1) Where a person having bought or agreed to buy goods obtains, with the consent of the seller, possession of the goods or the documents of title to the goods, the delivery or transfer by that person, or by a mercantile agent acting for him, of the goods or documents of title, under any sale, pledge, or other disposition thereof, to any person receiving the same in good faith and without notice of any lien or other right of the original seller in respect of the goods, has the same effect as if the person making the delivery or transfer were a mercantile agent in possession of the goods or documents of title with the consent of the owner.

(2) For the purposes of subsection (1) above—

(*a*)   the buyer under a conditional sale agreement is to be taken not to be a person who has bought or agreed to buy goods, and

(*b*)   "conditional sale agreement" means an agreement for the sale of goods which is a consumer credit agreement within the meaning of the Consumer Credit Act 1974 under which the purchase price or part of it is payable by instalments, and the property in the goods is to remain in the seller (notwithstanding that the buyer is to be in possession of the goods) until such conditions as to the payment of instalments or otherwise as may be specified in the agreement are fulfilled.

(3) Paragraph 9 of Schedule 1 below applies in relation to a contract under

which a person buys or agrees to buy goods and which is made before the appointed day.

(4) In subsection (3) above and paragraph 9 of Schedule 1 below references to the appointed day are to the day appointed for the purposes of those provisions by an order of the Secretary of State made by statutory instrument.

26. Supplementary to sections 24 and 25

In sections 24 and 25 above "mercantile agent" means a mercantile agent having in the customary course of his business as such agent authority either—

(*a*)   to sell goods, or
(*b*)   to consign goods for the purpose of sale, or
(*c*)   to buy goods, or
(*d*)   to raise money on the security of goods.

INSOLVENCY ACT 1986
(c. 45)

Part II

Administration Orders

Part III

Receivership

Part VII

Interpretation for First Group of Parts

Appendix

Making, etc. of administration order

Power of court to make order

8.—(1) Subject to this section, if the court—

(a) is satisfied that the company is or is likely to become unable to pay its debts (within the meaning given to that expression by section 123 of this Act), and

(b) considers that the making of an order under this section would be likely to achieve one or more of the purposes mentioned below,

the court may make an administration order in relation to the company.

(2) An administration order is an order directing that, during the period for which the order is in force, the affairs, business and property of the company shall be managed by a person ("the administrator") appointed for the purpose by the court.

(3) The purposes for whose achievement an administration order may be made are—

(a) the survival of the company, and the whole or any part of its undertaking, as a going concern;

(b) the approval of a voluntary arrangement under Part 1;

(c) the sanctioning under section 425 of the Companies Act of a compromise or arrangement between the company and any such persons as are mentioned in that section; and

(d) a more advantageous realisation of the company's assets than would be effected on a winding up;

and the order shall specify the purposes for which it is made.

Application for order

9.—(1) An application to the court for an administration order shall be by petition presented either by the company or the directors, or by a creditor or creditors (including any contingent or prospective creditor or creditors), or by all or any of those parties, together or separately.

(2) Where a petition is presented to the court—

(a) notice of the petition shall be given forthwith to any person who has appointed, or is or may be entitled to appoint, an administrative receiver of the company, and to such other persons as may be prescribed, and

(b) the petition shall not be withdrawn except with the leave of the court.

Note
For the "other persons" in s.9(2)(a), see the Insolvency Rules 1986, r. 2.6.

(3) Where the court is satisfied that there is an administrative receiver of the company, the court shall dismiss the petition unless it is also satisfied either—

(a) that the person by whom or on whose behalf the receiver was appointed has consented to the making of the order, or

(b) that, if an administration order were made, any security by virtue of which the receiver was appointed would—

  (i) be liable to be released or discharged under sections 238 to 240 in Part VI (transactions at an undervalue and preferences),

  (ii) be avoided under section 245 in that Part (avoidance of floating charges), or

  (iii) be challengeable under section 242 (gratuitous alienations) or 243 (unfair preferences) in that Part, or under any rule of law in Scotland.

(4) Subject to subsection (3), on hearing a petition the court may dismiss it, or adjourn the hearing conditionally or unconditionally, or make an interim order or any other order that it thinks fit.

(5) Without prejudice to the generality of subsection (4), an interim order under that subsection may restrict the exercise of any powers of the directors or of the company (whether by reference to the consent of the court or of a person qualified to act as an insolvency practitioner in relation to the company, or otherwise).

Effect of application

10.—(1) During the period beginning with the presentation of a petition for an administration order and ending with the making of such an order or the dismissal of the petition—

(a) no resolution may be passed or order made for the winding up of the company;

(b) no steps may be taken to enforce any security over the company's property, or to repossess goods in the company's possession under any hire-purchase agreement, except with the leave of the court and subject to such terms as the court may impose; and

(c) no other proceedings and no execution or other legal process may be commenced or continued, and no distress may be levied, against the company or its property except with the leave of the court and subject to such terms as aforesaid.

(2) Nothing in subsection (1) requires the leave of the court—

(a) for the presentation of a petition for the winding up of the company,

(b) for the appointment of an administrative receiver of the company, or

(c) for the carrying out by such a receiver (whenever appointed) of any of his functions.

(3) Where—

(a) a petition for an administration order is presented at a time when there is an administrative receiver of the company, and

(b) the person by or on whose behalf the receiver was appointed has not consented to the making of the order,

the period mentioned in subsection (1) is deemed not to begin unless and until that person so consents.

(4) References in this section and the next to hire-purchase agreements include conditional sale agreements, chattel leasing agreements and retention of title agreements.

(5) In the application of this section and the next to Scotland, references to execution being commenced or continued include references to diligence being carried out or continued, and references to distress being levied shall be omitted.

Effect of order

11.—(1) On the making of an administration order—

(a) any petition for the winding up of the company shall be dismissed, and
(b) any administrative receiver of the company shall vacate office.

(2) Where an administration order has been made, any receiver of part of the company's property shall vacate office on being required to do so by the administrator.

(3) During the period for which an administration order is in force—

(a) no resolution may be passed or order made for the winding up of the company;
(b) no administrative receiver of the company may be appointed;
(c) no other steps may be taken to enforce any security over the company's property, or to repossess goods in the company's possession under any hire-purchase agreement, except with the consent of the administrator or the leave of the court and subject (where the court gives leave) to such terms as the court may impose; and
(d) no other proceedings and no execution or other legal process may be commenced or continued, and no distress may be levied, against the company or its property except with the consent of the administrator or the leave of the court and subject (where the court gives leave) to such terms as aforesaid.

(4) Where at any time an administrative receiver of the company has vacated office under subsection (1)(b), or a receiver of part of the company's property has vacated office under subsection (2)—

(a) his remuneration and any expenses properly incurred by him, and
(b) any indemnity to which he is entitled out of the assets of the company,

shall be charged on and (subject to subsection (3) above) paid out of any property of the company which was in his custody or under his control at that time in priority to any security held by the person by or on whose behalf he was appointed.

(5) Neither an administrative receiver who vacates office under subsection (1)(b) nor a receiver who vacates office under subsection (2) is required on or after so vacating office to take any steps for the purpose of complying with any duty imposed on him by section 40 or 59 of this Act (duty to pay preferential creditors).

Notification of order

12.—(1) Every invoice, order for goods or business letter which, at a time when an administration order is in force in relation to a company, is issued by or on behalf of the company or the administrator, being a document on or in which the company's name appears, shall also contain the administrator's name and a statement that the affairs, business and property of the company are being managed by the administrator.

(2) If default is made in complying with this section, the company and any of the following persons who without reasonable excuse authorises or permits the default, namely, the administrator and any officer of the company, is liable to a fine.

Administrators

Appointment of administrator

13.—(1) The administrator of a company shall be appointed either by the administration order or by an order under the next subsection.

(2) If a vacancy occurs by death, resignation or otherwise in the office of the administrator, the court may by order fill the vacancy.

(3) An application for an order under subsection (2) may be made—

(a) by any continuing administrator of the company; or
(b) where there is no such administrator, by a creditors' committee established under section 26 below; or
(c) where there is no such administrator and no such committee, by the company or the directors or by any creditor or creditors of the company.

General powers

14.—(1) The administrator of a company—

(a) may do all such things as may be necessary for the management of the affairs, business and property of the company, and

(b) without prejudice to the generality of paragraph (a), has the powers specified in Schedule 1 to this Act;

and in the application of that Schedule to the administrator of a company the words "he" and "him" refer to the administrator.

(2) The administrator also has power—

(a) to remove any director of the company and to appoint any person to be a director of it, whether to fill a vacancy or otherwise, and

(b) to call any meeting of the members or creditors of the company.

(3) The administrator may apply to the court for directions in relation to any particular matter arising in connection with the carrying out of his functions.

(4) Any power conferred on the company or its officers, whether by this Act or the Companies Act or by the memorandum or articles of association, which could be exercised in such a way as to interfere with the exercise by the administrator of his powers is not exercisable except with the consent of the administrator, which may be given either generally or in relation to particular cases.

(5) In exercising his powers the administrator is deemed to act as the company's agent.

(6) A person dealing with the administrator in good faith and for value is not concerned to inquire whether the administrator is acting within his powers.

Power to deal with charged property, etc.

15.—(1) The administrator of a company may dispose of or otherwise exercise his powers in relation to any property of the company which is subject to a security to which this subsection applies as if the property were not subject to the security.

(2) Where, on an application by the administrator, the court is satisfied that the disposal (with or without other assets) of—

(a) any property of the company subject to a security to which this subsection applies, or

(b) any goods in the possession of the company under a hire-purchase agreement,

would be likely to promote the purpose or one or more of the purposes specified in the administration order, the court may by order authorise the administrator to dispose of the property as if it were not subject to the security or to dispose of the goods as if all rights of the owner under the hire-purchase agreement were vested in the company.

(3) Subsection (1) applies to any security which, as created, was a floating charge; and subsection (2) applies to any other security.

(4) Where property is disposed of under subsection (1), the holder of the

security has the same priority in respect of any property of the company directly or indirectly representing the property disposed of as he would have had in respect of the property subject to the security.

(5) It shall be a condition of an order under subsection (2) that—

(a)   the net proceeds of the disposal, and
(b)   where those proceeds are less than such amount as may be determined by the court to be the net amount which would be realised on a sale of the property or goods in the open market by a willing vendor, such sums as may be required to make good the deficiency,

shall be applied towards discharging the sums secured by the security or payable under the hire-purchase agreement.

(6) Where a condition imposed in pursuance of subsection (5) relates to two or more securities, that condition requires the net proceeds of the disposal and, where paragraph (b) of that subsection applies, the sums mentioned in that paragraph to be applied towards discharging the sums secured by those securities in the order of their priorities.

(7) An office copy of an order under subsection (2) shall, within 14 days after the making of the order, be sent by the administrator to the registrar of companies.

(8) If the administrator without reasonable excuse fails to comply with subsection (7), he is liable to a fine and, for continued contravention, to a daily default fine.

(9) References in this section to hire-purchase agreements include conditional sale agreements, chattel leasing agreements and retention of title agreements.

Operation of s.15 in Scotland

16.—(1) Where property is disposed of under section 15 in its application to Scotland, the administrator shall grant to the disponee an appropriate document of transfer or conveyance of the property, and—

(a)   that document, or
(b)   where any recording, intimation or registration of the document is a legal requirement for completion of title to the property, that recording, intimation or registration,

has the effect of disencumbering the property of or, as the case may be, freeing the property from the security.

(2) Where goods in the possession of the company under a hire-purchase agreement, conditional sale agreement, chattel leasing agreement or retention of title agreement are disposed of under section 15 in its application to Scotland, the disposal has the effect of extinguishing, as against the disponee, all rights of the owner of the goods under the agreement.

General duties

17.—(1) The administrator of a company shall, on his appointment, take into his custody or under his control all the property to which the company is or appears to be entitled.

(2) The administrator shall manage the affairs, business and property of the company—

(a) at any time before proposals have been approved (with or without modifications) under section 24 below, in accordance with any directions given by the court, and

(b) at any time after proposals have been so approved, in accordance with those proposals as from time to time revised, whether by him or a predecessor of his.

(3) The administrator shall summon a meeting of the company's creditors if—

(a) he is requested, in accordance with the rules, to do so by one-tenth, in value, of the company's creditors, or

(b) he is directed to do so by the court.

Note
For the rules relevant for s.17(3), see the Insolvency Rules 1986, rr. 2.21 *et seq.*

Discharge or variation of administration order

18.—(1) The administrator of a company may at any time apply to the court for the administration order to be discharged, or to be varied so as to specify an additional purpose.

(2) The administrator shall make an application under this section if—

(a) it appears to him that the purpose or each of the purposes specified in the order either has been achieved or is incapable of achievement, or

(b) he is required to do so by a meeting of the company's creditors summoned for the purpose in accordance with the rules.

(3) On the hearing of an application under this section, the court may by order discharge or vary the administration order and make such consequential provisions as it thinks fit, or adjourn the hearing conditionally or unconditionally, or make an interim order or any other order it thinks fit.

(4) Where the administration order is discharged or varied the administrator shall, within 14 days after the making of the order effecting the discharge or variation, send an office copy of that order to the registrar of companies.

(5) If the administrator without reasonable excuse fails to comply with subsection (4), he is liable to a fine and, for continued contravention, to a daily default fine.

Vacation of office

19.—(1) The administrator of a company may at any time be removed from office by order of the court and may, in the prescribed circumstances, resign his office by giving notice of his resignation to the court.

Note
For the prescribed circumstances, see the Insolvency Rules 1986, r. 2.53.

(2) The administrator shall vacate office if—

(a) he ceases to be qualified to act as an insolvency practitioner in relation to the company, or
(b) the administration order is discharged.

(3) Where at any time a person ceases to be administrator, the next two subsections apply.

(4) His remuneration and any expenses properly incurred by him shall be charged on and paid out of any property of the company which is in his custody or under his control at that time in priority to any security to which section 15(1) then applies.

(5) Any sums payable in respect of debts or liabilities incurred, while he was administrator, under contracts entered into or contracts of employment adopted by him or a predecessor of his in the carrying out of his or the predecessor's functions shall be charged on and paid out of any such property as is mentioned in subsection (4) in priority to any charge arising under that subsection.

For this purpose, the administrator is not to be taken to have adopted a contract of employment by reason of anything done or omitted to be done within 14 days after his appointment.

Release of administrator

20.—(1) A person who has ceased to be the administrator of a company has his release with effect from the following time, that is to say—

(a) in the case of a person who has died, the time at which notice is given to the court in accordance with the rules that he has ceased to hold office;
(b) in any other case, such time as the court may determine.

Note
The relevant rule for s.20(1)(a) is the Insolvency Rules 1986, r. 2.54.

(2) Where a person has his release under this section, he is, with effect from the time specified above, discharged from all liability both in respect of acts or omissions of his in the administration and otherwise in relation to his conduct as administrator.

(3) However, nothing in this section prevents the exercise, in relation to a person who has had his release as above, of the court's powers under section 212 in Chapter X of Part IV (summary remedy against delinquent directors, liquidators, etc.).

Appendix

Ascertainment and Investigation of Company's Affairs

Information to be given by administrator

21.—(1) Where an administration order has been made, the administrator shall—

(a) forthwith send to the company and publish in the prescribed manner a notice of the order, and

(b) within 28 days after the making of the order, unless the court otherwise directs, send such a notice to all creditors of the company (so far as he is aware of their addresses).

(2) Where an administration order has been made, the administrator shall also, within 14 days after the making of the order, send an office copy of the order to the registrar of companies and to such other persons as may be prescribed.

Note
See the Insolvency Rules 1986, r. 2.10.

(3) If the administrator without reasonable excuse fails to comply with this section, he is liable to a fine and, for continued contravention, to a daily default fine.

Statement of affairs to be submitted to administrator

22.—(1) Where an administration order has been made, the administrator shall forthwith require some or all of the persons mentioned below to make out and submit to him a statement in the prescribed form as to the affairs of the company.

Note
See the Insolvency Rules 1986, r. 2.11.

(2) The statement shall be verified by affidavit by the persons required to submit it and shall show—

(a) particulars of the company's assets, debts and liabilities;

(b) the names and addresses of its creditors;

(c) the securities held by them respectively;

(d) the dates when the securities were respectively given; and

(e) such further or other information as may be prescribed.

(3) The persons referred to in subsection (1) are—

(a) those who are or have been officers of the company;

(b) those who have taken part in the company's formation at any time within one year before the date of the administration order;

(c) those who are in the company's employment or have been in its employment within that year, and are in the administrator's opinion capable of giving the information required;

(d) those who are or have been within that year officers of or in the employment of a company which is, or within that year was, an officer of the company.

In this subsection "**employment**" includes employment under a contract for services.

(4) Where any persons are required under this section to submit a statement of affairs to the administrator, they shall do so (subject to the next subsection) before the end of the period of 21 days beginning with the day after that on which the prescribed notice of the requirement is given to them by the administrator.

(5) The administrator, if he thinks fit, may—

(a) at any time release a person from an obligation imposed on him under subsection (1) or (2), or

(b) either when giving notice under subsection (4) or subsequently, extend the period so mentioned;

and where the administrator has refused to exercise a power conferred by this subsection, the court, if it thinks fit, may exercise it.

(6) If a person without reasonable excuse fails to comply with any obligation imposed under this section, he is liable to a fine and, for continued contravention, to a daily default fine.

Administrator's proposals

Statement of proposals

23.—(1) Where an administration order has been made, the administrator shall, within 3 months (or such longer period as the court may allow) after the making of the order—

(a) send to the registrar of companies and (so far as he is aware of their addresses) to all creditors a statement of his proposals for achieving the purpose or purposes specified in the order, and

(b) lay a copy of the statement before a meeting of the company's creditors summoned for the purpose on not less than 14 days' notice.

(2) The administrator shall also, within 3 months (or such longer period as the court may allow) after the making of the order, either—

(a) send a copy of the statement (so far as he is aware of their addresses) to all members of the company, or

(b) publish in the prescribed manner a notice stating an address to which members of the company should write for copies of the statement to be sent to them free of charge.

(3) If the administrator without reasonable excuse fails to comply with this section, he is liable to a fine and, for continued contravention, to a daily default fine.

Consideration of proposals by creditors' meeting

24.—(1) A meeting of creditors summoned under section 23 shall decide whether to approve the administrator's proposals.

(2) The meeting may approve the proposals with modifications, but shall not do so unless the administrator consents to each modification.

(3) Subject as above, the meeting shall be conducted in accordance with the rules.

(4) After the conclusion of the meeting in accordance with the rules, the administrator shall report the result of the meeting to the court and shall give notice of that result to the registrar of companies and to such persons as may be prescribed.

(5) If a report is given to the court under subsection (4) that the meeting has declined to approve the administrator's proposals (with or without modifications), the court may by order discharge the administration order and make such consequential provision as it thinks fit, or adjourn the hearing conditionally or unconditionally, or make an interim order or any other order that it thinks fit.

(6) Where the administration order is discharged, the administrator shall, within 14 days after the making of the order effecting the discharge, send an office copy of that order to the registrar of companies.

(7) If the administrator without reasonable excuse fails to comply with subsection (6), he is liable to a fine and, for continued contravention, to a daily default fine.

Approval of substantial revisions

25.—(1) This section applies where—

(a) proposals have been approved (with or without modifications) under section 24, and
(b) the administrator proposes to make revisions of those proposals which appear to him substantial.

(2) The administrator shall—

(a) send to all creditors of the company (so far as he is aware of their addresses) a statement in the prescribed form of his proposed revisions, and

(b) lay a copy of the statement before a meeting of the company's creditors summoned for the purpose on not less than 14 days' notice;

and he shall not make the proposed revisions unless they are approved by the meeting.

(3) The administrator shall also either—

(a) send a copy of the statement (so far as he is aware of their addresses) to all members of the company, or

(b) publish in the prescribed manner a notice stating an address to which members of the company should write for copies of the statement to be sent to them free of charge.

(4) The meeting of creditors may approve the proposed revisions with modifications, but shall not do so unless the administrator consents to each modification.

(5) Subject as above, the meeting shall be conducted in accordance with the rules.

(6) After the conclusion of the meeting in accordance with the rules, the administrator shall give notice of the result of the meeting to the registrar of companies and to such persons as may be prescribed.

Miscellaneous

Creditors' committee

26.—(1) Where a meeting of creditors summoned under section 23 has approved the administrator's proposals (with or without modifications), the meeting may, if it thinks fit, establish a committee (**"the creditors' committee"**) to exercise the functions conferred on it by or under this Act.

(2) If such a committee is established, the committee may, on giving not less than 7 days' notice, require the administrator to attend before it at any reasonable time and furnish it with such information relating to the carrying out of his functions as it may reasonably require.

Protection of interests of creditors and members

27.—(1) At any time when an administration order is in force, a creditor or member of the company may apply to the court by petition for an order under this section on the ground—

(a) that the company's affairs, business and property are being or have been managed by the administrator in a manner which is unfairly prejudicial to the interests of its creditors or members generally, or of some part of its creditors or members (including at least himself), or

(b) that any actual or proposed act or omission of the administrator is or would be so prejudicial.

(2) On an application for an order under this section the court may, subject as follows, make such order as it thinks fit for giving relief in respect of the matters complained of, or adjourn the hearing conditionally or unconditionally, or make an interim order or any other order that it thinks fit.

(3) An order under this section shall not prejudice or prevent—

(a) the implementation of a voluntary arrangement approved under section 4 in Part I, or any compromise or arrangement sanctioned under section 425 of the Companies Act; or

(b) where the application for the order was made more than 28 days after the approval of any proposals or revised proposals under section 24 or 25, the implementation of those proposals or revised proposals.

(4) Subject as above, an order under this section may in particular—

(a) regulate the future management by the administrator of the company's affairs, business and property;

(b) require the administrator to refrain from doing or continuing an act complained of by the petitioner, or to do an act which the petitioner has complained he has omitted to do;

(c) require the summoning of a meeting of creditors or members for the purpose of considering such matters as the court may direct;

(d) discharge the administration order and make such consequential provision as the court thinks fit.

(5) Nothing in sections 15 or 16 is to be taken as prejudicing applications to the court under this section.

(6) Where the administration order is discharged, the administrator shall, within 14 days after the making of the order effecting the discharge, send an office copy of that order to the registrar of companies; and if without reasonable excuse he fails to comply with this subsection, he is liable to a fine and, for continued contravention, to a daily default fine.

PART III

RECEIVERSHIP

Administrative receivers: general

Power to dispose of charged property, etc.

43.—(1) Where, on an application by the administrative receiver, the court is satisfied that the disposal (with or without other assets) of any relevant property which is subject to a security would be likely to promote a more advantageous realisation of the company's assets than would otherwise be effected, the court may by order authorise the administrative receiver to dispose of the property as if it were not subject to the security.

(2) Subsection (1) does not apply in the case of any security held by the person by or on whose behalf the administrative receiver was appointed, or of any security to which a security so held has priority.

(3) It shall be a condition of an order under this section that—

(a) the net proceeds of the disposal, and
(b) where those proceeds are less than such amount as may be determined by the court to be the net amount which would be realised on the sale of the property in the open market by a willing vendor, such sums as may be required to make good the deficiency,

shall be applied towards discharging the sums secured by the security.

(4) Where a condition imposed in pursuance of subsection (3) relates to two or more securities, that condition shall require the net proceeds of the disposal and, where paragraph (b) of that subsection applies, the sums mentioned in that paragraph to be applied towards discharging the sums secured by those securities in the order of their priorities.

(5) An office copy of an order under this section shall, within 14 days of the making of the order, be sent by the administrative receiver to the registrar of companies.

(6) If the administrative receiver without reasonable excuse fails to comply with subsection (5), he is liable to a fine and, for continued contravention, to a daily default fine.

(7) In this section **"relevant property"**, in relation to the administrative receiver, means the property of which he is or, but for the appointment of some other person as the receiver of part of the company's property, would be the receiver or manager.

Part VII

Interpretation for First Group of Parts

Expressions used generally

251. "retention of title agreement" means an agreement for the sale of goods to a company, being an agreement—

(a) which does not constitute a charge on the goods, but
(b) under which, if the seller is not paid and the company is wound up, the seller will have priority over all other creditors of the company as respects the goods or any property representing the goods.

Appendix

COMPANIES ACT 1989
(c. 40)

PART IV

REGISTRATION OF COMPANY CHARGES

Introduction

92. The provisions of this Part amend the provisions of the Companies Act 1985 relating to the registration of company charges—

(a) by inserting in Part XII of that Act (in place of sections 395 to 408 and 410 to 423) new provisions with respect to companies registered in Great Britain, and

(b) by inserting as Chapter III of Part XXIII of that Act (in place of sections 409 and 424) new provisions with respect to oversea companies.

Registration in the companies charges register

Charges requiring registration

93. The following sections are inserted in Part XII of the Companies Act 1985—

268

"Registration in the company charges register

Introductory provisions

395.—(1) The purpose of this Part is to secure the registration of charges on a company's property.

(2) In this Part—

"charge" means any form of security interest (fixed or floating) over property, other than an interest arising by operation of law; and "property", in the context of what is the subject of a charge, includes future property.

(3) It is immaterial for the purposes of this Part where the property subject to a charge is situated.

(4) References in this Part to "the registrar" are—

(a) in relation to a company registered in England and Wales, to the registrar of companies for England and Wales, and

(b) in relation to a company registered in Scotland, to the registrar of companies for Scotland;

and references to registration, in relation to a charge, are to registration in the register kept by him under this Part.

Charges requiring registration

396.—(1) The charges requiring registration under this Part are—

(a) a charge on land or any interest in land, other than—
  (i) in England and Wales, a charge for rent or any other periodical sum issuing out of the land,
  (ii) in Scotland, a charge for any rent, ground annual or other periodical sum payable in respect of the land;

(b) a charge on goods or any interest in goods, other than a charge under which the chargee is entitled to possession either of the goods or of a document of title to them;

(c) a charge on intangible movable property (in Scotland, incorporeal moveable property) of any of the following descriptions—
  (i) goodwill,
  (ii) intellectual property,
  (iii) book debts (whether book debts of the company or assigned to the company),
  (iv) uncalled share capital of the company or calls made but not paid;

(d) a charge for securing an issue of debentures; or

(e) a floating charge on the whole or part of the company's property.

(2) The descriptions of charge mentioned in subsection (1) shall be construed as follows—

(a) a charge on a debenture forming part of an issue or series shall not be treated as falling within paragraph (a) or (b) by reason of the fact that the debenture is secured by a charge on land or goods (or on an interest in land or goods);

(b) in paragraph (b) "goods" means any tangible movable property (in Scotland, corporeal moveable property) other than money;

(c) a charge is not excluded from paragraph (b) because the chargee is entitled to take possession in case of default or on the occurrence of some other event;

(d) in paragraph (c)(ii) "intellectual property" means—

(i) any patent, trade mark, service mark, registered design, copyright or design right, or

(ii) any licence under or in respect of any such right;

(e) a debenture which is part of an issue or series shall not be treated as a book debt for the purposes of paragraph (c)(iii);

(f) the deposit by way of security of a negotiable instrument given to secure the payment of book debts shall not be treated for the purposes of paragraph (c)(iii) as a charge on book debts;

(g) a shipowner's lien on subfreights shall not be treated as a charge on book debts for the purposes of paragraph (c)(iii) or as a floating charge for the purposes of paragraph (e).

(3) Whether a charge is one requiring registration under this Part shall be determined—

(a) in the case of a charge created by a company, as at the date the charge is created, and

(b) in the case of a charge over property acquired by a company, as at the date of the acquisition.

(4) The Secretary of State may by regulations amend subsections (1) and (2) so as to add any description of charge to, or remove any description of charge from, the charges requiring registration under this Part.

(5) Regulations under this section shall be made by statutory instrument which shall be subject to annulment in pursuance of a resolution of either House of Parliament.

(6) In the following provisions of this Part references to a charge are, unless the context otherwise requires, to a charge requiring registration under this Part.

Where a charge not otherwise requiring registration relates to property by virtue of which it requires to be registered and to other property, the references are to the charge so far as it relates to property of the former description."

The companies charges register

94. The following section inserted in Part XII of the Companies Act 1985—

"The companies charges register

397.—(1) The registrar shall keep for each company a register, in such form as he thinks fit, of charges on property of the company.

(2) The register shall consist of a file containing with respect to each charge the particulars and other information delivered to the registrar under the provisions of this Part.

(3) Any person may require the registrar to provide a certificate stating the date on which any specified particulars of, or other information relating to, a charge were delivered to him.

(4) The certificate shall be signed by the registrar or authenticated by his official seal.

(5) The certificate shall be conclusive evidence that the specified particulars or other information were delivered to the registrar no later than the date stated in the certificate; and it shall be presumed unless the contrary is proved that they were not delivered earlier than that date."

Delivery of particulars for registration

95. The following sections are inserted in Part XII of the Companies Act 1985—

"Company's duty to deliver particulars of charge for registration

398.—(1) It is the duty of a company which creates a charge, or acquires property subject to a charge—

(a) to deliver the prescribed particulars of the charge, in the prescribed form, to the registrar for registration, and

(b) to do so within 21 days after the date of the charge's creation or, as the case may be, the date of the acquisition;

but particulars of a charge may be delivered for registration by any person interested in the charge.

(2) Where the particulars are delivered for registration by a person other than the company concerned, that person is entitled to recover from the company the amount of any fees paid by him to the registrar in connection with the registration.

(3) If a company fails to comply with subsection (1), then, unless particulars of the charge have been delivered for registration by another person, the company and every officer of it who is in default is liable to a fine.

(4) Where prescribed particulars in the prescribed form are delivered to the registrar for registration, he shall file the particulars in the register and shall note, in such form as he thinks fit, the date on which they were delivered to him.

(5) The registrar shall send to the company and any person appearing from the particulars to be the chargee, and if the particulars were delivered by another person interested in the charge to that person, a copy of the

271

particulars filed by him and of the note made by him as to the date on which they were delivered.

Effect of failure to deliver particulars for registration

399.—(1) Where a charge is created by a company and no prescribed particulars in the prescribed form are delivered for registration within the period of 21 days after the date of the charge's creation, the charge is void against—

(a) an administrator or liquidator of the company, and

(b) any person who for value acquires an interest in or right over property subject to the charge,

where the relevant event occurs after the creation of the charge, whether before or after the end of the 21 day period.

This is subject to section 400 (late delivery of particulars).

(2) In this Part "the relevant event" means—

(a) in relation to the voidness of a charge as against an administrator or liquidator, the beginning of the insolvency proceedings, and

(b) in relation to the voidness of a charge as against a person acquiring an interest in or right over property subject to a charge, the acquisition of that interest or right;

and references to "a relevant event" shall be construed accordingly.

(3) Where a relevant event occurs on the same day as the charge is created, it shall be presumed to have occurred after the charge is created unless the contrary is proved.

Late delivery of particulars

400.—(1) Where prescribed particulars of a charge created by a company, in the prescribed form, are delivered for registration more than 21 days after the date of the charge's creation, section 399(1) does not apply in relation to relevant events occurring after the particulars are delivered.

(2) However, where in such a case—

(a) the company is at the date of delivery of the particulars unable to pay its debts, or subsequently becomes unable to pay its debts in consequence of the transaction under which the charge is created, and

(b) insolvency proceedings begin before the end of the relevant period beginning with the date of delivery of the particulars,

the charge is void as against the administrator or liquidator.

(3) For this purpose—

(a) the company is "unable to pay its debts" in the circumstances specified in section 123 of the Insolvency Act 1986; and

(b) the "relevant period" is—

(i) two years in the case of a floating charge created in favour of a person connected with the company (within the meaning of section 249 of that Act).

(ii) one year in the case of a floating charge created in favour of a person not so connected, and

(iii) six months in any other case.

(4) Where a relevant event occurs on the same day as the particulars are delivered, it shall be presumed to have occurred before the particulars are delivered unless the contrary is proved."

Delivery of further particulars

96. The following section is inserted in Part XII of the Companies Act 1985—

"Delivery of further particulars

401.—(1) Further particulars of a charge, supplementing or varying the registered particulars, may be delivered to the registrar for registration at any time.

(2) Further particulars must be in the prescribed form signed by or on behalf of both the company and the chargee.

(3) Where further particulars are delivered to the registrar for registration and appear to him to be duly signed, he shall file the particulars in the register and shall note, in such form as he thinks fit, the date on which they were delivered to him.

(4) The registrar shall send to the company and any person appearing from the particulars to be the chargee, and if the particulars were delivered by another person interested in the charge to that other person, a copy of the further particulars filed by him and of the note made by him as to the date on which they were delivered."

Effect of omissions and errors in registered particulars

97. The following section is inserted in Part XII of the Companies Act 1985—

"Effect of omissions and errors in registered particulars

402.—(1) Where the registered particulars of a charge created by a company are not complete and accurate, the charge is void, as mentioned below to the extent that rights are not disclosed by the registered particulars which would be disclosed if they were complete and accurate.

(2) The charge is void to that extent, unless the court on the application of the chargee orders otherwise, as against—

(a) an administrator or liquidator of the company, and

  (b) any person who for value acquires an interest in or right over property subject to the charge,

where the relevant event occurs at a time when the particulars are incomplete or inaccurate in a relevant respect.

  (3) Where a relevant event occurs on the same day as particulars or further particulars are delivered, it shall be presumed to have occurred before those particulars are delivered unless the contrary is proved.

  (4) The court may order that the charge is effective as against an administrator or liquidator of the company if it is satisfied—

  (a) that the omission or error is not likely to have misled materially to his prejudice any unsecured creditor of the company, or
  (b) that no person became an unsecured creditor of the company at a time when the registered particulars of the charge were incomplete or inaccurate in a relevant respect.

  (5) The court may order that the charge is effective as against a person acquiring an interest in or right over property subject to the charge if it is satisfied that he did not rely, in connection with the acquisition, on registered particulars which were incomplete or inaccurate in a relevant respect.

  (6) For the purposes of this section an omission or inaccuracy with respect to the name of the chargee shall not be regarded as a failure to disclose the rights of the chargee."

Memorandum of charge ceasing to affect company's property

  98. The following section is inserted in Part XII of the Companies Act 1985—

"Memorandum of charge ceasing to affect company's property

403.—(1) Where a charge of which particulars have been delivered ceases to affect the company's property, a memorandum to that effect may be delivered to the registrar for registration.

  (2) The memorandum must be in the prescribed form signed by or on behalf of both the company and the chargee.

  (3) Where a memorandum is delivered to the registrar for registration and appears to him to be duly signed, he shall file it in the register, and shall note, in such form as he thinks fit, the date on which it was delivered to him.

  (4) The registrar shall send to the company and any person appearing from the memorandum to be the chargee, and if the memorandum was delivered by another person interested in the charge to that person, a copy of the memorandum filed by him and of the note made by him as to the date on which it was delivered.

  (5) If a duly signed memorandum is delivered in a case where the charge in fact continues to affect the company's property, the charge is void as against—

(a) an administrator or liquidator of the company, and

(b) any person who for value acquires an interest in or right over property subject to the charge,

where the relevant event occurs after the delivery of the memorandum.

(6) Where a relevant event occurs on the same day as the memorandum is delivered, it shall be presumed to have occurred before the memorandum is delivered unless the contrary is proved."

Further provisions with respect to voidness of charges

99. The following sections are inserted in Part XII of the Companies Act 1985—

"Further provisions with respect to voidness of charges

Exclusion of voidness as against unregistered charges

404.—(1) A charge is not void by virtue of this Part as against a subsequent charge unless some or all of the relevant particulars of that charge are duly delivered for registration—

(a) within 21 days after the date of its creation, or

(b) before complete and accurate relevant particulars of the earlier charge are duly delivered for registration.

(2) Where relevant particulars of the subsequent charge so delivered are incomplete or inaccurate, the earlier charge is void as against that charge only to the extent that rights are disclosed by registered particulars of the subsequent charge duly delivered for registration before the corresponding relevant particulars of the earlier charge.

(3) The relevant particulars of a charge for the purposes of this section are those prescribed particulars relating to rights inconsistent with those conferred by or in relation to the other charge.

Restrictions on voidness by virtue of this Part

405.—(1) A charge is not void by virtue of this Part as against a person acquiring an interest in or right over property where the acquisition is expressly subject to the charge.

(2) Nor is a charge void by virtue of this Part in relation to any property by reason of a relevant event occurring after the company which created the charge has disposed of the whole of its interest in that property.

Effect of exercise of power of sale

406.—(1) A chargee exercising a power of sale may dispose of property to a purchaser freed from any interest or right arising from the charge having become void to any extent by virtue of this Part—

(a) against an administrator or liquidator of the company, or
(b) against a person acquiring a security interest over property subject to the charge;

and a purchaser is not concerned to see or inquire whether the charge has become so void.

(2) The proceeds of the sale shall be held by the chargee in trust to be applied—

> First, in discharge of any sum effectively secured by prior incumbrances to which the sale is not made subject;
> Second, in payment of all costs, charges and expenses properly incurred by him in connection with the sale, or any previous attempted sale, of the property;
> Third, in discharge of any sum effectively secured by the charge and incumbrances ranking *pari passu* with the charge;
> Fourth, in discharge of any sum effectively secured by incumbrances ranking after the charge;

and any residue is payable to the company or to a person authorised to give a receipt for the proceeds of the sale of the property.

(3) For the purposes of subsection (2)—

(a) prior incumbrances include any incumbrance to the extent that the charge is void as against it by virtue of this Part; and
(b) no sum is effectively secured by a charge to the extent that it is void as against an administrator or liquidator of the company.

(4) In this section—

(a) references to things done by a chargee include things done by a receiver appointed by him, whether or not the receiver acts as his agent;
(b) "power of sale" includes any power to dispose of, or grant an interest out of, property for the purposes of enforcing a charge (but in relation to Scotland does not include the power to grant a lease), and references to "sale" shall be construed accordingly; and
(c) "purchaser" means a person who in good faith and for valuable consideration acquires an interest in property.

(5) The provisions of this section as to the order of application of the proceeds of sale have effect subject to any other statutory provision (in Scotland, any other statutory provision or rule of law) applicable in any case.

(6) Where a chargee exercising a power of sale purports to dispose of property freed from any such interest or right as is mentioned in subsection (1) to a person other than a purchaser, the above provisions apply, with any necessary modifications, in relation to a disposition to a purchaser by that person or any successor in title of his.

(7) In Scotland, subsections (2) and (7) of section 27 of the Conveyancing and Feudal Reform (Scotland) Act 1970 apply to a chargee unable to obtain

a discharge for any payment which he is required to make under subsection (2) above as they apply to a creditor in the circumstances mentioned in those subsections.

Effect of voidness on obligation secured

407.—(1) Where a charge becomes void to any extent by virtue of this Part, the whole of the sum secured by the charge is payable forthwith on demand; and this applies notwithstanding that the sum secured by the charge is also the subject of other security.

(2) Where the charge is to secure the repayment of money, the references in subsection (1) to the sum secured include any interest payable."

Additional information to be registered

100. The following sections are inserted in Part XII of the Companies Act 1985—

"Additional information to be registered

Particulars of taking up of issue of debentures

408.—(1) Where particulars of a charge for securing an issue of debentures have been delivered for registration, it is the duty of the company—

  (a) to deliver to the registrar for registration particulars in the prescribed form of the date on which any debentures of the issue are taken up, and of the amount taken up, and

  (b) to do so before the end of the period of 21 days after the date on which they are taken up.

(2) Where particulars in the prescribed form are delivered to the registrar for registration under this section, he shall file them in the register.

(3) If a company fails to comply with subsection (1), the company and every officer of it who is in default is liable to a fine.

Notice of appointment of receiver or manager, etc.

409.—(1) If a person obtains an order for the appointment of a receiver or manager of a company's property, or appoints such a receiver or manager under powers contained in an instrument, he shall within seven days of the order or of the appointment under those powers, give notice of that fact in the prescribed form to the registrar for registration.

(2) Where a person appointed receiver or manager of a company's property under powers contained in an instrument ceases to act as such receiver or manager, he shall, on so ceasing, give notice of that fact in the prescribed form to the registrar for registration.

(3) Where a notice under this section in the prescribed form is delivered to the registrar for registration, he shall file it in the register.

(4) If a person makes default in complying with the requirements of subsection (1) or (2), he is liable to a fine.

(5) This section does not apply in relation to companies registered in Scotland (for which corresponding provision is made by sections 53, 54 and 62 of the Insolvency Act 1986).

Notice of crystallisation of floating charge, etc.

410.—(1) The Secretary of State may by regulations require notice in the prescribed form to be given to the registrar of—

(a) the occurrence of such events as may be prescribed affecting the nature of the security under a floating charge of which particulars have been delivered for registration, and

(b) the taking of such action in exercise of powers conferred by a fixed or floating charge of which particulars have been delivered for registration, or conferred in relation to such a charge by an order of the court, as may be prescribed.

(2) The regulations may make provision as to—

(a) the persons by whom notice is required to be, or may be, given, and the period within which notice is required to be given;

(b) the filing in the register of the particulars contained in the notice and the noting of the date on which the notice was given; and

(c) the consequences of failure to give notice.

(3) As regards the consequences of failure to give notice of an event causing a floating charge to crystallise, the regulations may include provision to the effect that the crystallisation—

(a) shall be treated as ineffective until the prescribed particulars are delivered, and

(b) if the prescribed particulars are delivered after the expiry of the prescribed period, shall continue to be ineffective against such persons as may be prescribed,

subject to the exercise of such powers as may be conferred by the regulations on the court.

(4) The regulations may provide that if there is a failure to comply with such of the requirements of the regulations as may be prescribed, such persons as may be prescribed are liable to a fine.

(5) Regulations under this section shall be made by statutory instrument which shall be subject to annulment in pursuance of a resolution of either House of Parliament.

(6) Regulations under this section shall not apply in relation to a floating charge created under the law of Scotland by a company registered in Scotland."

Copies of instruments and register to be kept by company

Copies of instruments and register to be kept by company

101. The following sections are inserted in Part XII of the Companies Act 1985—

"Copies of instruments and register to be kept by company
Duty to keep copies of instruments and register

411.—(1) Every company shall keep at its registered office a copy of every instrument creating or evidencing a charge over the company's property.

In the case of a series of uniform debentures, a copy of one debenture of the series is sufficient.

(2) Every company shall also keep at its registered office a register of all such charges, containing entries for each charge giving a short description of the property charged, the amount of the charge and (except in the case of securities to bearer) the names of the persons entitled to it.

(3) This section applies to any charge, whether or not particulars are required to be delivered to the registrar for registration.

(4) If a company fails to comply with any requirement of this section, the company and every officer of it who is in default is liable to a fine.

Inspection of copies and register

412.—(1) The copies and the register referred to in section 411 shall be open to the inspection of any creditor or member of company without fee; and to the inspection of any other person on payment of such fee as may be prescribed.

(2) Any person may request the company to provide him with a copy of—

(a) any instrument creating or evidencing a charge over the company's property, or

(b) any entry in the register of charges kept by the company, on payment of such fee as may be prescribed.

This subsection applies to any charge, whether or not particulars are required to be delivered to the registrar for registration.

(3) The company shall send the copy to him not later than ten days after the day on which the request is received or, if later, on which payment is received.

(4) If inspection of the copies or register is refused, or a copy requested is not sent within the time specified above—

(a) the company and every officer of it who is in default is liable to a fine, and

(b) the court may by order compel an immediate inspection of the copies or register or, as the case may be, direct that the copy be sent immediately."

Appendix

Supplementary provisions

Power to make further provision by regulations

102. The following section is inserted in Part XII of the Companies Act 1985—

"Supplementary provisions
Power to make further provision by regulations

413.—(1) The Secretary of State may by regulations make further provision as to the application of the provisions of this Part in relation to charges of any description specified in the regulations.

Nothing in the following provisions shall be construed as restricting the generality of that power.

(2) The regulations may require that where the charge is contained in or evidenced or varied by a written instrument there shall be delivered to the registrar for registration, instead of particulars or further particulars of the charge, the instrument itself or a certified copy of it together with such particulars as may be prescribed.

(3) The regulations may provide that a memorandum of a charge ceasing to affect property of the company shall not be accepted by the registrar unless supported by such evidence as may be prescribed, and that a memorandum not so supported shall be treated as not having been delivered.

(4) The regulations may also provide that where the instrument creating the charge is delivered to the registrar in support of such a memorandum, the registrar may mark the instrument as cancelled before returning it and shall send copies of the instrument cancelled to such persons as may be prescribed.

(5) The regulations may exclude or modify, in such circumstances and to such extent as may be prescribed, the operation of the provisions of this Part relating to the voidness of a charge.

(6) The regulations may require, in connection with the delivery of particulars, further particulars or a memorandum of the charge's ceasing to affect property of the company, the delivery of such supplementary information as may be prescribed, and may—

(a) apply in relation to such supplementary information any provisions of this Part relating to particulars, further particulars of such a memorandum, and

(b) provide that the particulars, further particulars or memorandum shall be treated as not having been delivered until the required supplementary information is delivered.

(7) Regulations under this section shall be made by statutory instrument

which shall be subject to annulment in pursuance of a resolution of either House of Parliament."

Other supplementary provisions

103. The following sections are inserted in Part XII of the Companies Act 1985—

"Date of creation of charge

414.—(1) References in this Part to the date of creation of a charge by a company shall be construed as follows.

(2) A charge created under the law of England and Wales shall be taken to be created—

(a) in the case of a charge created by an instrument in writing, when the instrument is executed by the company or, if its execution by the company is conditional, upon the conditions being fulfilled, and

(b) in any other case, when an enforceable agreement is entered into by the company conferring a security interest intended to take effect forthwith or upon the company acquiring an interest in property subject to the charge.

(3) A charge created under the law of Scotland shall be taken to be created—

(a) in the case of a floating charge, when the instrument creating the floating charge is executed by the company, and

(b) in any other case, when the right of the person entitled to the benefit of the charge is constituted as a real right.

(4) Where a charge is created in the United Kingdom but comprises property outside the United Kingdom, any further proceedings necessary to make the charge valid or effectual under the law of the country where the property is situated shall be disregarded in ascertaining the date on which the charge is to be taken to be created.

Prescribed particulars and related expressions

415.—(1) References in this Part to the prescribed particulars of a charge are to such particulars of, or relating to, the charge as may be prescribed.

(2) The prescribed particulars may, without prejudice to the generality of subsection (1), include—

(a) whether the company has undertaken not to create other charges ranking in priority to or *pari passu* with the charge, and

(b) whether the charge is a market charge within the meaning of Part VII of the Companies Act 1989 or a cr rge to which the provisions of that Part apply as they apply to a market charge.

(3) References in this Part to the registered particulars of a charge at any

time are to such particulars and further particulars of the charge as have at that time been duly delivered for registration.

(4) References in this Part to the registered particulars of a charge being complete and accurate at any time are to their including all the prescribed particulars which would be required to be delivered if the charge were then newly created.

Notice of matters disclosed on register

416.—(1) A person taking a charge over a company's property shall be taken to have notice of any matter requiring registration and disclosed on the register at the time the charge is created.

(2) Otherwise, a person shall not be taken to have notice of any matter by reason of its being disclosed on the register or by reason of his having failed to search the register in the course of making such inquiries as ought reasonably to be made.

(3) The above provisions have effect subject to any other statutory provision as to whether a person is to be taken to have notice of any matter disclosed on the register.

Power of court to dispense with signature

417.—(1) Where it is proposed to deliver further particulars of a charge, or to deliver a memorandum of a charge ceasing to affect the company's property, and—

(a) the chargee refuses to sign or authorise a person to sign on his behalf, or cannot be found, or

(b) the company refuses to authorise a person to sign on its behalf,

the court may on the application of the company or the chargee, or of any other person having a sufficient interest in the matter, authorise the delivery of the particulars or memorandum without that signature.

(2) The order may be made on such terms as appear to the court to be appropriate.

(3) Where particulars or a memorandum are delivered to the registrar for registration in reliance on an order under this section, they must be accompanied by an office copy of the order.

In such a case the references in sections 401 and 403 to the particulars or memorandum being duly signed are to their being otherwise duly signed.

(4) The registrar shall file the office copy of the court order along with the particulars or memorandum."

Interpretation, etc.

104. The following sections are inserted in Part XII of the Companies Act 1985—

"Regulations

418. Regulations under any provision of this Part, or prescribing anything for the purposes of any such provision—

(a) may make different provision for different cases, and

(b) may contain such supplementary, incidental and transitional provisions as appear to the Secretary of State to be appropriate.

Minor definitions

419.—(1) In this Part—

"chargee" means the person for the time being entitled to exercise the security rights conferred by the charge;

"issue of debentures" means a group of debentures, or an amount of debenture stock, secured by the same charge; and

"series of debentures" means a group of debentures each containing or giving by reference to another instrument a charge to the benefit of which the holders of debentures of the series are entitled *pari passu*.

(2) References in this Part to the creation of a charge include the variation of a charge which is not registrable so as to include property by virtue of which it becomes registrable.

The provisions of section 414 (construction of references to date of creation of charge) apply in such a case with any necessary modifications.

(3) References in this Part to the date of acquisition of property by a company are—

(a) in England and Wales, to the date on which the acquisition is completed, and

(b) in Scotland, to the date on which the transaction is settled.

(4) In the application of this Part to a floating charge created under the law of Scotland, references to crystallisation shall be construed as references to the attachment of the charge.

(5) References in this Part to the beginning of insolvency proceedings are to—

(a) the presentation of a petition on which an administration order or winding-up order is made, or

(b) the passing of a resolution for voluntary winding up.

Index of defined expressions

420. The following Table shows the provisions of this Part defining or otherwise explaining expressions used in this Part (other than expressions used only in the same section)—

| charge | sections 395(2) and 396(6) |

charge requiring registration	section 396
chargee	section 419(1)
complete and accurate (in relation to registered particulars)	section 415(4)
creation of charge	section 419(2)
crystallisation (in relation to Scottish floating charge)	section 419(4)
date of acquisition (of property by a company)	section 419(3)
date of creation of charge	section 414
further particulars	section 401
insolvency proceedings, beginning of	section 419(5)
issue of debentures	section 419(1)
memorandum of charge ceasing to affect company's property	section 403
prescribed particulars	section 415(1) and (2)
property	section 395(2)
registered particulars	section 415(3)
registrar and registration in relation to a charge	section 395(4)
relevant event	section 399(2)
series of debentures	section 419(1)."

Charges on property of oversea company

105. The provisions set out in Schedule 15 are inserted in Part XXIII of the Companies Act 1985 (oversea companies), as a Chapter III (registration of charges).

SCHEDULE 15

CHARGES ON PROPERTY OF OVERSEA COMPANIES

[Section 105]

The following provisions are inserted in Part XXIII of the Companies Act 1985—

"CHAPTER III—REGISTRATION OF CHARGES

Introductory provisions

703A.—(1) The provisions of this Chapter have effect for securing the registration in Great Britain of charges on the property of a registered oversea company.

(2) Section 395(2) and (3) (meaning of "charge" and "property") have effect for the purposes of this Chapter.

(3) A "registered oversea company", in relation to England and Wales or Scotland, means an oversea company which has duly delivered documents to the registrar for that part of Great Britain under section 691 and has not subsequently given notice to him under section 696(4) that it has ceased to have an established place of business in that part.

(4) References in this Chapter to the registrar shall be construed in accordance with section 703E below and references to registration in relation to a charge, are to registration in the register kept by him under this Chapter.

Charges requiring registration

703B—(1) The charges requiring registration under this Chapter are those which if created by a company registered in Great Britain would require registration under Part XII of this Act.

(2) Whether a charge is one requiring registration under this Chapter shall be determined—

(a) in the case of a charge over property of a company at the date it delivers documents for registration under section 691, as at that date,

(b) in the case of a charge created by a registered oversea company, as at the date the charge is created, and

(c) in the case of a charge over property acquired by a registered oversea company, as at the date of the acquisition.

(3) In the following provisions of this Chapter references to a charge are, unless the context otherwise requires, to a charge requiring registration under this Chapter.

Where a charge not otherwise requiring registration relates to property by virtue of which it requires to be registered and to other property, the references are to the charge so far as it relates to property of the former description.

The register

703C.—(1) The registrar shall keep for each registered oversea company a register, in such form as he thinks fit, of charges on property of the company.

(2) The register shall consist of a file containing with respect to each such charge the particulars and other information delivered to the registrar under or by virtue of the following provisions of this Chapter.

(3) Section 397(3) to (5) (registrar's certificate as to date of delivery of

particulars) applies in relation to the delivery of any particulars or other information under this Chapter.

Company's duty to deliver particulars of charges for registration

703D.—(1) If when an oversea company delivers documents for registration under section 691 any of its property is situated in Great Britain and subject to a charge, it is the company's duty at the same time to deliver the prescribed particulars of the charge, in the prescribed form, to the registrar for registration.

(2) Where a registered oversea company—

(a)   creates a charge on property situated in Great Britain, or

(b)   acquires property which is situated in Great Britain and subject to a charge,

it is the company's duty to deliver the prescribed particulars of the charge, in the prescribed form, to the registrar for registration within 21 days after the date of the charge's creation or, as the case may be, the date of the acquisition.

This subsection does not apply if the property subject to the charge is at the end of that period no longer situated in Great Britain.

(3) Where the preceding subsections do not apply and property of a registered oversea company is for a continuous period of four months situated in Great Britain and subject to a charge, it is the company's duty before the end of that period to deliver the prescribed particulars of the charge, in the prescribed form, to the registrar for registration.

(4) Particulars of a charge required to be delivered under subsections (1), (2) or (3) may be delivered for registration by any person interested in the charge.

(5) If a company fails to comply with subsection (1), (2) or (3), then, unless particulars of the charge have been delivered for registration by another person, the company and every officer of it who is in default is liable to a fine.

(6) Section 398(2), (4) and (5) (recovery of fees paid in connection with registration, filing of particulars in register and sending of copy of particulars filed and note as to date) apply in relation to particulars delivered under this Chapter.

Registrar to whom particulars, etc. to be delivered

703E.—(1) The particulars required to be delivered by section 703D(1) (charges over property of oversea company becoming registered in a part of Great Britain) shall be delivered to the registrar to whom the documents are delivered under section 691.

(2) The particulars required to be delivered by section 703D(2) or (3) (charges over property of registered oversea company) shall be delivered—

(a) if the company is registered in one part of Great Britain and not in the other, to the registrar for the part in which it is registered, and

(b) if the company is registered in both parts of Great Britain but the property subject to the charge is situated in one part of Great Britain only, to the registrar for that part;

and in any other case the particulars shall be delivered to the registrars for both parts of Great Britain.

(3) Other documents required or authorised by virtue of this Chapter to be delivered to the registrar shall be delivered to the registrar or registrars to whom particulars of the charge to which they relate have been, or ought to have been, delivered.

(4) If a company gives notice under section 696(4) that it has ceased to have an established place of business in either part of Great Britain, charges over property of the company shall cease to be subject to the provisions of this Chapter, as regards registration in that part of Great Britain, as from the date on which notice is so given.

This is without prejudice to rights arising by reason of events occurring before that date.

Effect of failure to deliver particulars, late delivery and effect of errors and omissions

703F.—(1) The following provisions of Part XII—

(a) section 399 (effect of failure to deliver particulars),

(b) section 400 (late delivery of particulars), and

(c) section 402 (effect of errors and omissions in particulars delivered),

apply, with the following modifications, in relation to a charge created by a registered oversea company of which particulars are required to be delivered under this Chapter.

(2) Those provisions do not apply to a charge of which particulars are required to be delivered under section 703D(1) (charges existing when company delivers documents under section 691).

(3) In relation to a charge of which particulars are required to be delivered under section 703D(3) (charges registrable by virtue of property being within Great Britain for requisite period), the references to the period of 21 days after the charge's creation shall be construed as references to the period of four months referred to in that subsection.

Delivery of further particulars or memorandum

703G. Sections 401 and 403 (delivery of further particulars and memorandum of charge ceasing to affect company's property) apply in relation to a charge of which particulars have been delivered under this Chapter.

Further provisions with respect to voidness of charges

703H.—(1) The following provisions of Part XII apply in relation to the voidness of a charge by virtue of this Chapter—

(a) section 404 (exclusion of voidness as against unregistered charges),
(b) section 405 (restrictions on cases in which charge is void),
(c) section 406 (effect of exercise of power of sale), and
(d) section 407 (effect of voidness on obligation secured).

(2) In relation to a charge of which particulars are required to be delivered under section 703D(3) (charges registrable by virtue of property being within Great Britain for requisite period), the reference in section 404 to the period of 21 days after the charge's creation shall be construed as a reference to the period of four months referred to in that subsection.

Additional information to be registered

703I.—(1) Section 408 (particulars of taking up of issue of debentures) applies in relation to a charge of which particulars have been delivered under this Chapter.

(2) Section 409 (notice of appointment of receiver or manager) applies in relation to the appointment of a receiver or manager of property of a registered oversea company.

(3) Regulations under section 410 (notice of crystallisation of floating charge, etc.) may apply in relation to a charge of which particulars have been delivered under this Chapter; but subject to such exceptions, adaptations and modifications as may be specified in the regulations.

Copies of instruments and register to be kept by company

703J.—(1) Sections 411 and 412 (copies of instruments and register to be kept by company) apply in relation to a registered oversea company and any charge over property of the company situated in Great Britain.

(2) They apply to any charge, whether or not particulars are required to be delivered to the registrar.

(3) In relation to such a company the references to the company's registered office shall be construed as references to its principal place of business in Great Britain.

Power to make further provision by regulations

703K.—(1) The Secretary of State may by regulations make further provision as to the application of the provisions of this Chapter, or the provisions of Part XII applied by this Chapter, in relation to charges of any description specified in the regulations.

(2) The regulations may apply any provisions of regulations made under section 413 (power to make further provision with respect to application of Part XII) or make any provision which may be made under that section with respect to the application of provisions of Part XII.

Provisions as to situation of property

703L.—(1) The following provisions apply for determining for the purposes of this Chapter whether a vehicle which is the property of an oversea company is situated in Great Britain—

(a) a ship, aircraft or hovercraft shall be regarded as situated in Great Britain if, and only if, it is registered in Great Britain;

(b) any other description of vehicle shall be regarded as situated in Great Britain on a day if, and only if, at any time on that day the management of the vehicle is directed from a place of business of the company in Great Britain;

and for the purposes of this Chapter a vehicle shall not be regarded as situated in one part of Great Britain only.

(2) For the purposes of this Chapter as it applies to a charge on future property, the subject-matter of the charge shall be treated as situated in Great Britain unless it relates exclusively to property of a kind which cannot, after being acquired or coming into existence, be situated in Great Britain; and references to property situated in a part of Great Britain shall be similarly construed.

Other supplementary provisions

703M. The following provisions of Part XII apply for the purposes of this Chapter—

(a) section 414 (construction of references to date of creation of charge),
(b) section 415 (prescribed particulars and related expressions),
(c) section 416 (notice of matters disclosed on the register),
(d) section 417 (power of court to dispense with signature),
(e) section 418 (regulations) and
(f) section 419 (minor definitions).

Index of defined expressions

703N. The following Table shows the provisions of this Chapter and Part XII defining or otherwise explaining expressions used in this Chapter (other than expressions used only in the same section)—

charge	sections 703A(2), 703B(3) and 395(2)

charge requiring registration	sections 703B(1) and 396
creation of charge	sections 703M(f) and 419(2)
date of acquisition (of property by a company)	sections 703M(f) and 419(3)
date of creation of charge	sections 703M(a) and 414
property	sections 703A(2) and 395(2)
registered oversea company	section 703A(3)
registrar and registration in relation to a charge	sections 703A(4) and 703E
situated in Great Britain in relation to vehicles	section 703L(1)
in relation to future property	section 703L(2)."

INDEX

ADMINISTRATION
administrator. *See* Administrator
creditors, protection of interests of,
125–127
order. *See* Administration order

ADMINISTRATION ORDER
application, effect of, 120–122
conditions to be satisfied before making,
119
court, powers of, 118, 119
discharge of, 127, 128
enforcement of reservation of title
clauses, moratorium on, 117, 120–122
opposition to making, 118
other proceedings, effect on, 120
procedure, 118
puposes of, 118

ADMINISTRATIVE RECEIVER
agent of company, as, 90
reservation of title clauses, and, 128

ADMINISTRATOR
company's property, getting in, 127
discharge of, 127, 128
Factors Act, reliance on, 167, 168
property subject to reservation of title,
dealing with,
sale of goods, 122, 123, 127
open market, on, 123, 124
willing vendor, concept of, 124, 125
use of goods, 122
release from liability, 128

ADMIXTURE OF GOODS
accessio, 46, 47
accession,
annexation, degree and purpose of, 48
attachment, rights created by, 134, 135
cases of, 47, 48
destruction of utility test, 48
injurious removal test, 48–50, 134
meaning, 47
principal goods, belonging to owner of,
48
reservation of title context, in, 86
separate existence test, 48
wrongful interference cases, and, 50, 51
commixtio, 46, 47
commingling,
co-owners, remedies of, 54–56
dry mixtures, of, 47, 53, 54
good faith, in, 52
meaning, 47
physical identity,
processing involving loss of, 56–58,
83, 113–115

ADMIXTURE OF GOODS—*cont.*
commingling—*cont.*
physical identity—*cont.*
without loss of, 51–53, 83, 112
specific delivery order, 51
tenancy in common of goods, 52, 53
confusio, 46, 47
confusion,
co-owners, remedies of, 54–56
meaning, 47
physical identity,
processing involving loss of, 56–58,
83, 113–115
without loss of, 51–53, 83
specific delivery order, 51
wet mixtures, of, 47, 53, 54
manufactured goods, right to title to,
83–86
principles, application in tracing, 34
processing, 47, 56–58
products clause, 227–229
summary of principles, 58, 59
terminology, 46, 47
use of, 112

AGENCY
claim against proceeds of sale, as
foundation for, 43
del credere, 44, 46, 79
reservation of title cases, in, 45, 46
undisclosed principal,
concept of, 169, 170
contractual exclusion of, 170, 171
election to sue, 172, 173
judgment against agent, effect of, 172
liability to be sued, 173–175
personality of agent, and, 171, 172
ratification, not making, 170
trust receipt device, 174

AGENT
administrative receiver as, 90
alteration of nature of goods by, 45
fiduciary relationship, not in, 42, 43
mercantile, buyer acting as, 165
principal, separation of assets from, 44
sale of goods by, 43, 44

AGGREGATION CLAUSE
accession. *See* Admixture of goods
bill of sale, and, 133–136
generally, 2
charge, as, 112
physical identity,
commingling without loss of, 112
loss of, 113–115

291

Index